GW01458085

# "Jesus Chr

*An Examination of Victor Paul Wierwille
and His "The Way International,"
a Rapidly Growing
Unitarian Cult*

JUDITH ●●●●● ( 1985

# "Jesus Christ IS God!"

*An Examination of Victor Paul Wierwille
and His "The Way International,"
a Rapidly Growing
Unitarian Cult*

By Robert L. Sumner

**One of the most comprehensive works
defending the Deity of Christ, the Trinity,
and other fundamental doctrines
written in modern times**

BIBLICAL EVANGELISM PRESS
Murfreesboro, Tennessee 37133-1513

Copyright © 1983
BIBLICAL EVANGELISM

ISBN 0-914012-23-1
Library of Congress 83-072-498

Cover Design by Ron Sumner

Library of Congress Cataloging in Publication Date
Sumner, Robert L., 1922-

    Jesus Christ is God
    Bibliography: pp. 9-17
    Includes index

1. Theology, Deity of Christ—Holy Spirit—Bible—Life after death, etc.
2. Apologetics, The Way International—Victor Paul Wierwille
I Title

Printed in the United States of America

# DEDICATION

## DR. FRED M. BARLOW

Esteemed colleague, beloved personal friend, faithful servant of our Master. The memory of his dedicated life as an evangelist, author, Sunday school authority and fervent winner of souls remains to this hour. Although dead, his influence continues to speak to the world through his prolific, pungent, anointed writings.

# TABLE OF CONTENTS

# BIBLIOGRAPHY AND
# ABBREVIATION SYMBOLS

## A. Primary Sources

ADAN  *Are the Dead Alive Now?* Victor Paul Wierwille; The American Christian Press, New Knoxville, OH; © 1971, The Devin-Adair Company, assigned to The Way International in 1973; 1976 printing

BTMS  *Studies in Abundant Living, Volume I: The Bible Tells Me So,* Victor Paul Wierwille; American Christian Press, New Knoxville, OH; © 1971, The Way International; 1976 printing

JCNG  *Jesus Christ is NOT God,* Victor Paul Wierwille; The American Christian Press, New Knoxville, OH; © 1975, The Way International

NDC  *Studies in Abundant Living, Volume II: The New, Dynamic Church,* Victor Paul Wierwille; American Christian Press, New Knoxville, OH; © 1971, The Way, Inc.

PAL  *Power for Abundant Living,* Victor Paul Wierwille; The American Christian Press, New Knoxville, OH; © 1971, The Way International

RHST  *Receiving the Holy Spirit Today,* Victor Paul Wierwille; The American Christian Press, New Knoxville, OH; 1972, The Way International; 1976 edition

TWW  *Studies in Abundant Living, Volume III: The Word's Way,* Victor Paul Wierwille; The American Christian Press, New Knoxville, OH; © 1971, The Way, Inc.

WLL  *The Way, Living in Love,* Elena S. Whiteside; American Christian Press, New Knoxville, OH; © 1972, The Way International; Second Edition, 1976

WM  *The Way Magazine,* David C. Craley, Editor; published 6 times annually, New Knoxville, OH

## B. Commentaries, Dictionaries, Encyclopedias

AGT  *The Greek Testament,* Henry Alford; Moody Press, Chicago, IL; n.d.

BEE  *The Bible of the Expositor and the Evangelist,* William Bell Riley; Union Gospel Press, Cleveland, OH; Copyright, 1925, 1926, 1927, 1928, 1929, 1930, 1931, 1932, 1933, 1935, 1938

BNNT  *Barnes' Notes on the New Testament,* Albert Barnes; Kregel Publications, Grand Rapids, MI; 1963

DOTW  *Dictionary of Old Testament Words for English Readers,* Aaron Pick; Kregel Publications, Grand Rapids, MI; Originally published by Hamilton, Adams & Co., London, as *The Bible Students Concordance*

EBC  *The Expositor's Bible Commentary,* Frank E. Gaebelein, General Editor; Zondervan Publishing House, Grand Rapids, MI; © 1978, The Zondervan Corporation

| | |
|---|---|
| ECWB | *Ellicott's Commentary on the Whole Bible,* Edited by Charles John Ellicott; Zondervan Publishing House, Grand Rapids, MI; 1959 |
| EDNTW | *Expository Dictionary of New Testament Words,* W. E. Vine; Fleming H. Revell Company, Westwood, NJ; 1956 printing |
| EGT | *The Expositor's Greek Testament,* Edited by W. Robertson Nicoll; Wm. B. Eerdmans Publishing Company, Grand Rapids, MI; 1979 printing |
| EHHC | *Eerdman's Handbook to the History of Christianity,* Organizing Editor, Tim Dowley; Wm. B. Eerdmans Publishing Company, Grand Rapids, MI; © 1977, Lion Publishing |
| GABC | *Gray & Adams Bible Commentary,* James Comper Gray and George M. Adams; Zondervan Publishing House, Grand Rapids, MI; n.d. |
| ISBE | *The International Standard Bible Encyclopaedia,* James Orr, General Editor; Wm. B. Eerdmans Publishing Company, Grand Rapids, MI; Copyright 1939, 1956 |
| ISBER | *The International Standard Bible Encyclopedia, Fully Revised,* Geoffrey W. Bromiley, General Editor; William B. Eerdmans Publishing Company, Grand Rapids, MI; © 1979 |
| JFB | *Commentary Critical and Explanatory on the Whole Bible,* Robert Jamieson, A. R. Fausett, David Brown; Zondervan Publishing House, Grand Rapids, MI; n.d. |
| NICNT | *The New International Commentary on the New Testament,* F. F. Bruce, General Editor; Wm. B. Eerdmans Publishing Company, Grand Rapids, MI; © 1953, 1959, 1962, 1964, 1965, 1971, 1974, 1976, 1977, 1978 |
| NNT | *Notes on the New Testament Explanatory and Practical,* Albert Barnes, Edited by Robert Frew; Baker Book House, Grand Rapids, MI; 1961, 1962 |
| NSG | *A New Short Grammar of the Greek New Testament,* A. T. Robertson and W. Hersey Davis; Baker Book House, Grand Rapids, MI; Copyright 1931, 1933, 1958 by Harper & Brothers |
| OTWS | *Old Testament Word Studies, An English Hebrew and Chaldee Lexicon and Concordance,* William Wilson; Kregel Publications, Grand Rapids, MI; © 1978 |
| | *The Pulpit Commentary,* Edited by H. D. M. Spence and Joseph S. Exell; Wm. B. Eerdmans publishing company, Grand Rapids, MI; 1950 |
| RETG | *Ryle's Expository Thoughts on the Gospels,* J. C. Ryle; Zondervan Publishing House, Grand Rapids, MI; n.d. |
| RHD | *Random House Dictionary of the English Language, The Unabridged Edition;* Random House, New York, NY; 1966, Random House, Inc. |

SEC    *The Exhaustive Concordance of the Bible,* James Strong; Abingdon Press, New York/Nashville; 25th printing, March 1963

TOD    *The Treasury of David,* Charles Haddon Spurgeon; Zondervan Publishing House, Grand Rapids, MI; 1975 printing

TNTC    *Tyndale New Testament Commentaries,* R. V. G. Tasker, General Editor; Wm. B. Eerdmans Publishing Company, Grand Rapids, MI; © The Tyndale Press, 1978, 1979 printings

WFJ    *The Works of Flavius Josephus,* Translated by William Whiston; The S. S. Scranton Company, Hartford, CT; 1912

WPNT    *Word Pictures in the New Testament,* Archibald Thomas Robertson; Harper & Brothers, New York/London; Copyright 1930, Sunday School Board of the Southern Baptist Convention

WSNT    *Word Studies in the New Testament,* Marvin R. Vincent; Wm. B. Eerdmans Publishing Company, Grand Rapids, MI; 1977 printing

YAC    *Young's Analytical Concordance to the Bible,* Robert Young; Wm. B. Eerdmans Publishing Company, Grand Rapids, MI; 1975 printing

## C. Books

AF    *The Apostolic Fathers,* Edited by Jack Sparks; Thomas Nelson Publishers, Nashville/New York; © 1978

AOD    *Apostles of Denial,* Edmond C. Gruss; Presbyterian and Reformed Publishing Company, Nutley, NJ; Copyright 1970

APOC    *The Apocalypse,* Joseph A. Seiss; Zondervan Publishing House, Grand Rapids, MI; n.d.

ARMS    *ARMSTRONGISM: The "Worldwide Church of God" Examined in the Searching Light of Scripture,* Robert L. Sumner; Biblical Evangelism Press, Brownsburg, IN; © 1974, Biblical Evangelism

BEA    *Biblical Evangelism in Action,* Robert L. Sumner; Sword of the Lord Publishers, Murfreesboro, TN; Copyright 1966

BGNT    *Bypaths in the Greek New Testament,* Kenneth S. Wuest; Wm. B. Eerdmans Publishing Company, Grand Rapids, MI; Copyright 1940

BLH    *The Bible on Life Hereafter,* William Hendriksen; Baker Book House, Grand Rapids, MI; Copyright 1959

CAL    *Christianity and Liberalism,* J. Gresham Machen; Wm. B. Eerdmans Publishing Company, Grand Rapids, MI; Copyright 1923, Owned by the Trustees u/w J. Gresham Machen

CAYD    *Counterfeits At Your Door,* James Bjornstad; Regal Books, Glendale, CA; © 1979 by Gospel Light Publications

11

CBS    *Called to Be Saints*, Robert G. Gromacki; Regular Baptist Press, Schaumburg, IL; Copyright 1977, Baker Book House

CC    *Confronting the Cults*, Gordon R. Lewis; Baker Book House, Grand Rapids, MI; Copyright 1966, Presbyterian & Reformed Publishing Company

CCB    *Christ, Christianity and the Bible*, I. M. Haldeman; Charles C. Cook, New York, NY; Copyright 1912

CDP    *The Charismatics: A Doctrinal Perspective*, John F. MacArthur, Jr.; Zondervan Publishing House, Grand Rapids, MI; © 1978 by John F. MacArthur

CFC    *Commentary on the First Epistle to the Corinthians*, Frederic Louis Godet; Zondervan Publishing House, Grand Rapids, MI; 1957

CJG    *Commentary on John's Gospel*, Frederic Louis Godet; Kregel Publications, Grand Rapids, MI; © 1978

COH    *Commentary on Hebrews*, William Gouge; Kregel Publications, Grand Rapids, MI; Copyright © 1980

COM    *Commentaries*, John Calvin, Translated by John Pringle; Wm. B. Eerdmans Publishing Company, Grand Rapids, MI; 1948

COR    *Commentary on Romans*, Frederic Louis Godet; Kregel Publications, Grand Rapids, MI; 1977

CVGW    *The Christian View of God and the World*, James Orr; Charles Scribner's Sons; 1893

DCP    *Devotional Commentary on Philippians*, F. B. Meyer; Kregel Publications, Grand Rapids, MI; © 1979

DE    *Doom Eternal: The Bible and Church Doctrine of Everlasting Punishment*, Junius B. Reimensnyder; Nelson S. Quincy, Philadelphia, PA; 1880

DJCL    *The Deity of Jesus Christ Our Lord*, J. B. Rowell; published by the author, Victoria, BC, Canada; n.d.

EAER    *Explanatory Analysis of St. Paul's Epistle to the Romans*, Henry Parry Liddon;1977 reprint by James and Klock Christian Publishing Company, Minneapolis, MN

EGJ    *An Exposition of the Gospel of John*, Herschel H. Hobbs; Baker Book House, Grand Rapids, MI; Copyright 1968

EPJ    *The Epistles of St. Peter and St. Jude*, Charles Bigg; Charles Scribner's Sons, New York, NY; 1922

ERJC    *Exposition of the Revelation of Jesus Christ.* Walter Scott; Kregel Publications, Grand Rapids, MI; Fourth Edition

ETH    *The Epistle to the Hebrews*, Adolph Saphir; Loizeaux Brothers, Publishers, New York, NY; Seventh American Edition

ETHC    *The Epistle to the Hebrews: A Commentary*, Homer Kent, Jr.; Baker Book House, Grand Rapids, MI; © 1972

FEJ    *The First Epistle of John*, Robert S. Candlish; Zondervan Publishing House, Grand Rapids, MI; n.d.

| GASJ | *The Gospel According to St. John,* C. K. Barrett; Society for Promoting Christian Knowledge, London; 1967 |
|---|---|
| GCW | *Great Cloud of Witnesses,* E. W. Bullinger; Kregel Publications, Grand Rapids, MI; Copyright, © 1979 |
| GGNT | *Galatians in the Greek New Testament,* Kenneth S. Wuest; Wm. B. Eerdmans Publishing Company, Grand Rapids, MI; Copyright 1944 by Kenneth S. Wuest |
| GNG | *Golden Nuggets From the Greek New Testament,* Kenneth S. Wuest; Wm. B. Eerdmans Publishing Company, Grand Rapids, MI; Copyright 1940 by Kenneth S. Wuest |
| GST | *God Speaks Today,* Jerry Vine; Zondervan Publishing House, Grand Rapids, MI; © 1979, The Zondervan Corporation |
| GTLB | *Great Truths to Live By,* Kenneth S. Wuest; Wm. B. Eerdmans Publishing Company, Grand Rapids, Mi; Copyright 1952 |
| HGNT | *Hebrews In the Greek New Testament,* Kenneth S. Wuest; Wm. B. Eerdmans Publishing Company, Grand Rapids, MI; Copyright 1947 |
| HPP | *The High Priestly Prayer, A Devotional Commentary on the Seventeenth Chapter of St. John,* H. C. G. Moule; Baker Book House, Grand Rapids, MI; 1978 printing |
| HSHS | *A Help to the Study of the Holy Spirit,* William E. Biederwolf; Baker Book House, Grand Rapids, MI; Fourth edition, 1974 |
| HSTW | *The Holy Spirit In Today's World,* W. A. Criswell; Zondervan Publishing House, Grand Rapids, MI; © 1966 |
| HVV | *Hebrews Verse by Verse,* William R. Newell; Moody Press, Chicago, IL; Copyright 1947 by William R. Newell |
| IJG | *Is Jesus God?* John R. Rice; Sword of the Lord Publishers, Murfreesboro, TN; Copyright 1948 |
| JGGG | *Jesus: God, Ghost or Guru?* Jon A. Buell and O. Quentin Hyder; Zondervan Publishing House, Grand Rapids, MI/Probe Ministries International, Richardson, TX; 1978 by Probe Ministries International |
| LEPP | *Lectures Exegetical and Practical on the Epistle of Paul to the Philippians,* Robert Johnstone; Baker Book House, Grand Rapids, MI; 1955 printing |
| LFH | *The Lord From Heaven,* Robert Anderson; Kregel Publications, Grand Rapids, MI; © 1978 |
| LH | *The Lord From Heaven,* Leon Morris; InterVarsity Press, Downers Grove, IL; © 1974 |
| LID | *Light In Darkness,* Homer A. Kent, Jr.; Baker Book House, Grand Rapids, MI; Copyright 1974 |
| LOH | *Lectures on Hebrews,* Samuel Ridout; Loizeaux Brothers, New York, NY; n.d. |

| | |
|---|---|
| LST | *Lectures In Systematic Theology*, Henry C. Thiessen; Wm. B. Eerdmans Publishing Company, Grand Rapids, MI; Copyright 1949 |
| ML | *The Martyr Lamb*, F. W. Krummacher; Baker Book House, Grand Rapids, MI; 1978 printing |
| MOJ | *The Mother of Jesus: Her Problems and Her Glory*, A. T. Robertson; Baker Book House, Grand Rapids, MI; 1963 |
| NOT | *Notes on Thessalonians*, C. F. Hogg and W. E. Vine |
| OBAM | *Our Bible and the Ancient Manuscripts*, Frederic Kenyon; Harper & Brothers, New York, NY; Fourth edition, revised, rewritten and enlarged; 1941 printing |
| OPR | *The Origin of Paul's Religion*, J. Gresham Machen; Wm. B. Eerdmans Publishing Company, Grand Rapids, MI; Copyright 1925, Owned by the Trustees u/w J. Gresham Machen |
| OWC | *Oneness With Christ*, W. R. Nicholson; Kregel Publications, Grand Rapids, MI; Copyright 1903 by A. B. Simpson |
| PCF | *Pillars of the Christian Faith*, Abram M. Long; Fleming H. Revell Company, New York, NY; Copyright 1947 |
| PEG | *The Pastoral Epistles in the Greek New Testament*, Kenneth S. Wuest; Wm. B. Eerdmans Publishing Company, Grand Rapids, MI; Copyright 1952 |
| PIC | *Paul the Interpreter of Christ*, A. T. Robertson; Baker Book House, Grand Rapids, MI; © 1921 by George H. Doran |
| PS | *Pauline Studies*, Edited by Donald A. Hagner and Murray J. Harris; Wm. B. Eerdmans Publishing Company, Grand Rapids, MI; Copyright © The Paternoster Press, Ltd. |
| PWHS | *Person and Work of the Holy Spirit*, H. C. G. Moule; Kregel Publications, Grand Rapids, MI; 1977 |
| ROC | *The Rise of the Cults*, Walter R. Martin; Zondervan Publishing House, Grand Rapids, MI; Copyright 1955 |
| RR | *The Revision Revised*, John William Burgon; Conservative Classics, Paradise, PA; n.d. |
| SCP | *Studies in Colossians and Philemon*, W. H. Griffith Thomas; Baker Book House, Grand Rapids, MI © 1973 |
| SFL | *Stand Fast in Liberty*, Robert G. Gromacki; Baker Book House, Grand Rapids, MI; Copyright 1979 |
| SGS | *Saved by Grace. . .for Service!* Robert L. Sumner; Biblical Evangelism Press, Brownsburg, IN; © 1979 by Biblical Evangelism |
| SII | *Studies In Isaiah*, F. C. Jennings; Loizeaux Brothers, Neptune, NJ; 1935 |
| SOC | *The Supernaturalness of Christ*, Wilbur M. Smith; Baker Book House, Grand Rapids, MI; 1974 edition |
| SQD | *Seven Questions in Dispute*, William Jennings Bryan; Fleming H. Revell Company, New York, NY; Copyright 1924 |

SST    *Studies In II Timothy,* Handley C. G. Moule; Kregel Publications, Grand Rapids, MI; 1977

SVG    *Studies in the Vocabulary of the Greek New Testament,* Kenneth S. Wuest; Wm. B. Eerdmans Publishing Company, Grand Rapids, MI; Copyright 1945

TBT    *Tested by Temptation,* W. Graham Scroggie; Kregel Publications, Grand Rapids, MI; n.d.

TGI    *The Truth of God Incarnate,* Edited by Michael Green; Wm. B. Eerdmans Publishing Company, Grand Rapids, MI; © 1977

TMA    *Tongues of Men and Angels,* William J. Samarin; MacMillan Company, New York, NY; © 1972

TMM    *The Mormon Mirage,* Latayne Colvett Scott; Zondervan Publishing House, Grand Rapids, MI; © 1979 by The Zondervan Corporation

TOB    *The Open Bible;* Thomas Nelson Publishers, Nashville/Camden/New York; © 1975

TOF    *Truth on Fire,* Clark H. Pinnock; Baker Book House, Grand Rapids, MI; © 1972

TSC    *The Story of the Cross,* Leon Morris; Wm. B. Eerdmans Publishing Company, Grand Rapids, MI; 1957

TT    *The Trinity,* Edward Henry Bickersteth; Kregel Publications, Grand Rapids, MI; 1957; formerly published under the title, *The Rock of Ages*

VBC    *The Virgin Birth of Christ,* James Orr; Charles Scribner's Sons, New York, NY; Copyright 1907

VWST    *Vital Word Studies In I Thessalonians,* John Lineberry; Zondervan Publishing House, Grand Rapids, MI; Copyright 1960

WFWO    *We Found Our Way Out,* Edited by James R. Adair; Baker Book House, Grand Rapids, MI; Copyright 1964

WGBM    *When God Became Man,* George Lawlor; Moody Press, Chicago, IL; © 1978

WHH    *Whatever Happened to Hell?* Jon E. Braun; Thomas Nelson Publishers, Nashville/New York; © 1979 by Jon E. Braun

WIF    *What Is Faith?* J. Gresham Machen; Wm. B. Eerdmans Publishing Company, Grand Rapids, MI; Copyright 1925, Owned by the Trustees u/w J. Gresham Machen

YBEC    *Youth, Brainwashing, and the Extremist Cults,* Ronald Enroth; Zondervan Publishing House, Grand Rapids, MI; © 1977 by The Zondervan Corporation

## D. Newspapers, Magazines

AJC    *The Atlanta Journal & Constitution,* Atlanta, GA

BE    *The Biblical Evangelist,* Murfreesboro, TN

BS    *Bibliotheca Sacra,* Dallas, TX

| CE | *The Cincinnati Enquirer,* Cincinnati, OH |
|---|---|
| CN | *The Christian News,* New Haven, MO |
| CPN | *CP Newsletter,* Berkeley, CA |
| CT | *Christianity Today,* Carol Stream, IL |
| DIS | *The Discerner,* Minneapolis, MN |
| EC | *The Evangelical Christian,* Toronto, Canada |
| EG | *The Emporia Gazette,* Emporia, KS |
| GNB | *The Good News Broadcaster,* Lincoln, NE |
| IS | *The Indianpolis Star,* Indianapolis, IN |
| JPP | *The Journal of Pastoral Practice,* Phillipsburg, NJ |
| KB | *The King's Business,* Los Angeles, CA |
| LC | *The Living Church,* Milwaukee, WI |
| LIFE | *Life Magazine,* New York, NY |
| MM | *Moody Monthly,* Chicago, IL |
| OIB | *The Ohio Independent Baptist,* Xenia, OH |
| SL | *The Sword of the Lord,* Murfreesboro, TN |
| TM | *Time Magazine,* New York, NY |

## E. Bible Translations

ADAMS  *The Christian Counselor's New Testament,* Jay E. Adams; Baker Book House, Grand Rapids, MI; Copyright 1977 by Jay E. Adams

AMP  *The Amplified Bible;* Zondervan Publishing House, Grand Rapids, MI; © 1965

BECK  *An American Translation,* William F. Beck; Leader Publishing Company, New Haven, MO; © 1976 by Mrs. William F. Beck

BERK  *The New Berkeley Version in Modern English,* Revised Edition; Zondervan Publishing House, Grand Rapids, MI; 1969

CB  *The Complete Bible;* The University of Chicago Press, Chicago, IL; Copyright 1939 by University of Chicago

CON  *The Confraternity Revision of the New Testament;* St. Anthony Guild Press, Paterson, NJ; Copyright 1941 by Confraternity of Christian Doctrine

EVD  *The New Testament English Version for the Deaf;* Baker Book House, Grand Rapids, MI; Copyright © 1978 by World Bible Translation Center, Inc., Arlington, TX

HBP  *Holy Bible From the Peshitta,* George M. Lamsa; A. J. Holman Company, Philadelphia, PA; © 1957, eighth edition

MONT  *Centenary Translation of the New Testament,* Helen Barrett Montgomery; The American Baptist Publication Society, Philadelphia, PA; Copyright 1924

NASB  *New American Standard Bible, New Testament;* Broadman Press, Nashville, TN; © The Lockman Foundation, 1960, 1962, 1963

| | |
|---|---|
| NEB | *The New English Bible;* Oxford University Press/ Cambridge University Press; © 1961 |
| NIV | *New International Version;* Zondervan Bible Publishers, Grand Rapids, MI; © 1978 New York International Bible Society |
| NKJB | *New King James Bible, New Testament;* Thomas Nelson Publishers, Nashville/Camden/New York; © 1979 |
| NWT | *New World Translation of the Holy Scriptures,* Revised 1961; Watchtower Bible and Tract Society of New York, Inc., Brooklyn; Copyright 1961, Watchtower Bible & Tract Society of Pennsylvania |
| PHIL | *The New Testament in Modern English,* J. B. Phillips; Geoffrey Bles Ltd, London/William Collins Sons & Co. Ltd, Glasgow; © 1959 by J. B. Phillips |
| RSV | *Revised Standard Version;* Thomas Nelson & Sons, New York/Toronto/Edinburgh; Copyright 1952, Division of Christian Education of the National Council of the Churches of Christ in the United States of America |
| RV | *Revised Version of 1881, New Testament;* Thomas Nelson & Sons, New York/Henry Frowde, London/C. J. Clay, London |
| TEV | *Good News for Modern Man, the New Testament in Today's English Version;* American Bible Society, New York, NY; © American Bible Society 1966 |
| TLB | *The Living Bible;* Tyndale House Publishers, Wheaton, IL/ Coverdale House Publishers, London; © 1971 Tyndale House Publishers |
| WEY | *The Modern Speech New Testament,* Richard Francis Weymouth; The Pilgrim Press, Boston/James Clarke & Company, London; third edition |
| WILL | *The New Testament in the Language of the People,* Charles B. Williams; Moody Press, Chicago, IL; Copyright 1937, Bruce Humphries, Inc., assigned in 1949 to Moody Bible Institute |
| WUEST | *Wuest's Expanded Translation of the Greek New Testament; The Gospels,* Kenneth S. Wuest; Wm. B. Eerdmans Publishing Company, Grand Rapids, MI; Copyright 1956 |
| YOUNG | *Young's Literal Translation of the Bible,* Robert Young; Baker Book House, Grand Rapids, MI; revised edition |

AUTHOR'S NOTE: Listing of any title in the above is not to be construed as endorsement of the book, magazine or translation. For example, the "Jehovah's Witnesses" translation, *New World Translation of the Holy Scriptures,* is especially unreliable and is used for comparative purposes only.

# AN APOLOGIA

"The question has sometimes been proposed to me, how it is that some of us who hold the divinity of Christ manifest what is called uncharitableness toward those who deny Him. We do continually affirm that an error, with regard to the divinity of Christ, is absolutely fatal, and that a man cannot be right in his judgment upon any part of the gospel unless he think rightly of Him who is *personally* the very centre of all the purposes of Heaven, and the foundation of all the hopes of earth. Nor can we admit of any latitudinarianism here. We extend the right hand of fellowship to all those who love the Lord Jesus Christ in sincerity and truth; but we cannot exchange our Christian greetings with those who deny Him to be 'very God of very God'. . . .The Unitarians must, to be consistent, charge the whole of us, who worship Christ, with being idolators. Now idolatry is a sin of the most heinous character; it is not an offence against men, it is true, but it is an intolerable offence against the majesty of God. We are ranked by Unitarians, if they be consistent, with the Hottentots. 'No,' say they, 'we believe that you are sincere in your worship.' So is the Hottentot; he bows down before his Fetich, his block of wood or stone, and he is an idolator; and although you charge us with bowing before a man, yet we do hold that you have laid at our door a sin insufferably gross, and we are obliged to repel your accusation with some severity. You have so insulted us by denying the Godhead of Christ, you have charged us with so great a crime that you can not expect us to sit coolly down and blandly smile at the imputation. It matters not what a man worships; if it be not God, he is an idolator. There is no distinction in principle between worship to a god of mud and a god of gold; nay, further, there is no distinction between the worship of an onion and the worship of the sun, moon, and stars. These are alike idolatries. And though Christ be confessed by the Socinian to be the best of men, perfection's own self; yet if He be nothing more, the vast mass of the Christian world is deliberately assailed with the impudent accusation of being idolators. Yet those who charge us with idolatry, expect us to receive them with cordial kindness. It is not in flesh and blood for us to do so, if we take the low ground of reason; it is not in grace or truth to do so, if we take the high ground of revelation. As men, we are willing to show them respect, we regard them, we pray for them, we have no anger or enmity against them. But when we come to the point of theology, we cannot, as we profess to be followers of Christ,

19

tamely see ourselves charged with an offence so dreadful and so heinous as that of idol worship.

"I confess I would almost rather be charged with a religion that extenuated murder, than with one that justified idolatry. Murder, great as the offence is, is but the slaying of man; but idolatry is, in its essence, the killing of God; it is the attempt to thrust the Eternal Jehovah out of His seat, and to foist into His place the work of His own hand, or the creature of my own conceit. Shall a man charge me with being so besotted as to worship a mere man? Shall he tell me I am so low and grovelling in my intellect, that I should stoop down to worship my own fellow creature? and yet does he expect me after that to receive him as a brother professing the same faith? I cannot understand his presumption. The charge against our sanctity of heart is so tremendous, the accusation is so frightful, that if there have been some severity and bitterness of temper in the controversy, the sin lies upon our opponent, and not on us. For he has charged us with a crime so dreadful, that an upright man must repel it as an insult. . . .If Jesus Christ be not the Son of God, co-equal, co-eternal with the Father, He so spake as to induce that belief in the minds of His own disciples, and of His adversaries likewise . . . .Now, if Christ were but a good man and a prophet, why did He not speak more decisively? Why has He not left on record a war cry for the Christian, which would be as explicit and decisive as that of Mahomet? If Christ did not mean to teach that He Himself is God, at least He was not very clear and definite in His denial, and He has left His disciples extremely in the dark, the proof whereof is to be found in the fact, that at the present day, nine hundred and ninety-nine out of every thousand of the whole of the professed followers of Christ, do receive Him, and bow down before Him, as being the very God. And if He is not God, I deny His right to be esteemed as a prophet. If He is not God, He was an imposter, the grandest, the greatest of deceivers that ever existed. This, of course, is no argument to the man who denies the faith, and does not avow himself to be a follower of Christ. But to the man that is Christ's follower, I do hold that the argument is irresistible, that Christ could not have been a good and great prophet, if He were not what He certainly led us to believe Himself to be, the Son of God, who thought it not robbery to be equal with God—,the very God, by whom all things were made, and without whom was not any thing made that is made."

—*Charles Haddon Spurgeon (1834-1892)*
*Metropolitan Tabernacle, London*

# AUTHOR'S PREFACE

My introduction to The Way International, formerly The Chimes Hour Youth Caravan, came about during a revival crusade in Emporia, Kansas when I sought to witness to an attractive, vivacious waitress during lunch at the local Holiday Inn. Her name was Teresa. When I gave her a copy of my Scripture-sated booklet, *Heaven Can Be Yours*, she thumbed through it until she noted my address, then exclaimed, "Oh, you are from Indiana; my home is in Franklin!"

A few more moments of congenial conversation revealed that she was from a good, fundamental, Bible-believing church and had attended Baptist High, a church-supported arm of the large Indianapolis Baptist Temple where my friend, Dr. Greg Dixon, has long pastored so successfully. Yet, here she was, completely *wrapped up in* and *sold out to* a heretical, Christ-denying cult, enthusiastically attending its college and planning to make her allegiance a lifelong commitment.

Later, dining at the Emporia Ramada Inn and hoping to turn it into a witness for Christ, I opened a friendly interchange with another waitress. Her name was LeAnne. Prominently displayed on the back of her right hand was a huge, full-color dove. (The Way International has chosen this, rather than the cross, as its symbol of Christianity.) Since it appeared tatooed, I curiously inquired whether it would wash off or if it were permanent.

Embarrassedly, or so it seemed to me, she confessed it was on her hand for life. Following an unwise impulse, I ventured a prediction that later she would wear gloves quite frequently. I say unwise because it closed the door to further conversation or hope of witness. LeAnne left abruptly and did not return to my table again, even sending the busboy with my check at the completion of my meal.

Also that week in Emporia I visited a barber shop and started talking to the barber about his need of Christ. He quickly convinced me he was a born-again Christian, actively seeking to serve Christ, so our talk turned to the local college. He passed on a number of very interesting things about the students.

By way of example, he told of one young man who came into the shop one day for a haircut and, in the process, asked if the barber would like to hear him talk in tongues. Without waiting for a reply, the youth started jabbering with indistinguishable vowels. After rattling on for awhile, he stopped to inquire, "Did you understand what I said?"

"No. What *did* you say?"

And the student laughingly responded, "Oh, I don't know. Only God knows."

It was a direct result of these incidents that the conviction burned into my heart and gripped my soul that someone should write an exposé of The Way. My meeting with Teresa especially burdened me. Poor, poor Teresa! Here was a lovely young woman, seemingly trained in the very finest of fundamental Bible tradition, yet so unstable as to be swept off her feet by a vicious cult which eliminates the very core of Christianity, the very foundation of the New Testament church, the Rock on which it rests—the absolute deity of our Lord and Saviour Jesus Christ.

*This book is the result!*

# INTRODUCTION

Lake Jackson is a comfortable southeast Texas community of about 15,000 souls situated a dozen miles or so inland from the Gulf of Mexico, directly below Houston. One of its chief claims to fame is a unique naming of major downtown thoroughfares. One is called "That Way," another is "This Way," a third is "Any Way," and one on which a mainline church is located has been designated "His Way."

If we were to sum up very briefly the religious thoroughfare of Victor Paul Wierwille (pronounced *we're will*) and his The Way International (hereafter identified by its initials, TWI), we would immediately designate it: **"Wrong Way!"** We are confident that long before the reader reaches the conclusion of this volume he will see the irony in Wierwille's statement regarding others, "How wrong people can be and still think they are right."[1]

Could a church organization, claiming to be Christian, be anything but wrong when the cornerstone of its doctrinal superstructure is a denial that Jesus Christ is God? The founder and president, not especially noted for his humility anyway, has boasted: "Before I finish, my life may stir up the biggest beehive in Roman Catholicism and Protestantism since the religious leaders took a shot at Martin Luther."[2]

*Why?*

Because of his teaching—although it contains an almost total lack of originality, dating back to the heretics of the first and second centuries[3]—that Jesus Christ is merely a created being, hav-

---

1. TWW, p. 63 [See bibliography for abbreviation symbols.]
2. AJC, November 26, 1977; on Reformation Sunday in 1977, Wierwille and his followers, in a crude imitation of Martin Luther, nailed a thesis to the door of the local United Church of Christ in New Knoxville, saying, "JESUS CHRIST IS NOT GOD never was and never will be." It also challenged "theologians, Bible scholars and clergymen to refute" TWI's position by "the revealed Word and will of God." Wierwille was the first signer, claiming to be a descendant of the Huguenots and adding, "Wierwilles have a legacy of courage and fidelity for truth." Yet if what he teaches today is *truth*, his ancestors were defenders of *heresy!*
3. Joel A. MacCollam sums it up: "The teaching has a historical basis in what has always been held as heresy; Wierwille also manages to touch upon Christian Science, Unity thoughts, and pious humanism. He is Gnostic and very much appears to be in the Ebionite tradition. He is certainly a Monarchian, for he totally denies the Trinity. . .he has learned much from Marcion, the second-century Gnostic who started his own movement apart from the church, while rejecting the Old Testament for Christians"; LC, October 10, 1976; pp. 11,12

23

ing His beginning in Bethlehem's manger, not equal with God the Father or thought to be God in any sense. He has written: "Jesus Christ is similar to God in many aspects, but Jesus Christ and God are not identical. They are not one and the same; they are not co-equal."[4] In a newspaper article, although saying his group "worships one God and His son, Jesus Christ our Lord and Savior," he hastened to explain: "We don't worship Jesus Christ as God or the Holy Spirit as God, even though God is holy and spirit."[5]

He claims that those who attribute deity to Christ "substantiate their beliefs by isolating bits of biblical texts."[6] Quite the contrary, the Word of God is saturated with the teaching—as we shall see in this study. What *Expositor's* says about Paul's "declarations of the divinity of the Eternal Son" is true of all Scripture, namely, ". . .the proofs that St. Paul held Christ to be God Incarnate do not lie in a few disputable texts, but in the whole attitude of his soul towards Christ, and in the doctrine of the relation of Christ to mankind which is set forth in his epistles."[7]

### What Is "The Way International"?

Legally, TWI goes back to October 30, 1947 when it was launched under the laws of the State of Ohio with the name The Chimes Hour Youth Caravan, Incorporated. Dorthea Wierwille, Lawrence G. Lee and Victor Paul Wierwille were named as incorporators and it was not until June 26, 1974 that an amendment was filed changing its name to The Way, Incorporated. However, as doctrinally structured today, the birth of the movement really dates back only to 1953 when Wierwille was pastoring a small Evangelical and Reformed congregation at Van Wert, Ohio.[8] Thinking he had discovered "new truth" and dissatisfied with the deadness in his own denomination, Wierwille started "Power for Abundant Living" classes. This was followed, in 1957, by his

---

4. JCNG, p. 28
5. AJC, November 26, 1977
6. JCNG, p. 81
7. EGT, Vol. IV, p. 196
8. Wierwille speaks of being a former United Church of Christ minister, but this is not true. He had been asked to leave the E & R about 3 years before it became a part of the new UCC movement. Leaders of the latter group are emphatic that he was *never* one of its ministers.

resignation from the church—which he says "died" shortly thereafter—and a decision to devote full time to the movement. In 1961 TWI headquarters—currently staffed by about 400 workers—was moved to the old homestead, a 147-acre family farm just outside of New Knoxville, in northwestern Ohio. Wierwille's grandfather settled the land back in 1850, shortly after arriving in America from his native Germany.

Since the cult claims to have no membership and TWI authorities refused to give us any data, attendance figures are hard to obtain and not necessarily accurate. We judge there are currently 100,000 or so adherents scattered throughout all 50 states and 50 foreign countries. (Most of them, we think, as with disciples in other cults, are caught up in its web without really understanding what is happening until they are trapped—and it is too late.[9]) TWI publishes a bimonthly magazine, *The Way*, with a circulation of about 10,000. There are over 2,000 Word Over the World [WOW] Ambassadors representing the movement across the country and around the world, donating a year of their time to the cause.[10] These kids are expected to completely support themselves with part-time jobs and still "witness" eight hours a day.

In 1974 the organization purchased the 41-acre defunct College of Emporia, a United Presbyterian school founded in 1892, renaming it The Way College of Emporia. It was obtained by merely paying off the $504,000 mortgage and $190,000 in delinquent bills, including the back salaries of former teachers. TWI also owns The Way College of Biblical Research, near Rome City, Indiana; The International Fine Arts and Historical Center at Sidney, Ohio; Camp Gunnison, a 105-acre ranch near Gunnison, Colorado; "survival camps" near Roswell, New Mexico and Fresno, California; plus numerous lesser properties for offices in various states where TWI operates. According to an April 5, 1981 article in *The Indianapolis Star*, assets total $50 million and annual income is believed to be slightly under $10 million.

TWI did not really catch fire until after it had been operating for a decade or so. Two things helped spark it: (1) Wierwille had his "Power for Abundant Living" class put on film in 1968.

---

9. See, for example, the story of Marie Leonetti; YBEC, pp. 122-132
10. These figures, other than the "50 states and 50 foreign countries," are several years old and from secondary sources. TWI refused to give us any current information whatsoever.

(2) The same year he went to the Haight-Ashbury district in San Francisco, where the Jesus Movement was seeing such phenomenal success among the long-haired scruffy kids freaked out on drugs and alcohol. His bizarre doctrine proved to be right up their alley! Dave Anderson, a former TWI leader who helped put Abundant Living on film, called it "hippie time."

In fact, Wierwille frankly confesses that his message proves effective, for the most part, only with the young. In a local newspaper interview at the time TWI purchased the Kansas campus, he said of his early years: "Most of the people I taught were church-goers in the old ritual syndrome. They would hear the Word, but then they would go back to the same old church rituals. And I was gearing my teaching, my approach, to those people—not the young, or those outside of the church. I did that for 15 years. It took me time to wise up."[11]

Translated into plain English, what he is saying is that he couldn't fool those who had been grounded in the Word of God. He found that he needed young, immature people—or those older who were completely ignorant of what the Bible teaches— to deceive. And the soil was especially fertile for the seeds of his heresy at Haight-Ashbury.

Perhaps this is one reason why his rallies feature music with the jungle beat of the world. The first festival was held at the farm in 1971 with about 1,000 in attendance. Three years later it had been moved to a county fairgrounds and 5,500 showed up. The following year saw a crowd of 8,300 paying an admission fee of $25 each for the 4-day show. By 1980 officials of the group were claiming 16,000 in attendance. Regional festivals are now in vogue and in one 3-month period 2,000 gathered in Marin, California for a Western Regional festival; 3,200 assembled in Muncie, Indiana for a Midwestern Regional festival; and another 2,200 met in Wichita, Kansas for the Southwestern Regional festival, which was also televised throughout part of Kansas. Music at these "happenings" are provided by groups with such names as "Cookin' Mama," "The Dove," "Selah," "Joyful Noise" and "Pressed Down, Shaken Together & Running Over." A rock band, Takit, tours the country making the cult's pitch to high school students.

Wierwille and other leaders in TWI are insistent that their

---

11. EG, October 22, 1974; " 'The Way' Founder Tells His Story: Part II," by E. N. Earley

movement is not a cult, a religious sect, a denomination—or even a church. Yet the organization ordains ministers, both male and female. They, in turn, are authorized to perform weddings, funerals, baptisms (but only if specifically requested), and other functions normally handled by recognized church leaders. To call TWI a cult, as we are correctly doing in this study, is especially upsetting to Wierwille and calls forth strong denunciation and denial. In a magazine editorial about deprogramming he offered his own definition and conclusion about a cult, saying:

"What is a cult? In its broadest definition, a cult is a group of people expressing devotion to some person, idea or thing. No doubt the Lutherans fit the definition when they dissented from the Roman Catholic Church in the 15th century, in response to what they saw as 'a better way.' No doubt the followers of the Wesley Brothers fit the definition when they dissented from the Church of England in the 18th century. No doubt the Pilgrims fit the definition when they set sail for the New World in 1620 in search of religious freedom."[12]

But he is wrong in his definition. To use a secular source, the unabridged *Random House Dictionary of the English Language* offers seven definitions of "cult," one of which is: "religion that is considered or held to be false or unorthodox, or its members."[13] That is exactly how the word is used throughout Christendom.

Scholarly and spiritual definitions agree. For example, Dr. Walter R. Martin, a recognized authority on the subject, has defined cults as religious groups who hold "doctrines which are pointedly contradictory to orthodox Christianity and which yet claim the distinction of tracing their origin to orthodox sources."[14]

Dr. Gordon R. Lewis, in his excellent study, *Confronting the Cults*, adds to the understanding of the word: "The term cult here designates a religious group which claims authorization by Christ and the Bible but neglects or distorts the gospel, the

---

12. WM, March-April, 1977; "Some parents ought to be deprogrammed," p. 30; incidentally, it was the 16th century, not the 15th, when Luther and his followers broke with Rome, but the error is typical of Wierwille's careless, sloppy research. Tom Jenkinson, chief executive officer of the cult's Camp Gunnison, where Way Corps members are trained, said, "We're classified as a cult and considered a three-eyed monster. But we're neither" (CN, December 15, 1980)
13. P. 353
14. *The Rise of the Cults;* quoted in "The Truth About Error" by John A. Witmer, BS, Vol. 124, No. 495, July-September, 1967; p. 249

central message of the Savior and the Scripture."[15]

Although both of these definitions were penned before Wierwille and TWI made any significant splash on the religious scene, one could easily suppose they were written yesterday to specifically describe TWI. Wierwille, like other cultic leaders, claims to have gone to the very foundations of orthodoxy for his doctrines, yet he has carved out and removed the very heart of Christianity in his denial of the absolute deity of Jesus Christ. And his understanding of *cult* seems to be those who are merely devoted to a cause and who may only disagree with the mainstream on some minor matters.

Wierwille argues, "The followers of Jesus Christ were slandered as a cult by the Pharisees and Sadducees."[16] He fails to give "chapter and verse" for this erroneous claim, probably for the simple reason that the Bible says no such thing—although it well may have been true. They called it a "sect" [Greek, *hairesis*], but the same word was used of their own groups. And for him to place himself in the same class with Martin Luther, John and Charles Wesley, the Pilgrims, and New Testament followers of Jesus Christ is certainly missing the point. None of them denied the absolute deity of our Lord; in fact, any one of them would have fiercely and bitterly opposed any and every Wierwille of his day who did!

Nor is Wierwille correct in his assessment as to why TWI is labeled a cult and opposed by true Bible believers. In his deprogramming editorial he blamed it on Satan's fear of TWI and what it is accomplishing. After quoting another writer, Wierwille says:

"Of course, the Adversary doesn't care about the dope dealers or the seminaries or the Vatican or the Black Muslims. It is the accuracy and integrity of the Word on the lips of sons of God [*by this he means his own followers*] that concerns him. It is the courageous stand of our Ambassadors in the streets and public places of Minnesota, Michigan and around the world that has him with his back to the wall. He fights, using the denominations as his respectable 'cover' and a few distraught, deluded parents as his leverage of consent."[17]

15. P. 3; John E. Dahlin, an expert in this field, answering the question, "What is the best way of identifying a cult or a false system of religion?" [DIS, April-June, 1980; p. 16], replied, "The basic test is on the matter of the Deity of Jesus Christ (I John 4:3). Every cult in our time has a defective concept with regard to this vital doctrine."
16. WM, op. cit.
17. Ibid.

But is this really logical, even from Wierwille's viewpoint? Far more efforts have been made to deprogram Moonies, Hare Krishnas, "Moses David" Berg's "Children of God" and other cult-snared youth than have ever been directed at TWI followers. Yet we are confident he doesn't think their actions are upsetting to Satan, or that these cults have Satan "with his back to the wall."

Perhaps we should take a closer look at the founder and president of TWI.

### Who Is Victor Paul Wierwille?

*Time* magazine called him ". . .a crackerbarrel theological promoter who grandiosely claims to have done the only 'pure and correct' interpretation of the Bible since the First Century."[18] As lacking in the grace of humility as such an idea is, it corresponds completely with Wierwille's own evaluation and with that of his followers.

In an interview with Wierwille which was published in *The Emporia Gazette* at the time he purchased Emporia College, the author, E. N. Earley, wrote: "His followers see him as a biblical Jeremiah, struggling in a corrupt world; an Old Testament Samuel, selected by God to teach a spiritually-ignorant world; an Apostle Paul reborn, guiding the lost sheep back to the Good Shepherd."[19] This is not even slightly an overstatement.

In his book, *Power for Abundant Living,* Wierwille argues:

"Some people contend that when the New Testament apostles died, there were no more apostles or prophets. This cannot be the case because God said that 'When he [Christ] ascended up on high, he led captivity captive, and gave gifts' to the Church. We live during the Church Administration so these gifts must still be given to us. Ephesians says that He gave (1) apostles, (2) prophets, (3) evangelists, (4) pastors and (5) teachers. If there are any pastors left, there must be some prophets; if there are any evangelists left, there must be some apostles, prophets, pastors and teachers."[20]

---

18. September 6, 1971; another media voice said TWI "preaches a version of Christianity tinged with hatred and fear," but then described it as a "show business approach to religion" and Wierwille "a dazzler, a showman who. . .understands the techniques of audience manipulation" (IS, April 5, 1981)

19. October 21, 1974; " 'The Way' Founder Tells His Story: Part I"; he apparently sees himself this way and a former associate, Dave Anderson, declared: "He bought his own hype. He really began to believe that he was the greatest man of God since the Apostle Paul" (IS, April 5, 1981)

20. P. 352

Overlooking the obvious flaw in his reasoning—which ignores the fact that the ministry of the apostles and prophets pertained only to the *foundation* of the church, according to the same Book of Ephesians (2:19-22)—it is very apparent whom Wierwille and his followers believe holds the rank of apostle in the 20th century. We say this for three reasons: (1) He alone in TWI, as far as we know, claims to have had God commission him audibly by a voice from Heaven. (2) His definition of the office fits his claim for himself ["An *apostle* is one who brings new light to his generation. It may be old revelation, but it is new to the generation to whom he speaks"[21]], ignoring the New Testament qualifications. (3) The testimonies of his devotees take the claim for granted. One of his disciples, Elena S. Whiteside, who herself calls him "the man who initially believed," in a book released in 1972, *The Way, Living in Love,* quotes one hippie convert to the cult as enthusing, "I see Dr. Wierwille as the next man of God to rise up after Paul's death. It's taken that long to rise up in believing."[22] A heady comment, indeed. And she quotes another as saying, "Nowhere else can you get this knowledge of how to read and understand God's Word."[23] The latter added, "This is the closest thing you'll find to the first century Church anywhere in the world."[24]

Although family tradition called for the youngest child to take over the farm—and Victor Paul, born on the final day of 1916, was the last in a half-dozen descendants (Otto, Lydia, Sevilla, Harry and Reuben preceded him) of Ernest and Emma Rehn Wierwille—the budding apostle announced while still in high school that he wanted to be a minister and often, like Billy Graham says he did, went out into the woods and preached to the trees. Apparently to offset his father's disappointment over his decision, he agreed to attend the family's denominational college, Mission House College (now Lakeland College) in Sheboygan, Wisconsin. There he picked up a bride during his junior year, Dorothea "Dotsie" Kipp, tying the knot with his childhood sweetheart on July 2, 1937—although the happy tidings were kept secret for six months so he could continue playing basketball[25]—and a Bachelor of Divinity degree upon gradua-

---

21. Ibid.
22. P. 43
23. P. 29
24. P. 30
25. EG, October 22, 1974; op. cit.

tion. His union with Dotsie produced five offspring: Donald, Karen, Mary, John Paul and Sara.

V.P., as his intimates refer to him, took his graduate work at Princeton Theological Seminary and obtained a Master of Theology degree in practical theology. He also studied briefly at the University of Chicago Divinity School and even claims he took everything he could take at the evangelical Moody Bible Institute, through its correspondence courses—an assertion the latter school vigorously denies.[26] His Doctor of Theology, ostensibly obtained by correspondence and two summers at the institution, was granted from Pikes Peak Seminary, a nonaccredited institution considered by some to be little more than a degree mill.[27]

Obviously, the heart of Wierwille's education was liberal. The jacket of *Jesus Christ Is NOT God*—which is also given as an Epilogue of sorts in the body of his other books—notes men who have influenced his thinking, saying: "In his many years of research, Dr. Wierwille has studied with such men as Karl Barth, E. Stanley Jones, Glen(n) Clark, Bishop K. C. Pillai and George Lamsa." We do not recognize the name of one reliable, capable, trustworthy man in the group. Yet, at the same time, strangely, Wierwille is a *strong* dispensationalist with both a premillennial and pretribulation position—which helps add to the confusion about him. He also claims to have taught at the evangelical Gordon Divinity School.[28] And he says he wrote monthly articles

26. In a letter to the author (1/2/80), Eric Fellman, MBI public relations director, wrote: ". . .we are aware of his claim to have attended Moody Bible Institute. However, I have personally researched our files on this matter and am positive no one of that name ever attended any Day, Summer, Evening or Correspondence Classes as a bonafide registrant. Regrettably, this does not stop him from claiming to attend." However, his personal secretary, who has been with TWI since its inception, Rhoda Wierwille, wife of his brother Reuben, graduated from Moody in 1946; WLL, p. 88

27. ". . .the Colorado Commission on Higher Education reports that Pikes' Peak has no resident instruction, no published list of faculty, no accreditation, and is not under the supervision of any government agency. The degree program is offered by extramural methods, and the degree has only that status which the conferring school chooses to give it"; LC, op. cit., p. 11

28. WLL, p. 175; Gordon merged with Conwell School of Theology in 1969, becoming Gordon-Conwell Theological Seminary. Lloyd A. Kalland, executive vice-president of the institution, kindly sent us photo copies of the 1946-47 catalog, showing Wierwille listed as a "Summer School Guest Professor," teaching *Homiletics D10, Radio Preaching,* 2 hours, and *Christian Education D10, History of Religious Education,* 2 hours.

for the evangelical Higley Press of Butler, Indiana.[29]

The entire TWI movement bases its appeal to recruits on the idea of intellectualism. Converts are assured they will be receiving the very latest and finest scholarship in Bible teaching available anywhere. Yet the exact opposite is sadly true.

James Bjornstad, executive director of the Institute of Contemporary Christianity, calls Wierwille's scholarship "an abomination." To illustrate, he says: "To make a point he will go to the extreme of saying, 'Now in the Sanskrit it says. . . .' There's no Sanskrit manuscript, but he uses that language to show unique interpretations. To the person who doesn't have any scholastic background, it sounds great."[30] Or Wierwille may say something like, "The Telegu translation of Proverbs 29:18 reads: 'Where there is no knowledge of God the people wander aimlessly.' "[31] But this is translating from Hebrew into an Indian dialect and then retranslating into English—a very unsatisfactory method when accuracy of meaning is desired. In legal parlance it could be called "double jeopardy" in translation! However, perhaps his most common copout, when faced with Scripture refuting his teaching, is to say, "A literal translation of this verse would be. . . ," then offer a meaning entirely contrary to what the passage is plainly saying. Or he might say, if it stretches credulity too far for even him to call it literal, "A literal translation *according to usage is*. . . ."

Another popular evasion is his repeated reference to the Aramaic. For example, quoting John 19:40, when he wants the burial of Jesus to be exclusively the act of Nicodemus, apart from any assistance by Joseph of Arimathea, he says, "In the Aramaic text the word 'they' is the word 'he.' "[32] Often, as in this case, his Aramaic authority, George S. Lamsa, does not agree

29. Ibid., p. 177
30. Quoted by Shirl Short in "The menace of the new cults" MM, July-August, 1977, p. 29; see also John Juedes, who concludes: "Let this sampling of Wierwille's merciless mutation of biblical scholarship be sufficient warning against his overall perversion of God's Word regarding Christ's nature" (JPP, Vol. IV, No. 1, 1980, "Wierwille's Way with the Word," p. 97)
31. BTMS, p. 10; this reference to an Indian dialect reminds us that in 1955-6, while still pastoring an E & R church, he and his family made an overseas missionary tour, including 3 months in India where, "because of certain remarks which he made criticizing the church and the government of India, a riot erupted. . .resulting in destruction of considerable property" (IS, April 5, 1981)
32. TWW, p. 262

with him. But that seems a trivial matter to him! Still another habit is his custom, which most Bible believers and all scholars find horribly obnoxious, of saying, after brutally mutilating, taking completely out of context, or rewriting some passage: "How beautiful and accurate is God's matchless Word when properly understood!" The words of Jon Braun are pertinent here: "Biblical word games may be entertaining, but they do not change the meaning of words."[33]

Perhaps some of his liberty in changing and twisting biblical meaning comes from a license he feels inherent with his special "call" for TWI ministry. That call dates back to the fall of 1942 when, after pastoring for barely a year his first Evangelical and Reformed charge at Payne, Ohio, he was sitting in his office feeling frustrated, discouraged and ready to quit. He "told God outright," he claimed to an interviewer later, "that He could have the whole thing, unless there were real genuine answers that I wouldn't ever have to back up on. That's when He spoke to me audibly, just like I'm talking to you now. He said He would teach me the Word as it has not been known since the first century if I would teach it to others."[34] He said, "Father spoke to me and promised that He would teach me the Word. . . ."[35]

What was Wierwille's reaction to this prophet/apostle/biblical amanuensis-type call? He says, "Well, I nearly flew off my chair. I couldn't believe that God would talk to me." Then, to assuage the seeming phenomenon for the ears of his Gentile hearers, he adds, "But really why is it so strange? When you think about it, you see in the Bible that all through the ages God talked to people. God talked to Moses, and to all of the Prophets. God talked to Paul. All through the centuries, God has talked to people in times of great need."[36]

But this explanation ignores the clear scriptural teaching that the divine revelation is closed. The last chapter in the Bible plainly warns, "For I testify unto every man that heareth the words of the prophecy of this book, If any man shall add unto these things, God shall add unto him the plagues that are written in this book" (Rev. 22:18). If God were to speak from Heaven today **it would be an addition to His Word**—His mind and will to man. This cannot possibly be! And the fact that Wierwille's message is one so contradictory to the past revelation of God in the

33. WHH, p. 162
34. EG, October 22, 1974, op. cit.
35. EG, October 21, 1974, op. cit.

Bible makes its lack of authenticity a foregone conclusion!

We are willing to concede that Wierwille heard an audible voice—we know enough about demonism, for example, to make this concession—but we are **absolutely positive** the voice he heard was not the voice of God, nor was the message a revelation from God. It seems self-evident, since another quarter of a century rolled by before Wierwille's unorthodox message caught fire, that there is no valid spiritual connection between the 1942 "call" and the late 1960s "teaching."

*What was the voice?* Was it the voice of a demon? Did Wierwille fall asleep in his chair and experience a nightmare as an aftermath of lunching on lasanga and garlic bread? Who could say with certainty?

It reminds us of a humorous but true incident reported in the *Reader's Digest.* A gynecologist was using his battery-operated mini-dop on a pregnant patient, checking on the fetal heartbeat. While he knew the instrument occasionally picked up interference from either the radio or television in his waiting room he wasn't aware it would also pick up CB and walkie-talkie transmissions. Imagine his surprise, then, as he listened for the fetus' heartbeat, to hear a voice asking, "How are things out there?"

Along the same line, Rev. Austin Miles, pastor of an Assembly of God Church at Bath, New York, was challenging his people about the power of prayer, confidently assuring them that God would answer. No sooner had he spoken the words than a nearby CBer's message was picked up by the church public address system, flashing it to the startled congregation: "That's a big 10-4, good buddy." While the timing may have been perfect, the voice was not the voice of God.

That Wierwille may have fallen asleep and dreamed his commission is indicated by the confirmation he received the following day. Returning to his office, he said, "Lord, if it's really true what you said to me yesterday, if that was really you talking to me, you've got to give me a sign so that I really know, so that I can believe. Let me see snow." He insists today that when he closed his eyes the skies were bright and clear. When he opened them "the sky was so thick and white with snow, I couldn't see the tanks of the filling station on the corner, 75 feet away."[37]

---

36. EG, October 22, 1974, op. cit.; this entire account, given almost word-for-word the same, is also found in WLL, pp. 178,179

37. Ibid.; see also WLL, p. 180

Obviously, a period of time passed between his eyes closing and then reopening. While we can only offer a nap as a *possibility* of what happened, we are *dogmatic* in insisting that Wierwille's heretical teachings about Christ, the Trinity, the Holy Spirit and other matters—which date back to the days of Marcion and the Gnosticism Paul refuted in his Colossian writing—are definitely not of God, hence whatever experiences he had in the early fall of 1942 were not from God, either.

In many ways Wierwille reminds one—in claiming to be an apostle with a rediscovered New Testament message which, in reality, is far removed from biblical teaching—of another false prophet, Herbert W. Armstrong.[38] For example, both Armstrong and Wierwille are most liberal in their use of brackets. It seems that if one has a large enough supply, he can insert them into Bible verses right and left, making any passage say and mean whatever the bracket user wishes it to say and mean.

Consider a random illustration. If Wierwille is to establish a denial of our Lord's absolute deity, he must nullify the plain and unmistakable force of John 1:1-3, which says: "In the beginning was the Word, and the Word was with God, and the Word was God. The same was in the beginning with God. All things were made by him; and without him was not any thing made that was made." How could Wierwille's Christ—a created being who had no existence prior to Bethlehem—be with God in the beginning, yea, *be* God and create all things?

Out come the plentiful brackets and the passage is made to read: "In the beginning was the Word [God], and the [revealed] Word was with [*pros*] God [with Him in His foreknowledge yet independent of Him], and the Word was God. The same [revealed Word] was in the beginning with [*pros*] God. All things were made by him [God]; and without him [God] was not anything made that was made."[39]

We will comment on what he has done to this passage, showing how he has twisted the original—plus giving his "literal translation"—later in the book; we are only concerned here with showing his use of brackets. Through them—just like that, *ipso*

38. See the author's in-depth study, ARMSTRONGISM: THE "WORLDWIDE CHURCH OF GOD" EXAMINED IN THE SEARCHING LIGHT OF SCRIPTURE, © 1974, Biblical Evangelism, Brownsburg, IN 46112; 16 chapters, 424 pages, hardbound, $7.95
39. JCNG, pp. 87,91

*facto*—the meaning of the passage is reversed to harmonize with Wierwille's heretical teaching.

Another factor in common with Armstrong and other cultists is the use of "keys" to unlock spiritual truth, supposedly discovered by the "apostle" and available through no other teacher in our day. Wierwille, in his Introduction to *Power for Abundant Living,* writes: "This is a book containing Biblical keys. . . .it is designed to set before the reader the basic keys in the Word of God so that Genesis to Revelation will unfold and so that the abundant life which Jesus Christ came to make available will become evident to those who want to appropriate His abundance to their lives."[40] And Wierwille joins Armstrong and other cultists in the abominable practice of building imaginary strawmen, then gleefully tearing them apart—supposedly proving thereby the accuracy of their own teachings.

As indicated earlier, one of the prime factors in launching TWI successfully was the filming and taping of Wierwille's twelve "Power for Abundant Living" lessons, his "foundation course." *Time* magazine described it by saying he "unloaded 36 hours of rambling, folksy lectures," adding that he carried "Norman Vincent Peale's pious optimism a good bit further [than Peale]."[41] TWI charges each individual $85 for the 12 lessons and approximately 2,000 people a month are taking the course, assured by Mr. Wierwille, "After you take the class there is no amount of money that you will take for what you have learned."[42]

One of the disciples explains the TWI framework like this: "The Way organization also is designed with exactness. It is structured like a tree. When one or two followers of The Way meet together, that is called a twig meeting. Twigs come from a tree and that was Doctor Wierwille's vision for this ministry years ago.

---

40. P. 4; a sample of Herbert W. Armstrong's use of keys: ". . .the vital KEY, needed to unlock prophetic doors to understanding, had become lost. That KEY is a definite knowledge of the true identity of the American and British peoples in biblical prophecy," *The United States and the British Commonwealth in Prophecy,* Copyright, 1954; p. 1
41. Op. cit.; actually, although Wierwille filmed 36 hours, it was edited to only 33; see WLL, p. 229
42. EG, October 21, 1974, op. cit.; the fee was later raised to $100 and is currently believed to be $200—and an "advanced" course is available for $250 (IS, April 5, 1981)

"The life of a tree is in its twigs—its individual leaves or new leaves (Way followers). Three twigs in an area form a branch of The Way (districts) and then the branches form a limb (states or regions). The limbs join the trunks (countries) and the trunks all lead to the roots, which is the international headquarters where research is done."[43]

In preparing this book we endeavored to obtain information from TWI as to the approximate number of trunks, limbs, branches, twigs and leaves the movement currently operates, but were refused even a hint. Regardless of the number, it is safe to say that these people, mostly high school and college youth, have a dedication to their cause that is so often characterized by cults. Some are members of The Way Corps, which involves volunteering for a 4-year work stint on the Ohio farm without remuneration. Others volunteer for WOW (Word Over the World) ambassadorships and this is a 1-year commitment to accept assignments wherever the leadership desires to send them, moving out "on a day or even on a one-hour notice."

Followers of TWI work hard and study diligently. Unfortunately, since the teaching they are receiving is erroneous, the deeper they drink at that fountain the more dangerous and damaging it is. As with all cults, not everything taught by TWI is error, but such a mingling of truth and falsehood only makes the wrong more dangerous.

It is interesting that the secret for mind control[44] which is being practiced by many of the eastern religions sweeping American campuses—*keep the kids so dog tired they can't think for themselves*—is also followed by TWI. A normal day on the Ohio farm sees members of the Way Corps rising at 5 a.m., followed by strenuous excercises. Most run any where from one to four miles each morning, following with the typical toe-touching excercises

---

43. Ibid.; Wierwille has announced his retirement as head of the cult on October 3, 1982 in order to travel and teach, appointing 32-year-old Craig Martinsdale, current director of The Way Corps, as his successor; Wierwille's son, Donald, will remain in his vice-president capacity (CT, March 13, 1981)
44. A bill dealing with cults before the Minnesota House, introduced by Representatives Reding and Kalis, defined mind alteration as the "use of subtle psychological techniques. . .[such as] deprivation of sleep, continual observance, interference with privacy, group peer pressure to discourage contrary thought questioning, monotonous chanting and singing, and inadequate diets which are designed to, or have the effect of, diminishing or eliminating the potential convert's or convert's free will and ability to rationally decide. . . ."

which are accompanied by such chants as, "One, two, three for the Lord; four, five, six for His glory."

This is only the prelude to the hard day's labor. Then, after the evening meal, the disciples are sent into area communities to "witness." Bedtime, a welcome relief, does not arrive until after 11 p.m.; then at 5 the following morning it is "rise and shine" all over again. Miss Whiteside acknowledges that they "do with six hours sleep a night." Coupled with the constant activity and laborious hours are the stern disciplines and regimentation which usually accompany mind-captive cults. One critic, Ken Altekruse, explains it: "When Wierwille gets done with them, they all think like him, or, rather, don't think."[45]

On the matter of mind control—and the extent to which loyal followers of Wierwille obey his every whim—perhaps we should note a letter he sent to his Way Corps workers on May 24, 1979. To honor his 42nd wedding anniversary, Wierwille wanted these devotees to write essays cataloging key events in their lives, including minute descriptions of past indiscretions. He instructed them: "I want the where, what, who, when, why and how regarding every major decision point in your life from birth that brought you to the point of entering The Way Corps. For example: I got into sex in the sixth grade; I started drugs when I was 12; I robbed the local liquor store; I was in the Baptist Church; my basketball coach taught me something that changed my life. Paint the picture of what you were in, and vividly relate how you were delivered."[46]

As Duddy noted: "The overt intent of this letter is to rouse to public light foul, closeted skeletons of the Way Corps' sinful pasts that beg the silence of definite burial." And he rightly concludes: "First, the 'sin bank' lifts, not one occasion of confession, but the entire ignominious record, out of the confessors' personal control. Although Wierwille writes, 'The information you send me will be confidential unless you give me permission to use it,' he does not explain how confidentiality will be maintained. The Corps carte blanche, in compliance with their leader's request, will deliver private confessional data into the hands of a third party or parties who might use it in broad, unknown contexts.

"Second, the temptation for Way staff to sinfully use the con-

---

45. IS, April 5, 1981; Bill Henline, a Lutheran minister's son, said his experience in the cult made him "a non-person" (Ibid.)
46. CPN, July-August 1979; "Holding the Corps High!?" by Neil Duddy

fessions is an explosive possibility. If an agitator or defector emerges from the Corps, a few appropriate phone calls or letters to employers or neighbors, tapping the 'sin bank,' could effectively silence those dissenters and would undoubtedly deter other waffling Corps patriots from voicing their criticism. In addition, material siphoned from the 'sin bank' could be powerfully used to coerce members in certain circumstances that would compromise their standards."[47]

This mind control—called by some "a network of deceit" and "mental violence"—is further illustrated by the fact that the followers are required to implicitly obey the leadership in all areas as "the will of God." Not to do so is considered rebellion against God Himself and results in the loss of His blessing and power! Dr. Wierwille's assistant and one of the group's ordained ministers, Rev. Walter Cummins, uses the falling out between Barnabas and Paul to prove the point. Since Barnabas is not mentioned again in Acts, He interprets this silence as teaching that he was out of the will of God in disagreeing with Paul and fell by the wayside. So Cummins sums it up: "[Barnabas and Paul] both thought they were right, had their good reasons, but you see, from all indications in the Word, Paul the apostle was the spiritual leader. He was responsible to God. And anyone else goes with the spiritual leader. That's why **we go with the leader, believing God he's receiving the necessary guidance from God**."[48] That, of course, nullifies and ignores the individual priesthood of every believer, provided through the work of our Lord Jesus Christ on the cross. Each child of God today can

---

47. Ibid.
48. WLL, p. 111, emphasis added; John Desmond, who was dismissed from The Way Corps, which he described as "an SS training camp," when he refused to sign a blank 3" x 5" file card promising unquestioned obedience to leaders, says, "You follow the leader, right or wrong," and Wendy Ford, who quit TWI, explained, "We were up at 5 and told what to do every minute of the day" (IS, April 5, 1981; state Editor Joan Richardson, who research and wrote the *Star* articles, said: "Called the largest and most dangerous cult in the country today.The Way has been accused of brainwashing its followers into a mindless obedience as intense as the suicidal loyalty Jim Jones once commanded"; she gives chilling evidence TWI followers may be willing to kill at the command of its leaders); *U.S. News & World Report* quoted one source as saying Way followers are taught "to hit a bull's-eye from three different position—prone, sitting and standing"

determine the will of God for himself; he is not dependent upon a pope, a priest, a preacher—or *any* third party.

It is understandable that such "mind control" devotion keeps the coppers freely flowing into TWI coffers. As far back as 1971, *Time* magazine quoted Harry Wierwille, brother of the founder and treasurer of the group, to the effect that "Sunday services take in as much as $10,000 a night."[49] It is small wonder that Wierwille is now able to "roam the range" in a $750,000 twin-engine turbojet.[50]

\* \* \* \* \*

We will close this Introduction with words Wierwille wrote about the citizens of Emporia in his President's Newsletter a few months after TWI purchased the campus in that city. He said:

"In Emporia, the church leaders are beginning to spread the usual baloney that so often sprouts up like weeds whenever our people hold forth the Word with boldness.

"Some are saying that I am a devil worshipper and that we who are followers of The Way are a bunch of heretics. Let them talk. Paul ran into some of the same flak.

". . .It is always the religious element in a community that starts the rumors and the backbiting. They will do anything to stop you from teaching the accuracy of the Word. Like the Pharisees and Sadducees in Jesus' day, they can't tolerate the truth because the great light of it always reproves the error of their theology."[51]

We are releasing this book to throw the "great light" of Truth upon the age-old errors of heresy which Victor Paul Wierwille and The Way International have revived.

*We are confident of the final outcome!*

---

49. Op. cit.
50. IS, April 5, 1981
51. EG, November 16, 1974

## Chapter One
# THE FATAL FLAW, REJECTION OF CHRIST'S DEITY

*Can one honor the Lord Jesus Christ and, at the same time, deny His absolute deity?* Wierwille and his followers in TWI think so. He says, "To say Jesus Christ is not God does not degrade the importance and significance of Jesus Christ in any way, it simply elevates to God the position that the Bible places Him."[1]

**The testimony of history's evangelical scholarship could not disagree more vehemently!**

Dr. I M. Haldeman, noted defender of the Faith and long pastor of the historic First Baptist Church in New York City, where President George Washington was baptized, put it well: "If Jesus Christ were not God, then he was not a redeemer and saviour. All the beautiful things that have been taught about him as such are false. All the hopes of heaven, the beauty of the celestial city, the tree of life, the river of crystal, the company of the saints, the arch-angelic song, the meeting and the knowing of those who long ago have left us—none of these things are so.

"If he were not God, then it is not true that he sits upon the throne, high and lifted up, listening to the plaints of the weakest heart that shall trust him, and hearing the sound of every falling tear.

"If Jesus Christ be not God, then the whole system of Christianity built upon his person and work falls to the ground, is broken into fragments, and like wind-swept dust can never be gathered.

"If Jesus Christ be not God, the New Testament record of him is untrue. The New Testament impeached in its prime particular becomes a worthless book—a book full of exhortations to holiness and truth, in the name of him who is proven to be (if he ever lived at all) a blasphemer, a deceiver of men and the concrete of human wickedness. If the New Testament is not true, neither is the Old; for the Old Testament finds its meaning and value only in the Christ of the New Testament. Take Jesus Christ out of the Old Testament (which you must do if you set aside the New; for he alone fulfills the types, the symbols and the prophecies of the Old Testament; he alone makes its testimony and history intelligible; he alone gives unity, harmony and authoritative meaning

---

1. AJC, November 26, 1977

*41*

to its exhortations)—take Christ out of the Old Testament and you take away its one and only key.

"And mark you—*when Christ goes out of the Bible as God— God goes out of the Bible.* The deity which has preserved it, the power which has made it living and unchangeable in the midst of change and death, will have been dethroned.

"Without Christ as God you are without any sane and satisfying knowledge of God."[2]

One of America's finest statesmen—Congressman, Secretary of State under Woodrow Wilson, 3-time Democrat nominee for President, famed for his 3-hour "Cross of Gold" speech— William Jennings Bryan, put it bluntly: "The Bible, from beginning to end, teaches the deity of Christ. In the Old Testament, His coming is foretold and His Divine character is plainly announced."[3]

Sir Robert Anderson, another outstanding Christian gentleman, a devout scholar of Scripture, and a member of London's famed Scotland Yard—probably in that same order of importance—authored a classic book on the deity of Christ. It permeates with the investigative thoroughness of a Scotland Yard member. Referring to those in his day who denied it, he noted: "That the New Testament teaches the Deity of Christ is so indisputable that the infidel accepts the fact, and the task he sets himself is to disparage the testimony of the writers."[4] In the case of Wierwille, however, he refuses to face this fact so obvious that even infidels acknowledge it, and writes reams of material to twist and distort that which on the surface is so self-evident and plain to an honest reader.

Thirty years ago the founder and director of the American Prophetic League, Dr. Keith L. Brooks, declared: "We do not hesitate to assert that the deity of Jesus Christ is so interwoven with the whole texture of the New Testament that any honest person who would deny His deity, must first destroy the New Testament or resort to strange devices to dispose of plain language."[5] Since Wierwille professes to believe in biblical inerrancy and to take what it says literally, he is guilty of the second rather than the first. In this chapter we will see some of the truly

---

2. CCB, pp. 27,28
3. SQD, p. 33
4. LFH, p. 21
5. KB, March, 1949; "How Could Christ Be A Mere Man?" p. 8

"strange devices to dispose of plain langauge" to which he resorts.

Wierwille is strong and vitriolic in his denunciation of Jesus Christ as God. In his major work, *Jesus Christ Is NOT God,* which he describes as "a summation of my personal quest to test the doctrine of the trinity to see whether it be a man-made or a God-breathed doctrine,"[6] he loses no time launching his attack. On the opening pages of his Introduction he writes: "I have checked God's Word hundreds of times over, and thus I am convinced beyond a shadow of a doubt that Jesus Christ is not God . . . .I am saying that Jesus Christ is not God. . . .Jesus Christ was not literally with God in the beginning; neither does he have all the assets of God."[7]

In the initial chapter he endeavors to align history with his position, giving numerous quotations from early writings to that effect. Since there have always been heretics numbered within professing Christendom, he is able to amass several strong statements, of course. But he sums up the chapter with a blatantly false assertion: "Clearly, historians of Church dogma and systematic theologians agree that the idea of a Christian trinity was not a part of the first century Church. The twelve apostles never subscribed to it or received revelation about it."[8] And it was not until the peak of Constantine's power, Wierwille says, "that the idea of Jesus Christ's being co-equal with God the Father began to gain a wide base of support."[9]

Such a conclusion is reached only through biased, slanted, one-sided reporting of the data which would make today's liberal news media green with envy. In dealing with the facts of history, no more dispassionate, neutral, nonpartisan witness dating back closer to the days of Christ and His apostles could be called to testify than Flavius Josephus. Since he was an Israelite, a member of the Jewish establishment and not a follower of Christ in any sense, when he speaks as a historian what he says is certainly worthy of our careful attention.

In his *Antiquities of the Jews,* written in the first century, Josephus says of our Lord: "Now, there was about this time Jesus, a wise man, if it be lawful to call him a man, for he was a doer of wonderful works,—a teacher of such men as receive the

---

6. P. 7
7. Ibid., pp. 3-5
8. Ibid., p. 25
9. Ibid., p. 22

truth with pleasure. He drew over to him both many of the Jews and many of the Gentiles. He was [the] Christ; and when Pilate, at the suggestion of the principal men among us, had condemned him to the cross, those that loved him at the first did not forsake him, for he appeared to them alive again the third day, as the divine prophets had foretold these and ten thousand other wonderful things concerning him; and the tribe of Christians, so named from him, are not extinct at this day."[10]

This is a most remarkable authentication about Christ from one who, if anything, would have been prejudiced as a Jew against our Lord. Yet he sets forth clear indication that many in that time considered Jesus Christ to be God ("if it be lawful to call him a man"), using language to confess even his own uncertainty that He was not. He also acknowledged the validity and historicity of Christ's miracles ("he was a doer of wonderful works"), and he considered the resurrection a historical fact ("he appeared to them alive again the third day, as the divine prophets had foretold"). While all three affirmations are significant, we call special attention to this first century, unbiased testimony that our Lord's followers considered Him to be God.

In a letter that Pliny the Younger, who was governor of Bithynia from A.D. 111 to 113, sent to the Emperor Trajan, he makes it quite clear that the followers of Christ considered Him to be God. Part of that letter declares: "They were in the habit of meeting on a certain fixed day before it was light, **when they sang an anthem to Christ as God**, and bound themselves by a solemn oath (*sacramentum*) not to commit any wicked deed, but to abstain from all fraud, theft and adultery, never to break their word, or deny a trust when called upon to honor it: after which it was their custom to separate, and then meet again to partake of food, but food of an ordinary and innocent kind."[11] This letter, remember, was written in the very first century following our Lord's life, death and resurrection—and only a few years after the New Testament was written.

One of the earliest witnesses among the church fathers was Ignatius of Antioch, the second bishop of this city which was such a key one in early Christendom—where the disciples were first called Christians (Acts 11:26) and the one from whence the famous missionary team of Paul and Barnabas was commissioned (Acts 13:1-3). Eusebius reveals that Ignatius was made

10. WFJ, Book XVII, Chapter III, paragraph 3, p. 548
11. *Letters* x. 96; quoted in EHHC, p. 124, emphasis added

bishop at Antioch about 69 A.D., meaning that he assumed this responsibility just a few years after Paul's martyrdom, the date of which was as early as 64 A.D. or as late as 68 A.D. At any rate, Ignatius, apparently a prolific writer, takes us back to the cradle of our Faith and seven letters he penned while on the way to martyrdom have been preserved to this hour.

What did this contemporary of the Apostle John have to say about the person of Jesus Christ? To the Ephesians, he praised them "because no heresy dwells among you; indeed, you do not even listen to anyone unless he speaks truly of Jesus Christ" (6:2), then two verses later described that nonheretical view of Him:

> "both flesh and spirit,
> begotten and unbegotten,
> in man, God,
> in death, true life,
> both from Mary and from God,
> first passible and then impassible,
> Jesus Christ our Lord."

He also said, "For our God, Jesus the Christ, was conceived by Mary in accordance with the plan of God" (18:2), and "God was becoming manifest in human form for the newness of eternal life" (19:3).

To the church at Tralles, also in Asia, he spoke of those who were "inseparable from the God Jesus Christ" (7:1). To the Romans he said, "our God Jesus Christ appears all the more clearly because he is in the Father" (3:3). To the church at Smyrna he wrote, "I give glory to Jesus Christ, the God who made you so wise" (1:1). And "to Polycarp, bishop of the church of the Smyrnaeans," he pleaded: "Wait for him who is above a moment of time—

> eternal,
> invisible, for our sake visible,
> intangible,
> impassible, for our sake passible—
> him who in every way endured on our behalf" (3:2).

And in closing, he told Polycarp, "I bid you farewell always in our God Jesus Christ" (8:3). There is not the slightest doubt about Ignatius' firm commitment to and belief in the absolute deity of Jesus Christ.[12]

---

12. Quotes taken from AF, pp. 79,80,83,94,99,110,117,119

Speaking of Polycarp, whose stinging retort to Marcion as "the firstborn of Satan" and his thrilling refusal to recant and save his life at the time of martyrdom are well known to multitudes even today, Irenaeus, bishop of Lyons late in the second century, tells us he personally knew several who had seen Christ in the flesh— indeed, had even been the disciple of John the Beloved. In the account of the martyrdom of Polycarp, taken from the writings of Irenaeus, we find that he refused to say "Caesar is Lord" (8:2), indicating that he understood such to be a title reserved for deity, and that he declared at the time of his death, "we shall never find it possible either to abandon Christ. . .or to worship any other. For him we worship as the Son of God" (17:2,3).[13] Here is clear and definite testimony to the fact that the early Christians worshiped Christ as Lord, one who is deity.

However, since all ages—past, present and undoubtedly future—have had and will have both orthodox and heterodox professors of Christianity, quotations can liberally be found on both sides of the theological fence. This issue can only be settled by the "Thus saith the Lord" as revealed in the Word of God. What does the Bible teach?

Wierwille's argument for denying deity to Christ is based primarily on his hypothesis that if Christ is the Son of God, He cannot be God the Son [which, we presume, would also conclusively prove that ten cents and a dime are not equal, either]. He says: "In the Bible the phrase *Son of God*, referring to Jesus Christ, is found 50 times. At no place is there *God the Son*. Without 'God the Son,' Jesus Christ cannot be God."[14] He says again: "To say that 'Son of God' means or equals 'God the Son' totally negates the rules of language, leaving it utterly useless as a tool of communication."[15]

While this argument may appear strong to Gentiles untrained in biblical language now living in the 20th century, it would have proven illogical and foolish to Jewish students of Scripture living in New Testament days. It is anything but a scholarly argument and, while Wierwille may claim equating *Son of God* with *God the Son* "totally negates the rules" of today's English, according to "the rules of biblical usage" the exact opposite is true. The terms were interchangeable and equal; our Lord was ascribing deity to Himself when He called Himself the Son of God.

---

13. Ibid., pp. 142,148
14. JCNG, p. 27, emphasis his
15. Ibid., p. 5

As Sir Robert Anderson points out in his discussion of the "Son of God" title: "The only meaning that can be given to it is that which it conveyed to those who heard His teaching, those among whom He lived and died. Just as by 'Son of Man' He claimed to be man in the highest and most absolute sense, so by 'Son of God' He laid claim to Deity. His disciples understood it thus, and they worshipped Him as divine; and those who refused to believe in Him understood it thus, and they crucified Him as a blasphemer."[16]

A twentieth century Jewish writer highlights the same truth. Answering the claim of a pamphlet that Jesus was merely the Son of God, neither God nor preexistent, he pointed out: "Whatever meaning this term conveys to this particular writer, it certainly is not that which the Holy Scripture teaches concerning the Son of God. . . .any article which sets out to prove that Jesus Christ was not God is *a priori* erroneous, for it shows that the writer has absolutely no conception of the Hebrew Messiah as taught in the Bible, and has no spiritual perception of what the prophets and seers teach concerning the subject in the Old Testament Scriptures.

". . .This statement [that 'Son of God' denies deity] shows how utterly unfamiliar that writer is with Hebrew language, Hebrew Messianic expectancy and Hebrew phraseology. Anyone reading John 10:30-33 can see that Jesus claimed in verse 30 that 'I and my Father are one,' and by declaring that He is the Son of God He made Himself equal with God, and therefore God. That is why He was accused of blasphemy. That is why the Jews attempted to stone Him. It stands to reason that if the Jews thought that Jesus claimed to be an ordinary man or even superman, it was not an utterance that deserved the extreme penalty of stoning.

". . .[This writer] arrives at erroneous conclusions because of his lack of appreciation and knowledge of Hebrew Messianic terminology, and that is why he makes the incorrect statement that Jesus denied the charge against Him in John 10:33. It shows lack of spiritual as well as judicial perception. Jesus, in verses 34, 35 and 36 does not deny the charge, but affirms it by declaring He is the 'Son of God.' 'Therefore they sought *again* to take Him' (verse 39) not because He denied He was God, but because in no uncertain terms He affirmed that He was the Son of God, which to all Jews was a term equal to God.

---

16. Op. cit., pp. 45,46

"Ancient Jewish Rabbis in their mystic writings, as well as the Prophets in the Old Testament, believed that Messiah, the Redeemer of Israel, is none other but God. That is precisely the reason for the accusation in John 10:33, and that is why they took up stones to stone Him, that is, to kill Him with the death prescribed in the Law of Moses for utterances of blasphemy. Otherwise, the attitude and action of the Jews in the case cannot be understood and the alternative is error and misconception."[17]

John R. Rice points out the position of historic Christianity: ". . .Jesus boldly affirmed His deity. That is what Jesus meant when He claimed to be in a peculiar sense the Son of God. It is a modern idea—not even hinted at in the Bible. . .—that Jesus could be the Son of God as He claimed to be without actually being deity, the God-man."[18]

It is the same regarding Christ's claim that God was His Father. Kenneth S. Wuest, who was professor of Greek at the Moody Bible Institute when Wierwille claims to have taken courses there, comments: "We have in John 5:18, the words (A.V.) 'Therefore the Jews sought the more to kill Him, because He not only had broken the Sabbath, but said also that God was His Father, making Himself equal with God.' The Jews here are the Jewish religious leaders, well educated, learned in the Old Testament scriptures. They had heard Jesus claim that God was His Father. The pronoun 'his' does not bring out the full force of the Greek here. This English word is the translation of the ordinary pronoun of the third person in the genitive case in Greek. It expresses the general idea of ownership. But this construction does not appear in the original here. The word is *idios*, which means 'one's own private, unique, individual possession.' That is, Jesus claimed to own God as His Father in a way different from the way in which believers have God as their Father. His relationship to God as His Son was different, uniquely different, from that relationship sustained by every other person who claims sonship. These astute theologians saw clearly that in making this claim, Jesus was making Himself equal with God. And any person equal with God, must be God. On another occasion, Jesus differentiated between the sonship of believers and that of Himself. He said to Mary, 'Go to my brethren, and say to them, I ascend to my Father, and your Father, and to my God,

17. EC, December, 1950; "The Pre-Existent Christ is God" by M. Zeidman; pp. 578-579
18. IJG, p. 23

and your God' (John 20:17.)"[19]

Yet, on the basis of his unscholarly confusion about Messianic and Hebrew phraseology, Wierwille develops a monstrous strawman which he, purportedly by Scripture, proceeds to demolish. Much of his chapter, "Who Is Jesus Christ?" is devoted to this argument, quoting various ones in Scripture who called Christ the Son of God, offering it as proof that they denied His deity. He quotes John, Paul, God's angel, John the Baptist, Simon Peter, Nathanael, Martha, the man born blind, the disciples in the ship, Philip and the Ethiopian, the centurion, and even "devil spirits" as calling Jesus the Son of God, ending each quote with the words: "make it known that [he/she/they] believed Jesus Christ to be the Son of God, not God."[20] Yet not one single time in any of the 38 verses he quotes on these 7 pages does anyone quoted deny that Jesus Christ is God. The claim is entirely a figment of Wierwille's imagination and his lack of understanding about the term "Son of God." One might as well quote verses calling Jesus Christ "the Son of Man" as proof that He is not the Son of God!

Equally dishonest and unscholarly is Wierwille's statement, "Jesus Christ made it known that he believed himself to be the Son of God, not God. And he should have known."[21] His only proof again is to quote 8 verses where our Lord referred to Himself as the Son of God. Not a single time did our Lord deny that He was God the Son.

This misunderstanding of "Son of God" surfaces again with the explanation of John's Gospel. Wierwille writes: "Have you ever asked why various scriptures were recorded? The express purpose for the Word of God regarding Jesus Christ is that men may know that he is not God the Creator, but the Son of God.

"John 20:31:

But these are witten, that ye might believe that Jesus is the Christ, the Son of God; and that believing ye might have life through his name.

"The Scriptures were written not that we might believe that Jesus is God, but rather that we might believe that he is the Son of God."[22] Wierwille has missed the point completely!

We sum up the title "Son of God" by quoting Anderson again:

19. GTLB, p. 37
20. JCNG, pp. 38-44
21. Ibid., p. 44
22. Ibid., p. 36

"No one who accepts the Scriptures as divine is entitled to deny that in His personal ministry the Lord Jesus laid claim to Deity. And the crucifixion is a public proof that He did in fact assert this claim. . . .And as regards His declaring Himself to be the Son of God, the question is not what these words might convey to English readers today, but what He Himself intended His hearers to understand by them."[23] The very fact that our Lord never corrected those who understood His use of the term to mean a claim of deity and equality with the Father is proof positive of what He *intended* them to understand. As Canon Henry Parry Liddon pointed out: "The motive of their indignation was not disowned by Him. They believed Him to mean that He Himself was a divine Person; and He never repudiated that construction of His language."[24] To Wierwille and TWI we can only ask, *"Why didn't Jesus set them straight if they merely misunderstood His use of the title 'Son of God'?"*

Along the same line, the title "Lord" is further indication of Christ's absolute deity. While it may be used lightly or as an indication of mere submission (see Matthew 7:22,23; I Peter 3:6), in its true sense it is the New Testament name (Greek, *kurios*) for the Old Testament Jehovah (Hebrew, *yahweh*; never pronounced, but read *Adonai*), and was the regular word for Jehovah in the Septuagint, the Greek translation of the Old Testament which was in use during the days of Christ and the apostles.[25] It is with this in mind that Paul told the saints in Corinth, "I give you to understand, that no man speaking by the Spirit of God calleth Jesus accursed: and that no man can say that Jesus is the Lord [Greek, *kurios*], but by the Holy Ghost" (I Cor. 12:3). It is only through the Holy Spirit that one can acknowledge Jesus Christ as Jehovah, one who is absolute deity. Perhaps this is why one of TWI's leaders, in a personal letter to this writer, referred to "our lord Jesus Christ," using Lord without a capital letter.

---

23. Op. cit., p. 88
24. *The Divinity of Our Lord,* p. 189; quoted in DJCL, p. 10
25. William Gouge, calling attention to the fact that Genesis 19:24 declares "the Lord [Jehovah] rained. . .brimstone and fire from the Lord [Jehovah] out of heaven," noted that "Jehovah the Son is said to rain fire from Jehovah the Father," adding, "Some of the ancient fathers, assembled in a council, were so confident of the truth of the application of that title *Jehovah,* twice used, once to the Father, and again to the Son, as they denounced anathema against such as should expound it otherwise"; COH, p. 8

Wierwille, it should be noted, avoids any discussion of the title "Lord" as if it were some form of spiritual *pasteurella pestis*. The nearest he came to dealing with it, at least in his writings we examined, was to infer that it was merely a synonym for "Master." It is not difficult to understand his reluctance to face this issue. One of the 20th century's greatest scholars, J. Gresham Machen, observes: ". . .the title 'Lord,' at Antioch, at Tarsus, and everywhere in the Greco-Roman world, was clearly a title of divinity. Indeed, it may be added, the word 'lord' was no whit inferior in dignity to the term 'god.' When the early Christian missionaries, therefore, called Jesus 'Lord,' it was perfectly plain to their pagan hearers everywhere that they meant to ascribe divinity to Him and desired to worship Him.

". . .when the Christian missionaries used the word 'Lord' of Jesus, their hearers knew at once what they meant. They knew at once that Jesus occupied a place which is occupied only by God. For the word 'Lord' is used countless times in the Greek scriptures as the holiest name of the covenant God of Israel, and these passages were applied freely to Jesus."[26]

As for any idea that "Lord" is simply a synonym for "Master," Machen insists: ". . .it is not in accordance with New Testament usage when Jesus is called, by certain persons in the modern Church, 'the Master,' rather than 'the Lord'. . . . sometimes the modern fashion is adopted by devout men and women with the notion that the English word 'Lord' has been worn down and that the use of the word 'Master' is a closer approach to the meaning of the Greek Testament. This notion is false. . . .The religious associations of the English word 'Lord' are due to Bible usage; and the religious associations of the New Testament word 'kyrios' were also due to Bible usage—the usage of the Septuagint. The Christian, then, should remember that 'a little learning is a dangerous thing.' The uniform substitution of 'the Master' for 'the Lord' in speaking of Jesus has only a false appearance of freshness and originality. In reality it sometimes means a departure from the spirit of the New Testament usage."[27]

Machen developed this same thought in another work, arguing: ". . .the really outstanding fact is that in the Epistles of Paul, Jesus is everywhere separated from ordinary humanity; the deity of Christ is everywhere presupposed. It is a matter of small

---

26. OPR, pp. 306,308
27. Ibid., pp. 308,309

consequence whether Paul ever applies to Jesus the Greek word which is translated 'God' in the English Bible; certainly it is very difficult, in view of Rom. ix. 5, to deny that he does. However that may be, the term 'Lord,' which is Paul's regular designation of Jesus, is really just as much a designation of deity as is the term 'God.' It was a designation of deity even in the pagan religions with which Paul's converts were familiar; and (what is far more important) in the Greek translation of the Old Testament which was current in Paul's day and was used by the Apostle himself, the term was used to translate the 'Jahwe' of the Hebrew text. And Paul does not hesitate to apply to Jesus stupendous passages in the Greek Old Testament where the term Lord thus designates the God of Israel. But what is perhaps most significant of all for the establishment of the Pauline teaching about the Person of Christ is that Paul everywhere stands in a religious attitude toward Jesus. He who is thus the object of religious faith is surely no mere man, but a supernatural Person, and indeed a Person who was God.

". . .the view which Paul had of Jesus was also the view which was held by Jesus' intimate friends. The fact appears in the Pauline Epistles themselves, to say nothing of other evidence. Clearly the Epistles presuppose a fundamental unity between Paul and the original apostles with regard to the Person of Christ; for if there had been any controversy about this matter it would certainly have been mentioned. Even the Judaizers, the bitter opponents of Paul, seem to have had no objection to Paul's conception of Jesus as a supernatural Person. The really impressive thing about Paul's view of Christ is that it is not defended. Indeed it is hardly presented in the Epistles in any systematic way. Yet it is everywhere presupposed. The inference is perfectly plain—Paul's conception of the Person of Christ was a matter of course in the primitive Church. With regard to this matter Paul appears in perfect harmony with all Palestinian Christians. The men who had walked and talked with Jesus and had seen Him subject to the petty limitations of earthly life agreed with Paul fully in regarding Him as a supernatural Person, seated on the throne of all Being."[28]

But it is not merely the title "Lord" that unites Him in Scripture with Jehovah; there are scores of Old Testament references to Jehovah that are applied to Christ in the New Testament.

28. CAL, pp. 97,98

Perhaps it would prove helpful to quote from the author's big manual on soul winning, used as a textbook in numerous Bible institutes, colleges and seminaries. We said there:

"Actually, it is a simple matter to show that many passages about Jehovah in the Old Testament are applied to Jesus Christ in the New Testament, indicating Jehovah and Jesus are one and the same. For example, you might want to use some of the following: (1) Isaiah 44:6 and Isaiah 48:12 with Revelation 1:8,11,17,18 and Revelation 2:8; (2) Jeremiah 17:10 with John 2:24,25 and Revelation 2:18,23; (3) Deuteronomy 31:8 with Matthew 28:20; (4) Malachi 3:6 with Hebrews 13:8; (5) Genesis 17:1 with Revelation 1:8. The latter verse, incidentally, is helpful in answering the Jehovah's Witness when he acknowledges that Jesus is called a Mighty God, but protests He is never called the Almighty God; (6) Isaiah 43:3, where Jehovah is called the Holy One, with Acts 3:14; (7) Genesis 1:1 with John 1:1,3; (8) Isaiah 44:24 with Colossians 1:16; (9) Proverbs 16:4 with the latter part of Colossians 1:16; (10) I Kings 8:39 with John 2:24,25 and Revelation 2:23; (11) Genesis 18:25 with John 5:22; (12) Psalm 83:18 with Philippians 2:9 and Colossians 1:18; (13) Psalm 103:19 with Acts 10:36; (14) Psalm 11:5,6 with II Thessalonians 1:7-9; (15) Isaiah 40:10 with Revelation 22:12; (16) Psalm 119:28 with Philippians 4:13; (17) Psalm 39:7 with I Timothy 1:1; (18) Jeremiah 17:7 with Psalm 2:12 and Colossians 1:27; (19) Psalm 91:4 with Matthew 23:37; (20) Isaiah 43:11 with Matthew 1:21, I Timothy 1:15, Acts 15:11, I Thessalonians 1:10, Hebrews 7:25, II Peter 3:18 and Acts 4:12; (21) Isaiah 49:26 with Titus 2:13,14; (22) Psalm 130:7,8 with Titus 2:14; (23) Psalm 36:9 with John 1:4 and John 8:12; (24) Isaiah 25:8 with II Timothy 1:10; (25) Hosea 13:14 with Hebrews 2:14,15 and I Corinthians 15:54-57; (26) Isaiah 45:21 with John 1:1; (27) Exodus 34:7 with Mark 2:5; (28) Psalm 107:29 with Matthew 8:26; (29) Jeremiah 31:25 with Matthew 11:28,29; (30) Joel 2:28 with John 16:7; (31) Psalm 73:24 with John 14:3 and John 17:22; (32) Malachi 1:6 with Matthew 23:8,10; (33) Deuteronomy 10:20 with Colossians 3:24; (34) Isaiah 54:5 with John 3:29 and Revelation 21:9; (35) Psalm 119:11 with Colossians 3:16; (36) Psalm 23:1 with Hebrews 13:20 and I Peter 5:4; (37) Ezekiel 34:15 with John 10:14,16; (38) Ezekiel 34:16 with Luke 19:10; (39) Psalm 23:2 with Revelation 7:17; (40) Proverbs 3:12 with Revelation 3:19; (41) Micah 4:5 with Colossians 3:17; (42) Isaiah 24:15 with II Thessalonians 1:12; (43) Proverbs 18:10

with Matthew 12:21; (44) Isaiah 61:10 with I Peter 1:8,9 and II Corinthians 5:21; (45) Psalm 145:18 with I Corinthians 1:2 and Romans 10:13; (46) Isaiah 40:3 with Matthew 3:3; (47) Isaiah 8:13,14 with I Peter 2:7,8; (48) Zechariah 12:10 (noting verse one to see who is speaking) with John 19:37; (49) Isaiah 45:23 with Romans 14:10,11; (50) Jeremiah 10:10 with I John 5:20; (51) Deuteronomy 6:4 and Zechariah 14:9 with I Corinthians 8:6."[29]

We think it would be extremely difficult—if not impossible—for an honest individual to study the above verses and then deny the absolute deity of our Lord Jesus Christ. If He is not Almighty God, then neither is the Jehovah of the Old Testament. This truth is driven home with special force in the light of Isaiah 42:8, "I am the Lord [Jehovah]: that is my name: and my glory will I not give to another. . . ."[30]

In light of our Lord's names and their significance in Scripture, John Lineberry offers some excellent thoughts on the title "Lord Jesus Christ." Writing about the phrase as found in I Thessalonains 1:1, he says: " 'Lord' is *Kurios*, 'the sovereign Lord of the universe,' blessed and worthy designation of our Saviour who is 'very God of very God,' possessor of fullest deity. 'Jesus' is *Iesou*, the Greek transliteration of the Hebrew *Joshua* which means, 'God saves.' Matthew 1:21, historical fulfillment of Genesis 3:15, Isaiah 7:14, *et al.*, reads, 'And she shall bring forth a son, and thou shalt call his name JESUS: for he shall save his people from their sins.' This means that God in Christ saves sinners by Himself (Mark 10:45; Luke 19:10). The salvation of our God is an eternal work, permanent and unchangeable (Eccles. 3:14). In order to save, the Lord Jesus must possess deity. In order to save, He must be man. In order to save, the Lord Jesus must die to settle the sin question. All of which means that in the one word *Jesus*, 'God saves,' there are three fundamental truths; namely, (1) the deity of Christ; (2) the humanity of Christ; and (3) His propitiatory sacrifice upon the Cross. 'Christ' is from *Christos*, 'the anointed one.' The verb, *chrio*, means 'to anoint,' 'to touch with the hand.' The picture is that of the Old Testament prophet, priest, and king being anointed with oil, which spoke of being empowered by the Holy Spirit to carry out the will

---

29. BEA, pp. 189,190
30. Note it relates especially to His name that He jealously guards His glory. How strange, then, for Wierwille to say: "Jesus Christ is the sweetest name I know. . ." [BTMS, p. 21]. If He is not God, why wouldn't Jehovah, or one of the Father's other names, be sweetest?

of God in each respective office (Lev. 8:30; I Sam. 2:35; I Sam. 16:13). The Lord Jesus Himself was anointed with the Holy Spirit at the baptismal scene in the Jordan River (Matt. 3:16-17) as He began His ministry to carry out the ordained, redemptive plan of God in the mediatorial offices of Prophet, Priest, and King. All of these wonderful truths are brought out in the word, *chrio*, 'to anoint.' The Hebrew equivalent is the word *Messiah*. The Lord Jesus is God's anointed Saviour, in whom alone there is salvation (Acts 4:12). The church, then, in the city of Thessalonica has spiritual life in God our Father and the Lord Jesus Christ. The Father and the Son are co-equal in adorative worship, in power, and in honor (John 5:23). God the Father planned our salvation. God the Son, in accordance with the Father's plan, willingly laid down His life (Heb. 10:7) and purchased our salvation, that we might live through Him, once we are made alive by God the Holy Spirit."[31] W. Neil concludes, "The whole name, therefore, *Lord Jesus Christ*, and the significance of each of its component parts and all of them in conjunction, was essentially pre-Pauline, the faith of the church from the beginning."[32]

Wierwille seeks to dismiss all of this by simply saying, "Names given to Christ such as *Jesus*, meaning 'God our Saviour,' and *Emmanuel*, meaning 'God with us,' emphasize his service to mankind. They do not indicate that Jesus is God any more than Joshua's name, meaning 'God our Saviour,' signifies that Joshua was God or that a girl named Barbara means she is a barbarian."[33] But Joshua was not given his name by Jehovah as identity for his person and work, nor has He ever named any girl Barbara as significance for hers. If God had said to Nun, the father of Joshua, "Call his name Joshua, for he will save people from sins," then Wierwille might have a parallel. He did not, of course. But He did say to Joseph, ". . .thou shalt call his name JESUS: for he shall save his people from their sins. Now all this was done, that it might be fulfilled which was spoken of the Lord by the prophet, saying, Behold, a virgin shall be with child, and shall bring forth a son, and they shall call his name Emmanuel, which being interpreted is, God with us" (Matt. 1:21-23). Both Jesus and Emmanuel were names given to Christ to indicate and highlight His deity.

---

31. VWST, p. 25
32. Quoted by Leon Morris, NICNT, *First Thessalonians;* p. 48, fn #5
33. JCNG, p. 138

Before leaving the thought of our Lord's names and titles, we might note Wierwille's strange understanding of Jesus as the Christ. He writes: "According to Acts 10:38, 'God anointed Jesus of Nazareth with the Holy Ghost.' This anointing made Jesus the Christ, the promised anointed one (*Messiah*) to Israel."[34] No, that anointing did not *make* Him the Christ. He was *born* the Christ! As the angel told the shepherds watching their flocks near Bethlehem on the night the Saviour came to earth: "Fear not: for, behold, I bring you good tidings of great joy, which shall be to all people. For unto you is born this day in the city of David a Saviour, which is Christ the Lord" (Luke 2:10,11). And a few weeks later, when Mary and Joseph brought the baby Jesus to the temple at Jerusalem for the offering of the sacrifices required by law, the "just and devout" Simeon, of whom the divine record says "it was revealed unto him by the Holy Ghost, that he should not see death, before he had seen the Lord's Christ," picked Him "up in his arms, and blessed God, and said, Lord, now lettest thou thy servant depart in peace, according to thy word: For mine eyes have seen thy salvation" (Luke 2:25-30). Our Lord Jesus did not *become* the Christ; He was *born* the Christ!

Earlier we quoted Wierwille as saying, "Jesus Christ. . .does [not] have all the assets of God."[35] While we can only guess what he meant by "assets," we assume he referred to the *attributes* of deity. If so, he could not be more mistaken. To quote an outstanding theologian and scholar, Dr. Henry Clarence Thiessen, on the matter:

"Divine attributes are ascribed to Him and manifested by Him. There are five distinctively divine attributes. These are eternity, omnipresence, omniscience, omnipotence, and immutability. Christ possesses all these. He is eternal. He was not only before John (John 1:15), before Abraham (John 8:58), and before the world came into being (John 17:5,24); but He is 'the firstborn of every creature' (Col. 1:15), being in existence 'in the beginning' (John 1:1; I John 1:1); and, in fact, 'from the days of eternity' (Micah 5:2, marg.). And as to the future, He continues forever (Heb. 1:11; Isa. 9:6; Rev. 1:11). The Father's communication of life to Him is an eternal process (John 5:26; 1:4).

"He is omnipresent and omniscient. He was in heaven while on earth (John 3:13, A.V., A.S.V.), and is on earth while He is in heaven (Matt. 18:20; 28:20). He fills all (Eph. 1:2,3). As for His

34. NDC, p. 201
35. JCNG, p. 5

omniscience, we read that He knows all things (John 16:30; 21:17). He knew what was in man (John 2:24,25). He saw Nathanael under the fig tree (John 1:49); He knew the history of the Samaritan woman (John 4:29), the thoughts of men (Luke 6:8; cf. 11:17), the time and manner of His exit out of this world (Matt. 16:21; John 12:33; 13:1), who would betray Him (John 6:66), the character and certain termination of the present age (Matt. 24:25), the Father (Matt. 11:27); and 'in him are all the treasures of wisdom and knowledge hidden' (Col. 2:3). In Mark 13:32 He is said to be ignorant of the day of His return. On the basis of this statement some would have us believe that He was ignorant on many other points also. But we must remember that while He had the attributes of deity, He had surrendered the independent exercise of them. He went to a fig tree, 'if haply he might find anything thereon' (Mark 11:13); He marvelled at their unbelief (Mark 6:6). All due to the fact that the Father did not allow Him to exercise His divine attributes in these instances. But He, no doubt, now knows the time of His coming.

"He is omnipotent. Jesus says: 'I am the Almighty' (Rev. 1:8), and, 'The Son can do nothing of himself, but what he seeth the Father doing, for what things soever he doeth, these the Son also doeth in like manner' (John 5:19). He upholds all things with the word of His power (Heb. 1:3); all authority is given to Him (Matt. 28:18). He had power over demons (Mark 5:11-15), disease (Luke 4:38-41), death (Matt. 9:25; Luke 7:14,15; John 11:43,44), the elements (Matt. 8:26,27), nature (John 2:11; Matt. 21:19), and all things (Matt. 28:18; Rev. 1:8). If it be objected that Christ performed His miracles through the Spirit (Matt. 12:28), we reply that they are, nevertheless, frequently cited as proofs of His deity (John 5:36; 10:25,38; cf. 20:30,31).

"He is also immutable (Heb. 13:8; 1:12). This is true of His plans, promises, and person. But this does not preclude the possibility of a variety of manifestations on His part, nor of a restriction of some of His instructions and purposes to particular ages and persons."[36]

Perhaps a simple illustration of His divine attributes would fall into the classification of *hearing* and *answering* prayer. Paul wrote, in I Corinthians 1:2, "Unto the church of God which is at Corinth, to them that are sanctified in Christ Jesus, called to be saints, with all that in every place call upon the name of Jesus

---

36. LST, pp. 139,140

Christ our Lord, both their's and our's." We suppose that, right now, as you read these lines, literally millions of people all over the world are praying, this very moment, to Christ. If He is not God, how can He *hear* them, to say nothing of *answering*? The attributes of omnipresence, omniscience and omnipotence are all involved. This is why we insist our Roman Catholic friends are grossly mistaken and deceived in praying to the Virgin Mary and to the saints. Since they are not God, possessing the attributes of God, there is no possible way for them to hear or help. Not so with our Lord Jesus Christ. He is Almighty God!

Did Jesus claim to be God? In their book, *Jesus: God, Ghost or Guru?* Jon A. Buell and O. Quentin Hyder have a chapter entitled "Jesus' Self-Conception" in which His words, behavior and audience response are evaluated. They offer the conclusion: "To summarize, we have seen a picture of formidable consistency as we have looked at four lines of evidence presenting the position that *Jesus claimed to be Messiah-God, the logos, or message to mankind from beyond the natural realm.* First, Jesus behaved as if he were divine (he forgave sins and claimed he would be involved in the final judgment of mankind). Second, his audience received his words as if he were claiming divinity. (Some worshiped him, while others accused him of blasphemy or urged him to reject the worship he was receiving.) Third, he quoted Scripture and religious terms regarding deity and applied them to himself. And, lastly, his close, long-term associates (including his own brother) became convinced that Jesus was God, some to the point of putting their convictions into writing."[37] The Son of God truly claimed to truly be God the Son!

As already indicated, Wierwille and TWI vehemently deny the Trinity, relegating it to the heathenism of the ages. *Time* magazine said: "Wierwille dismisses the doctrine of the Trinity as a throwback to paganism, because it proposes, he says, 'three Gods.' "[38] Instead, here is how he sees it: "The Bible, which is God's revealed Word and will, does not once mention the word 'trinity,' although biblically there are three: (1) God, who is

---

37. P. 39
38. September 6, 1971. Incredibly, in another secular magazine interview [*National Courier,* April, 1977], Wierwille sought to make Martin Luther join his denial of Christ's deity and the Trinity; such an inane suggestion is annihilated by Douglas Morton in "The Way: Ancient Heresies Modernized," JPP, Vol. IV, No. 1, 1980, pp. 86-88

Holy Spirit, the Father of our Lord Jesus Christ, (2) Jesus Christ, the Son of God, and the son of man, and (3) the holy spirit, God's gift, which God made available on the day of Pentecost."[39] The reader will note that in Wierwille's "three," only the first is God. The second, Jesus Christ, is not considered God, as we have already discovered. The third, spoken of by him without capital letters ("the holy spirit") is not even considered a person, merely an influence emanating from the Father.

As for his charge that the Bible "does not once mention the word 'trinity,' " this we readily concede. It is a theological term (literally meaning tri-unity) developed over the years to describe a Bible truth. We find abundant evidence that the Father is God. We find abundant evidence that the Son is God. And we find abundant evidence that the Holy Spirit is God. Since they, we learn from Scripture, are co-equal, co-eternal, etc., "the same in substance but distinct in subsistence," theologians have coined the word "Trinity" to describe them. There is nothing wrong with this and Christians today use scores of theological words, not themselves found in the Bible but which describe biblical truth. For example, we have just spoken of such divine attributes as omniscience, omnipotence and omnipresence. They are abundantly taught in Scripture, but the words are not found a single time. Again, did you know that our English term "Holy Bible" is not found in the Word of God even once? Yet no one objects to another speaking of the Scriptures in this way since Bible simply means *book* and we reverently consider it to truly be God's *holy* book. The same is true with our reference to the Trinity.

Wierwille opens his anti-God book with an anti-Trinitarian attack, saying:

"Long before the founding of Christianity the idea of a triune god or a god-in-three persons was a common belief in ancient religions. Although many of these religions had many minor deities, they distinctly acknowledged that there was one supreme God who consisted of three persons or essences. The Babylonians used an equilateral triangle to represent this three-in-one god, now the symbol of modern three-in-one believers.

"The Hindu trinity was made up of the gods Brahma, Vishnu and Shiva. The Greek triad was composed of Zeus, Athena and Apollo. These three were said by the pagans to 'agree in one.' One of the largest pagan temples built by the Romans was constructed at Baalbek (situated in present-day Lebanon) to their trinity of Jupiter, Mercury

---

39. JCNG, p. 123

and Venus. In Babylon the planet Venus was revered as special and was worshipped as a trinity consisting of Venus, the moon and the sun. This triad became the Babylonian holy trinity in the fourteenth century before Christ."[40]

But why should the fact that other religions may have honored "trinities" preclude the truth of a biblical Trinity? Nearly all religions have some form of sacrifices to deities. Should that rule out the validity and truth of Christ's sacrifice at Calvary? And if the story of creation be true in the Genesis account, and TWI professes belief that this is so, why wouldn't the matter of a Trinity who created this world and all therein (the "us" of Genesis 1:26) have been verbally handed down from generation to generation? This is why most ancient peoples, no matter what section of the world they made their homes, had "localized" accounts of the Garden of Eden, the fall, the flood, and other matters later accurately told in the Word of God. Would Wierwille have us believe, for example, that because the Babylonian religion had its own account of the flood, the story of Noah and his ark is untrue?

However, to compare the pagan triads with the biblical Trinity is not altogether honest. As the scholarly Benjamin B. Warfield noted: "Triads of divinities, no doubt, occur in nearly all polytheistic religions, formed under very various influences. Sometimes, as in the Egypt triad of Osiris, Isis and Horus, it is the analogy of the human family with its father, mother and son which lies at their basis. Sometimes they are the effect of mere syncretism, three deities worshipped in different localities being brought together in the common worship of all. Sometimes, as in the Hindu triad of Brahma, Vishnu and Shiva, they represent the cyclic movement of a pantheistic evolution, and symbolize the three stages of Being, Becoming and Dissolution. Sometimes they are the result apparently of nothing more than an odd human tendency to think in threes, which has given the number three widespread standing as a sacred number (so H. Usener). It is no more than was to be anticipated, that one or another of these triads should now and again be pointed to as the replica (or even the original) of the Christian doctrine of the Trinity. Gladstone found the Trinity in the Homeric mythology, the trident of Poseidon being its symbol. Hegel very naturally found it in the Hindu Trimurti, which indeed is very like his pantheizing notion

---

40. Ibid., pp. 11,12

of what the Trinity is. Others have perceived it in the Buddhist Triratna (Soderblom); or (despite their crass dualism) in some speculations of Parseeism; or, more frequently, in the notional triad of Platonism (e.g. Knapp); while Jules Martin is quite sure that it is present in Philo's neo-Stoical doctrine of the 'powers,' esp. when applied to the explanation of Abraham's three visitors. Of late years, eyes have been turned rather to Babylonia; and H. Zimmern finds a possible forerunner of the Trinity in a Father, Son, and Intercessor, which he discovers in its mythology. **It should be needless to say that none of these triads has the slightest resemblance to the Christian doctrine of the Trinity. The Christian doctrine of the Trinity embodies much more than the notion of 'threeness,' and beyond their 'threeness' these triads have nothing in common with it."**[41]

Wierwille says there are only "two scriptures which in our modern versions of the Bible contain a trinitarian formula."[42] While this is horribly untrue,[43] the two he lists are I John 5:6-8 and Matthew 28:19. He dismisses the first on the basis of textual authority for verse 7, not telling the whole truth when he says it is "not found in any of the Greek manuscripts before the sixteenth century,"[44] but he ignores the fact that, even discrediting

---

41. ISBE, Vol. V, p. 3012, emphasis added
42. JCNG, p. 18
43. Edmond Charles Gruss says: "The doctrine of the Trinity is not based on a few isolated proof texts. Warfield writes: 'It is not a text here and there that the New Testament bears its testimony to the doctrine of the Trinity. The whole book is Trinitarian to the core; all its teaching is built on the assumption of the Trinity; and its allusions to the Trinity are frequent, cursory, easy and confident' "; Benjamin B. Warfield, *Biblical and Theological Studies,* p. 32; quoted in AOD, p. 110; passages where Father, Son and Holy Spirit are treated as equals include Ephesians 2:18; I Corinthians 12:4-6; Ephesians 3:14-17; Hebrews 6:4-6; Ephesians 4:4-6; II Thessalonians 2:13-16; I John 3:21-24; Jude 20,21; I John 4:1,2
44. JCNG, p. 18; Wierwille apparently "borrowed," without giving credit or checking sources, from the Jehovah's Witnesses' book, *Let God Be True,* a quote credited to "a Greek Scripture translator, Benjamin Wilson," that I John 5:7 "is not contained in any Greek manuscript which was written earlier than the fifteenth century" (p. 103). If he had checked the JW authority he would have discovered Wilson to have been misquoted. He said "earlier than the fifth century," not the fifteenth! (See Gruss, op. cit., p. 111.) Gruss also says: "Two fourth century writers, Priscillian and Varimadum, quote the verse as though genuine"; ibid., p. 112; source credited: *The Greek New Testament,* ed. by Kurt Aland, Matthew Black, *et al* (New York: American Bible Society, 1966), p. 824

verse 7, the fact of the Trinity is seen all around it, both before and after. As Stuart E. Lease points out: ". . .the truth of the Trinity is clearly presented in the verses immediately preceding and following I John 5:7. Verse 4 says, 'Whatsoever is born of God'; verse 5 says, 'Jesus is the Son of God'; and the latter part of verse 6 says, 'And it is the Spirit.' Thus God, Jesus as the Son of God and the Spirit are all mentioned in these three verses preceding I John 5:7. Verse 8 also mentions 'the Spirit,' and the end of verse 9 speaks of 'the witness of God which he hath testified of his Son.' Therefore, the verses which follow I John 5:7 also clearly set forth the Trinity."[45]

His handling of the second verse is even more shoddy. He says:

"All extant manuscripts do contain this verse in Matthew 28, the oldest dating from the fourth century during which century trinitarianism was becoming a part of formal doctrine and writing. It would not have been difficult for scribes to insert 'in the name of the Father, and of the Son, and of the Holy Ghost,' in place of the original 'in my name.' This must have been what happened because earlier manuscripts from which Eusebius (who died in 340 A.D.) quoted in the early part of the fourth century could not have used the trinitarian words."[46]

*This is the usual Wierwille cop-out!* Whenever a passage is mentioned that seems to contradict his position, it immediately is described as "not having good textual authority," or it "probably" has been "tampered with" and changed by some bygone scribe. Incidentally, the Eusebius Wierwille mentions here [of Caesarea, A.D. 263-339, approximately], was one of the formulators of the Creed of Nicaea, which strongly defended the Trinity, giving special emphasis to the deity of the Son as "God from God, Light from Light, Very God from Very God." Eusebius makes a very poor witness for Wierwille's cause.

In fact, Eusebius, to whom modern scholarship is deeply indebted through his prolific writings, especially his 10-volume *Historia Ecclesiastica*, indicates that the earliest corruptions of manuscripts were by those who, like Wierwille, were the enemies of our Lord's deity, seeking to discredit biblical claims to its truth! He quotes the very ancient church father, Caius (or Gaius, writing about A.D. 175), answering the Arian heresy of

45. GNB, December, 1979; "Reality of the Trinity," p. 23
46. JCNG, pp. 19,20; for evidence of Wierwille's confusion about Eusebius and the baptismal formula, see Douglas Morton, op. cit., pp. 78-80

Theodotus and others, as follows: " 'The Divine Scriptures,' he says, 'these heretics have audaciously *corrupted*:. . .laying violent hands upon them under pretence of *correcting* them. That I bring no false accusation, any one who is disposed may easily convince himself. He has but to collect the copies belonging to these persons severally; then, to compare one with another; and he will discover that their discrepancy is extraordinary. Those of Asclepiades, at all events, will be found discordant from those of Theodotus. Now, plenty of specimens of either sort are obtainable, inasmuch as these men's disciples have industriously multiplied the (so-called) *"corrected"* copies of their respective teachers, which are in reality nothing else but *"corrupted"* copies. With the foregoing copies again, those of Hermophilus will be found entirely at variance. As for the copies of Apollonides, they even contradict one another. Nay, let any one compare the fabricated text which these persons put forth in the first instance, with that which exhibits their *latest* perversions of the Truth, and he will discover that the disagreement between them is even excessive.

" 'Of the enormity of the offence of which these men have been guilty, they must needs themselves be fully aware. Either they do not believe that the Divine Scriptures are the utterances of the HOLY GHOST,—in which case they are to be regarded as unbelievers: or else, they account themselves wiser than the HOLY GHOST,—and what is that, but to have the faith of devils? As for their denying their guilt, the thing is impossible, seeing that the copies under discussion are their own actual handywork; and they know full well that not such as these are the Scriptures which they received at the hands of their catechetical teachers. Else, let them produce the originals from which they made their transcripts. Certain of them indeed have not even condescended to falsify Scripture, but entirely reject Law and Prophets alike.' "[47]

Keep this truth in mind whenever Wierwille speaks of poor textual authority. However, we think it strange that Wierwille, in listing "trinitarian formulas" found in Scripture, did not list one of the most prominent and frequently quoted of all, the "Apostolic Benediction." Perhaps it was because he knew no way to explain it away on "textual" or "corrupted manuscript" grounds. At any rate, this noteworthy benediction, used as a formal closing in so many church services of all denominations,

47. V. 28 (ap. Routh's *Reliqq.* ii. 132-4); quoted in RR, pp. 323,324

says: "The grace of the Lord Jesus Christ, and the love of God, and the communion of the Holy Ghost, be with you all. Amen" (II Cor. 13:14). According to TWI theology, this benediction must be changed in essence to something like, "The grace of an elevated man, and the love of God, and the communion of an impersonal energy, be with you all. Amen."

Philip E. Hughes comments on this verse: "This final benediction is trinitarian in form, but spontaneously so. The doctrine of the Trinity is not, in fact, systematically and as it were self-consciously formulated in the New Testament. It is there, none the less, and indeed is one of the clearest inferences to be drawn from Scripture. Like other great doctrines of the faith, it is not, and could not be, a construction of unaided natural reason. The being of God, because of its transcendence, cannot be confined descriptively within the categories of man's mundane thought. In the New Testament the teaching of a trinitarian distinction within the Godhead is primarily practical in its impact. It is related to the human situation, for it is within the framework of redemption that is disclosed to fallen man. And therefore it is a truth which is confirmed by the knowledge of the believer's experience. Hence Paul's mention of the grace, the love, and the fellowship that flow from the three Persons of the one God. The meaning of the Trinity is learnt (or one might more accurately say relearnt) in response, through personal faith, to what God, Father, Son, and Holy Spirit, have done for our redemption.

"But the meaning of the Trinity is not exhausted by an understanding of the economy of redemption. It is a truth which defines an eternal relationship within the Godhead and which exists quite independently of man. The Triune God, as Scripture testifies, was active at the Creation; the glory of the Son is a glory of Trinitarian harmony enjoyed before the world was; the love of the Father for the Son existed in eternity before the foundation of the world (Jn. 17:5,24). It is a truth which reveals the very constitution of the Godhead. However much, therefore, it transcends the limits of man's finite mind, to man, precisely because he is created in the divine image, the truth of the Trinity is, in this sense, a truth of his very constitution, and the foundation of all his knowledge of the being and mind of God. The revelation of the trinitarian nature of the Godhead is not, accordingly, the manifestation of a new truth, but the re-affirmation, in the very act of mercy (which is the act of re-creation), of the age-old foundation truth which man in his sin has sought to suppress. He who knows in his heart the saving activity of Father, Son, and Holy Spirit is in fact re-established in the truth of the Trinity and is restored to that divine image from which he had fallen."[48]

Incidentally, the trinitarian order is different in this apostolic benediction from that in Matthew 28:19. Here it is Son, Father and Holy Spirit; in the baptismal formula it is Father, Son and Holy Spirit. This highlights the fact that there is no special order of importance, that the three are co-equal. In fact, in the one Wierwille ignores, the Son is listed first, thus given the most prominent place!

But is Wierwille right? Is the Trinity suggested only in isolated instances in the Word of God? B. B. Warfield, discussing the teaching of the Trinity in the Old Testament, said:

"The older writers discovered intimations of the Trinity in such phenomena as the pl. form of the Divine name *Elohim*, the occasional employment with reference to God of pl. pronouns ('Let us make man in our image,' Gen. 1:26; 3:22; 11:7; Isa. 6:8), or of pl. verbs (Gen 20:13; 35:7), certain repetitions of the name of God which seem to distinguish between God and God (Gen 19:27; Ps 45:6,7; 110:1; Hos 1:7), threefold liturgical formulas (Dt 16:4; Nu 6:24,26; Isa 6:3), a certain tendency to hypostatize the conception of Wisdom (Prov 8), and esp. the remarkable phenomena connected with the appearances of the Angel of Jeh (Gen 16:2-13; 22:11,16; 31:11,13; 48:15,16; Ex 3:2,4,5; Jgs 13:20-22). The tendency of more recent authors is to appeal, not so much to specific texts of the OT, as to the very 'organism of revelation' in the OT, in which there is perceived an underlying suggestion 'that all things owe their existence and persistence to a threefold cause,' both with reference to the first creation, and, more plainly, with reference to the second creation. Passages like Ps 33:6; Isa 61:1; 63:9-12; Hag 2:5,6, in which God and His Word and His Spirit are brought together, co-causes of effects, are adduced. A tendency is pointed out to hypostatize the Word of God on the one hand (e.g. Gen 1:3; Ps 33:6; 107:20; 119:87; 147:15-18; Isa 55:11); and, esp. in Ezk and the later Prophets, the Spirit of God, on the other (e.g. Gen 1:2; Isa 48:16; 63:10; Ezk 2:2; 8:3; Zec 7:12). Suggestions—in Isa for instance (7:14; 9:6)—of the deity of the Messiah are appealed to. And if the occasional occurrence of pl. verbs and pronouns referring to God, and the pl. form of the name *Elohim*, are not insisted upon as in themselves evidence of

---

48. NICNT, *The Second Epistle to the Corinthians*, pp. 488,489

a multiplicity in the Godhead, yet a certain weight is lent them as witnesses that 'the God of revelation is no abstract unity, but the living, true God, who in the fulness of His life embraces the highest variety' (Bavinck). The upshot of it all is that it is very generally felt that, somehow, in the OT development of the idea of God there is a suggestion that the Deity is not a simple monad, and that thus a preparation is made for the revelation of the Trinity yet to come. It would seem clear that we must recognize in the OT doctrine of the relation of God to His revelation by the creative Word and the Spirit, at least the germ of the distinctions in the Godhead afterward fully made known in the Christian revelation. And we can scarcely stop there. After all is said, in the light of the later revelation, the Trinitarian interpretation remains the most natural one of the phenomena which the older writers frankly interpreted as intimations of the Trinity; esp. of those connected with the descriptions of the Angel of Jeh, no doubt, but also even of such a form of expression as meets us in the 'Let us make man in our image' of Gen 1:26—for surely ver 27: 'And God created man in his own image,' does not encourage us to take the preceding verse as announcing that man was to be created in the image of the angels. This is not an illegitimate reading of NT ideas back into the text of the OT; it is only reading the text of the OT under the illumination of the NT revelation. The OT may be likened to a chamber richly furnished but dimly lighted; the introduction of light brings into it nothing which was not in it before; but it brings out into clearer view much of what is in it but was only dimly or even not at all perceived before. The mystery of the Trinity is not revealed in the OT; but the mystery of the Trinity underlies the OT revelation, and here and there almost comes into view. Thus the OT revelation of God is not corrected by the fuller revelation which follows it, but only perfected, extended and enlarged."[49]

Warfield notes that this truth is emphasized by how the New Testament writers treated it. He says,

"It is an old saying that what becomes patent in the NT was latent in the OT. And it is important that the continuity of the revelation of God contained in the two Testaments should not be overlooked or obscured. If we find some difficulty in perceiving

---

49. ISBE, Vol. V, p. 3014; all Warfield's abbreviations will be understood by the average reader, we think, with the possible exception of *Jeh* (Jehovah)

for ourselves, in the OT, definite points of attachment for the revelation of the Trinity, we cannot help perceiving with great clearness in the NT abundant evidence that its writers felt no in-.congruity whatever between their doctrine of the Trinity and the OT conception of God. The NT writers certainly were not conscious of being 'setters forth of strange gods.' To their own apprehension they worshipped and proclaimed just the God of Israel; and they laid no less stress than the OT itself upon His unity (Jn 17:3; I Cor 8:4; I Tim 2:5). They do not, then, place two new gods by the side of Jeh, as alike with Him to be served and worshipped; they conceive Jeh as Himself at once Father, Son and Spirit. In presenting this one Jeh as Father, Son and Spirit, they do not even betray any lurking feeling that they are making innovations. Without apparent misgiving they take over OT passages and apply them to Father, Son and Spirit indifferently. Obviously they understand themselves, and wish to be understood, as setting forth in the Father, Son and Spirit just the one God that the God of the OT revelation is; and they are as far as possible from recognizing any breach between themselves and the Fathers in presenting their enlarged conception of the Divine Being. This may not amount to saying that they saw the doctrine of the Trinity everywhere taught in the OT. It certainly amounts to saying that they saw the Triune God whom they worshipped in the God of the OT revelation, and felt no incongruity in speaking of their Triune God in the terms of the OT revelation. The God of the OT was their God, and their God was a Trinity, and their sense of identity of the two was so complete that no question as to it was raised in their minds."[50]

As for the New Testament, Warfield says, "It is not in a text here and there that the NT bears its testimony to the doctrine of the Trinity. The whole book is Trinitarian to the core; all its teaching is built on the assumption of the Trinity; and its allusions to the Trinity are frequent, cursory, easy and confident . . . .we have said in effect that the whole mass of the NT is evidence for the Trinity."[51] We sincerely suggest any who question the idea of the Trinity being a biblical doctrine read the ten full, huge pages—much of it in small type—on the subject by Warfield in *The International Standard Bible Encyclopaedia.* In our judgment, no honest person could do so and ever again question its truth.

---

50. Ibid.
51. Ibid., pp. 3014,3015

## The Devastating John 1 Passage

Obviously, if TWI is to destroy the teaching of our Lord's deity, something must be done to explain away the force of John's tremendous declaration and defense of that truth in the opening verses of his Gospel, where he refers to a beginning that had no beginning. Wierwille dedicates an entire chapter to such an attempt in his book, *Jesus Christ Is NOT God*. It is one of the most amazing twistings of plain Scripture one will ever read anywhere, no matter the cult he is studying.

How majestic, how sublime are the words chosen to introduce the theme in John's Gospel: "In the beginning was the Word, and the Word was with God, and the Word was God. The same was in the beginning with God. All things were made by him; and without him was not any thing made that was made" (vss. 1-3). How could Wierwille—or anyone else—destroy their force? He attempts it in two principal ways: (1) chopping it up and twisting its meaning through the use of his ever-present and plentiful bracket insertions; (2) denying its *literal* meaning.

The identification of our Lord Jesus Christ as "the Word" in John 1 is so obvious that, for the most part, Wierwille cannot deny it—although he does to a certain extent. This Word is the one who "was made flesh, and dwelt among us" (vs. 14). He is the one who became flesh and blood through the incarnation, described in I John 1:1 with the words: "That which was from the beginning, which we have heard, which we have seen with our eyes, which we have looked upon, and our hands have handled, of the Word of life." And He is the one who will one day come from Heaven with His armies to set up an everlasting kingdom of righteousness on this earth, as described in Revelation 19:13: "And he was clothed with a vesture dipped in blood: and his name is called The Word of God."

Wierwille starts his explaining away by saying: "When John 1:1 says, '. . .and the Word was with God,' it refers to the manifested, revealed *logos*: (1) the written Word which has come to us as the Bible and (2) the created Word which is Jesus Christ. 'In the beginning was the Word [God] and the [revealed] Word was with God. . . .' "[52] By the simple insertion of brackets, he has changed the clear identification of the Word from the one who "was made flesh, and dwelt among us" (vs. 14) to the Father first, then to the Bible and a created being. In-

---

52. JCNG, p. 84

cidentally, note how he makes "Word" *separate from* God and *part of* God at will, whichever best suits his purpose.

Wierwille offers what he calls a "literal translation according to usage" of the opening three verses in this fashion:

"In the beginning (before the creation) God was the Word, and the revealed Word was in God's foreknowledge (which was later communicated to man in spoken Words, written Words and the incarnate Word). This Word absolutely was in the beginning before the foundation of the world together with the one true God in His foreknowledge yet distinctly independent of Him. All things without exception were made by God who was the cause of their existence. And without God not one thing came into being that has existed or does exist presently."[53]

Scholars everywhere will be astounded at one calling this a "literal translation," even with the addition of the strange "according to usage" qualification. *It is anything but such!* In fact, while on the one hand it might be called a paraphrase, on the other hand it contains too much foreign to the Greek or even the context to properly designate as a paraphrase. Since Wierwille often refers to Robert Young as a Greek authority, it might be well to quote those same three verses from his highly respected literal translation of the Bible, thus giving the reader an insight into what a *true* literal translation might be: "In the beginning was the Word, and the Word was with God, and the Word was God; this one was in the beginning with God; all things through him did happen, and without him happened not even one thing that hath happened."

As additional evidence of what Wierwille has done, it might be helpful also to quote from an expanded translation. Using the one from the pen of a Greek professor at a school where he says he studied, we find: "In the beginning the Word was existing. And the Word was in fellowship with God the Father. And the Word was as to His essence absolute deity. This Word was in the beginning in fellowship with God the Father. All things through His intermediate agency came into being, and without Him there came into being not even one thing which has come into existence."[54]

---

53. Ibid., pp. 91,93. John Juedes notes of this: "While the Greek text of John 1:1-3 has only 36 words and the KJV uses 42, Wierwille's 'literal translation according to usage' contains 91. His 'literal translation' of John 1:12 follows suit: he has 44 words compared to the KJV's 25 and the Greek's 16"; JPP, Vol. IV, No. 1, 1980, "Wierwille's Way With the Word," p. 92
54. WUEST

But even with Wierwille's weird translation and reidentifying of the Word, he is still stuck with his created Christ being with God "in the beginning." How does he destroy the truth of Christ's preexistence? *By denying its literalness!* [His "literal" translation according to usage becomes nonliteralness!] Wierwille writes: "How was this revealed Word with God? The Word was with God in His foreknowledge. . . .This is what John 1:1 literally says: The revealed 'Word was with God' in His foreknowledge; the revealed Word was later to be manifested in writing as the Bible and in the flesh as Jesus Christ."[55] He says again: "Jesus Christ, who is God's communication of Himself in a person, had a beginning when he was born, yet in God's foreknowledge Jesus Christ was in the beginning."[56] And again: "In John 1:1 the *logos*, which is God, has reference to the thoughts and ideas conveyed by the spoken Words, the written Words and the incarnate Word. All the spoken, written and incarnate Words were with God in His foreknowledge."[57] Earlier we saw where he flatly stated, "Jesus Christ was not literally with God in the beginning. . . ."

Now, that kind of scholarship might fool and impress Haight-Ashbury hippies, but it most certainly will not a serious, informed student of the Word of God. No one, of course, denies God's foreknowledge as part of His omniscience. But could the Word be understood only in this sense? Hitler was in God's foreknowledge. Could it be said therefore that "Hitler was in the beginning. . .with God"? The blasphemy of such a thought would startle the average individual into stunned silence.

Many Bible students have noted the similarity between the opening of John's Gospel and Genesis. The former says, "In the beginning was the Word. . . ," and the latter, "In the beginning God created the heaven and the earth." It would be every bit as logical to assume that Genesis 1:1 describes only God's foreknowledge, not a literal creation, as it would to suppose that John 1:1 refers to an uncreated being existing merely in divine foreknowledge. This is not to deny that God foreknew His creative acts; quite the contrary. But Genesis 1:1 does not speak of that foreknowledge; it declares the literal act of creation. And, by the same token, John 1:1 speaks of Christ literally being with the Father in eternity past.

---

55. JCNG, pp. 84,85
56. Ibid., pp. 88,89
57. Ibid., p. 89

In one reference to this foreknowledge, Wierwille says:

"Where was Jesus Christ before he was born to Mary? Jesus Christ was with God in His foreknowledge. The first epistle of Peter makes this clear.

"I Peter 1:20:

Who [Christ] verily was foreordained [Carefully note this word 'foreordained' in its context.] before the foundation of the world, but was manifest in these last times for you."[58]

We trust every reader will take him up on his suggestion and note the context of this verse. Putting the previous two verses with it and omitting the Wierwille brackets, here is what we have: "Forasmuch as ye know that ye were not redeemed with corruptible things, as silver and gold, from your vain conversation received by tradition from your fathers; But with the precious blood of Christ, as of a lamb without blemish and without spot: Who verily was foreordained before the foundation of the world, but was manifest in these last times for you" (vss. 18-20).

Contrary to saying that our Lord Jesus Christ merely existed in God's foreknowledge before the foundation of the world, it is saying that His act of atonement through His blood, the crucifixion, existed in that divine foreknowledge. Peter has *an event* in view, not *the Person!* The world still awaits a single Scripture from Wierwille or his associates in the Way International Biblical Research & Teaching Center which offers the slightest indication that Jesus Christ existed before Bethlehem only in the Father's foreknowledge.

Such an explanation of John 1:1 will not "wash," to use a slang expression of our British friends. For example, in discussing the preposition "with" in John 1:1,2, Wierwille says: "There are a vast number of different Greek prepositions translated 'with,' but only *pros* could fit here. *Pros* means 'together with and yet having distinct independence'; 'intimate and close intercommunion, together with distinct independence.' "[59] How in the name of sanity could God the Father have "intimate and close intercommunion" with mere foreknowledge?

Fortunately, that is not what our Lord had in mind when, during His high priestly prayer of John 17, He said to the Father, "And now, O Father, glorify thou me with thine own self with the

---

58. Ibid., p. 28
59. Ibid., p. 86

glory which I had with thee before the world was" (vs. 5). Could foreknowledge have "glory" with the Father? Would Christ be asking for mere restoration to the Father's foreknowledge? Even an amateur student of the Bible would acknowledge such as being patently absurd!

Bishop Handley C. G. Moule of Durham (1841-1920) translated John 17:5, "Glorify Thou Me, by Thine own side, with the glory which I had, before the universe was, by Thy side." And he offered as a paraphrase, "Give Me now that exaltation in My Human Nature which is Mine eternally in My Divine Nature; let Me be *'the Son of Man* at the right hand of God,' upon 'the throne of God *and of the Lamb.*' "[60] He offers Acts 7:56 and Revelation 22:1 as justification for the latter part of the paraphrase.

But, regarding the preposition "with" [*pros*], Dr. Kenneth S. Wuest, a Greek scholar of no little repute, calls it "active communion" and has this to say: "The word 'with' is from a preposition meaning literally 'facing.' Thus the Word is a Person facing God the Father. The article appears before the word 'god' in the Greek, which indicates that the First Person of the Trinity is meant. Thus, John is speaking of the fellowship between the Word, Jesus Christ, and the Father, a fellowship that existed from all eternity and will exist to all eternity, and which was never broken except at that dark mysterious moment at Calvary when the Son cried, 'My God, my God, why hast thou forsaken me?' "[61] The Greek authorities, Robertson and Davis, offer the phrase as *"the Logos was face to face with God."*[62]

Dr. Herschel H. Hobbs pursues the same thought, saying:

"The Greek phrase rendered 'with God' is *pros ton Theon*, face to face with God. This entails both equality and intimacy. In ancient times if one entertained two guests of equal rank they must be seated on an equal basis. If one were tall and the other short, the latter was seated on pillows so that when he looked at the former their eyes met on an even line. Neither must look down upon or up to the other. They saw eye to eye. They were *pros*, face to face, with each other. They were equal. So when John said that the Word was *pros ton Theon* he meant that they were equal. So Christ was not a lesser created being of God. He was equal with God."[63]

60. HPP, p. 44
61. GNG, p. 51
62. NSG, p. 260
63. EGJ, pp. 25,26

Surely mere foreknowledge could not be described as enjoying "face to face," "intimate and close intercommunion" with the Father.

Additional comment is offered by Leon Morris:

"If the preposition is to be taken literally it means 'the Word was towards God.' John thinks of no opposition between the Word and the Father. The whole existence of the Word was oriented towards the Father. Probably we should understand from the preposition the two ideas of accompaniment and relationship. That the thought is of importance and is no casual expression is indicated by the fact that the statement is repeated in v. 2. It marks an advance on the previous statement (*cf.* also I John 1:2). There John established the personal existence of the Word. Now he goes on to the Word's personal character in relation to the Father. Not only did the Word exist 'in the beginning,' but He existed in the closest possible connection with the Father. . . .

"The high point is reached in the third affirmation: 'the Word was God.' Nothing higher could be said. All that may be said about God may fitly be said about the Word. This statement should not be watered down."[64]

Dr. Marvin R. Vincent offers his conclusion: "Thus John's statement is that the divine Word not only *abode* with the Father from all eternity, but was in the living, active relation of communion with Him."[65] This completely rules out mere foreknowledge.

Along this line, Wierwille has an interesting explanation of John 1:2. He writes: "Verse 2 is a repetition of what we just noted in verse 1. Why the repetition? To establish what has been said. Whenever God doubles a revelation in the Word, the absoluteness is established."[66] And he has a footnote referring to Genesis 41:32 and Pharaoh's two-part dream as proof of his statement. Ignoring for the moment Wierwille's confusion over "dream" and "revelation"—God has only to give a revelation *once* for it to be "established"—we would like to point out that he is wrong in calling it mere repetition. As C. K. Barrett notes, it is a clarification of the point that "the Word does not *come to be* with God; the Word *is* with God in the beginning."[67] And as

64. NICNT, *The Gospel According to John,* pp. 75,76
65. WSNT, Vol. II, p. 34
66. JCNG, p. 86
67. *The Gospel According to St. John* (London, 1967), p. 130; quoted in LID, p. 27

for the repetition in Pharaoh's dream, it had to do with *time* ("God will shortly bring it to pass"), not merely with it being *established.*

Actually, there is considerable, clear, unmistakable evidence to the preexistence of Christ in the Word of God. One of the very strongest and most positive, Micah 5:2, Wierwille makes absolutely no reference to in his book dealing with the deity of Christ. Since he goes to so much trouble to explain away other statements, we found this a little surprising. In fact, it reminded us of Neiman-Marcus, the famous Dallas department store with such unique gifts in its Christmas catalog. In 1977 it featured an 11-foot collapsible aluminum pole—complete with black leatherette carrying case—for $50. It was for people facing things so bad they wouldn't touch them with a 10-foot pole! Wierwille has seemingly refused to touch Micah 5:2 with a 10-foot pole.

It says, "But thou, Beth-lehem Ephratah, though thou be little among the thousands of Judah, yet out of thee shall he come forth unto me that is to be ruler in Israel; whose goings forth have been from of old, from everlasting." That this prophecy refers to Christ is not even debatable (see Matt. 2:4-6; Luke 2:4,11,15; John 7:42), as Wierwille himself acknowledges elsewhere.[68] And Micah distinctly says Messiah's goings forth have been "from everlasting"; that is, "from the days of eternity." Wordsworth was right in saying, "This is an illustrious testimony to the Divine generation, before all time, of Christ the Eternal Son of God."[69] Commenting on the words "going forth. . .from everlasting," Jamieson, Fausset and Brown observe, ". . .the plain antithesis of this clause, to 'come forth out of thee' (*from Beth-lehem*), shows that the eternal generation of the Son is meant. The terms convey the strongest assertion of infinite duration of which the *Hebrew* language is capable (cf. Psalm 90.2; Proverbs 8.22,23; John 1.1). Messiah's generation as man coming forth unto God to do His will on earth is *from Beth-lehem*; but as Son of God, His goings forth are *from everlasting.*"[70]

The noted German scholar Krummacher has some expressive comments on this passage about the incarnation:

"Who then comes out of Bethlehem? . . .'*the Man Jehovah,*' the Man who is God the Lord in the highest. . . .It brings into

---

68. ADAN, p. 32; however, he makes the "from everlasting" and "from the days of eternity" to be "from Bethlehem"!

69. Quoted in GABC, Vol. III, p. 806

70. P. 692

connexion two natures as different from each other as heaven and earth. They join together in *one*, God and man. Unheard of combination! Most astonishing alliance, scarcely to be believed! A thousand obstacles seem to lie between, but in a moment they are all overcome. God might have revealed himself in a visible form, amidst lightning splendour in the clouds; or, by a voice from heaven, manifested himself still more clearly to mortals. He might have instructed men by heavenly messengers, or disclosed himself by means of wonders and signs to the blind and deaf throughout the world. Had he willed to appear personally, he might have assumed long ago the form of a holy angel, or taken upon him the unfallen and glorious nature of the first of our species. But no! such was not the Eternal counsel! Not God and angel—not God and Adam—but God and our disorganized nature, were joined together in one! The whole Bible declares to us that it so happened. Oh, unutterable mystery! The Eternal become a creature of time! The Unapproachable, an object which we have seen with our eyes, looked upon, and handled! The Lord of lords, a brother and a relative of miserable sinners! The All-holy One, a partaker of our misery, and a sojourner in our vale of tears! The Disposer of every creature tended by a mortal mother! The Consoler of all affliction, weeping with those that weep, and suffering along with them! The Thunderer amidst the clouds, at whose reproof the heavens tremble—a lisping, stammering child on the bosom of the Virgin! And he who gives life and breath to all, become for our sakes needy and helpless—an infant requiring the hands of men to guide him, and the love of a mother to watch over him! All this is now clear as day; it is the perfection and the crown of the wonders of God! Here we stand upon a height beyond which neither the spirit of man nor of seraph can soar! And this incarnation of God did not take place merely in appearance; it took place in deed and in truth, and is now an historical fact. In order to believe and comprehend it, one must be God himself, or else a simple child; yet, whether it is believed or not, let us still cry Hallelujah! for we know that it has been done!"[71]

Another key verse for Christ's preexistence is Paul's statement in II Corinthians 8:9, "For ye know the grace of our Lord Jesus Christ, that, though he was rich, yet for your sakes he became poor, that ye through his poverty might be rich." The obvious

---

71. ML, pp. 75-77

question to ask TWI and all others who deny an existence for Christ before Bethlehem is: **When was He rich?** If He *was* rich, yet *became* poor for our sakes, He obviously had those riches before He ever came to this earth, was born in a stable, raised in poverty, ministered without a place to lay His head, owned only the clothes on His back when He died, then was buried in a borrowed tomb. If He *became* poor, when was He rich? The only answer lies in the biblical one: *He was wealthy with the riches of eternity past when He shared the glory of His Father!*

Then there is the specific language of Isaiah 9:6 and Galatians 4:4,5. The former says: "For unto us a child is born, and unto us a son is given: and the government shall be upon his shoulder: and his name shall be called Wonderful, Counsellor, The mighty God, The everlasting Father, The Prince of Peace." Ignoring the names for now, notice that there is a dual reference to "a child" and "a son." The *child*, which speaks of His humanity, was *born*; it had its beginning at Bethlehm. But the *son*, which speaks of His deity, was *given*; it couldn't originate at Bethlehem since He was from everlasting. The same careful terminology is used in Galatians 4:4,5: "But when the fulness of the time was come, God sent forth his Son, made of a woman, made under the law, To redeem them that were under the law, that we might receive the adoption of sons." *"Made of a woman"*; there is His humanity. *"God sent forth his Son"*; there is His deity. The humanity was "made"; it had a beginning at Bethlehem. The Son, who was eternal and had no beginning, was "sent forth." How could it be said of the Son of God that He was sent forth in the incarnation if He had no prior existence?

Another interesting verse is Paul's warning to the Corinthians, "Neither let us tempt Christ, as some of them also tempted, and were destroyed of serpents" (I Cor. 10:9), referring to Numbers 21 and the Israelites' murmuring against Moses and against Jehovah. Did they merely murmur against foreknowledge, or was Christ existing in those Old Testament days with the other two persons of the Trinity?

In Colossians 1:17 Paul emphasized that Christ was "before" everything. He declared: "And he is before all things, and by him all things consist." Lawlor notes: "The preposition 'before' (*pro*) denotes that which is prior in time to all other things. Although superiority, sovereignty, and exaltation are implied in the context, it is the idea of *priority* that is emphasized. The One through whom everything was called into existence necessarily existed before all else was created. Prior to this creative work, Christ filled all the unmeasured periods of an unbeginning eternity. He preexisted all matter and material things. Everything is posterior to Him. All created things celebrate a point of origin. Christ does not, in terms of His divine existence. Notice also that the present tense is employed in the first clause of verse 17— 'And he *is* before all things,' not He *'was.'* This further emphasizes that at every point of His existence it may be said of Him that 'He *is.*' "[72] And he added in a footnote: "The Greek has the emphatic pronoun *autos* ('He Himself') in verse 17. Unless this pronoun is added for emphasis, there is no satisfactory explanation for its presence in the sentence. It has been suggested by Lightfoot that *autos estin* ('He Himself is') corresponds exactly with *ego eimi* ('I Myself am') in John 8:58. Whatever may be held with regard to this point, the fact remains that 'firstborn' (Col 1:15), the differentiation between Christ and the creation (v. 16), the 'before all things' (v. 17*a*), and the 'by him all things consist' (v. 17*b*) all point out with great clarity the preexistence of our Lord Jesus Christ."[73]    And as for Christ's preexistence, what means His repeated assertion to the people of His day that He "came down from heaven" if Bethlehem launched His beginning? In John 3:13 He said to Nicodemus, "No man hath ascended up to heaven, but *he that came down from heaven*, even the Son of man which is in heaven." In John 6, in His great discourse on the bread of life, He said, "For the bread of God is *he which cometh down from heaven. . . . I came down from heaven*, not to do mine own will, but the will of *him that sent me.* . . .I am the bread *which came down from heaven. . . .I came down from heaven. . . .*I am the living bread *which came down from heaven. . . .*This is that bread *which came down from heaven*" (vss. 33,38,41,42,51,58). And at the conclusion of His sermon, when some of His disciples murmured, He said: "Doth this offend you? What and if ye shall see the Son of man *ascend up where he was before?*" (vss. 61,62). This "up" of His previous existence ["was," Greek *en*] is the Heaven referred to throughout the chapter.

In John 8:42, answering the false allegations of those claiming to be the children of God, He said: "If God were your Father, you would love me: for *I proceeded forth and came from God*; neither came I of myself, but *he sent me.*" Then in John 16:27,28 He told

72. WGBM, p. 39
73. Ibid.

His disciples, "For the Father himself loveth you, because ye have loved me, and have believed that *I came out from God. I came forth from the Father, and am come into the world:* again, I leave the world, and go to the Father." In His prayer for His disciples, He said to the Father: "I have given unto them the words which thou gavest me; and they have received them, *and have known surely that I came out from thee,* and they have believed that *thou didst send me*" (John 17:8). And He told Pilate, who had asked if He were a king, "To this end was I born, and for this cause *came I into the world,* that I should bear witness unto the truth" (John 18:37). All of these passages in John become totally devoid of meaning apart from a preexistent, preincarnate Christ.

It speaks of His coming to this earth, and what was involved to make it possible, in Hebrews 10:5 as well. There we read, "Wherefore when he cometh into the world, he saith, Sacrifice and offering thou wouldest not, but a body hast thou prepared me." In order for the eternal Son, who always existed as Spirit, to enter into our world *and die,* a "body" had to be prepared for Him. He had to be "made a little lower than the angels for the suffering of death" (Heb. 2:9). Neither deity nor angels could die; to accomplish this it was necessary for Him to become man, made of flesh and blood. Far from proving inferiority or lack of deity, it merely explains His humanity. And He received that prepared body through the miracle of the virgin birth.

Jesus Christ not preexistent? It seems incredible that an honest man could believe the Bible says what it means and means what it says, as Wierwille says he does, and deny it! As a leading voice of the 19th century denial of the deity of Jesus Christ, Dr. Noah Worcester, expressed it: "It is amazing that the preexistence of Christ should be denied by any man who professes a respect for the oracles of God."[74]

Coming back to John 1:1, it is interesting that the phrase "the Word was God" is *theos en ho logos* in the original, with God appearing first. It is literally "God was the Word." Homer A. Kent, Jr., comments about this: "By placing *theos* first in the clause, John gave it the emphatic position, and by employing it without the article he stressed the qualitative sense of the noun. His point was: 'The Word was deity.' "[75] Yet the KJV translators were correct in the way they worded it since, "When the substan-

---

74. *The Doctrine of the Trinity* by Richard N. Davies, Hunt & Eaton, New York, 1891; quoted in WGBM, p. 41
75. LID, p. 27

tive has the article and the adjective has not, the adjective is generally predicate. . . . As a rule the article is not used with the predicate noun even if the subject is definite. The article with one and not with the other means that the articular noun is the subject. . . . So in Jo. 1:1 [*theos en ho logos*] the meaning has to be *the Logos was God*, not *God was the Logos*."[76]

The absence of the article does not go unnoticed by Wierwille, but he wrongly concludes: "The third phrase 'the Word was God' ties together the first two phrases in this verse. The word 'God' has no article for grammatical reasons rather than thought content. 'The Word, which was with God in His foreknowledge and later became spoken, written and incarnate, was God.' "[77] But it has reasons *both* grammatical and of thought content for its omission. For one thing, if there were a definite article in John 1:1 before God, it would rule out deity forever for both the Father and the Holy Spirit, since the article in this place would have made the Word God *exclusive* of all others. Contrary to the argument from its absence that the Word is merely "a god," it is the only way essence of deity could grammatically be described without excluding the Father and the Holy Spirit. Or, as Kent says, "If he had used the article with *theos*, he would have expressed the error of Sabellianism which held that the Son and the Father were one person, and thus would have contradicted his previous statement which distinguished them."[78] The same lack of a definite article before God is seen in verses 6, 12, 13 and 18 of the same chapter—and for the same reason! As Wuest says, "The absence of the article qualifies, shows nature, essence."[79] Thought content *is* in view here most definitely; the Word **was** God!

Before we leave John 1:1 we would like to quote one of the greatest scholars of the 19th century, Frederic Louis Godet. In his huge work on the Gospel of John, considered a classic on this Book, he wrote: "*In the beginning was the Word, and the Word was with God, and the Word was God.* These three propositions follow each other like oracles; they enunciate, each of them, one of the features of the greatness of the Logos before His coming in the flesh. The ascending progression which binds them together is indicated, after the Hebrew manner, by the simple copula

---

76. NSG, p. 279
77. JCNG, p. 90
78. LID, p. 27
79. GTLB, p. 23

[kai, kai], and, and. . . . The imperfect [emi], was, must designate, according to the ordinary meaning of this tense, the simultaneousness of the act indicated by the verb with some other act. This simultaneousness is here that of the *existence* of the Word with the fact designated by the word *beginning*. 'When everything which has begun began, the Word *was*.' Alone then, it did not begin; the Word *was* already. Now that which did not begin with *things*, that is to say, with time, the form of the development of things, belongs to the eternal order. . . . The idea of this first proposition is, therefore, that of the *eternity* of the Logos.

"The salient word of the second proposition is the preposition [pros], which, with the objective word in the accusative, denotes the movement of approach towards the object or the person serving to limit it. . . . This proposition is chosen in order to express under a local form, as the prepositions in general do, the direction, the tendency, the moral movement of the being called the Word. His aspiration tends towards God. . . . This use of the preposition [pros] has evidently no meaning except as it is applied to a personal being. We believe that we hear in this an echo of that plural of Genesis which indicates intimate communion (i.26): 'Let *us* make man in *our* image.' So in the 18th verse the term *Son* will be substituted for *Word*, as *Father* will take the place of *God*. It is not of abstract beings, of metaphysical principles, that John is here pointing out the relation, but of persons . . . . The idea of this second proposition is that of the *personality* of the Logos and of His intimate communion with God. But thus there is found lying in the Divine existence a mysterious duality. This duality is what the third proposition is designed to resolve.

"In this third proposition we must not make [theos] (*God*) the subject, and [ho logos] (the Word) the predicate, as if John meant to say: And God was the Word. John does not propose in this prologue to explain what God is, but what the Word is. . . . The word [theos], *God*, is used without an article, because it has the sense of an adjective and designates, not the person, but the quality. . . . The Logos is something different from the most perfect of men or the most exalted of angels; He partakes of [theiotes] (*deity*). It is when this proposition is thus understood, that it answers its purpose, that of bringing back to unity the duality posited in God in the preceding clause. The idea contained in the third proposition is thus that of the essential *divinity* of the Word.

"To the plenitude of the divine life, therefore, there appertains the existence of a being *eternal* like God, *personal* like Him, *God* like Him; but dependent on Him, aspiring towards Him, living only for Him."[80]

And later he added: "In applying to Jesus the name Word, John. . .wished to describe Jesus Christ as the *absolute revelation* of God to the world, to bring back all divine revelations to Him as their living centre, and to proclaim the matchless grandeur of His appearance in the midst of humanity."[81]

When Wierwille arrived at verse three he was faced with another serious problem, since John declares Christ the Word created *all* things—without one single exception. How does he evade the force of this obvious declaration? He, with a little help from his limitless supply of brackets, says:

"Verse 3 continues the information divulged in the first two verses of John 1.

"All things were made by him [God]; and without him [God] was not any thing made that was made.

" 'Him' is the pronoun *autou* controlled by its closest associated noun which is 'God.' Therefore, we must always remember that only God was in the beginning as stated in Genesis 1:1."[82]

We have no argument with the statement that "only God was in the beginning" since we have already conclusively seen from the opening verses that the Word, Jesus Christ, is God. Our objection here relates to his attempt to interpret Greek through rules of English grammar. The *subject* of these opening verses is "the Word" and it is to Him that verse three clearly points. It is as illogical to say the pronoun "him" refers to God the Father, as the "closest associated noun," as it would be to claim, using a random illustration, that the pronoun "who" in II Thessalonians 1:9 refers to the "closest associated noun," the Lord Jesus Christ! There is no reason to interpret John 1:3 in any sense apart from the understanding orthodox Christians have always given it. Incidentally, regarding this pronoun *autou*, Robertson and Davis point out: "The use of [*autou*] is usually emphatic 'he' in the nominative often to be expressed in English by the tone of voice. . . ."[83] So, speaking of Christ, John is saying emphatically,

---
80. CJG, pp. 244-246, italics in the original
81. Ibid., p. 290, italics in the original
82. JCNG, pp. 91,92
83. NSG, p. 265

"All things were made by **Him** and without **Him** was not anything made that was made!" No doubt the reason Wierwille is so anxious to nullify the force of this verse is because, as Anderson expressed it, ". . .if this does not assert His Deity, I again repeat, words have no meaning."[84]

Wierwille follows this erroneous understanding all the way down the passage about the Word, helped along by his inexhaustible supply of brackets, changing the meaning from the Word, Christ Jesus, to God the Father. Here is what he comes up with:

"In him [God] was life; and the life was the light of men. And the light [God] shineth in darkness; and the darkness comprehended it not. There was a man sent from God, whose name *was* John. The same [John] came for a witness, to bear witness of the Light [God], that all *men* through him [John] might believe. He [John] was not that Light [God], but *was sent* to bear witness of that Light [God]. *That* was the true Light [God], which lighteth every man that cometh into the world. He [God] was in the world [by the revealed Word], and the world was made by him [God], and the world knew him [God] not. He [God] came unto his own [Israel], and his own received him not. But as many [of Israel] as received him [God], to them gave he [God] power to become the sons of God, *even* to them that believe on [unto] his name [namesake, Jesus Christ]."[85]

You will note that things start getting a little sticky for Wierwille in verse ten, which speaks of the Word coming into the world and not being recognized by the world He made. Thanks to his unending supply of brackets, however, he palms this off as merely God coming into the world through His "revealed Word," making the entire passage devoid of intelligent meaning except through the directed eyes of TWI researchers. But he descends from the utterly foolish to the supremely ridiculous in verse 12, which speaks of sinners becoming children of God through faith in Christ the Word, by his bracket change of the word "name" to "namesake, Jesus Christ." Obviously, if the "He" in the verse is the Father, the "believe on his name" must be the Father also— unless Wierwille can come up with a gimmick to change it. Hence the brackets and the change of "name" to "namesake."

This is done completely apart from any textual authority whatsoever. The word "name" here is the Greek *onoma*. It is found 226 times in the New Testament and not one single place

84. LFH, p. 12
85. JCNG, pp. 93,94,95,96,97,98

is it translated "namesake," nor could it be so translated. Wierwille's only real warrant for the change is that "necessity is the mother of invention." It is this type of "fast and loose" handling of Sacred Scripture that forfeits his right to any reasonable claim to scholarship.

Why does Wierwille attempt to foist such a Greek blunder on his readers? Apparently only so he can use the next verse to prop up his contention that the Word, Jesus Christ, is merely a created being. With the help of his brackets, he makes verse 13 to read: "Which were [who was] born [conceived], not of blood, nor of the will of the flesh, nor of the will of man, but of God." He explains: "The first word, 'which,' must be the word 'who,' referring to the 'namesake' of verse 12, Jesus Christ. There are no manuscripts indicating this although second century writers ascribed to it which shows that an earlier text must have had a rendering of 'who' instead of 'which.' An itacism of this nature or text corruption due to misunderstanding is not uncommon. Nevertheless, this scripture must be in harmony with all related scriptures."[86]

Translated from Wierwillese into plain English, what he is saying is: "I do not have one single manuscript authority, out of over 5,000 known manuscripts, but some 'unnamed' writers said something which makes me conclude I have proof the Greek text we have today is corrupted. Anyway, this Scripture must be made to conform to my teaching about other Scriptures."

Probably his reference is to the fact that *one* Latin *translation* uses a singular pronoun instead of a plural and a few of the church fathers, notably Tertullian, argued for this reading from a conviction that it supported a teaching by the Apostle John of the virgin birth. In reply, we offer two indisputable facts: (1) there is not one single Greek manuscript in existence which supports the singular reading—all give it in the plural, making the evidence overpoweringly telling; (2) if the rendering of the singular were accepted and understood to be a reference to Christ, the context ("not of blood, nor of the will of the flesh, nor of the will of man") would not only rule out a human father, it would eliminate a human mother as well! However, the relative pronoun does not point back to "name" (or "namesake"), as Wierwille indicates, but to the neuter substantive, "children of God." So his interpretation could not possibly be correct.

But then Wierwille gets to the heart of his purpose, saying:

---

86. Ibid., pp. 99,100

"The word 'born' is the same word as 'begotten': 'Who was born [begotten], not of blood. . . .' You and I are born of blood. All Israel was born of blood. Hebrews 2:14 says, '. . .children are partakers of flesh and blood. . . .' The only one who did not partake as the natural man in the life of the flesh, which is in the blood, was Jesus Christ. Therefore, John 1:13 refers only to Jesus Christ. It was Jesus Christ 'who was born, not of blood, nor of the will of the flesh, nor of the will of man, but of God.' Jesus Christ was conceived by God's creating soul-life. God created, brought into existence, a sperm in an ovum in Mary."[87]

There are several serious blunders here. The first, and the one which should be the most obvious even to the casual Bible student, is that Wierwille has taken verse 13 completely out of context. He makes it refer to *physical* birth when the context is clearly speaking of *spiritual* birth, a rebirth. The verse immediately preceding this one describes sinners trusting Christ and becoming "the sons of God." Wierwille ignores this fact and takes verse 13 completely out of context, describing it as a birth of "flesh and blood."

Second, his reference to Hebrews 2:14 must be, one can only conclude, a deliberate attempt to deceive his readers. He lifts the words "children are partakers of flesh and blood" out of that verse, then says Jesus Christ was the "only one who did not partake as the natural man in the life of the flesh, which is in the blood." Yet the moment one turns to Hebrews 2:14 and reads the entire verse, which Wierwille conveniently does not give, he finds it saying, "Forasmuch then as the children are partakers of flesh and blood, **he also himself likewise took part of the same**; that through death he might destroy him that had the power of death, that is, the devil" (emphasis added). Contrary to proving Wierwille's point, it emphatically disproves it. In fact, the very purpose of the verse is not to point out that all babies partake of flesh and blood, *but that Jesus Christ did!* And He did so that He might die for sinners and provide a redemption for them through the defeat of Satan. Quite frankly, we are at a loss to understand how his followers could note such dishonest handling of the Word of God and still consider Wierwille a biblical scholar or researcher—to say nothing of remaining his disciples!

Third, a look at any translation in existence will quickly show a failure to render John 1:13 as Wierwille suggests. Although we do not concur with George M. Lamsa—especially in his claim that Aramaic was the language in which the Gospels were

---

87. Ibid., p. 100

originally written—we quote him here because Wierwille lists him as one of the scholars under whom he studied. Does Lamsa concur with a singular "who," referring to Christ? No, he opens the verse with a plural "those," pointing to the ones who have by faith received Christ.

Other translators, both liberal and evangelical, follow the same pattern. Edgar J. Goodspeed, a radical liberal who once wrote and called this writer a murderer and tried to get his daily broadcast in Texas off the air because we dared object to his faulty textual criticism, translated John 1:12,13: "But to all who did receive him and believe in him he gave the right to become children of God, owing their birth not to nature nor to any human or physical impulse, but to God "(CB).

Richard Francis Weymouth, another liberal, has rendered the two verses, "But all who have received Him to them—that is, to those who trust in His name—He has given the privilege of becoming children of God; who were begotten as such not by human descent, nor through an impulse of their own nature, nor through the will of a human father, but from God "(WEY).

J. B. Phillips has it: "Yet wherever men did accept him he gave them the power to become sons of God. These were the men who truly believed in him, and their birth depended not on the course of nature nor on any impulse or plan of man, but on God "(PHIL).

The New International Version translates it: "Yet to all who receive him, to those who believed in his name, he gave the right to become children of God—children born not of natural descent, nor of human decision or a husband's will, but born of God." The New Berkeley Version in Modern English offers it: "But to those who did receive Him He granted authority to become God's children, that is, to those who believe in His name, who owe their birth neither to human blood, nor to physical urge, nor to human design, but to God." And The New Testament English Version for the Deaf gives it: "Some people did accept him. They believed in him. He gave something to those people who believed. He gave them the right to become children of God. These children were not born like little babies are born. They were not born from the wish or plan of a *mother* and father. These children were born from God." While other translations could easily be appealed to, this should suffice for our purpose and establish our point.

Going back to Wierwille's bracket correction of verse 4, "In him [God] was life; and the life was the light of men," this changes the verse's obvious intent and makes John the Baptist coming to "bear witness of" the Father, not the Word, Jesus Christ. This identification of the Father as the Light becomes confusion personified when verses 7 and 8 are reached: "The same came for a witness, to bear witness of the Light, that all men through him might believe. He was not that Light, but was sent to bear witness of that Light."

Why would anyone need the explanation that John was not God the Father? The whole thrust and impact of the passage is nullified. Some thought John was the Messiah, the Christ (see vss. 19-21), but no one mistook him for Jehovah God! Wierwille's interpretation simply does not make sense.

Too, it was the Christ, the Messiah, for whom John was the forerunner, the voice. He said in verse 23, responding to the demand of the priests and Levites who were sent from the Pharisees at Jerusalem that he say plainly who he was, "I am the voice of one crying in the wilderness, Make straight the way of the Lord, as said the prophet Esaias." The reference being, of course, to Isaiah 40:3, "The voice of him that crieth in the wilderness, Prepare ye the way of the Lord, make straight in the desert a highway for our God."

But it is even plainer that Wierwille is wrong in supposing the Light was God the Father. As we saw in verse seven, it says John "came for a witness, to bear witness of the Light," then in verse 15, after speaking of how "the Word was made flesh, and dwelt among us," it says: "John bare witness of him, and cried, saying, This was he of whom I spake, He that cometh after me is preferred before me: for he was before me." So it is settled beyond controversy that the Light John bore witness to was Jesus Christ, not God the Father. Wierwille as much as admits this when he confesses that verse 15 speaks of Christ. He says: "Verse 15 says that Jesus was preferred before John."[88]

It is when Wierwille enlarges on this fact that Jesus was preferred before John the Baptist, "for he was before me," that his foreknowledge theory really backfires. How could Jesus be "before" John, yet "younger"? Wierwille says: "Jesus Christ was preferred before John because John was an Israelite and Israel was first 'called in Jacob'; Jesus Christ had already been called in God's foreknowledge from the beginning. Jesus Christ came after John in the sense that John was six months old when Jesus

---

88. Ibid., p. 106

was born."[89] He offers Genesis 35:10-12 as his scriptural proof, but this passage has nothing whatsoever to do with a "calling," merely a renaming.

Are we to suppose that Jacob (Israel) and John the Baptist were not in God's foreknowledge from eternity past? Was John's ministry a surprise to the Father, or did He foresee it only at the time of Genesis 35? *The thought is absurd!* Absolutely the only way Jesus Christ could have been "before" John is in the light of true scriptural teaching; that is, He is the eternal one, "from everlasting" (Micah 5:2).

The road gets rocky for Wierwille's human Christ in John 1:16, "And of his fulness have all we received, and grace for grace." He comments about this: "It is out of his complete fullness that we were filled to capacity when we were born again of God's Spirit and **received Christ in us**. The word 'received' is from the root *lambano* which means 'to receive to the end that we manifest that which is received.' We not only received the fullness of Christ in us, but we also receive him into manifestation as we walk on God's Word and exercise the power of God's gift, holy spirit."[90]

But if Jesus Christ is not God, how could He be received in us? Could we receive Elijah in us? or John? or Moses? or Paul? And if He is not God, how can we be in Him? Paul spoke of his kinsmen, Andronicus and Junia, who "were in Christ before me" (Rom. 16:7). And our hope of Heaven lies in Christ being in us, since Colossians 1:27 insists, ". . .which is Christ in you, the hope of glory." How difficult it is to imagine singing, for example,

> **"Isaiah liveth in me!**
> **Isaiah liveth in me!**
> **Oh, what a salvation, this**
> **That Isaiah liveth in me!"**[91]

When discussing John 1:18, "No man hath seen God at any time; the only begotten Son, which is in the bosom of the Father, he hath declared him," Wierwille reverts to his foreknowledge theory to soften the impact. He says, "Jesus Christ was in the bosom of the Father, not by pre-existence, but in the foreknowledge of God."[92] One might as well claim that when the

---

89. Ibid., p. 106,107
90. Ibid., p. 107, emphasis added
91. With apologies to Daniel W. Whittle (1840-1901), author of "Christ Liveth in Me"
92. JCNG, p. 116

beggar died he departed into Abraham's foreknowledge (Luke 16:22). Anyway, John 1:18 does not say He "**was** in the bosom of the Father," which would be necessary if it referred to foreknowledge, but "**is** in the bosom," which indicates the attribute of deity, omnipresence. Morris, commenting about the phrase "is in the bosom of the Father," says: "This final expression expresses the closeness of the Father and the Son. It also carries overtones of affection (*cf.* our 'the wife of his bosom'). The copula 'is' expresses a continuing union. The only begotten is continually in the bosom of the Father."[93]

In fact, this one verse could be one of the most damaging in the Word of God to the cause of those who deny the deity of Jesus Christ. There is strong evidence that, instead of "only begotten Son," it should be "God only begotten." Dr. Kenneth S. Wuest translates this verse, "Deity in its invisible essence no one has ever yet seen. God only begotten, the one who is constantly in the bosom of the Father, that One has fully explained God." Then he comments: "The words 'God only begotten' refer to Jesus of Nazareth. He is God only begotten, proceeding by eternal generation as the Son of God from the Father in a birth that never took place because it always was. This one, John says, fully explained Deity. The Greek word translated 'fully explained' means literally 'to lead out.' Jesus in the incarnation led Deity out from back of the curtain of its invisibility, showing the human race in and through a human life, what God was like. Our word 'exegesis' is the transliteration of the Greek word here. The science of exegesis is that of fully explaining in detail the meaning of a passage of Scripture. In the incarnation, Jesus of Nazareth fully explained God so far as a human medium could explain the infinite, and human minds and hearts could receive that revelation. And He could do that only because He was God Himself."[94]

Wuest is not alone in this understanding of how John 1:18 should be rendered. The New American Standard has it: "No man has seen God at any time; the only begotten God, who is in the bosom of the Father, He has explained Him." Williams renders it: "No one has ever seen God; the only Son, Deity Himself, who lies upon His Father's breast, has made him known." Even the translations of liberal scholars, such as the Revised Standard Version and The New English Bible,

93. NICNT, *The Gospel According to John,* p. 114
94. GTLB, p. 30

acknowledge this possibility. The Amplified Bible has a footnote regarding "the only-begotten God," quoting the Greek scholar Vincent that such a rendering is supported by "a great mass of ancient evidence." And so it is!

Along this line, Dr. H. W. Watkins, Archdeacon of Durham and Canon of Durham Cathedral, writing in *Ellicott's Commentary on the Whole Bible,* notes that soon after the middle of the second century the reading "only begotten *God"* became prominent and "has at least an equal, if not a superior, claim to be considered the original text." Here is part of his comment, quoting for the most part only evidence supporting it, to save space; those interested in the entire passage may check the commentary for themselves:

"The external evidence, judged by the testimony of MSS., of versions, and of quotations in extant works, must be admitted to be in favour of the reading, 'only begotten *God.'*

"Of the chief uncial MSS. (comp. p. xvi.), the Sinaitic, the Vatican, and the Codex Ephraem at Paris, support it; while against it are the Alexandrian MS. now in the British Museum, and a reading of Codex Ephraem from the hand of a later scribe. The preponderance in weight is, however, much greater than it seems to be numerically.

"Of the Versions the Revised Syriac (Peshito), the margin of the Philoxenian Syriac, the AEthiopic (?), read 'only begotten God.'. . . The Revised Syriac must here be regarded as having special weight from the fact that its evidence agrees with that of MSS. from which it usually differs.

"Of the Fathers 'only begotten God' is read certainly by Irenaeus, Clement of Alexandria, Origen, Epiphanius, Didymus *de Trinitate,* Basil, Gregory of Nyssa, Cyril of Alexandria. . . . The uncertain text of many of the Fathers makes their witness doubtful; but this at least seems clear, that the decided weight of Patristic evidence is in favour of 'only begotten God.'. . .

"The external evidence being thus in favour of 'only begotten God,' we have to inquire whether there is any sufficient ground on which it can be set aside. We are at once met by the fact that the term is unique, and therefore, it is often said, not likely to occur; whereas 'the only begotten Son' is perfectly natural, and occurs in St. John in chap. iii. 16, 18, and I John iv.19. But we are to remember that what is unnatural to us would have been so to copyists and translators; and the fact that we have an unusual term strongly supported by external evidence is of weight just in proportion as the term is unusual. Nor need a unique term be a matter of suspicion in this Prologue, where we have found so much that is not paralleled in other parts of the New Testament. . . .

"*A priori* reasons would seem, then, to unite with external evidence in favour of the unfamiliar reading, 'only begotten God.' We find it beyond all question soon after the middle of the second century. It is almost impossible to believe that it was of set purpose, and quite impossible to believe that it was by accident, read instead of 'only begotten Son,' and the only alternative is that it is part of the original Gospel."[95]

Watkins offers a simple and logical explanation as to how the text became corrupted from "only begotten God" to "only begotten Son," then observes: "But although the term 'only begotten God' is unfamiliar to us, it is not foreign to the thought of the Prologue, the very central idea of which is that the Logos was with God, and was God. The eternal Sonship of the Logos is expressed in the parallel sentence 'in the bosom of the Father,' and in this term 'only begotten God' the Prologue repeats emphatically at its conclusion the text with which it opened: 'In the beginning was the Logos, and the Logos was with God, and the Logos was God.' The omission of the article gives the sentence a meaning which it is difficult to express in translation, but which in Greek makes the term 'only begotten God' an assertion—'No man hath seen God at any time; only begotten God as He is, He who is in the bosom of the Father, *He* hath declared Him.' "[96]

The reading "only begotten God" is the one adopted by Westcott and Hort in their Greek text, and it would have been adopted in the English Revised Version of 1881 if they had had their way, instead of being merely a marginal reading, Sir Robert Anderson tells us.[97] And Watkins referred to a "remarkable *Dissertation* upon it, read before the University of Cambridge by Dr. Hort in 1876," which he hoped would "turn the current of thoughtful opinion in favour of reading" *only begotten God.*[98]

### Other Passages Wierwille Notes

We have taken considerable space to deal with the passage in

---

95. Vol. VI, pp. 554, 555, Excursus B
96. Ibid., p. 555
97. LFH, p. 42
98. Op. cit., p. 555

John 1 because we deem it pivotal to the entire TWI issue. But other trinitarian references and statements about the absolute deity of Jesus Christ are explained away by the cult with equal dexterity—or lack of it, depending upon your point of view.

One of these deals with the fact that the opening chapter in the Bible describes the Creator through the use of both plural pronouns and a plural name. Wierwille writes:

> "The people who hold or have held this idea that God is Jesus and Jesus is God substantiate their beliefs by isolating bits of biblical texts. Genesis 1:26 is their initial scripture where God says, 'Let us make man in our image. . . .' 'Us' and 'our' are interpreted to mean 'God in conjunction with Jesus Christ.'
>
> "Truly, this scripture is no proof of Jesus' existence in the beginning. The first person plural pronouns, 'we' and 'us,' are used to indicate the magnitude of the incident to which God related Himself. When a plural noun or pronoun is used but the singular case is true to fact, it is the figure of speech *heterosis*. The plural is used for the singular when great excellence or magnitude is denoted."[99]

First of all, Wierwille is incorrect in saying the trinitarians' "initial scripture" is Genesis 1:26. Our first Scripture is the opening verse of the Word of God: "In the beginning God. . . ." The word *God* here is *Elohim*. Not only is it one of the primary names of deity—used some two and a half thousand times in the Old Testament—it is a uni-plural noun, not singular. And it is Elohim in Genesis 1:26 also, just as it is throughout this creation chapter. In creation we have our Trinitarian God working in unity. This is borne out in other Scriptures where each member of the Godhead is described as being active in creation. God the Father is pictured in Isaiah 42:5, "Thus saith God the Lord, he that created the heavens, and stretched them out; he that spread forth the earth, and that which cometh out of it; he that giveth breath unto the people upon it, and spirit to them that walk therein." God the Son is pictured in Psalm 102:25-27, a passage the Father ascribed to the Son in Hebrews 1: "Of old hast thou laid the foundation of the earth: and the heavens are the work of thy hands. They shall perish, but thou shalt endure: yea, all of them shall wax old like a garment; as a vesture shalt thou change them, and they shall be changed. But thou art the same, and thy years shall have no end." And God the Holy Spirit is pictured in Elihu's testimony: "The Spirit of God hath made me, and the

---

99. JCNG, pp. 81,82

breath of the Almighty hath given me life" (Job 33:4). Other passages could be cited, of course, but these are taken at random as illustrative. What we have in Genesis 1:26 is far more than the "figure of speech" Wierwille imagines.

In fact, this uni-plural name for God, Elohim, is used in the very passages insisting He is One. We read in Deuteronomy 6:4, for example: "Hear, O Israel: The Lord [Jehovah] our God [Elohim] is one Lord [Jehovah]." This truth has amazed, startled and even confused Jews and other monotheistic peoples down through the ages. How could God be *singular* and *plural* at the same time? The biblical teaching of the Trinity is the answer! Not only so, but as Lease points out, "The Hebrew word *echad*, translated 'one' Lord in Deuteronomy 6:4, is the very same word found in Numbers 13:23, where it relates to 'one' cluster of grapes. Thus, *echad* allows for many, or a plurality, within its unity and indeed plurality is required in the Numbers 13:23 reference."[100]

In the second place, Wierwille is wrong in passing off the force of the passage by claiming that the "plural is used for the singular when great excellence or magnitude is denoted." This is another argument borrowed from the Jehovah's Witnesses, but it simply is not true. As G. A. F. Knight pointed out, "Some have suggested, for example, that the word is a plural of majesty. But surely that is to read into Hebrew speech a modern way of thinking. The Kings of Israel and Judah are **always** addressed in the singular in our Bible records."[101] And Thomas Whitelaw adds about the plural of majesty explanation: "[It is] a usage which the best Hebraists affirm to have no existence in the Scriptures . . . ."[102]

One verse which Wierwille admits is "thorny" to his unitarian position is Isaiah 9:6, "For unto us a child is born, unto us a son is given: and the government shall be upon his shoulder: and his name shall be called Wonderful, Counsellor, The mighty God, The everlasting    Father, The Prince of Peace." He says of it: "The words 'Jesus Christ' are not specifically used in this scrip-

100. GNB, op. cit., p. 22
101. *A Biblical Approach to the Doctrine of the Trinity* (Scottish Journal of Theology Occasional Papers No. 1, Edinburgh: Oliver and Boyd Ltd., 1953), p. 20, emphasis added; quoted in AOD, p. 128. Gruss points out that the Hebrew word for absolute oneness, *yachid,* although found a dozen times in the Old Testament, is **never** used of the unity of Jehovah God.
102. PC, Vol. I, p. 2

ture; however, many people believe it is a prophecy referring to him." This is subterfuge on Wierwille's part. Of course the words "Jesus Christ" are not specifically used here, nor are they used anywhere in the Old Testament. But he goes on: "If indeed this is the case, then the following facts apply: the quotation saying, 'His name shall be called,' means that this is the definition of his name."[103]

*Ah, but what name is it defining, if definition it be?* This child to be born, this son to be given was previously mentioned by Isaiah two chapters earlier in that great Messianic promise about the virgin birth. He wrote: "There the Lord himself shall give you a sign; Behold, a virgin shall conceive, and bear a son, and shall call his name Immanuel" (7:14). Immanuel is literally, "God with us," as the Angel of Jehovah explained to Joseph in Matthew 1:23. Now Isaiah is telling his readers more about who this Immanuel is, this God with us. Consider it well: Wonderful! Counsellor! The Mighty God! The Everlasting Father! The Prince of Peace! No one with an unbiased mind could read these names ascribed to Messiah and doubt or deny for one moment His absolute deity.

He is *El Gibbohr* [The Mighty God], the one of whom the next chapter says, "The remnant shall return, even the remnant of Jacob, unto the mighty God" (10:21). F. C. Jennings was right when he said of *El Gibbohr*, "It is as simple, clear, unequivocal a claim of supreme deity for Messiah as could be expressed in human language, yet not more so than in every word He said, every act He did."[104] He is *Avi-ad* [The everlasting Father], literally, "The Father of Eternity!" No mere created being whose existence commenced in a Bethlehem stable is He; He is the one whose "goings forth have been from of old, from everlasting" (Micah 5:2). He is also *Sar-Shalohm* [The Prince of Peace], the only one who can and will produce the peace this sin-wracked, war-weary old world so desperately needs. *What a Saviour!* **What a God!**

Speaking of the Virgin Birth, it seems incredible that one would teach it, as Wierwille does, yet deny Christ's full deity. The two go together like hand and glove, fire and heat, peaches and cream. As the late Wilbur M. Smith noted: "Another point to be remembered in our discussion of the Virgin Birth of our Lord is that it is in perfect conformity to all that we know of the

---

103. JCNG, p. 35
104. SII, p. 117

subsequent life, and all that we know of the Person, of the Lord Jesus Christ. Even such a critic as Dr. Charles A. Briggs was forced to admit that, 'historically and logically, the divinity of Christ and the Incarnation are bound up with the Virgin Birth, and no man can successfully maintain any one of them without maintaining all.' "[105] And Sir William M. Ramsay added: "That in the man Jesus Christ the Divine nature was incarnate, is an essential and fundamental part of the Christian religion: 'the Word was made flesh and dwelt among us.' This fundamental principle is common to all the four Gospels and to the New Testament as a whole. If you try to eliminate it, there remains practically nothing: that is the result clearly demonstrated in many attempts which have been made to cut out the superhuman and Divine from the life of Jesus. . . . That Jesus was not merely human but truly superhuman and Divine is the Christian teaching and faith and belief, and to deny that is to separate one's self from Christianity."[106]

Perhaps that is why, although Wierwille says he believes in the virgin birth, what he more accurately believes in is a virgin *conception*. He flatly denies that Mary was a virgin when she gave birth to the Baby Jesus. In what must be considered a most bizarre understanding of the event, Wierwille wrote, in his comments on Matthew 1:

"Some commentaries and theologians declare that Mary was a virgin when she brought forth her first Son. According to verse 23, Mary was a virgin when she became pregnant. But verse 24 records that Joseph 'took unto him his wife,' according to the angel's command. Even though Joseph took unto him his wife, 'he knew her not.' 'Knew her not' specifically has to do, not with sexual intercourse alone, but with sexual intercourse producing pregnancy. Even though Joseph had sexual relations with Mary while she was pregnant with Jesus, Mary never conceived by Joseph until after Jesus Christ was born."[107]

The observing reader will note that Wierwille not only makes up new meanings for Hebrew and Greek words, but English as well. To him, "virgin" does not mean "one who has never had sexual intercourse"; it merely means "woman of marriageable age."[108] According to that definition, all the prostitutes at the local whorehouse are "virgins." And we still burst out laughing

---

105. SOC, p. 89
106. VBC, Appendix II, p. 243
107. TWW, p. 168
108. Ibid., p. 162

every time we think of Wierwille's claim that "to know" with regard to sex relations means "sexual intercourse producing pregnancy." Try to understand it that way in Genesis 19:5 ("And they called unto Lot, and said unto him, Where are **the men** which came in to thee this night? **bring them out unto us, that we may know them**")! The Sodomites having "intercourse producing pregnancy" with those men visiting in the home of Lot would have been something, indeed. And were the men of Jebus, when they demanded of the old man entertaining the Levite, "Bring forth **the man** that came into thine house, **that we may know him**" (Judges 19:22, emphasis added), insisting upon "intercourse producing pregnancy"? We think not.

But Wierwille's understanding does violence to the actual statements of the divine record. Mary's status when she conceived child of the Holy Spirit was as "espoused to Joseph" (Matt. 1:18). The word espoused is the Greek *mnesteuo* and means, Vine says, "to woo a woman and ask for her in marriage" when in the active voice. However, the only three times it is used in the New Testament it is in the passive voice and means "to be promised in marriage."[109] It is rendered "betrothed" uniformly in the Revised Version. So, at the time of conception, Mary was only espoused, *betrothed* to Joseph. We say "engaged" today, although the espousal of that time involved far more than our engagements do today, obviously, since Mary is called "espoused *wife*" and Joseph is described as "husband." And that espousal was so binding it took a "bill of divorcement" to break, as is implied by Joseph's initial thought to "put her away." And what was Mary's relation to Joseph when the baby Jesus was actually born? Luke 2:6, describing the arrival of Joseph and Mary at Bethlehem on the eve of His birth, says: "To be taxed with Mary his espoused wife, being great with child." So there had been no change in their relationship; Mary was still only Joseph's "espoused" or "betrothed" wife. Her status was still the same.

Matthew 1:23 should also be noted. It says: "Behold a virgin shall be with child, and shall bring forth a son. . . ." What about this virgin? She would "be with child" *as a virgin*. However, the phrase "bring forth a son" is still related to the virginity: "Behold a virgin. . .shall bring forth a son." In other words, she was a virgin at conception **and she was still a virgin when the child was born!** "Poof" goes Wierwille's claim of sexual intercourse between the pregnant Mary and Joseph!

---

109. EDNTW, Vol. I, p. 122

Is there any validity to his interpretation that when Joseph "took unto him his wife" it means they had sexual relations? Not in the *slightest*! It simply refers to one part of the espousal, the betrothal. E. H. Plumptre explains "took unto him his wife" as follows: "These few words cover a great deal. They imply the formal ratification of the betrothal before witnesses; the benediction by a priest; the marriage-feast; the removal from the house that had hitherto been her home to that of Joseph."[110] But there is no thought or suggestion of sex relations, as the very next words in the record bear out: "And knew her not till she had brought forth her firstborn son." That is how the passage has been understood by Bible believers from New Testament days to the present hour, Wierwille's bizarre interpretation notwithstanding. We might also point out that the conjunction "till" [Greek, *heos*] means "up to" and intelligently would only apply to virginity, not impregnancy. The thought is not that she was immediately impregnated by Joseph following the birth of the baby Jesus, but that normal marital relationships were begun after that birth.

Before leaving this thought of the virgin-born Saviour, permit a quote from the classic on the subject by James Orr. Speaking of how it has been understood universally as a means for blending the true humanity and the true deity of Jesus Christ, Orr wrote: "This is the ground taken up by Irenaeus, by Tertullian, by Clement of Alexandria, by Hippolytus, by Origen—by *all* who discuss the subject. Gnosticism, with its denial, or explaining away, of the Virgin Birth, Irenaeus speaks of as a 'system with neither the prophets announced, nor the Lord taught, nor the Apostles delivered.' Two of the headings of his chapters are: 'Jesus Christ was not a mere man begotten from Joseph in the ordinary course of nature, but was very God, begotten of the Father Most High, and very man, born of the Virgin'—'Christ assumed human flesh, conceived and born of the Virgin.' Here is a characteristic passage from Tertullian. I do not ask you to accept the reasoning, but only to note the belief that is in the heart of it. 'It was not fit,' he says, 'that the Son of God should be born of a human father's seed, lest, if He were wholly the Son of Man, He should fail to be also the Son of God. . . . In order, therefore, that He who was already the Son of God—of God the Father's seed, i.e., the Spirit—might also be the Son of Man, He only wanted to assume flesh, of the flesh of man, without the seed of a man; for the seed

110. ECWB, Vol. VI, p. 4

of a man was unnecessary for One who had the seed of God.' "[111]
We repeat again that Christ's deity and the virgin birth go
together; no wonder Wierwille wishes to soften the impact of the
latter.

One idea Wierwille advances to disprove our Lord's absolute
deity is summed up:

> "Another difference between God and Jesus Christ regards that of
> knowledge. God is omniscient, but Jesus Christ knew only those things
> which he ascertained from his knowledge of the Scriptures and from the
> rest of the senses world, plus that which God revealed to him.
>
> "Mark 13:32:
> > "But of that day and *that* hour knoweth no man, no, not the angels
> > which are in heaven, neither the Son, but the Father."
>
> "This clearly shows the limitations of Jesus Christ's knowledge."[112]

No, *not in the slightest!* Kindly observe the context of this
statement and it is readily discovered that our Lord was speaking in view of His humanity, not His deity. Six verses previous,
speaking on the same subject of His second coming, He said,
"And then shall they see **the Son of man** coming in the clouds
with great power and glory" (vs. 26). And two verses after,
launching another parable on the same theme, He declared, "For
**the Son of man** is as a man taking a far journey. . ." (vs. 34). He
was not speaking as the Son of God, but as the Son of man. His
humanity was involved, not His deity. This limitation of
knowledge in His humanity was part of the great voluntary "setting aside" described by Paul in Philippians 2, which we will look
at closely in a moment.

When it came to our Lord's deity, His disciples, at the end of
their long instruction at His feet and observing His life and actions, could say, "Now are we **sure** that thou **knowest all
things**, and needest not that any man should ask thee: by this we
believe that thou camest forth from God" (John 16:30). And
Peter could say with confident assurance to the resurrected
Christ: "Lord, **thou knowest all things**; thou knowest that I love
thee" (John 21:17). No wonder Paul exclaimed of Him, "In
whom are hid **all** the treasures of wisdom and knowledge" (Col.
2:3). In His humanity, His knowledge was limited; in His deity,
it knows no limitations or boundaries whatsoever.

Wierwille also thinks the fact Jesus was tempted by Satan

111. VBC, pp. 148,149
112. JCNG, p. 47

proves He was not God. After quoting James 1:13, which says, "Let no man say when he is tempted, I am tempted of God: for God cannot be tempted with evil, neither tempteth he any man," he observes:

"God cannot be tempted, yet Jesus Christ was in all points tempted.

"Luke 4:1,2,13:
"And Jesus being full of the Holy Ghost returned from Jordan, and was led by the Spirit into the wilderness,

"Being forty days tempted of the devil. . . .

"And when the devil had ended all the temptation, he departed from him for a season.

"Hebrews 4:15:
"For we have not an high priest which cannot be touched with the feeling of our infirmities; but was in all points tempted like as *we are, yet* without sin.

"Jesus Christ was tempted in all points as we are, yet God is never tempted; indeed, cannot be tempted."[113]

Wierwille errs on several important points in this reasoning. First of all, it was as a man, with the same human frailties as any other earthling, that Jesus Christ was tempted. The first Adam was tempted by Satan in the garden and fell, yielding to the temptation. The last Adam was tempted in the same way by the same force of evil and was triumphant, gaining the victory over every thrust from the tempter. Enduring temptation as a man was one of the purposes in the incarnation. Hebrews 2:16-18 make clear that our Lord's temptation was in His humanity: "For verily he took not on him the nature of angels; but he took on him the seed of Abraham. Wherefore in all things it behooved him to be made like unto his brethren, that he might be a merciful and faithful high priest in things pertaining to God, to make reconciliation for the sins of the people. For in that he himself hath suffered being tempted, he is able to succour them that are tempted."

W. Graham Scroggie emphasizes that it was in His humanity that He was tempted. Commenting on Matthew 4:1 ("Then was Jesus led up of the Spirit into the wilderness to be tempted of the devil"), he observed: "*Jesus*, the name in this connection is of great importance. It was not as the Divine Son of God clothed with glory that He entered into the wilderness, although the

_____
113. Ibid., pp. 46,47

Father had recently borne witness to His Sonship; neither was it as the Christ anointed for service, although He had just received that anointing with the Holy Spirit; neither was it as the Lord, 'Who, by inheritance has obtained a better name and place than the angels,' and before Whom all yet must bow and own His Lordship, though that name is guaranteed to Him by the Father. But it was Jesus, the name that tells us of His humanity, that brings Him into sympathetic touch with us and announces His purpose to save. From this we see that Jesus was led into the conflict as man, and not as God. In the fourth Gospel, which opens with a sublime declaration of Christ's Deity, there is no reference to the temptation. . . ."[114]

Second, as for God being tempted, we think a word from the respected Greek scholars, Hogg and Vine, would help here: "James 1:13-15 seems to contradict other statements of Scripture in two respects, saying (a) that 'God cannot be tempted with evil,' and (b) that 'He Himself tempteth no man.' But God tempted, or tried, Abraham, Heb. 11:17, and the Israelites tempted or tried, God, I Cor. 10:9. Ver. 14, however, makes it plain that, whereas in these cases the temptation, or trial, came from without, James refers to temptation, or trial, arising within, from uncontrolled appetites and from evil passions, cp. Mark 7:20-23. But though such temptation does not proceed from God, yet does God regard His people while they endure it, and by it tests and approves them."[115] One who is God may be tempted from *without*, but never from *within*! It is this fact that shows, through Christ's victory in the temptation, the very opposite of what Wierwille charges. Instead of the temptation proving Him not to be God, His victory proves that He was God! He *couldn't* be tempted from within to do evil; He had no inner desire, no urge, no compulsion to submit to the wrong Satan suggested. "Who did no sin, neither was guile found in his mouth" (I Pet. 2:22).

James Adamson's translation of verse 13 is helpful in showing this meaning: "Let no one under trying assault of evil say, 'My trial by assault of evil comes from God.' For God is invincible to assault of evils, and himself subjects no one to assault of evil."[116] So the complete triumph of Jesus Christ against Satan's assaults

---

114. TBT, pp. 6,7
115. *Notes on Thessalonians*, p. 97; quoted in EDNTW, Vol. IV, p. 116
116. NICNT, *The Epistle of James*, p. 66

of evil, showing Him to be invincible, is in itself a major evidence of His absolute deity.

Finally, it should be pointed out that God *can* and *is* tempted in the sense that Jesus Christ was tempted. Of God the Son, Mark 1:13 says: "And he was there in the wilderness forty days, tempted [Greek, *peirazo*] of Satan. . . ." Of God the Holy Spirit, Acts 5:9 says: "How is it that ye have agreed together to tempt [Greek, *peirazo*] the Spirit of the Lord?" And of God the Father, Acts 15:10 questions, "Now therefore why tempt [Greek, *peirazo*] ye God, to put a yoke upon the neck of the disciples, which neither our fathers nor we were able to bear?" Recall also the testimony of Psalm 78:40,41 about God's earthly people: "How oft did they provoke him in the wilderness, and grieve him in the desert! Yea, they turned back and **tempted God**, and limited the Holy One of Israel."

Wierwille thinks he sees a problem in our Lord's claim to deity by a disavowal of goodness to the rich young ruler. He quotes Luke 18:18,19, "And a certain ruler asked him, saying, Good Master, what shall I do to inherit eternal life? And Jesus said unto him, Why callest thou me good? none is good, save one, that is, God," then says, "This verse clearly shows Jesus correcting the ruler for calling him 'good master.' "[117]

We think not! In the first place, the use of the epithet "Good Master" (literally, "Good Teacher") was most remarkable and unusual. Even the most revered, the most respected, the most famous rabbis were never addressed thus by their pupils. Contrary to the way we lightly use the word today—speaking of good women, good men, good boys and good girls—it was a title of deep reverence. And the emphasis in our Lord's reply was, "**Why** do **you** call **me** good?"

He was saying in effect, "You do not consider Me God, but merely a man. Why do you use such a lofty title? Only God is good and you are not willing to call Me God." And to this reasoning we heartily concur. If Jesus Christ is not God, let us not call Him good. He is an imposter, a blasphemer, a liar, a fraud and a charlatan not worthy of anyone's respect. One could not make the claims He made and, if false, be a good man! And if He were on earth today He would say to Wierwille, the TWI disciples, and to all other unitarians: "Don't call Me good. You will not acknowledge My deity and so I will not and cannot accept your professions of respect and honor. If I am not God, I am not good."

---

117. JCNG, p. 139

Incidentally, you will note that the Lord did not deny His deity. He simply asked the rich young ruler why he called Him good, since he did not believe He was God. If Wierwille were right, Jesus should have added a disclaimer of deity. He did not.

Wierwille offers a strange interpretation of John 3:13, which says, "And no man hath ascended up to heaven, but he that came down from heaven, even the Son of man which is in heaven," claiming, "The oldest extant manuscripts delete the last four words in verse 13, 'which is in heaven.' The son of man came down by God's miraculous conception."[118] And he said earlier, " 'Came down from heaven' was the conception or creation of life in Mary for the Son of God."[119]

We will overlook the statement about the omission in some manuscripts of the phrase "which is in heaven"—even though there is good authority for it—since Wierwille would want it out no matter how strong its case. It is a clear statement of deity's attribute of omnipresence: *Christ was in Heaven even as He conversed on earth with Nicodemus!* This would be utterly impossible for any but deity. As Bishop J. C. Ryle observed: "The expression 'which is in heaven,' deserves particular notice. It is one of those many expressions in the New Testament which can be explained in no other way than by the doctrine of Christ's divinity. It would be utterly absurd and untrue to say of any mere man, that at the very time he was speaking to another on earth he was in heaven! But it can be said of Christ with perfect truth and propriety. He never ceased to be very God, when He became incarnate. He was 'with God and was God.' As God He was in heaven while He was speaking to Nicodemus."[120]

However, the phrase "he that came down from heaven" is proof both positive and conclusive of His preincarnation. The Revised Version of 1881 makes it even plainer, "And no man hath ascended into heaven, **but he that descended out of heaven**, even the Son of man, which is in heaven." It would be impossible to get a mere physical birth conception—even divine insemination—from this verse without doing violence to all the rules of language as a means of communicating truth. Could it be said of me, "Robert L. Sumner came down from Heaven" at the time of my physical conception? Nonsense!

Dr. H. R. Reynolds has it: "**No one hath ascended into**

118. Ibid., p. 140
119. Ibid., p. 118
120. RETG, Vol. III, p. 153

**heaven except he who has by living there as in his eternal home come down from heaven.** Meyer, Luthardt, Westcott, etc., all call attention to other and analogous usage of [*ei me*], which fastens upon a part of the previous negative, not the whole assertion, and therefore here upon the idea of living in heaven and coming thence. . . .*he who has descended from heaven*, having been there before his manifestation in the flesh, having been 'in God,' 'with God,' 'in the bosom of the Father,' and having come thence, not losing his essential ego, his Divine personality, even though calling himself **the Son of man.** For any other to have come down from heaven, it was necessary that he should first have ascended thither; but the Son of man has descended without having ascended. He calls himself 'Son of man,' and he claims to have come down from heaven without ceasing to be what he was before. . . . By using the term, 'Son of man,' Christ emphasized the exalted dignity that is involved in the extent of his self-humiliation and complete sympathy with us. He was 'the second Adam, the Lord from heaven.' "[121]

Wierwille only takes a passing shot at John 5:17-19, which says: "But Jesus answered them, My Father worketh hitherto, and I work. Therefore the Jews sought the more to kill him, because he not only had broken the sabbath, but said also that God was his Father, making himself equal with God. Then answered Jesus and said unto them, Verily, verily, I say unto you, The Son can do nothing of himself, but what he seeth the Father do: for what things soever he doeth, these also doeth the Son likewise." This is, of course, a tremendous declaration of His deity and those to whom He spoke understood it exactly that way—nor did He correct them when they assumed it to mean He was "making himself equal with God."

Wierwille merely offers two sentences in reply, following the usual unitarian position of "inferiority" for the Son. He says: "The Son could only walk with the power and authority of his Father, as belonging to him, if he obeyed and carried out what his Father said. The context makes the distinction between Father and Son clear."[122]

Quite the contrary, the context makes clear the truth of equality with the Father; only by lifting the phrase "the Son can do nothing of himself" out of the context is inferiority implied. As Dr. J. B. Rowell pointed out: "Our Lord claimed God as *His*

---

121. PC, Vol. XVII, p. 120
122. JCNG, p. 141

*own Father.* His claim to equality was grounded on His oneness of essence with the Father. He was so truly one in will and sympathy with the Father, that 'self-originated action is impossible, not by reason of defect of power, but by reason of unity of being.' The Son can do nothing of Himself, that is, independently of the Father; and this, because of His *oneness* with the Father. When He does act, it is 'in like manner' with the Father (John 5:19, A.S.V.). The identity of action is based on the identity of nature. What an amazing Scripture this is! What an answer to the denial of Christ's deity!"[123] It would be equally in harmony with the thought and teaching of Scripture to say, "The Father can do nothing of Himself, without the Son," so in oneness is their unity. The blessed Trinity exercises no independence of action.

Bishop J. C. Ryle offers some pertinent comments about the phrase "the Son can do nothing of Himself," then adds valuable observations of other scholars, writing: "This opening verse declares the complete unity there is between God the Father and God the Son. The Son, from His very nature and relation to the Father, 'can do nothing,' independently or separately from the Father. It is not that He lacks or *wants* the power to do, but that He *will* not do. (Compare Gen. xix.22.) When the angel said, 'I cannot do anything till Thou be come thither;' it means of course 'I will not do.'—'Of Himself' does not mean without help, or unassisted but 'from Himself,' from His own independent will. He can only do such things as, from His unity with the Father, and consequent ineffable knowledge, He 'seeth' the Father doing. For the Father and the Son are so united,—one God though two Persons,—that whatsoever the Father does the Son does also. The acts of the Son therefore are not His own independent acts, but the acts of His Father also.

"The Greek word which we render 'likewise' must not be supposed to mean nothing more than 'also, as well.' It is literally 'in like manner.'

"Bishop Hall paraphrases this saying of our Lord thus:—'I and the Father are one indivisible essence, and our acts are no less inseparable. The Son can do nothing without the will and act of the Father; and, even as He is man, can do nothing but what He seeth agreeable to the will and purpose of His heavenly Father.'

"Barnes remarks,—'The words "what things soever" are without limit; all that the Father does, the Son likewise does. This is as high an assertion as possible of His being equal with

---

123. DJCL, pp. 15,16

God. If one does all that another does, or can do, then there is proof of equality. If the Son does all that the Father does, then, like Him, He must be almighty, omniscient, all-present, and infinite in every perfection; or, in other words, He must be God.'

"Augustine remarks,—'Our Lord does not say, whatsoever the Father doeth the Son does other *things like* them, but the very *same things*. . . . If the Son doeth the same things, and in like manner, then let the Jew be silenced, the Christian believe, the heretic be convinced: the Son is equal with the Father.'

"Hilary, quoted in the *'Catena Aurea,'* remarks,—'Christ is the Son because He does nothing of Himself. He is God because whatsoever things the Father doeth, He doeth the same. They are one because They are equal in honour. He is not the Father, because He is sent.'

"Diodati remarks,—'The phrase, "what He seeth the Father do," is a figurative term, showing the inseparable communion of will, wisdom, and power, between the Son and the Father in the internal order of the most holy Trinity.'

"Toletus remarks,—'When it is said "the Son can do nothing of Himself," this does not mean want of power, but the highest power. Just as it is a mark of omnipotence not to be able to die, or to be worn out, or to be annihilated, because there is nothing that can injure omnipotence, so likewise, "to be unable to do anything of Himself" is no mark of impotence, but of the highest power. It means nothing less than having one and the same power with the Father, so that nothing can be done by the One which is not equally done by the Other.' "[124]

And Dr. H. W. Watkins adds: "The key to this and the following verses is in the relation of Father and Son, from which they start. The Jews saw in this equality with God blasphemy, and sought to kill Him. Men have since seen and now see in it inferiority, and a proof that Christ did not claim for Himself the glory which the Apostle claims for Him in the prologue (chap. i. 1-18), and which the Church has ever in reverent adoration placed as a crown upon His brow. The words 'Son,' 'Father,' are the answer to both. Did they accuse Him of blasphemy? He is a Son. The very essence of blasphemy was independence of, and rivalry with, God. He claimed no such position, but was as a Son subject to His Father's will, was as a Son *morally* unable to do anything of Himself, and did whatever He saw the Father do. Yea, more. He thought not His equality with God a thing to be

---

124. RETG, Vol. III, pp. 286,287

seized, but emptied Himself and became, as they then saw Him, in the form of a servant, and in the likeness of men."[125] Far from contradicting His deity, this passage establishes it!

Another strong claim of deity, just a few verses on in the same passage, is dismissed by Wierwille in a dozen or so words. In John 5:23, our Lord said: "All men should honour the Son, even as they honour the Father. He that honoureth not the Son honoureth not the Father which hath sent him." To this Wierwille responds: "If someone did not respect your son, you too might be insulted and disturbed."[126] But this ignores the key phrase, the main impact of the declaration: **"even as they honour the Father!"** Every believer is a son of God, yet it could hardly be said that the world should honor us as they honor the Father. I would never say, "All men should honor Robert L. Sumner, even as they honor God the Father. Any one who does not honor Robert L. Sumner does not honor God the Father." Only absolute deity could make that claim!

Well did Albert Barnes remark, "If our Saviour here did not *intend* to teach that he ought to be *worshipped*, and to be esteemed as *equal* with God, it would be difficult to teach it by any language which we could use."[127] In this same context (vss. 21-29), our Lord not only assumed equal honor with the Father, He claimed the power to raise the dead at the resurrection, have all authority for judgment, and to have "life in himself," even as the Father has life in Himself. This could be the language of none but deity.

Christ's claim to be the eternal "I Am" of the Old Testament is also dismissed with little more than a passing remark by Wierwille. He writes:

" 'It is I' is 'I am' in the Greek. This no more shows that Jesus Christ is God than my saying 'I am' proves that I am God.

"John 8:58:

"Jesus said unto them, Verily, verily, I say unto you, Before Abraham was, I am.

"Christ was with God in His foreknowledge before Abraham was born. Compare notes on Exodus 3:14. John 9:9 and John 18:6 contain the same common error in understanding."[128]

---

125. ECWB, Vol. VI, p. 418
126. JCNG, p. 141
127. BNNT, p. 289
128. JCNG, p. 141

While it would be interesting to make a list of all the things Wierwille discards under the label of "foreknowledge," his explanation completely ignores the context, especially verses 56 and 57: "Your father Abraham rejoiced to see my day: and he saw it, and was glad. Then said the Jews unto him, Thou are not yet fifty years old, and hast thou seen Abraham?" To accept Wierwille's explanation of "foreknowledge" credits the attribute of deity, omniscience [foreknowledge], to Abraham, not God the Father. Jesus said, "**Abraham** rejoiced to see my day: and **he saw it**, and was glad." Did Abraham see Him in foreknowledge? Hardly! And while Wierwille's explanation of English usage probably satisfies his young followers, it is no credit to his scholarship, especially his claim as an authority on Greek.

Actually, our Lord was not merely claiming preexistence to Abraham, He was insisting upon **eternal** existence! As Dr. Kenneth S. Wuest expressed it: "The AV reports our Lord as saying to the Jews, 'Before Abraham was, I am' (John 8:58 AV). 'Was' is *ginomai*, the verb of 'becoming,' not *eimi*, the verb of being. It is ingressive aorist, signifying entrance into a new condition. Our Lord said, 'Before Abraham came into existence, I am.' He does not contrast Abraham's previous existence with His eternity of existence, but Abraham's coming into existence with His eternal being. There is a contrast between Abraham as a created being and our Lord as uncreated, the self-existent, eternal God."[129]

Lawlor says: "The significance of 'was' (*genesthai*) and 'I am' (*ego eimi*) is important and instructive. The distinction between the two should be carefully marked. Christians must understand the importance of this item of Greek grammar because it is vital to their correct knowledge of the person of Christ. The first verb, used to describe the existence of Abraham, connotes an existence that has an origin. It could be rendered 'was born.' Or it might be translated 'came to be, entered the realm of human life.' But the verb which Christ applies to Himself (*eimi*), along with the emphatic personal pronoun (*ego*), speaks of an existence that has no origin. There is no implied beginning in the verb *eimi*. It is the signature of the eternal God who identified Himself to Moses as the 'I AM' (Exod. 3:14). Bishop Lightfoot remarks: 'The *becoming* only can be rightly predicted of the patriarch, the *being* is reserved for the eternal Son alone.' Thus, in the simplest terms,

---

129. BS, Vol. 119, No. 475; July-September, 1962; "The Deity of Jesus in the Greek Texts of John and Paul," pp. 220,221

Christ testified to the eternal, divine preexistence of His person."[130]

Godet adds: "By the terms [*ginomai*], *became*, and [*eimi*], *I am*, Jesus, as *Weiss* says, contrasts His eternal existence with the historical beginning of the existence of Abraham. *To become* is to pass from nothingness to existence; *I am* designates a mode of existence which is not due to such a transition. Jesus goes still further; He says, not *I was*, but *I am*. Thereby He attributes to Himself, not a simple priority as related to Abraham, which would still be compatible with the Arian view of the Person of Christ, but existence in the absolute, eternal, Divine order. This expression recalls that of Ps.xc.2: *'Before the mountains were brought forth and thou hadst founded the earth, from eternity to eternity,* THOU ART, *O God!'* "[131]

Dr. John A. Witmer points out the same: "The most emphatic claim of Jesus to deity is the statement in His discussion with the Jews, 'Before Abraham was born, I am' (John 8:58, A.S.V.). The Jews brought the name of Abraham, their physical and spiritual father, into the conversation (vss. 52-53). Jesus seized upon it to lead on to His final claim in the verse already quoted, startling the Jews by saying: 'Your father Abraham rejoiced to see my day; and he saw it, and was glad' (vs. 56). When the Jews responded with a question as to how a man as young as Jesus could have seen Abraham, 'Jesus claims eternal existence with the absolute phrase used of God' [Archibald Thomas Robertson, *Word Pictures in the New Testament* V, 158-59]. Jesus did not claim mere pre-existence to Abraham, but eternal existence, the self-existence that belongs to God alone. Jehovah applied this same phrase to Himself as His name in His revelation and call to Moses at the burning bush (Ex. 3:14).[132]

And *The Open Bible* sums up its usage here and throughout the entire Gospel (more than 20 times), saying: "Throughout John's Gospel there is a cycle of 'I AM' sayings: Jesus said, 'I am the light of the world'; 'I am the bread of life'; 'I am the good shepherd.' The phrase 'I AM' is a very significant phrase in the Old Testament. It is the Divine Name revealed to Moses at the burning bush, because the name *Yahweh* (Jehovah) is built on the verb I AM.' Clearly, these 'I AM' sayings are identifying

---

130. WGBM, pp. 36,37
131. CJG, p. 682
132. BS, Vol. 125, No. 498; April-June, 1968; "Did Jesus Claim to Be the Son of God?" pp. 152,153

Jesus with the God of the Covenant, the God who brought Israel out of Egypt, the God of Abraham, Isaac, and Jacob. Early Christian Jews identified Jesus with God the Father Creator: 'I and the Father are one,' Jesus said; and 'He that hath seen me hath seen the Father.' "[133]

Discussing "I AM" as the name of God in Exodus 3:14, Abram M. Long points out: "The Hebrew root of this form, 'I AM THAT I AM,' is the verb *Hawah*, which means 'to be,' 'to exist.' The origin of this word, according to the illustrious scholar Gesenius, 'lies in the idea of breathing,' whence to live, to be. It is this word that is the root of most sacred Hebrew names for God, Jehovah. Hence, a little later on, when God confirms the commission with special promises of divine support, He says, again to Moses, 'and I appeared unto Abraham, unto Isaac, and unto Jacob, by the name of God Almighty (*El Shaddai*), but by my name Jehovah (Yehowah) was I not known unto them (Genesis 6:3). Like its root *hawah*, Jehovah means the Eternal One, the Always-Existing One, the Immutable One. In other words, Jehovah is the 'I AM' One, the Eternally-Existing One.

"This name Jehovah was the most sacred of all names for God. It is this name which for several centuries before the Christian era the Jews refused even to pronounce. Whether it was, as Gesenius suggests, due to a false interpretation of Exodus 20:7, or whether it was mere superstition on the part of the Jews, we shall probably never know. Nevertheless, they regarded this name too sacred even to be uttered, and in its place they put a substitute, both for reading and speaking—the Hebrew word *Adhonai*, another name for God, which meant Lord. The Septuagint translators followed the same scruple and uniformly substituted the Greek word Kurios, Lord. The name Jehovah was the ineffable name, too sacred for human lips to form. With this background, then, let us turn to John 8. . . . Now bear in mind the sacredness of that 'I AM' One, and hear Jesus' reply, 'Verily, verily, I say unto you, Before Abraham was, I AM!' Blasphemy of blasphemies! The prophet of Nazareth had dared to take to Himself this ineffable name and to draw the plain inference that He and Jehovah were one and the same! The divine record bears witness that in their fury the Jews 'took up stones therefore to cast at him: but Jesus hid himself, and went out of the temple.' And lest there should be any doubt in the minds of the Jews concerning the real implication of this assertion, He plainly tells

---

133. TOB, p. 984

them a little later at the Feast of Dedication, 'I and my Father are one' (John 10:30). When the Jews took up stones again to stone Him, they explained their wrath. 'For a good work we stone thee not, but for blasphemy and because that thou, being a man, makest thyself God' (v. 33). The fact that Jesus identified Himself with the 'I AM' One would have passed over the heads of a Gentile audience without producing a ripple; but the Jews knew all too well what the implication meant."[134]

One of the key statements in the Gospel of John relative to the deity of Jesus Christ is in His claim of oneness with the Father. Wierwille attempts to discredit this by saying:

"The scriptures which say that Jesus Christ and his Father are one do not indicate that Jesus Christ was God, but rather that Jesus Christ and God had unity of purpose, they worked in a unified effort. These same scriptures also specify that we can be one with them—not that we become God, but that we have a unity of purpose with God and His Son, Jesus Christ.

"John 10:30
"I and *my* Father are one.

" 'One' is the Greek word *hen*, neuter, meaning one in purpose, not one person which would be *heis*, masculine. This is the climax of Jesus' claim of oneness with the Father, and this oneness is of purpose."[135]

While they certainly did have oneness *of purpose*, our Lord's statement, "I and my Father are one," is the climax of His claim of oneness *in unity* with the Father. A. T. Robertson called it "the climax of Christ's claims concerning the relation between the Father and himself."[136] If this were only a claim of "oneness in purpose" it would do horrible violence to the context, and to the Greek as well.

It would violate the context since it makes it clear that the Jews to whom He spoke understood it as a clear claim of deity, an insistence of equality with the Father. Although they were upset over His claims of deity elsewhere, this is the only time in the entire Gospel they accused him of blasphemy, saying, "For a good work we stone thee not; but for blasphemy; and because that thou, being a man, makest thyself God" (vs. 33). They, unlike Wierwille, understood exactly what our Lord was saying. And, unless He were deity incarnate, they were right in wanting

---

134. PCF, pp. 39-41
135. JCNG, p. 50
136. Quoted in EGJ, p. 170

to stone Him. Moses, in Leviticus 24:16, had put down the will of God in this matter: "He that blasphemeth the name of the Lord, he shall surely be put to death, and all the congregation shall certainly stone him: as well the stranger, as he that is born in the land, when he blasphemeth the name of the Lord, shall be put to death." Remember, too, that the context deals with the right and ability of Jesus Christ to give eternal life to fallen men and women. No one could do this but God. Wierwille claims to have oneness of purpose with the Father, but could he say, "I and my Father are one"? Could he say, "I give unto them eternal life; and they shall never perish" (vs. 28), as Jesus did in this passage? *Of course not!*

But mere oneness of purpose not only does violence to the context, it does abuse to the Greek as well. Dr. J. B. Rowell wrote: "In answer to the question, 'If thou be the Christ, tell us plainly,' Christ made special claim to deity when He said, 'I and my Father are one' (John 10:24,30). Here, 'one' is used with a plural verb, proving both *unity of nature but difference of person.* It must be also emphasized that the word 'one' is neuter, not masculine. Hence, not 'I and my Father are one person,' but, 'I and my Father are *one in essence,*' speaking of unity in nature. As Dr. Marvin R. Vincent says, 'It implies unity of *essence,* not merely of *will* or of *power*' ('Word Studies,' vol. ii, p. 197)."[137] And Morris adds: "The bracketing of 'I' and 'the Father' is significant in itself quite apart from the predicate. Who else could be linked with God the Father in this fashion? 'One' is neuter, 'one thing' and not 'one person'. Identity is not asserted, but essential unity is. These two belong together. The statement does not go beyond the opening words of the Gospel, but it can stand with them. It is another statement which puts Jesus Christ with God rather than with man. It may be true that this ought not to be understood as a metaphysical statement, but it is also true that it means more than that Jesus' will was one with the Father's. As Hoskyns remarks, 'the Jews would not presumably have treated as blasphemy the idea that a man could regulate his words and actions according to the will of God'. But they did regard this as blasphemy as the next verse shows. They had asked Jesus for a plain assertion of His messiahship, and they got more than they had bargained for."[138]

Perhaps most significant of all, as Canon Liddon expressed it,

---

137. DJCL, p. 8
138. NICNT, *The Gospel According to John,* pp. 522,523

"The motive of their indignation was not disowned by Him. They believed Him to mean that He Himself was a divine Person; and He never repudiated that construction of His language."[139]

James Bjornstad, in refuting the Jehovah's Witnesses on this point, observed: "From the very beginning of His ministry Jesus Christ claimed equality with God in very clear and unmistakable statements.

"He equated a person's attitude to Himself with the person's attitude to God. He told people that—

in seeing Him, they were seeing God (see John 14:9);

in knowing Him, they were knowing God (see John 8:19);

in believing in Him, they were believing in God (see John 12:44);

in receiving Him, they were receiving God (see Mark 9:37);

in honoring Him, they were honoring God (see John 5:23);

in hating Him, they were hating God (see John 15:23)."[140]

How could language emphasize equality of essence any more forcefully or dogmatically than this?

Another important passage dealing with Christ's absolute deity is John 14. Wierwille writes:

"John 14:1,8,9,16:

"Let not your heart be troubled: ye believe in God, believe also in me.

"Philip saith unto him, Lord, shew us the Father, and it sufficeth us.

"Jesus said unto him, Have I been so long time with you, and yet has thou not known me, Philip? he that hath seen me hath seen the Father; and how sayest thou *then*, Shew us the Father?

"And I will pray the Father, and he shall give you another Comforter, that he may abide with you for ever.

"These verses clearly show the Father, His Son, and the gift of holy spirit, not as identities, but as three working in unison with singleness of purpose."[141]

Frankly, these verses deserve more attention than the single sentence with which Wierwille dismisses them. He is attempting, of course, to discredit the Trinity and we will examine his reference to the Holy Spirit as a mere impersonal force later. We wish to emphasize here the claim Jesus made that His disci-

---

139. Op. cit., p. 189; quoted in DJCL, p. 10
140. CAYD, pp. 18,19
141. JCNG, pp. 142,143

ples should believe in Him exactly as they believe in Jehovah. He said, ". . .ye believe in God, believe also in me." The Amplified Bible has it: "You believe in *and* adhere to *and* trust in *and* rely on God, believe in *and* adhere to *and* trust in *and* rely also on Me." Could you, or I, or Wierwille, or any mere mortal tell others to place faith and trust in us just as in Jehovah God? Of course not!

Neither could any of us use His words in verse 9, "Have I been so long time with you, and yet hast thou not known me, Philip? **he that hath seen me hath seen the Father**; and how sayest thou then, Shew us the Father?" In this case, we can only agree with Hobbs, "How any one can read these words and question whether or not Jesus ever claimed deity is beyond comprehension. Like Philip, such look at Jesus without really seeing Him."[142] Only deity could *manifest* deity.

What about verses which indicate that Christ is inferior to God? Wierwille writes:

"John 14:28 and I Corinthians 11:3 boldly indicate that God is superior to Jesus Christ.

"John 14:28
"Ye have heard how I said unto you, I go away, and come *again* unto you. If ye loved me, ye would rejoice, because I said, I go unto the Father: for my Father is greater than I.

"I Corinthians 11:3:
"But I would have you know, that the head of every man is Christ; and the head of the woman *is* the man; and the head of Christ *is* God."[143]

The second passage no more declares Christ to be *inferior* to the Father than it says women are *inferior* to men! Paul is not saying a woman is less of a *person* than man, nor is He saying Christ is less *God* than the Father. As for our Lord's statement— in His humanity, remember—that "my Father is greater than I," it must be viewed in the context of His self-emptying described in Philippians 2, which we shall consider in more detail later. Bishop J. C. Ryle observed: "What did our Lord mean by saying, 'My Father is greater than I'? I answer that the words of the Athanasian Creed contain the best reply. Christ is no doubt 'equal to the Father as touching His Godhead, and inferior to the Father as touching His manhood.' This we may freely and fully

---

142. EGJ, p. 221
143. JCNG, p. 51

admit, and yet not give up a hair's breadth to Arians and Socinians, who always throw this text in our teeth. The enemies of the doctrine of Christ's divinity forget that Trinitarians maintain the humanity of Christ as strongly as His divinity; and never shrink from admitting that while Christ as God is equal to the Father, as man He is inferior to the Father. And it is in this sense that He here says truly, 'My Father is greater than I.' It was specially spoken of the time of His incarnation and humiliation. When the Word was 'made flesh' He took on Him 'the form of a servant.' This was temporary and voluntarily assumed inferiority. (Phil. ii. 7.)"[144]

A strong passage dealing with our Lord's preexistence is lightly dismissed by Wierwille as follows:

"John 16:27-30:

"For the Father himself loveth you, because ye have loved me, and have believed that I came out from God.

"I came forth from the Father, and am come into the world: again, I leave the world, and go to the Father.

"His disciples said unto him, Lo, now speakest thou plainly, and speakest no proverb.

"Now are we sure that thou knowest all things, and needest not that any man should ask thee: by this we believe that thou comest forth from God.

"There have been many others sent forth from God but none were conceived of God as Jesus was in Mary."[145]

This is a strange explanation for one who professes to accept the Bible as saying what it means and meaning what it says! Note the specific language: "I came out from God"; "I came forth from the Father"; "I. . .am come into the world"; "we believe that thou camest forth from God." The 28th verse makes it especially clear, saying, "I came forth from the Father, and am come into the world; again, I leave the world, and go to the Father." Here are contrasts: coming and going. If "come into the world" does not signify a personal, literal coming from another place to this world, then neither would "leave the world, and go to the Father" speak of a personal, literal leaving to go to a specific place. If "go to the Father" is to be understood as a literal going to where the Father is, then "came forth from the Father" must be understood equally as literal, a coming from

144. RETG, Vol. IV, p. 324
145. JCNG, p. 144

where the Father was. And note that this is clearly "no proverb," but our Lord speaking "plainly" (vs. 29). What He said is to be taken at face value.

The historic confession of Christ's deity by Thomas is one of the major such statements in Scripture. Even Wierwille lists it as one of the four major apparent contradictions to his theory. He comments thusly:

"The third instance of Jesus Christ's being referred to as God is done so by the Apostle Thomas when he first sees the resurrected Christ.

"John 20:28:

"And Thomas answered and said unto him, My Lord and my God.

"This scripture is a natural follow-up of Hebrews 1:8 where Thomas acknowledged Jesus Christ in an exalted position by placing himself in lower status. 'My Lord and my God' pays greatest homage to the resurrected one.

"However, an even greater truth is shown by the usage of Thomas' addressing Jesus Christ as 'my Lord and my God.' It brings to light the precision of a figure of speech. The specific figure of speech is called *hendiadys*. Literally, the figure *hendiadys* means 'one by means of two.' Whenever two words are used but only one idea intended, it is the figure *hendiadys*. One of the two words expresses the fact and the other intensifies it to the superlative degree, thus making the statement especially emphatic. This method gives considerable cogency to an expression. When Thomas exclaimed 'My Lord and my God,' he was observing the resurrected Christ as 'my godly Lord.' The word 'lord' expresses the fact and the word 'godly' intensifies 'lord' to the superlative degree. Indeed my godly Lord is exactly what Jesus Christ is."[146]

Wierwille is confused here in several areas. In the first place, Thomas was not merely giving Christ an exalted position by placing himself in a lower one. Should a wife address her husband as "My God" in order to express her submission to his position as her head? We think not. Not only so, Wierwille again shows his unfamiliarity with Jewish customs and Jewish language prevalent in New Testament times. Thomas would have never called Jesus "Lord" without meaning deity (just as Judas Iscariot **never** did!), since it was an acknowledged title of deity—one used by citizens all throughout the Roman empire of Caesar. When Thomas did so, as Wuest points out, "This was enough to involve him in serious trouble with the Roman authorities had they known of it, for he was acknowledging Jesus

---

146. Ibid., pp. 34,35

of Nazareth as his Lord and his God instead of Caesar. Polycarp, who lived A.D. 156, was confronted with the question by the Roman official, 'What is the harm in saying "lord Caesar"?' And because he refused to acknowledge Caesar as lord, he was martyred. Festus (Acts 25:26) said regarding Paul, 'Of whom I have no certain thing to write unto my lord.' His lord was Caesar, 'lord' in the sense that Festus recognized Nero, who was then Caesar, as the emperor-god to whom worship was due."[147] Thomas would **never** have fallen into such a trap!

No, this was not merely a flattering expression of homage; here was a positive declaration of absolute deity. As Ryle observes: "The noble exclamation which burst from the lips of Thomas, when convinced that his Lord had risen indeed,—the noble exclamation, 'My Lord and my God,'—admits of only one meaning. It was a distinct testimony to our blessed Lord's divinity. It was a clear unmistakable declaration that Thomas believed Him, whom He saw and touched that day, to be not only man, but God. Above all, it was a testimony which our Lord received and did not prohibit, and a declaration which He did not say one word to rebuke. When Cornelius fell down at the feet of Peter and would have worshipped him, the Apostle refused such honour at once: 'Stand up: I myself also am a man.' (Acts x. 26.) When the people of Lystra would have done sacrifice to Paul and Barnabas, 'they rent their clothes, and ran in among the people, saying, Sirs, why do ye these things? We also are men of like passions with you.' (Acts xiv. 14.) But when Thomas says to Jesus, 'My Lord and my God,' the words do not elicit a syllable of reproof from our holy and truth-loving Master. Can we doubt that these things were written for our learning?

"Let us settle it firmly in our minds that the divinity of Christ is one of the grand foundation truths of Christianity, and let us be willing to go to the stake rather than let it go. Unless our Lord Jesus is very God of very God, there is an end of His mediation, His atonement, His advocacy, His priesthood, His whole work of redemption. These glorious doctrines are useless blasphemies, unless Christ is divine."[148]

Ryle said again: "The text before us is one of those which are justly quoted, as an unanswerable proof of the divinity of our Lord Jesus Christ. He is called 'God' in the presence of ten witnesses, and He accepts the language, and does not say one

147. BGNT, pp. 23,24
148. RETG, Vol. IV, p. 679

word to reprove the person who uses it. Unless a person is prepared to deny the inspiration of St. John's Gospel generally, or the genuineness and correctness of this text in particular, it is hard to see how the force of the sentence in favour of Christ's divinity can be evaded."[149]

Wierwille is equally confused in calling Thomas' declaration a mere "figure of speech." In this matter he should have checked with E. W. Bullinger, whom he quotes later (p. 82) as an authority on biblical figures of speech. According to Bullinger, there is no mistaking what Thomas meant about Christ's deity. In fact, he calls attention to the emphatic manner in which Thomas says, "MY Lord and MY God!"[150]

Wierwille fails to note that Thomas did not say, "My Lord and God," but "My Lord and my God." Instead of "one by means of two," there are two distinct titles used by Thomas. But even if it were merely a figure of speech, "Lord" comes before "God" in both the English and the Greek. It would not be "my godly Lord," as Wierwille thinks, but "my lordly God!" And is it not significant that the most skeptical of all the apostles— "doubting" Thomas, he has been called for centuries—is the one who eventually made the strongest declaration as to our Lord's deity?

In this matter we cannot but concur with Sir Robert Anderson: "But the faith of the little band of the Lord's disciples was far removed from the creeds and hopes of carnal men. 'Thou art the Christ, the Son of the living God' (Matt. 16:16); 'Thou art the Son of God, thou art the King of Israel' (John 1:49): these were typical confessions. None but the Christ could be King of Israel, and Christ was the Son of God in the pregnant sense which that title signified. The confession of Thomas, 'My Lord and my God' was the full expression of it. **And if anyone can suppose that devout Jews could have uttered such words to a fellow-creature, or that the Lord would have tolerated them had He not claimed to be divine, we have no common ground for a discussion of the question.**"[151]

Wierwille has a brief comment about the martyr Stephen's dying prayer of faith. He says:

"Acts 7:59:

---

149. Ibid., p. 688
150. Quoted by Ryle, ibid.
151. LFH, p. 68, emphasis added

"And they stoned Stephen, calling upon *God*, and saying, Lord Jesus receive my spirit.

"The Critical Greek texts contain no word 'god' in the above. The Greek texts read, 'And they stoned Stephen, invoking and saying, Lord Jesus, receive my spirit.' The Aramaic text also omits 'God.' "[152]

But whether the King James translators did or did not have justification for inserting "God" in the text, this verse strongly asserts the absolute deity of Jesus Christ. When a man is dying, *he prays to deity!* No substitute will do for a time like that. Just as Jesus, dying on the cruel cross at Golgotha, committed His spirit to the Father ("Father, into thy hands I commend my spirit"; Luke 23:46), so Stephen, dying outside the same city by cruel stoning, committed his spirit to God the Son ("Lord Jesus, receive my spirit").

Bickersteth well questions: "Again, what was the dying act of the proto-martyr Stephen, but the truest adoration of the Son of God? Realize, I pray you, that scene. Stephen, full of the Holy Ghost, looked up stedfastly into heaven and saw the glory of God, and Jesus standing on the right hand of God, and said, 'Behold, I see the heavens opened, and the Son of man standing on the right hand of God.' Then they cried out. . . .and stoned Stephen invoking, and saying, 'Lord Jesus, receive my spirit.' And he kneeled down and cried with a loud voice, 'Lord, lay not this sin to their charge.' And when he had said this, he fell asleep. The Holy Ghost, who inspired David's devout affiance— 'Into thine hand I commit my spirit: thou hast redeemed me, O Lord God of truth'—and who had dictated Solomon's declaration, 'The spirit shall return unto God who gave it'—now, in the plenitude of his grace, prompted the dying martyr to pray not to God the Father alone, nor to the Father through Christ, but to pray to Christ, worshipping him with his latest breath as very and eternal God."[153]

One extremely important passage dealing with Jesus Christ's absolute deity is found in Philippians 2:5-11. We will quote it in its entirety first, so the reader can get the grasp of it, then note how Wierwille dismisses it. Paul extolled:

*"Let this mind be in you, which was also in Christ Jesus: Who, being in the form of God, thought it not robbery to be equal with God: But made himself of no reputation, and took upon him the*

---

152. JCNG, p. 145
153. TT, pp. 59,60

*form of a servant, and was made in the likeness of men: And being found in fashion as a man, he humbled himself, and became obedient unto death, even the death of the cross. Wherefore God also hath highly exalted him, and given him a name which is above every name: That at the name of Jesus every knee should bow, of things in heaven, and things in earth, and things under the earth; And that every tongue should confess that Jesus Christ is Lord, to the glory of God the Father.*"

As Lawlor points out: "The apostle, under inspiration, insists upon the preexistence of Christ, His deity, His equality with God the Father, His incarnation, His true humanity, His atoning death upon the cross, His resurrection from the dead (by inference), and His ascension and exaltation in glory."[154] What a tremendous passage of Scripture!

How does Wierwille treat it? He comments on verse 6 first, saying:

"How can Jesus Christ be equal with God and yet, according to other scriptures, God be superior to Jesus Christ?

"The word 'equal' in Philippians 2:6 is the Greek word *isos* from which is derived the English word 'isosceles.' An isosceles triangle has two angles which contain the exact same number of degrees. Even though equal, the angles are not identical."[155]

Does it seem strange that he would refer to a *Greek* word and attempt its definition by a word from *another* language? That is only because, if you will forgive the expression, staying with the Greek would have cooked his goose! *Young's Analytical Concordance* gives the meaning of *isos* as "equal to, the same as."[156] Vine points out that *isos* in Philippians 2:6 "is in the neuter plural, lit., 'equalities'."[157] Jac J. Muller says a better translation would be "existence in a manner equal to God."[158] And Gifford calls attention to the fact that "in the R.V. the words are translated 'on an equality with God,' instead of 'equal with God,' as in the A.V. The change is of great importance to the right interpretation of the whole passage. The rendering, 'equal with God,' is evidently derived from the Latin Version. . . . It was apparently due at first to the fact that the Latin language had no

154. WGBM, p. 14
155. JCNG, p. 52
156. P. 305
157. EDNTW, Vol. II, p. 38
158. NICNT, *The Epistles of Paul to the Philippians and to Philemon,* p. 79

adequate mode of representing the exact form and meaning of the Greek. The neuter plural denotes the various modes or states in which it was possible for the nature of Deity to exist and manifest itself as Divine."[159]

Michael Green described it as "another very careful piece of writing," and explained: "There are two Greek words which express the participle 'being.' The weaker is *on*; the stronger, *huparchon* (meaning 'being from the beginning'). It is the latter which Paul uses when he says that Jesus had always been in the 'form' of God. Likewise 'form' has two Greek words which do duty for it. There is the word *schema* which indicates the external appearance, whether or not it corresponds exactly to the inner reality. Paul does not use that word. Instead, he chooses the stronger word, *morphe*, which indicates the outer form while implying that it gives precise expression to the inner reality. So the meaning of this amazingly profound 'hymn' to Christ in Philippians 2 is this, in a nutshell. It means that Jesus had always been one with God; that he voluntarily laid aside those aspects of his deity that would have been impossible to combine with sharing our human condition; that he became one of us, shared our death, even death on a cross. And that the Father has openly bestowed on him the sacred name of God, for it is to the divine love and judgment as brought to us by God-become-flesh that every knee will eventually bow. A mind-boggling claim! But that is what the earliest Christians believed. . . .to argue that the full deity of Christ was only gradually asserted after decades had rolled by is not only inaccurate, it is very bad scholarship."[160]

No wonder John Calvin exclaimed: ". . .that man is utterly blind who does not perceive that [Christ's] eternal divinity is clearly set forth in these words. . . .where can there be *equality with God* without *robbery*, excepting only where there is the essence of God. . . ."[161] Was it "robbery" for Christ to claim equality with the Father? He did not think so! And Wuest points out that the word for thought here, *hegeomai*, "refers to a judgment based upon facts."[162]

But note how Wierwille only commented on the word "equal," ignoring the heart of Paul's claim that Christ was "in the form of

159. Quoted by Vine, op. cit., Vol. II, p. 38
160. TGI, pp. 23,24
161. COM, *The Philippians, Colossians, and Thessalonians*, p. 56, emphasis his
162. BGNT, p. 83

God." Zeroing in on this, A. T. Robertson wrote: "A vast literature has grown up around the famous passage in Phil. 2:5-11. Here Paul definitely asserts that in Christ's Preincarnate state He was 'existing in the form of God.' In this state Christ Jesus 'counted the being on an equality with God' *as a fact*. First get that clearly. It was a fact, a conscious fact to Christ Jesus before his Incarnation, just as we have it in John 1:1. We need not split hairs over the distinctions between 'form' of God (see also 'form of a servant'), 'likeness of men,' 'in fashion as a man.' These refinements do not affect the broad statement in the sentence that Jesus in his Preincarnate state was on a par with God just as the Jews accused him of claiming, 'making himself equal with God' (John 5:18). The deity which Christ had was just as actual as the humanity which he took upon himself. Whatever is meant by 'emptied himself' Paul cannot mean to say that Jesus divested himself of his divine nature and Sonship. That he could not do as no earthly son can rid himself of his father's nature. The thing to which Jesus did not 'cling' was his place in heaven beside the Father and on the Throne of God. He gave up the habiliments of Deity, but not the reality and not the power, although the Incarnation inevitably imposed limitations of time and place and knowledge, and human weariness and weakness to which the Gospels bear ample witness. But in this great passage Paul sets forth in masterly fashion the Deity and the Humanity of Jesus Christ, the Son of God and the Son of Man, with the added glory and honor which came after the Humiliation. The supreme exaltation will be 'that every tongue should confess that Jesus Christ is Lord, to the glory of God the Father.' "[163] As Augustine aptly expressed it: "He emptied Himself not by losing what He was, but by taking to Him what He was not."[164]

Regarding the statement that Christ was in the form of God, F. B. Meyer writes: "The Greek word translated 'form' means a great deal more than the external appearance; it stands for the essence of God's nature, so that we may say that Jesus Christ possessed the essence of the Divine quality and nature from all eternity. This exactly agrees with other words of Scripture, as when we are told, He is *the image of the invisible God.*' Again, '*Being the effulgence of His glory,*' i.e. He was the outshining beam of the Father's glory; 'and the *very image of His sub-*

---

163. PIC, pp. 57,58
164. *Homilies on the Gospel of John,* xvii. 16; quoted by Leon Morris, NICNT, *The Gospel According to John,* p. 114, footnote 121

stance,' i.e. He corresponded to the Divine Nature, as a seal to the die. Again, *'The Word was with God, and the Word was God.' 'All things were made by Him.'* And then, as we overhear that marvellous communion between the Son and the Father, in John xvii., we notice His reference to the glory He had with the Father before the worlds were made, and with which He asks the Father to glorify Him in His human nature again. All these deep words prove that whatever God was in the uncreated eternity of the past,—the infinite, the incomprehensible, the all-holy, and the all-blessed,—that was Jesus Christ, who was absolutely one with Him, as spirit and soul are one in the organisation of our nature."[165]

The Edinburgh scholar, Robert Johnstone, added: "That any mere creature should be spoken of as 'in the form of God'— taking these words in any natural or adequate sense—is utterly inconceivable; and to exhibit, as an evidence of sublime condescension, the not reckoning equality of glory with God the Father to be a possession of supreme value, would plainly be totally unmeaning, unless this equality of glory were a true and rightful possession."[166]

The New International Version translates Philippians 2:5-7 as follows: "Your attitude should be the same as that of Christ Jesus: Who, being in very nature God, did not consider equality with God something to be grasped, but made himself nothing, taking the very nature of a servant, being made in human likeness." Kent comments on this: "Two assertions are made: He existed in the form of God and he did not regard his existing in a manner of equality with God as a prize to be grasped or held onto. 'Being in very nature God' is, literally, 'existing in the form of God.' The term *morphe* denotes the outward manifestation that corresponds to the essence, in contrast to the noun *schema* (2:7), which refers to the outward appearance, which may be temporary.

'The participle *hyparchon* ('being' [NIV], in the sense of 'existing') is in the present tense and states Christ's continuing condition. To say that he was existing in the essential metaphysical form of God is tantamount to saying that he possessed the nature of God. The phrase is elaborated on by the words 'equality with God' *(isa theo)*. It should be noted that *isa* is an adverb (not the substantive *ison*), and hence describes the manner of existence.

---

165. DCP, pp. 82,83
166. LEPP, p. 148

This does not need to be regarded as precisely the same as 'the form of God,' for one's essential nature can remain unchanged, though the manner in which that nature is expressed can vary greatly through changing times and circumstances."[167]

Kent also points out that "being" (*hyparchon*) and "to be" (*einai*) are the only verb forms in the entire passage not aorists, adding, "The use of the two present forms is most appropriate for describing the timeless existence of the preincarnate Christ. Although these two verbs often seem interchangeable, the distinctive sense of each would be assumed in a context where both appear. 'In the one instance we have *existence* as such, in the other we have *being* in a condition which comports with that existence' (Lenski, in loc.)."[168]

Vine, in discussing *being* in the New Testament, notes: "When not part of another verb (usually the participle), or part of a phrase, this word translates one of the following: . . .(c) the present participle of *huparcho*, to exist, which always involves a pre-existent state, prior to the fact referred to, and a continuance of the state after the fact. Thus in Phil. 2:6, the phrase 'who being (*huparcho*) in the form of God,' implies His pre-existent Deity, previous to His Birth, and His continued Deity afterwards."[169]

And Vincent adds: "To say, then, that Christ was *in the form of God*, is to say that He existed as essentially one with God. The expression of deity through human nature (ver. 7) thus has its background in the expression of deity *as deity* in the eternal ages of God's being. Whatever the mode of this expression, it marked the being of Christ in the eternity before creation. As the *form* of God was identified with the *being* of God, so Christ, being in the form of God, was identified with the being, nature, and personality of God."[170]

Since Wierwille professes to have taken everything he could take at the Moody Bible Institute, through its correspondence courses, we will close these remarks on Philippians 2:5-11 with that school's noted Greek scholar's translation. Wuest called it "Paul's great, classic Christological passage" and said: "The Greek text literally leaps at one in the words: 'Let this mind be in you which was also in Christ Jesus, who subsisting permanently

167. EBC, Vol. XI, p. 123
168. Ibid., p. 126
169. EDNTW, Vol. I, p. 116; see also NICNT, *Philippians* by Jac J. Muller, p. 78
170. WSNT, Vol. III, p. 431

in that state of being in which He gives outward expression of the essence of deity, that outward expression coming from and being truly representative of His inner being, did not consider it a prize to be clutched, the being on an equality with deity (in the expression of the divine essence), but emptied Himself, having taken the outward expression of a bondslave, that expression coming from and being truly representative of His inner being, having become in the likeness of man. And having been found in outward guise as man, He humbled Himself, having become obedient to the extent of death, even such a death as that upon a cross; on which account also God super-eminently exalted Him, and in grace gave Him THE NAME which is above every name, to the end that at or to the NAME which Jesus possesses, every knee should bow, of those in heaven and those upon the earth, and those under the earth, and that every tongue should openly confess that Jesus Christ is Lord to the glory of God the Father.' "[171] We can only stand back in awe and marvel at such a clear statement of absolute deity!

Perhaps the fertile imagination—or should we call it *the devious cunning?*—of Wierwille is seldom more apparent than in his effort to discredit the truth in Colossians 1:14-18, describing our Lord as the Creator of all things. Admitting that verses 14, 15 and 18 refer to Christ, he turns verses 16 and 17, with the help of his liberal supply of brackets, into references to God the Father! He says: "Verses 16 and 17 of Colossians 1 form a parenthesis which is a figure of speech explaining in more detail one point in the text. When a parenthesis is employed, one must proceed in reading from the last word preceding the parenthesis to the first word after the parenthesis. No thought continuity is lost, and the truth is quickly evident."[172]

Our first response to this was: "What an incredible imagination!" There is not the slightest basis in either Greek or English for putting verses 16 and 17 into a parenthesis. It was done solely and absolutely for none other reason than to annihilate the truth regarding the creation of all things by Jesus Christ. In short, since this truth does not harmonize with Wierwille's teaching, *ipso facto*, it must go. We cannot conceive of a more apt illustration of what Paul called "handling the word of God deceitfully" (II Cor. 4:2). In one swoop of dishonesty, Wierwille has endeavored to rid the Colossian passage of truth

---

171. GTLB, p. 33
172. JCNG, pp. 118,119; see also pp. 146,147

regarding: (1) Christ's deity; (2) Christ's preexistence; (3) Christ as Creator.

But he cannot eliminate our Lord's absolute deity from this passage even by such subterfuge. The 15th verse, which Wierwille is forced to admit refers to Christ, clearly says: "Who is the image of the invisible God, the firstborn of every creature." The word "image" is the Greek *eikon*, which carries two ideas, one of representation and one of manifestation. Curtis Vaughan says of these ideas: "One is *likeness*, a thought brought out in some of the versions (e.g., Moff., Am. Trans., Wms., and Knox). Christ is the image of God in the sense that he is the exact likeness of God, like the imge on a coin or the reflection in a mirror (cf. Heb 1:3). The other idea in the word is *manifestation*. That is, Christ is the image of God in the sense that the nature and being of God are perfectly revealed in him (cf. John 1:18). Therefore Paul can boldly say that we have 'the light of the knowledge of the glory of God in the face of Christ' (2 Cor 4:6) and that believers, reflecting the Lord's glory, 'are being transformed into his likeness with ever-increasing glory' (2 Cor 3:18). Paul's statement leaves no place for the vague emanations and shadowy abstractions so prominent in the gnostic system."[173]

Bishop W. R. Nicholson rendered the phrase "the image of God the invisible," then said: "It will thus be seen that this word 'image,' as applied to Christ, is the expression of His Sonship to the Father, seeing that the Scriptures describe His derivation as being that of a son from his father. Nay, it is the expression of His *Eternal Sonship*, since, as we shall see hereafter, our text speaks of Him as the image of God *prior* to the creation of all things.

"In this word 'image,' then, as applied to Christ, we have these three teachings: He is *the Son* of God, He is the *Eternal* Son of God, He is *God*. And assurance is made doubly sure by what is said of this Image of God in the after words of our text: that 'in Him, and by Him, and unto Him, the universe was created.'

"As the image of God, He is God; even as the son of a man is man. But as the image of the Father, He is not the Father; even as a man's son is not himself. The person of Christ is distinct from the person of the Father; yet there is only one God. Godhead is not constituted of Deity alone; but of Deity *as it is in certain inter-relations.* Those relations are *within* the one Godhead; but, as relations, they *difference* the Son from the

173. EBC, Vol. XI, pp. 181,182

Father; therefore may the one be the image of the other."[174]

Wierwille's treatment of Colossians 2:9, the mighty declaration that in Jesus Christ "dwelleth all the fulness of the Godhead bodily," exhibits no more scholarship, but it is, mercifully, briefer. His only comment is: "God was in Christ. Colossians 1:27 says that Christ is in us. This does not make us Christ or God."[175] We can easily understand why Wierwille would want to skip over this passage as hurriedly as possible, since it was originally penned by Paul in defense of those who were attacking the absolute deity of Jesus Christ. Wuest calls the verse "very rich in meaning in the Greek text. 'Godhead' here is *theotetos* speaking of absolute deity. 'Dwelleth' is *katoikeo*. *Oikeo* means 'to live in a home.' *Kata*, the local meaning of which is 'down' adds the idea of permanency to the act of living in a home. Paul, in the use of this word is not saying that the fullness of absolute deity resides in our Lord as something conferred upon Him, but that *the essence of absolute deity is at home in Him*. It naturally resides in Him by virtue of who and what he is, and that in a permanent fashion. The translation reads, 'In Him there resides permanently and at home all the fullness of absolute deity corporeally.' "[176]

Hobbs offers as a literal translation: "For in him and him alone is permanently and abidingly at home all the essence of deity [*pleroma*], the state of being God, in bodily form."[177] The phrase "of the Godhead" is *tes theotetos* in the Greek and this is the only place *theotetos* is found in the entire New Testament. Vaughan calls it "an abstract term, meaning not just divine qualities and attributes but the very essence of God—'the whole glorious total of what God is, the supreme Nature in its infinite entirety' (H. C. G. Moule, p. 144)."[178]

The great reformer, John Calvin, commented: ". . .when he says that the *fulness of the Godhead* dwells in Christ, he means simply, that God is wholly found in him, so that he who is not contented with Christ alone, desires something better and more excellent than God. The sum is this, that God has manifested

174. OWC, pp. 72-73, italics in the original
175. JCNG, p. 147
176. BS, op. cit., pp. 225,226
177. EGJ, p. 33
178. EBC, Vol. XI, p. 199; the ancient Gouge (1575-1653) pointed out: "Not as in mere men, by assistance, efficacy, or power, but essentially and personally; that is, by union of the deity with the humanity in one person" (COH, p. 10).

himself to us fully and perfectly in Christ."[179] Bruce expresses it,
". . .the One in whom the plenitude of deity was embodied."[180]
Dr. W. R. Nicholson, a bishop in the Reformed Episcopal
Church, comments on this verse: "After the apostle describes the
philosophy of the world, he proceeds to set forth the true wisdom
of God in the words 'because in Him dwelleth permanently, in
bodily fashion, all the fulness of the Godhead.' That word
'because' is emphatic, as though Paul would say, He, Christ, is
Himself of necessity the true wisdom. Notice the word Godhead
here. It is a translation of the Greek word *theotes*, which means
Deity. . . . Let it not be overlooked that the 'fulness' of Deity
dwelt in Christ. The apostle said this in view of the Gnostic
teaching that the various emanations of Deity had only
*something* of Deity in them. Christ had its fulness. Could there
be a stronger possible assertion of Christ as God? And this
fulness of the Deity dwelt in Him in *bodily fashion*: i.e. in Him as
having a human body on earth, and still now in heaven. A
teaching this which reminds us of John I:1 and 14. And this
fulness of Deity dwelleth in Him *permanently*, and not transient-
ly. Cerinthus taught that the *pleroma*, or 'fulness,' came on
Christ at His baptism, and left Him before He died on the cross,
but Paul says it was permanently in Him. This word permanently, though not expressed in our English version, is the very
thought or word of the apostle."[181]

The noted scholar James Orr, in the Kerr Lectures of 1890-91,
discusses those who, like Wierwille, would make ascribing
"Godhead" to Christ a mere matter of God being in Him as He is
in every believer. Orr names several to whom ". . .Christ is an
archetyped man, ideal man, sinless man, the central individual
of the race, the founder of the Kingdom of God in humanity—but
He is not more than man. His humanity may be a 'God-filled
humanity'; still a God-filled man is one thing and God become
man is another. There may be participation in the divine life—
even in the divine nature—on the part of the ordinary believer;
but the man in whom God thus dwells does not on this account
regard himself as Divine, does not speak of himself as a divine
person, does not think himself entitled to divine honors, would
deem it blasphemy to have the term 'Godhead' applied to him
. . . .Incarnation is not simply the enduing of human nature with

---

179. COM, op. cit., p. 182
180. NICNT, *The Epistles to the Ephesians and Colossians,* p. 232
181. OWC, pp. 189-191

the highest conceivable plenitude of gifts and graces; it is not a mere dynamical relation of God to the human spirit, acting on it or in it with exceptional energy; it is not simply the coming to consciousness of the metaphysical unity all along subsisting between humanity and God; it is not even such moral union, such spiritual indwelling and the oneness of character and will, as subsists between God and the believer. . . . It is not the union simply of the divine nature with the human,—for that I acknowledge in the case of every believer through the indwelling Spirit,—but the entrance of a Divine Person into the human."[182]

One problem Wierwille has in denying the preexistence of Christ is that he must locate some passage which seems to imply that He was created. In a short appendix of approximately two pages in length, he lists what he calls "Scriptures Referring to Christ's Conception and Birth." These are simply listed, not quoted, and one of the four sections is as follows:

> B. The use of the words 'created' and 'made' in reference to the Lord Jesus Christ.
> 1. created—Greek *ktizo*—to produce, bring into being. Colossians 3:10.
> 2. made—Greek *ginomai*—to begin to be, to come into existence, or into any state, as implying origin. John 1:14; Romans 1:3; I Corinthians 15:45; Galatians 4:4; Philippians 2:7; Hebrews 1:4; 6:20; 7:16."[183]

The reader will note, first of all, that Wierwille offers but one reference relating to Jesus Christ being "created." And when he checks that lone verse he will be amazed to discover that it does not refer to Christ at all, but the "new creation," the "new man" of the believer. The verse says (with the preceding one, to understand the context): "Lie not one to another, seeing that ye have put off the old man with his deeds; And have put on the new man, which is renewed in knowledge after the image of him that created him." It is simply saying that as the believer grows in spiritual grace ("renewed in knowledge"), he is transformed more and more into the image God originally planned when He created him (Genesis 1:26,27). Colossians 3:10 has absolutely nothing to do with Jesus Christ being "created" and we are astounded, shocked, and even angered that Wierwille would seek to make it so.

As for *ginomai*, it has any number of meanings and certainly

182. CVGW, pp. 235-238
183. JCNG, p. 158

offers no proof whatsoever that Christ first came into being at Bethlehem. For example, the first time it is used in the Word of God we find: "And when the tempter came to him, he said, If thou be the Son of God, command that these stones be made [*ginomai*] bread" (Matt. 4:3). There is no thought here whatsoever of creating something, merely changing the form of something already existing (stones) to another form (bread). In Acts 1:20 it is used: "For it is written in the book of Psalms, Let his habitation be [*ginomai*] desolate, and let no man dwell therein: and his bishoprick let another take." Here it is used of an occupied dwelling place becoming unoccupied; there is no thought of creation. In Matthew 6:16 and Matthew 24:44 it is used only of an attitude on the part of one already existing. The first says, "Moreover when ye fast, be [*ginomai*] not as the hypocrites, of a sad countenance. . . ." And the second one says, "Therefore be [*ginomai*] ye also ready: for in such an hour as ye think not the Son of man cometh." In fact, it is translated "be" approximately 250 times in the King James version. And it is simply rendered "came to pass" or its equivalent over 80 times.

If the reader will trouble himself to check the references Wierwille offers for the use of *ginomai* with relation to Christ, he will discover it is used exclusively of His *humanity*, not His deity. Perhaps we should amend that to say *most* of the references, since one of them, I Corinthians 15:45, does not use the word *ginomai* of Christ at all, only of Adam. Readers will note that "was made" is in italics with reference to Christ, showing it was not in the Greek, but added by the translators.

Incidentally, while Wierwille obviously uses Galatians 4:4 in the above listing because of the phrase "made of a woman," the verse actually is a positive statement of our Lord's preexistence. Saying "the incarnation was a commissioned event," Gromacki notes: "The verb 'sent forth' (*exapesteilen*) literally means 'to send away from with a commission.' The addition of the prefix (*ex*) shows that God sent His son *out* of heaven to earth with a commission to turn servants into sons. Christ was God's apostle to a world of sinners. The departure from heaven to earth shows that Christ actually existed before Mary conceived in her womb."[184]

Wierwille also has a problem with Scriptures calling Jesus Christ our Saviour. Here is an attempt on his part to explain it:

---

184. SFL, p. 122

"I Timothy 2:3:
"For this *is* good and acceptable in the sight of God our Saviour.

"God is our Savior as the *author* of the plan of salvation. Jesus Christ made the new birth available as the *agent* of the plan of salvation and as the finisher of faith.

"Titus 1:3:
"But hath in due times manifested his word through preaching, which is committed unto me according to the commandment of God our Saviour.

"Again, God is our Savior as the *author* of the plan of salvation. Jesus Christ made the new birth available as the *agent* of the plan of salvation, the finisher of faith."[185]

There are several problems with this explanation. In the first place, the "author"/"agent" terminology is the invention of Wierwille; it is his attempt to weasel out of a serious problem. The fact of the matter is that both Father and Son are called Saviour indiscriminately throughout Scripture [*Saviour* is used 24 times in the New Testament; in all but 9 instances of the Son] and they are portrayed as equals in the salvation of sinners. As a matter of fact, the Son, Jesus Christ, is specifically stated to be *the author*—completely contrary to Wierwille's fanciful explanation. For example, Hebrews 5:8-10 say: "Though he were a Son, yet learned he obedience by the things which he suffered; And being made perfect, he became the author of eternal salvation unto all them that obey him; Called of God an high priest after the order of Melchisedec." Language could not be plainer that the Son is the author of salvation, as well as the agent!

We think I John 4:14 is pertinent here: "And we have seen and do testify that the Father sent the Son to be the Saviour of the world." But is the Son merely the *agent* for the Father? No, He *is* the Saviour. When we purchased our home, Lowell Wing, a good personal friend, was the realtor. He was our agent, passing on our offers and counter offers, doing all the leg work and, finally, handling the "closing" for us. But was he the buyer? Could it be said that "Lowell Wing bought a new house"? No, Mrs. Sumner and I were the buyers; Lowell was merely our agent. In like manner, Christ is the Saviour—specifically called the author—not just an agent, handling it for someone else.

Titus 1:3 is especially damaging to Wierwille's cause. The Saviour is called "God" and, lest someone misunderstand this

185. JCNG, pp. 147,148

reference as being of the Father, the Saviour is further identified as the one who committed to Paul the commandment to preach His Word. *And who was this?* The commission is given in Acts 9:15-17 and the commissioner is described as "the Lord, even Jesus." He is identified as strongly or stronger in Paul's account of that commissioning to King Agrippa, in Acts 26:14-19.

Why is Wierwille so anxious to make the Father the *author* and the Son merely an *agent?* The answer lies in the dogmatic claim of Jehovah God in Isaiah 43:11, "I, even I, am the Lord; and beside me there is no saviour." Here, in language that cannot be denied or explained away, Jehovah God insists that there is no Saviour but Himself. If Jehovah is not the triune God of Christendom, then Jesus Christ is a *false* Saviour. Wierwille cannot have it both ways; *either Jesus Christ is Jehovah God or He is a false Saviour, one not worthy of anyone's faith or trust!*

His comments on Titus 2:13, which describe Christ as *both* Saviour and God, are as follows:

"Titus 2:13:

"Looking for that blessed hope, and the glorious appearing of the great God and our Saviour Jesus Christ.

"Jesus Christ is part of the glory of his Father. In all Critical Greek texts and extant manuscripts this verse literally reads, 'Looking for that blessed hope and appearing of the glory of the great God even our Saviour Jesus Christ.' The glory of the great God is His Son."[186]

Wierwille errs in two major matters here. In the first place, if Jesus Christ is not the Jehovah God of the Old Testament, He cannot be "part of the glory" of the Father. Isaiah 42:8 specifically states: "I am the Lord: that is my name: and my glory will I not give to another. . . ." And Jehovah God adds in Isaiah 48:11, ". . .I will not give my glory to another." If Jehovah God is not the triune God of Christendom—with Jesus Christ a member of that    Godhead—there is no way Christ could share in the Father's glory as it relates to redemption.

His other major mistake relates to his reference to the "Greek texts and extant manuscripts," since the construction is irrelevant to the main point of our Lord's absolute deity. Regarding that point of deity, it matters little whether the verse says "the glorious appearing" or "the appearing of the glory." We object to Wierwille's changing of the Greek conjunction *kai* from "and" to "even" only once in the verse—when it appears twice—leaving it

---

186. Ibid., p. 148

"and" in the other instance, apparently only because it suited his cause, since the same rule of Greek grammar applies in both instances. But even that change does not alter the force of the claim for deity!

There is a familiar grammatical rule known to every Greek student as "Granville Sharp's rule." It says that when *kai* connects two terms in the same case, if the first has the article before it and the second does not, the two have reference to the same thing, the second being an additional description of the first. That rule applies twice in Titus 2:13, the first time indicating that "the glorious appearing" (or "the appearing of the glory") is an additional description of "the blessed hope." The other instance is the use of *kai* in the Greek to connect "great God" and "Saviour." Since even Wierwille acknowledges "Saviour" to refer to Christ, Granville Sharp's rule makes it: "our great God and Saviour Jesus Christ." The "Saviour Jesus Christ" is merely additional identification of "the great God." Middleton well says, "If here the sacred writer did not mean to *identify* the great God and the Saviour, he expressed himself in a manner which [could not but] mislead his readers."[187] Especially since "Moulton (Prol., p. 84) shows, from papyri writings of the early Christian era, that among Greek-speaking Christians this was 'a current formula' as applied to Christ. So in 2 Pet. 1:1 (cp. 1:1; 3:18)."[188]

D. Edmond Hiebert, in arguing for "our great God and Saviour" as the meaning, offers the following seven facts in support: "(1) Grammatically this is the most natural view since both nouns are connected by one article as referring to one person. (2) The combination 'god and savior' was familiar to the Hellenistic religions. (3) The added clause in v. 14 refers to Christ alone and it is most natural to take the entire preceding expression as its antecedent. (4) In the Pastorals the coming epiphany is referred to Christ alone. (5) The adjective 'great' of God is rather pointless but highly significant if applied to Christ. (6) This view is in full harmony with other passages such as John 20:28; Rom 9:5; Heb 1:8; and 2 Peter 1:1. (7) It is the view of the majority of the church fathers. This view takes the statement as an explicit assertion of the deity of Christ. Under the other view his deity is assumed, for the intimate association of his glory with that of God would be blasphemous for a monotheist like Paul if he did

---

187. Quoted in TT, p. 84
188. EDNTW, Vol. II, p. 161

not accept Christ's deity."[189] Anderson agrees, noting, "[It] cannot be evaded by rejecting the revised reading of the words; for, **however they are construed**, the Lord Jesus is here named with God in a way that to the Jewish mind would savor of blasphemy if He be not God."[190]

It might be helpful to note that the term "our Saviour" is used by Paul with reference to the Father three verses previously (vs. 10), then of Jesus Christ here (vs. 13). Bickersteth observes of this (and the same usage in 1:3,4 and 3:4,6): "Even if you refuse to admit the simple grammatical construction of ch. ii. 13, can you believe that the name Saviour is again and again applied in a lower and subordinate sense to the Son to that it bears when applied almost in the same breath to the Father?"[191]

At the conclusion of his remarks on "Titus 2:13 and the Deity of Christ," Murray J. Harris, lecturer in New Testament at the Bible College of New Zealand in Auckland, insisted: "In the light of the foregoing evidence, it seems probable that in Titus 2:13 Jesus Christ is called 'our great God and Saviour,' a verdict shared, with varying degrees of assurance, by almost all grammarians, and lexicographers, many commentators, and most writers on NT christology. . . . "Even if the early church had never applied the title [Theos] to Jesus, his deity would still be apparent in his being the object of human and angelic worship and of saving faith; the exerciser of exclusively divine functions such as creatorial agency, the forgiveness of sins, and the final judgment; the addressee in petitionary prayer; the possessor of all divine attributes; the bearer of numerous titles used of Yahweh in the OT; and the co-author of divine blessing. Faith in the deity of Jesus does not rest on the existence or validity of a series of 'proof-texts' in which Jesus may receive the title [Theos] but on the general testimony of the NT corroborated at the bar of personal experience. With this said, the significance of [Theos] as a christological appellation must not be minimized. The use of [Theos] in reference to Jesus confirms what may be established on other ground and makes explicit what is implied in other christological titles. . . ."[192]

One Scripture to which Wierwille gives major consideration, at least for him, is a verse in Paul's letter to young Timothy. Wierwille treats it like this:

189. EBC, Vol. XI, p. 441
190. LFH, pp. 75,76, emphasis added
191. TT, p. 45
192. PS, pp. 271, 272

"I Timothy 3 contains one of these four times when the word 'God' is used referring to Jesus Christ.'

"I Timothy 3:16:
"And without controversy great is the mystery of godliness: God |meaning Jesus Christ| was manifest in the flesh, justified in the Spirit, seen of angels, preached unto the Gentiles, believed on in the world, received up into glory.

"The word 'god' in the above verse is in Greek the relative pronoun *hos*, meaning 'which.' *Hos* is found in all Critical Greek texts except Stephens, the text used for the King James translation. How the error using 'god' instead of 'which' crept into Stephens is easy to perceive. The relative pronoun 'which' looks similar in Greek to our two English letters 'OC.' However, by putting a small horizontal line in the 'O' and a line over the top of the two letters OC, they produce the abbreviation for God found in the Greek uncials. The original text probably read *ho* rather than *hos*.

"And without controversy great is the mystery of godliness which |Jesus Christ| was manifest in the flesh. . . .

"The word 'God' could not have been in the original manuscripts. By using the original word 'which,' there remains no contradiction between this and the 50 clear verses about the Son of God."[193]

We will not quarrel with Wierwille about *hos* or *ho* although it might be pointed out that the later manuscripts and the great majority of the fathers who quote the passage in their writings give it as "God." Rather, we seek to emphasize the fact that, as far as the sense of the passage is concerned, it is the same whether rendered "God" or "Who" [not "which"]. It speaks of the deity of Jesus Christ in either phrase. As Anderson says: "At the coming of Christ He was 'manifested in flesh.' The somewhat doubtful revised reading of I Timothy 3:16 in no way affects the force of the passage. The statement that the Man of Nazareth 'was manifested in flesh' would be nothing better than a grandiloquent platitude. 'He who was manifested in flesh' must refer to God. The words are the equivalent of John 1:18, which tells us that the Son has declared Him."[194] Take the idea of God from the verse and it automatically is robbed of meaning and becomes totally devoid of any intelligent impact.

Rowell points out the same fact, then adds: ". . .without going into the various expositions, let us examine the grammatical construction, for it is this, with the context, which sheds the light

---

193. JCNG, pp. 30-32
194. LFH, p. 10

we need to give clear understanding concerning this controverted Scripture.

"The six-fold history, expressed in the six predicates, blend in one Person, viz. Christ; and, if these all meet in the Person of the personal pronoun *Who*, then which of the antecedents in verse 15 belongs to this pronoun? If this can be satisfactorily decided, then the central meaning of the passage should be clearly understood.

"There are three nouns in verse 15, 'the church,' 'the living God,' and 'the truth,' and one of these could be the antecedent to the pronoun 'Who.' Whichever it is, it must be in grammatical agreement with the pronoun 'Who,' which is of the masculine gender. This being the case, two of these nouns are ruled out as possible antecedents of 'Who,' since 'Church' is feminine, and also 'truth' is feminine. This leaves us with the third, which is 'the living God,' which is in grammatical agreement with 'Who,' both being in the masculine gender. Thus, it can be safely concluded that 'the living God' is the direct antecedent of 'Who,' and could read, 'The living God. . .Who was manifest in flesh.' "[195] There is no escaping the firm conclusion that the deity of our Lord Jesus Christ is taught and established in I Timothy 3:16.

Another critical passage relating to the deity of Jesus Christ is Hebrews 1. Wierwille writes:

"Hebrews 1 contains another erroneously interpreted passage which must be rightly divided in our study.

"Hebrews 1:1 and 2:

"God, who at sundry times [various times] and in divers [varied] manners [ways] spake in time past unto the fathers by the prophets.

"Hath in these last days [in this last time] spoken unto us by *his* Son, whom he [God] hath appointed heir of all things, by [for] whom also he made the worlds.

"Originally God created all things to His own satisfaction, knowing in His foreknowledge that His only-begotten Son would enjoy those things which God had created for Himself and for His appointed heir. The Greek word for 'by' is *dia*, and, in the genitive case, is translated 'on account of' or 'because of' or, according to current language, 'for.' 'Worlds' is the Greek word *aion* meaning 'ages.' God appointed His Son heir of all things, for whom also He made the ages. God structured the ages

195. DJCL, p. 34

because of the need for the redemptive work of Christ."[196]

We do not know Wierwille's Greek authority for the above, since he gives none, but what he says is erroneous. Obviously, he must discredit the statement that God made the worlds by His Son, since that would involve preexistence for Him and, if active in creation, deity. But Wierwille is either ignorant of the Greek or deliberately misrepresenting it in an attempt to establish error. Either is inexcusable in a man purporting to be a Bible scholar. While he is correct in saying that *dia* takes its object here in the genitive case, he is wrong about what it means in that case. According to Young, in the genitive case *dia* means "through, by means of."[197] God made the worlds "through, by means of" His Son. In the accusative case, *dia* would be through, on account of,"[198] but it would be *through* no matter the case! If the writer of Hebrews had wanted to say "for," or "in behalf of," he would have used the Greek word *huper*. The Son of God is clearly the Creator of the ages! (Whether it is "worlds" or "ages" is immaterial to the main point: **the Son made them!** This required His preexistence, that He be eternal. It means He had to be *God!*)

The noted Jewish scholar, Adolph Saphir, has an interesting comment on Hebrews 1:2,3 which highlights the Son's relation to *all* history. He observes: "It is of the incarnate place, to the *end* of all history, He is appointed the heir of all things; (2) to the *beginning* of all history, in Him God made the ages; (3) *before* all history, He is the brightness of His glory, and the express image of His being; (4) *throughout* all history, He upholdeth all things by the word of His power."[199]

The third verse in Hebrews 1 is one of the greatest, one of the most exact declarations of Christ's deity in the Word of God. It says of the Son: "Who being the brightness of his glory, and the express image of his person, and upholding all things by the word of his power, when he had by himself purged our sins, sat down on the right hand of the Majesty on high." This is lumped by

196. JCNG, pp. 120,121. Strangely, this contradicts the definition of *dia* given by Wierwille 28 pages earlier in the same book, where he defined it correctly!

197. YAC, p. 134; see also SEC, which describes *dia* as a primary preposition "denoting the *channel* of an act" ("Greek Dictionary of the New Testament," p. 22, #1223)

198. YAC, p. 134

199. ETH, Vol. I, p. 48, italics in the original

Wierwille with other passages and dismissed in two sentences: "The scriptures which say that Jesus Christ and his Father are one do not indicate that Jesus Christ was God, but rather that Jesus Christ and God had unity of purpose, they worked in a unified effort. These same scriptures also specify that we can be one with them—not that we become God, but that we have a unity of purpose with God and His Son, Jesus Christ."[200]

But is Hebrews 1:3 talking about unity of purpose and merely working together? *Not in the slightest!* It is claiming for the Son everything claimed for the Father. With the two statements about the Son in verse two, the five in verse three make a total of seven—the biblical number of perfection. And this sevenfold claim could be made for no one less than absolute deity: (1) the heir of all things; (2) the fashioner of the ages; (3) the brightness of the Father's glory; (4) the exact image of the Father's person; (5) the sustainer of the universe; (6) the purger of sins; (7) the honored on high at the Father's right hand. How one could consider these claims for Jesus Christ and still deny His deity goes beyond any intellectual depths we can fathom.

Note the phrase "the brightness of his glory." The word translated "brightness" is the Greek *apaugasma* and means "effulgence." *Expositor's* says it "seems to mean, not rays of light streaming from a body in their connection with that body or as part of it, still less the reflection of these rays caused by their falling upon another body, but rather rays of light coming out from the original body and forming a similar light-body themselves . . . . In the Arian controversy this designation of the Son was appealed to as proving that He is eternally generated and exists not by an act of the Father's will but essentially. . . . As the sun cannot exist or a lamp burn without radiating light, so God is essentially Father and Son.

". . .*Alford* says that 'the Son of God is, in this His essential majesty, the *expression* and the sole expression of divine light, not as in His incarnation, its reflection.' The word *apaugasma* is not preceded by the definite article, which fact makes the term highly descriptive of character or nature, all of which bears out the correctness of the above teaching."[201]

The framers of the Nicene Creed placed into that document on this verse: "God of God, Light of Light, Very God of Very God."

---

200. JCNG, p. 50
201. *The Expositor's Greek Testament,* edited by W. Robertson Nicoll, Alford's *Greek Testament;* quoted in HGNT, pp. 36,37

No less an exultation can do justice to it!

The word "glory" is the Greek *doxa* (from which we get our doxology) and is the one used by the Septuagint translators for Jehovah's splendor manifested to Moses on Mount Sinai, to Ezekiel in his visions, and the Shekinah glory of the holy of holies. Nothing less than the absolute deity of Jesus Christ can explain such an attribute credited to Him. This is the *doxa* accompanying the announcement to the shepherds of the Saviour's birth (Luke 2:9), the *doxa* Isaiah beheld (John 12:41) when he saw "the Lord sitting upon a throne, high and lifted up" (Isa. 6:1), the *doxa* of God which Abraham witnessed "when he was in Mesopotamia, before he dwelt in Charran" (Acts 7:2), the *doxa* of the uncorruptible God (Rom. 1:23), the *doxa* Stephen beheld at the time of his martyrdom (Acts 7:55), and the *doxa* that will light up the New Jerusalem to such an extent no sun or moon will be necessary (Rev. 21:23).

But note the even stronger phrase, "the express image of his person." Homer Kent translates this "the exact representation of his [God's] essence," then explains: ". . .thus is the perfect revealer. *Charakter* was the impress made by the engraving tool. This is its only occurrence in the New Testament, although the cognate *charagma* ('imprint,' 'image') appears eight times. As the imprint of the die perfectly represents the original design, so in Christ there is the display for those who have eyes to see of God's very essence. In a similar assertion in Colossians 1:15, Christ is set forth as the timeless image (*eikon*) of God. Jesus Himself said, 'He that hath seen me hath seen the Father' (John 14:9)."[202] Does one wish to know what God is like? Then let him examine the life and ministry of Jesus Christ! As Vincent says: "Here the essential being of God is conceived as setting its distinctive stamp upon Christ, coming into definite and characteristic expression in his person, so that the Son bears the exact impress of the divine nature and character."[203]

Bruce comments on this phrase: "He is the very image of the substance of God—the impress of His being. Just as the image and superscription on a coin exactly correspond to the device on the die, so the Son of God 'bears the very stamp of his nature' (RSV). The Greek word *charakter*, occurring here only in the New Testament, expresses this truth even more emphatically than *eikon*, which is used elsewhere to denote Christ as the

202. ETHC, p. 37
203. WSNT, Vol. IV, p. 383

'image' of God (II Cor. 4:4; Col. 1:15). Just as the glory is really in the effulgence, so the substance (Gk. *hypostasis*) of God is really in Christ, who is its impress, its exact representation and embodiment. What God essentially is, is made manifest in Christ. To see Christ is to see what the Father is like."[204]

Another evidence of His deity in this verse is seen in the fact that He is the sustainer, the maintainer, the upholder of all things. The Greek for upholding is *phero* and Wuest comments helpfully about it: ". . .while the word implies the idea of movement. It speaks of the act of sustaining something that is in constant movement. *Weiss* speaks of the act of sustaining as dealing 'with the all, in all its changes and transformations throughout the aeons.' This act has to do, not only with sustaining the weight of the universe, but also with maintaining its coherence and carrying on its development. Paul speaks of this same act of the Son in Colossians 1:17 where he says, 'By Him all things consist.' That is, all things maintain their coherence in Him. The Lord Jesus holds all things together and in their proper relationship to each other by His own power. The oceans are held in their beds. The rivers run down into the sea. The heavenly bodies are held in their orbits."[205]

How does He do it? We are told that it is "by the word of his power." Just as "the worlds were framed by the word of God" (Heb. 11:3)—"*For he spake, and it was done; he commanded, and it stood fast*" (Ps. 33:9)—so they are sustained and controlled today by that same word of Him who is the exact representation of the Father's essence. Hallelujah, what a Saviour!

Gouge notes that "word" here is not *logos* but *rhema*, "which importeth a command," and that "Christ is herein resembled to an absolute monarch, who at his word hath what he will [have] done. He needs no more but command."[206] His authority, as deity, is without limit.

And it is as savior/deity that He is described next: "when he had by himself purged our sins." Immediately comes to mind the cries of the Capernaumites when Jesus said to the man sick of the palsy, borne of four, lowered through the roof, "Son, thy sins be forgiven thee": "Why doth this man thus speak blasphemies? who can forgive sins but God only?" (Mark 2:7). The word

204. NICNT, *The Epistle to the Hebrews,* pp. 5,6
205. HGNT, pp. 38,39
206. COH, p. 18

"purged" is the Greek *katharismos* and speaks of a cleansing, carrying the thought of a purification through removal. Here is a God who can purify sinners by removing completely their defiling and damning sins! How could He? By "the sacrifice of Himself" (Heb. 9:26) at Calvary! This same epistle assures us: "By the which will we are sanctified through the offering of the body of Jesus Christ once for all. . . . But this man, after he had offered one sacrifice for sins for ever, sat down on the right hand of God. . . . For by one offering he hath perfected for ever them that are sanctified" (Heb. 10:10,12,14).

Hebrews 1:3 is truly holy ground, introducing mankind to deity Himself. The New International Version translates it: "The Son is the radiance of God's glory and the exact representation of his being, sustaining all things by his power word. After he had provided purification for sins, he sat down at the right hand of the Majesty in heaven." We join Samuel Ridout in exulting: "All that God is—not merely in His ways, but in His being—is expressed absolutely by the Son. . . . No one has grasped what the Son of God is until he has prostrated his soul before Him 'God over all, blessed forever'! (Rom. 9:5). I would that I could put it so strongly that every soul would bow to the truth of it, the absolutely essential, perfect divinity of the Son of God, our Lord Jesus Christ. We admit not one iota of a question, not one shadow of a doubt, not one bit of tarnish upon that glory which God has spread before us on this page."[207]

In light of Hebrews 1:3 it is not at all surprising that we find the Father addressing the Son as deity in verse 8: "But unto the Son he saith, Thy throne, O God, is for ever and ever: a sceptre of righteousness is the sceptre of thy kingdom." To this divine testimonial about the Son, Wierwille responds:

"This is apparently a quotation from Psalm 45:6 where the word 'God' refers to a man, a man in an exalted position, namely, the king.

". . .Every verse leading up to verse 8 in Hebrews 1 emphasizes the greatness of Christ and what he did; thus the title of 'God.' It is only a formal title, used here to indicate his power and glory."[208]

No, no! Go back and read the preceding verses, especially verse 3, and see if there is any way the Father calling the Son "God" in verse 8 could be merely a formal title. Such a thought is

---

207. *Lectures on Hebrews;* quoted in HVV, p. 11
208. JCNG, p. 32

absolutely incredible! **Totally impossible!** And when one compares Psalm 45:6,7 with Hebrews 1:8,9 he discovers something interesting: *the same Hebrew word for God is used for both Son and Father in the Psalm; both Son and Father are given the same Greek word for God in Hebrews!* Psalm 45:6,7 say: "Thy throne, O God [*Elohim*], is for ever and ever. . . .therefore God [*Elohim*], thy God [*Elohim*], hath anointed thee with the oil of gladness above thy fellows." And in the Hebrews passage: "But unto the Son he saith, Thy throne, O God [*Theos*], is for ever and ever. . . .therefore God [*Theos*], even thy God [*Theos*], hath anointed thee with the oil of gladness above thy fellows." The kind of deity the Father possesses is the quality of deity the Son possesses.

Another problem facing Wierwille and TWI in Hebrews 1 is the statement in verse 6: "And again, when he bringeth in the firstbegotten into the world, he saith, And let all the angels of God worship him." The Greek word for "worship" is *proskuneo* and it is the same word used by Satan in the temptation of Christ, where we read: "Again, the devil taketh him up into an exceeding high mountain, and sheweth him all the kingdoms of the world, and the glory of them: And saith unto him, All these things will I give thee, if thou wilt fall down and worship [*proskuneo*] me. Then saith Jesus unto him, Get thee hence, Satan: for it is written, Thou shalt worship [*proskuneo*] the Lord thy God, and him only shalt thou serve" (Matt. 4:8-10). If Jehovah God has demanded that worship be given only to Himself, then why or how could he command angels to worship [*proskuneo*] Christ unless the latter were God? One thinks here of the experience of John on the Isle of Patmos at the time of the Revelation. We read: "And I John saw these things, and heard them. And when I had heard and seen, I fell down to worship [*proskuneo*] before the feet of the angel which shewed me these things. Then saith he unto me, See thou do it not: for I am thy fellowservant, and of they brethren the prophets, and of them which keep the sayings of this book: worship [*proskuneo*] God" (Rev. 22:8,9).

But Wierwille and TWI are not free of Hebrews 1 yet. Verse 10 says, "And, Thou, Lord, in the beginning hast laid the foundation of the earth; and the heavens are the works of thine hands." Here the preexistence and creative power of Christ are both emphasized. How does Wierwille handle it? He dismisses it all with one short sentence: " 'And, Thou, Lord' addresses God who is the Creator of the heavens and the earth according to Genesis 1:1."[209] But this explanation does horrible violence to the context. All through the chapter the Son has been under discussion, statements about Him are made, and Old Testament passages are quoted and attributed to Him. This verse is just another in the series of Old Testament statements (taken from Psalm 102). Not only is this a continuation of these statements about the Son, it is added confirmation of His creative work as described in the earlier verses. Of the Son it may be said, "This is the true God!"

Which recalls the debate the unitarian clergyman and an evangelical preacher were having. The former declared heatedly that such an important doctrine as the deity of Jesus Christ, if true, would have to be stated in the Bible in such language that no one could misunderstand it.

The evangelical responded, "So, what language would you have used to reveal it?"

And the unitarian replied, "I would have described him as 'the true God.'"

"Wonderful!" shouted the Bible believer. "That is exactly what the Word of God calls Him in I John 5:20, 'And we know that the Son of God is come, and hath given us an understanding, that we may know him that is true, and we are in him that is true, even in his Son Jesus Christ. This is the true God, and eternal life.'"

As might be expected, Wierwille, with the help of his plentiful bracket supply, has an explanation to destroy the force of this statement. He opines: "The word 'even' is in italics indicating that it appears in no text. The words 'him that is true' are two Greek words, literally translated, 'the true.' 'True' is an objective used here as a noun and as such is translated 'true one.' In other words the verse reads: 'And we know that the Son of God is come, and hath given us an understanding that we may know the true One [God; John 1:18], and we are in the true One [God] by the work of his Son Jesus Christ. This [the true One] is the true God who is eternal life."[210] But even if we were to concede that he is right in his understanding of the "true one" being God the Father, we must saddle him with his own rules of grammar stated earlier in his book.[211] There we were told that the pronoun

---

209. Ibid., p. 149
210. Ibid., pp. 149,150
211. Ibid., p. 91

should be "controlled by its closest associated noun." Following Wierwille's rule of grammar, the pronoun "this" [*houtos*] must refer back to the noun, Jesus Christ.

Actually, in this case, it is good grammar to so understand it. Robert S. Candlish comments: "The Lord Jesus Christ is the person here meant. Such seems to be the fair inference from the use of the pronoun 'this'; which naturally and usually indicates the nearest person spoken of in the context; and therefore, in this instance, not 'him that is true,' but 'his Son Jesus Christ.'

"That inference indeed is so clear, in a merely grammatical and exegetical point of view, that there would not probably have been any doubt about it, were it not for its implying an assertion of our Lord's supreme divinity; an assertion which no sophistry or special pleading can evade or explain away. . . .It is a forced construction only that can get us past 'his Son Jesus Christ,' so as to send us back to him whose Son he is."[212]

Not only so, but trying to do it "makes the text rather tautologous: 'we are in him who is true. . . .He is the true God,' " as I. Howard Marshall points out. And he adds, "Further, it is Jesus who is the source of eternal life (1:2; Jn. 11:25; 14:6), and it is fitting that at the climax of the Epistle, as at the beginning and climax of the Gospel (Jn. 1:1; 20:28), full deity should be ascribed to Jesus. It is precisely because Jesus is the true God that the person who is in him is also in the Father."[213]

Yes, "he is the true God and eternal life" (I John 5:20, NIV).

### Other Important Deity Declarations

There are numerous other clear, positive statements about the absolute deity of Jesus Christ, in both Testaments, which Wierwille ignores. Before leaving this chapter, permit us to take a quick look as just a few of them.

For example, consider the tremendous vision Isaiah had of the Lord God Almighty at the time of his call and commission. While the entire sixth chapter is related to it, note especially verses 1, 3, 9 and 10: "In the year that king Uzziah died I saw also the Lord [*Elohim*] sitting upon a throne, high and lifted up, and his train filled the temple. . . . And one cried unto another, and said, Holy, holy, holy, is the Lord of hosts [*Jehovah Sabaoth*]: the whole earth is full of his glory. . . . And he said, Go, and tell this people,

---

212. FEJ, p. 564
213. NICNT, *The Epistles of John*, p. 254

Hear ye indeed, but understand not; and see ye indeed, but perceive not. Make the heart of this people fat, and make their ears heavy, and shut their eyes; lest they see with their eyes, and hear with their ears, and understand with their heart, and convert, and be healed." There is no possible mistaking or denying that this passage has reference to absolute deity.

Yet John applies this very Scripture to Jesus Christ and the reaction He and His ministry received at Jerusalem. He wrote: "But though he had done so many miracles before them, yet they believed not on him: That the saying of Esaias the prophet might be fulfilled, which he spake, Lord, who hath believed our report? and to whom hath the arm of the Lord been revealed? Therefore they could not believe, because that Esaias said again, He hath blinded their eyes, and hardened their heart; that they should not see with their eyes, nor understand with their heart, and be converted, and I should heal them. These things said Esaias, when he saw his glory, and spake of him" (John 12:37-41). When Isaiah beheld Jehovah's glory and spoke of Him, who was it? It was Jesus, John informs us!

We have the same idea in Isaiah 40:3-5, prophesying the ministry of John the Baptist: "The voice of him that crieth in the wilderness, Prepare ye the way of the Lord [*Jehovah*], make straight in the desert a highway for our God. Every valley shall be exalted, and every mountain and hill shall be made low: and the crooked shall be made straight, and the rough places plain: And the glory of the Lord [*Jehovah*] shall be revealed, and all flesh shall see it together: for the mouth of the Lord [*Jehovah*] hath spoken it." Here we are told that Jehovah would have a forerunner, a voice heralding His ministry in advance.

This prophecy was fulfilled, we are told in the New Testament, through the heralding of Jesus by John the Baptist. Matthew 3:1,3 reveal: "In those days came John the Baptist, preaching in the wilderness of Judaea, . . .For this is he that was spoken of by the prophet Esaias, saying, The voice of one crying in the wilderness, Prepare ye the way of the Lord, make his paths straight." It is unmistakable—yea, *undeniable*—that the voice crying in the wilderness of Isaiah's prophecy is John the Baptist, and that the Jehovah whose way he prepared was none other than our Lord Jesus Christ.

Who was the Jehovah the children of Israel tempted at Rephidim? Exodus 17:2 says, "Wherefore the people did chide with Moses, and said, Give us water that we may drink. And

Moses said unto them, Why chide ye with me? wherefore do ye tempt the Lord [*Jehovah*]?" And verse 7 adds, "And he called the name of the place Massah, and Meribah, because of the chiding of the children of Israel, and because they tempted the Lord [*Jehovah*], saying, Is the Lord [*Jehovah*] among us or not?" Who was that Jehovah among them on that occasion, bringing water out of the smitten rock? First Corinthians 10:4 informs us, "And did all drink the same spiritual drink: for they drank of that spiritual Rock that followed them: and that Rock was Christ."

A companion passage is found in Numbers 21:6,7 when, as a result of further complaining against Him, "the Lord [*Jehovah*] sent fiery serpents among the people, and they bit the people; and much people of Israel died. Therefore the people came to Moses, and said, We have sinned, for we have spoken against the Lord [*Jehovah*], and against thee; pray unto the Lord [*Jehovah*], that he take away the serpents from us. And Moses prayed for the people." Who was the Jehovah they temped, bringing the judgment of the poisonous snakes? It was Jesus, as I Corinthians 10:9 explains: "Neither let us tempt Christ, as some of them also tempted, and were destroyed of serpents."

And who was the Good Shepherd of the Old Testament? Psalm 23:1 exults, "The Lord [*Jehovah*] is my shepherd; I shall not want." Isaiah 40:10,11 add: "Behold, the Lord God [*Adonai Jehovah*] will come with strong hand, and his arm shall rule for him: behold, his reward is with him, and his work before him. He shall feed his flock like a shepherd: he shall gather the lambs with his arm, and carry them in his bosom, and shall gently lead those that are with young."

Who is this kind, considerate Shepherd, this Adonai Jehovah? Jesus said in John 10:11, "I am the good shepherd: the good shepherd giveth his life for the sheep." And the writer of Hebrews 13:20 calls Him "our Lord Jesus, that great shepherd of the sheep."

Incidentally, note that in Isaiah's prophecy Adonai Jehovah is coming with a strong hand, implying judgment; He is coming to reign; and His reward will be with Him when He comes. Compare this with the closing chapters of the Book of Revelation, about the coming of Jesus Christ back to this earth, and observe the very same wording in Revelation 22:12, "And, behold, I come quickly; and my reward is with me, to give every man according as his work shall be."

Remarkable, indeed, was the power and authority of Jesus Christ to forgive sin. In the case of the man sick of the palsy, brought by his four friends to Jesus at Capernaum, our Lord forgave his sin before He healed his body. The first thing He said to him was, "Son, be of good cheer; thy sins be forgiven thee" (Matt. 9:2). If He were not God, the inner reaction of the scribes was absolutely and undeniably correct: "This man blasphemeth" (vs. 3). Yet He went on to insist, ". . .the Son of man hath power. . .to forgive sins" (vs. 9.)

Forgiving sin is a prerogative of deity alone! Earlier we mentioned Isaiah 43:11, "I, even I, am the Lord [*Jehovah*]; and beside me there is no saviour." Verse 25 adds, "I, even I, am he that blotteth out thy transgressions for mine own sake, and will not remember thy sins." Joyce Kilmer was right when he penned, "only God can make a tree"; but, far more vital and to the point, only God can forgive sin. In the case of the palsied man, Jesus was either a blasphemer or absolute deity!

How are people saved? Both Old and New Testaments insist that it is through "the Lord their God." Hosea 1:7 says, "I will have mercy upon the house of Judah, and will save them **by the Lord their God**, and will not save them by bow, nor by sword, nor by battle, by horses, nor by horsemen." In the New Testament, the angel told Zacharias about the forerunner of the Messiah, John the Baptist, "Many of the children of Israel shall he turn **to the Lord their God**" (Luke 1:16). And, remember, when John the Baptist did come on the scene, "the Lord their God" to whom John pointed was "the Lamb of God," the Lord Jesus Christ (John 1:29).

On the day of Pentecost, Peter pointed men and women to Jesus Christ, quoting Joel 2:32, "And it shall come to pass, that whosoever shall call on the name of the Lord shall be saved" (Acts 2:21). And Romans 10:9 says, "If you confess with your mouth, 'Jesus is Lord,' and believe in your heart that God raised him from the dead, you will be saved" (NIV). Then verse 13 adds, "For whosoever shall call upon the name of the Lord shall be saved." The word for Lord in both passages is the Greek *Kurios*, the word used in the Septuagint for the "Jehovah" of Joel 2:32.

Significant to our subject is the worship ascribed to Christ. The Word of God is crystal clear in demanding that none but God receive worship. The first two of the Ten Commandments given by Jehovah to Moses on Sinai in tables of stone warned:

"Thou shalt have no other gods before me. Thou shalt not make unto thee any graven image, or any likeness of any thing that is in heaven above, or that is in the earth beneath, or that is in the water under the earth. Thou shalt not bow down thyself to them, nor serve them: for I the Lord thy God am a jealous God, visiting the iniquity of the fathers upon the children unto the third and fourth generation of them that hate me; And shewing mercy unto thousands of them that love me, and keep my commandments" (Exod. 20:3-6). That truth was repeated and emphasized with the giving of the second tables, "For thou shalt worship no other god: for the Lord, whose name is Jealous, is a jealous God" (Exod. 34:14).

Our Lord refused to worship Satan, saying, "Get thee hence, Satan: for it is written, Thou shalt worship the Lord thy God, and him only shalt thou serve" (Matt. 4:10; see also Luke 4:8). In I Corinthians 14:25 Paul speaks of it being right for a sinner to fall "down on his face [and] worship God." The Book of Revelation speaks of worshiping "him that liveth for ever and ever" (4:10; 5:14); worshiping God (7:11; 11:16); gives the instruction of the angel to "worship him that made heaven, and earth, and the sea, and the fountains of waters" (14:7); identifies part of the song of Moses and the Lamb as "all nations shall come and worship before thee" (15:4); along with other instructions and illustrations of worship to God (19:4,10; 22:9).

The last two references listed contain clear rebukes for worship directed to anyone other than God. In Revelation 19:10, when John fell at the angel's feet to worship him, he was told, "See thou do it not: I am thy fellowservant, and of thy brethren that have the testimony of Jesus: worship God: for the testimony of Jesus is the spirit of prophecy." Mounce says, "John is brought up sharply with the command, Don't do that."[214] Then in Revelation 22:9, when again he fell at the feet of the angel to worship, John was once more commanded: "See thou do it not: for I am thy fellowservant, and of thy brethren the prophets, and of them which keep the sayings of this book: worship God." All true worship is reserved for deity!

Yet worship was continuously given to Jesus Christ during His earthly sojourn. In only the second chapter of the New Testament we find the wise men from the east *worshiping* Him (Matt. 2:2,8,11). The leper, wanting healing, fell down before Him and *worshiped* Him (Matt. 8:2). The ruler of the synagogue, Jairus,

214. NICNT, *The Book of Revelation,* p. 341

wanting healing for his daughter, fell at His feet and *worshiped* Him (Matt. 9:18). The disciples, after seeing Him walk on the raging sea, invite Peter to join Him in that stroll, then quiet the tumultuous water, *worshiped* Him (Matt. 14:22-33). The woman of Tyre who wanted her demon-possessed daughter delivered, after first receiving a rebuff, *worshiped* Him and obtained the healing (Matt. 15:21-28). The demon-possessed maniac *worshiped* Him (Mark 5:6). The man who had been blind from birth, after his healing and discovery of who it was who performed the miracle, *worshiped* Him (John 9:38). He was *worshiped* by Salome, the mother of James and John (Matt. 20:20). He was *worshiped* by the women and the disciples after His resurrection (Matt. 28:9), then later by the eleven on the mountain (Matt. 28:16,17). The disciples *worshiped* Him at the time of His ascension into Heaven (Luke 24:51,52). And the Heavenly Father specifically instructed the angels to *worship* Him (Heb. 1:6).

In not one of these instances was it either directly or indirectly implied that such action was wrong. Quite the contrary, it was accepted and approved. If Jesus Christ were not God, He sinned grievously in accepting this worship; He should have said with the angel, "See thou do it not" (Rev. 19:10; 22:8). He should have responded like Peter, when Cornelius fell at his feet in worship, "Stand up; I myself also am a man" (Acts 10:25,26). The only conclusion possible, in the light of the oft-given, oft-received worship for Christ, is that He is, indeed, very God of very God and, as such, deserving of all worship from His creatures.

We are reminded of the story William Riley told about Charles Lamb, the English essayist, critic and poet. On an occasion when he was conversing on various topics with an assembly of friends, one asked, "What would you do if Plato, Aristotle or Shakespeare should enter the room at this moment?"

"I would rise," replied Lamb, "and receive them with great respect."

"And what," persisted the inquirer, "would you do if Christ should enter?"

Humbly and reverently Lamb responded, "I should kneel at His feet!"

Such is the honor reserved for deity.

Another clear, definite, positive statement of the deity of Jesus Christ is given by Paul in Romans 9:5. Our authorized version translates it, "Whose are the fathers, and of whom as concerning the flesh Christ came, who is over all, God blessed for ever. Amen." The New International Version words it: "Theirs are the patriarchs, and from them is traced the human ancestry of Christ, who is God over all, forever praised! Amen." The Lutheran scholar, William F. Beck, gives it, "They have the ancestors, and from them according to His body came Christ, who is God over everything, blessed forever. Amen." And Adams expresses it, "From them have come the patriarchs and, according to the flesh, Christ, the God who is over all and blessed forever. Amen."

In plain, unmistakable language Jesus Christ is acknowledged as possessing absolute deity. So strong is this declaration that unitarian enemies of our Lord have centered their fiercest and wildest assaults in attempting to discredit it, but all to no avail. Efforts have been made to change the punctuation, break up the sentence in the middle, or otherwise dull its force. Yet, as Dr. Gifford, writing in the *Speaker's Commentary*, correctly states, "it is the natural and simple construction, which every Greek scholar would adopt without hesitation, if no question of doctrine were involved."[215] Robertson sees it as a matter of logic to have "A clear statement of the deity of Christ following the remark about his humanity. This is the natural and the obvious way of punctuating the sentence. To make a full stop after *sarka* (or colon) and start a new sentence for the doxology is very abrupt and awkward."[216]

And J. Barmby, writing in *The Pulpit Commentary*, notes about the attempt to change the construction so that the words "God blessed for ever" refer to the Father, ". . .the idea of so unlikely a breaking up of the sentence may be dismissed as untenable," and calls the authorized version "certainly the most obvious meaning" and "the one understood by all ancient commentators."[217] He pointed out that not one single "one of the Greek or other Fathers, or any interpreter before Erasmus, is known to have understood it otherwise," and that such an in-

---

215. Quoted in RR, p. 214, footnote; see also NICNT, *The Epistle to the Romans* by John Murray, Vol. II, pp. 245-248, who concludes: ". . .there is no good reason to depart from the traditional construction and interpretation of this verse and, on the other hand, there are preponderant reasons for adopting the same."
216. WPNT, Vol. IV, p. 381
217. Vol. XVIII, p. 263

terpretation "gives the most obvious sense of the words themselves."[218] He summed up his arguments by saying, "The whole objection to the ancient interpretation rests solely on the views of modern critics as to what they think St. Paul was *likely* to mean—not on what his language most obviously intimates that he *did* mean—a very unsafe principle of interpretation. Our safe conclusion seems to be that modern criticism has not made out a sufficient case for departing from the unanimous ancient interpretation of this passage."[219]

Canon Henry Parry Liddon, whose book, *The Divinity of Our Lord & Saviour Jesus Christ*, was described by the noted literary authority Wilbur M. Smith as the greatest work on the deity of Christ every printed, discusses, in his commentary on Romans, the three principal ways Paul's doxology has been dealt with, concluding that the proper rules of grammar insist that "God blessed for ever" refer to Christ. He observes that "the authority of Christian antiquity is on the side" of this conclusion, then lists the following as evidence:

"S. Irenaeus, *adv. Haer.* iii. 16. n. 3 (vol. i. p. 506, ed. Stieren).
Tertullian, *adv. Prax.* c. 13,15 (vol. ii. pp. 669, 673, ed. Oehler).
Conc. Ant. A.D. 269, ap. Routh, *Rel. Sacr.* iii. 292 (ed. 1846).
Novatian, *De Trinitate*, c. 13,30 (pp. 43, 118, ed. Welchman).
S. Athanasius, *Contr. Arian. Orat.* i. 10; *Orat.* iv. I sub in. (vol. i. p. 415, ed. Ben.).
S. Athansius, *Epist. ad Epictetum* (vol. i. pt. ii. p. 908, ed. Ben.).
S. Epiphanius, *Haer.* 57.2, p. 483; 76, conf. 30 (p. 978).
S. Hilarius, *De Trinitate*, viii. c. 37,38 (p. 970, ed. Ben.).
S. Ambrosius, *De Spiritu Sancto*, i. 3.46 (vol. ii. p. 609, ed. Ben.).
S. Gregorius Nyss., *contra Eunom. Orat.* x. (volffii. p. 695, ed. Paris, 1638).
S. Augustinus, *De Trinitate*, ii. 13. n. 23 (vol. viii. p. 786, ed. Ben.).
S. Augustinus, *Contra Faustum*, iii. c. 6 (vol. viii. p. 192, ed. Ben.).
S. Hieronymus, *Ep. ad Algas.* Qu. ix. (vol. iv. p. 204, ed. Ben. Par.)."[220]

---

218. Ibid., p. 264
219. Ibid.
220. EAER, p. 151

The noted Swiss Protestant reformer and theologian, Frederic Louis Godet, argued the same, saying, "The entire primitive church seems to have had no hesitation as to the meaning to be given to our passage; comp. Irenaeus, Tertullian, Origen, Chrysostom, Augustine, Jerome, Theodoret; later, Luther, Calvin, Beza, Tholuck, Usteri, Olshausen, Philippi, Gess, Ritschl, Hofmann, Weiss, Delitzsch, Schultz."[221] And he concluded, "It seems to us, therefore, beyond doubt that Paul here points, as the crown of all the prerogatives granted to Israel, to their having produced for the world the Christ, who now, exalted above all things, is God blessed forever."[222]

Nearly a century ago, objecting to translations which tried to tone down this tremendous declaration of deity, John William Burgon, dean of Chichester, called attention to the vast textual and historical authority supporting the claim of deity. He wrote: "We refer to Manuscripts,—Versions,—Fathers: and what do we find? (1) It is demonstrable that *the oldest Codices, besides the whole body of the cursives*, know nothing about the method of 'some modern Interpreters.'—(2) 'There is absolutely not a shadow, *not a tittle of evidence, in any of the ancient Versions*, to warrant what they do.'—(3) How then, about the old Fathers? for the sentiments of our best modern Divines, as Pearson and Bull, we know by heart.

"We find that the expression *'who is over all* [things], *God blessed for ever'* is expressly acknowledged to refer to our SAVIOUR by the following 60 illustrious names:—

"Irenaeus,—Hippolytus in 3 places,—Origen,—Malchion, in the name of six of the Bishops at the Council of Antioch, A.D. 269,—ps.—Dionysius Alex., twice,—the *Constt. App.*,—Athanasius in 6 places,—Basil in 2 places,—Didymus in 5 places,—Greg. Nyssen. in 5 places,—Epiphanius in 5 places,—Theodorus Mops.,—Methodius,—Eustathius,—Eulogius, twice,—Caesarius, 3 times,—Theophilus Alex., twice,—Nestorius,—Theodotus of Ancyra,—Proclus, twice,—Severianus Bp. of Gabala,—Chrysostom, 8 times,—Cyril Alex., 15 times,—Paulus Bp. of Emesa,—Theodoret, 12 times,—Gennadius, Abp. of C. P.,—Severus, Abp. of Antioch,—Amphilochius,—Gelasius Cyz.,—Anastasius Ant.,—Leontius Byz., 3 times,—Maximus,—J. Damascene, 3 times. Besides of the Latins, Tertullian, twice,—Cyprian,—Novatian, twice,—Ambrose, 5 times,—

221. COR, p. 343
222. Ibid., p. 345

Palladius the Arian at the Council of Aquileia,—Hilary, 7 times,—Jerome, twice,—Augustine, about 30 times,—Victorinus,—the *Breviarium*, twice,—Marius Mercator,—Cassian, twice,—Alcimus Avit.,—Fulgentius, twice,—Leo, Bp. of Rome, twice,—Ferrandus, twice,—Facundus:—to whom must be added 6 ancient writers, of whom 3 have been mistaken for Athanasius,—and 3 for Chrysostom. All these see in Rom. ix.5, a glorious assertion of the eternal GODhead of CHRIST."[223]

Comments by two other scholars of note, Albert Barnes and Dean Henry Alford, might be noteworthy here. Barnes, discussing the phrase "God blessed for ever," observed: "This is evidently applied to the Lord Jesus; and it *proves* that he is Divine. If the translation is fairly made,—and it has never been proved to be erroneous,—it demonstrates that he is God as well as man. The doxology 'blessed for ever' was usually added by the Jewish writers after the mention of the name God, as an expression of reverence."[224] And Alford, with reference to the rendering "and of whom sprung Christ, as far as regards the flesh, Who is God over all, blessed for ever," noted: "The rendering given above is then not only that most agreeable to the usage of the apostles, but the *only one admissible by the rules of grammar and arrangement*. It also admirably suits the context: for, having enumerated the historic advantages of the Jewish people, he concludes by stating one which ranks far higher than all—that from them sprung according to the flesh, He who is God over all, blessed forever."[225]

Strangely, however, even though this is one of the strongest statements in Scripture relating to our Lord's deity, if Wierwille even once referred to it in an attempt to refute it, we were unable to locate it. None is listed in his index.

Ephesians 5:5 is another link in the chain of scriptural evidence establishing Christ's deity and Edward Henry Bickersteth, offering "the kingdom of [him who is] Christ and God" as a proper translation of the ending, quotes P. Smith as saying, "If this text had no relation to any controversy, and were judged of solely by the common law of Greek construction, no person would ever have disputed the propriety, or rather necessity, of considering the two concluding nouns as referring to one

223. RR, pp. 211-213
224. BNNT, p. 614
225. BS, op. cit., p. 221

and the same object."[226] If Granville Sharp's rule—that when two terms in the same case are preceded by the definite article, joined by *kai* (and), but the second term does not have the article before it, the two terms have reference to one and the same thing—were applied here, Bickersteth's translation would have to be the proper one. However, even those who do not think "Christ" and "God" refer to the same object here, acknowledge it to be a strong statement of deity nonetheless. For example, A. Skevington Wood observes, "On the other hand, that Christ and God, though distinct, are subsumed under the one definite article provides impressive evidence of our Lord's divinity."[227]

Biblical descriptions of the Gospel show how interchangeably the nouns Christ and God are used. There is only *one* Gospel, of course, and Paul pronounced the direst anathema upon anyone preaching any other gospel than the one he proclaimed (Gal. 1:7-9). Yet sometimes he referred to that gospel as "the gospel of Christ" (e.g., I Cor. 9:12,18; Phil. 1:27; I Thess. 3:2), sometimes as "the gospel of God" (e.g., I Thess. 2:2,8,9), and sometimes he used the two terms interchangeably in the same passage (e.g., Rom. 1:1,16; Rom. 15:16,19). And, like Paul, we rejoice in "the glorious gospel [lit. *the gospel of the glory*] of the blessed God, which was committed to my trust" (I Tim. 1:11).

Peter acknowledges deity for Jesus Christ also, opening his second epistle with a salutation to "them that have obtained like precious faith with us through the righteousness of God and our Saviour Jesus Christ" (1:1). That is literally, "our God and Saviour Jesus Christ." Why? Because, as B. C. Caffin points out in *The Pulpit Commentary*, "According to the strict grammatical construction of the passage, 'God' and 'Saviour' are both predicates of 'Jesus Christ,' as in Titus ii.13."[228] It is rendered "our God and Savior" in the Revised Version, the New International Version, the New Berkeley Bible, An American Translation, the New American Standard Bible, the Amplified Bible, Young's Literal Translation, and by Williams, Montgomery, Adams and a host of others. Even unreliable translations and paraphrases, including those with a definite liberal bias—such as the Revised Standard Version, Good News for Modern Man, the Living Bible, the New English Bible, Goodspeed and Lamsa—do the same. We note that even the Jehovah's Witnesses cult—like

226. TT, p. 83
227. EBC, Vol. XI, p. 73
228. Vol. XXII, p. 2

TWI, dedicated to fighting the truth of Christ's deity—in its monstrous New World Translation was compelled to render it the same, although a "the" was added in brackets before "Savior" to distract and confuse the reader from the momentous truth he was seeing.

Charles Bigg comments on this: "It has been much disputed whether Two Persons are here spoken of, or only One. . . . The argument has two branches, the grammatical and the historical. As regards the grammar, it may be urged:

"1. That the combination of the two substantives under one article is a very strong reason for regarding the two substantives as names of the same person. It is hardly open for anyone to translate in I Pet. i. 3 [ho theos kai pater] by 'the God and Father,' and yet here to decline to translate [ho theos kai soter] by 'the God and Saviour.' This point is rather strengthened than weakened by the addition of [hemon] to [theos]. It must be admitted that if the author intended to distinguish two persons, he has expressed himself with singular inaccuracy.

"2. If the author had intended to distinguish two persons, it is exceedingly doubtful whether he could have omitted the article before [soter]. [Soter] is used in the New Testament of God or of Christ twenty-three times. Of these instances, two are in St. Luke's Gospel; one in the Gospel, one in the Epistles of St. John; two in Acts; one in Philippians, ten in the Pastoral Epistles of St. Paul; five in 2 Peter; one in Jude. It is used eight times of God, fourteen times of Christ; one passage, Tit. ii.13, is doubted. As used of God, [soter] has the article five times, and dispenses with it three times (I Tim. i.1, iv.10, Jude 25). As used of Christ it is anarthrous in Luke ii.11; Acts v.31, xiii.23; I John iv.14, but in no one of these passages would the article be in place. In Phil. iii.20, also, it is anarthrous, and here possibly the article might have been used. Yet in this, the only passage where St. Paul uses [soter] outside of the Pastoral Epistles, the meaning may very well be 'we expect,' not *the* Saviour, but '*a* Saviour.'

"3. But what we have specially to regard is the usage not of other writers, but of 2 Peter. Five times the author uses [soter], and always in very similar phrases. . . . Though [soter] is one of his favourite words he never uses it alone, but always couples it under the same article with another name. There is strong reason for thinking that the two names always belong to the same person; undoubtedly they do so in four cases out of the five.

"Spitta and von Soden, two very keen critics, regard these

arguments as decisive. . . .the first and sovereign duty of the commentator is to ascertain, and to guide himself by the grammatical sense.

"The historical difficulty may be posed in the words of Kuhl. 'The immediate transfer of [*theos*] to Christ might find a parallel in Heb. i. 8, and in the doxologies addressed to Christ in Rom. ix. 5; Heb. xiii. 21; on the other hand, the immediate attributive connexion of [*theos*] with [*Iesous Christos*] is without analogy.' But there is really nothing startling in the phrase of 2 Peter, if we think of John i. 1, xx. 28; or the three, possibly five, doxologies addressed indifferently to Christ or Jesus Christ (Westcott, *Hebrews*, p. 464), one of which forms the conclusion of this Epistle; or the meaning of 'Lord' in 1 Peter; or the language of the Apocalypse. [*Soter*] itself is a divine title, transferred without hesitation from Jehovah to Jesus Christ. But after all, the question is not what other authors say, but what 2 Peter says.

"It may be argued that because 2 Peter is here speaking of one person, he belongs to the post-apostolic age—to that of Ignatius, who speaks of Jesus Christ as [*ho theos hemon*], Eph., Preface (see Lightfoot's note); but there is no sufficient reason for relegating this phrase to the second century.

"A final strong argument for supposing that St. Peter is here speaking of One Person only, is that those who consider him to be speaking of Two have great difficulty in explaining the word [*dikaiosune*]. Granting for the moment that Two Persons are here intended, is their righteousness the same, or different? Are we to say with Wiesinger that God is righteous in so far as He ordained the Atonement, Jesus Christ in so far as He accomplished it? or must we not think with Spitta, that the Atonement is not here in question at all; because it can hardly be meant that, on the ground of the Atonement, a faith has been given to the readers of the Epistle which is [*isotimos*] to that of the writer? The righteousness intended is not that which makes atonement, but that which gives equally. But, if the righteousness is one and the same, it becomes exceedingly difficult to keep God and Jesus Christ apart."[229]

The final book in the Bible, the Revelation of Jesus Christ, is a momentous tribute to His deity. In the salutation, Jesus Christ identifies Himself as "the Almighty" (1:8), a clear reference to Genesis 17:1, "And when Abram was ninety years old and nine,

229. EPJ, pp. 250-252; we have transliterated where Bigg used the Greek, making the argument more forceful to the English reader.

the Lord appeared to Abram, and said unto him, I am the Almighty God; walk before me, and be thou perfect." And the doxology of praise given Him in verse 6, "to him be glory and dominion for ever and ever. Amen," consists of the same identical words of praise given to the Father by Peter in his first epistle (I Pet. 5:11). Bickersteth well observes of this: "The words, both in Greek and English, are identical; the adoration is the same; and the Beings worshipped—the God of all grace, and the bleeding Saviour—are One indivisible Jehovah."[230]

Several times in the opening chapters He calls Himself "the first and the last" (1:11,17; 2:8), identifying Himself with the Jehovah of Isaiah 41:4 ("I am the Lord, the first, and with the last; I am he"), Isaiah 44:6 ("Thus saith the Lord the King of Israel, and his redeemer the Lord of hosts; I am the first, and I am the last; and beside me there is no God"), and Isaiah 48:12 ("Hearken unto me, O Jacob and Israel, my called; I am he; I am the first, I also am the last"). As Walter Scott notes: "This is essentially a divine title. Jehovah claims it three times exclusively for Himself in the prophecy of Isaiah. . . and Christ correspondingly three times in this book. . . . The application of this Jehovah title to the Son of Man is an absolute proof of His Deity. Eternal Self-Existence, with its necessary correlative, Absolute Supremacy, is thus intimated. As the 'FIRST,' He is before all, and above all, and from whom all proceed. As the 'LAST,' He is after all, and in Him all things centre. He is the source and sum of universal creation."[231]

It is in this opening chapter also that He announces, "I am he that liveth" (vs. 18). The words "I am" are in italics, indicating correctly that they are not in the original, but the phrase "he that liveth" is *ho zao*, which is literally "the living [one]." J. A. Seiss quotes *Trench on the Seven Epistles* as saying *ho zao* "expresses not so much that He, the Speaker, 'lived,' as that He was 'The Living One,' the Life (Jno. 1:4; 14:16)," then observed himself: "This is another title of Deity. It refers not to mere manifested life, but to life inherent and underived. The words do not relate simply to the fact of Christ's having lived in the flesh, but to his possession of a deeper and self-existing life, of which that was only one manifestation. The life here claimed by Christ is life coeval with the creation of the world, and which had an eternal subsistence with the Father before the world was. John

---

230. TT, p. 63
231. ERJC, pp. 47,48

tells us that in Christ was life, and that that life was the same eternal life which was with the Father. (I Jno. 1:1,2) All mere creatures are dying ones, except as their being is sustained by him who gave it; but God is the Living One, as life in him is self-existent. It needs no other to uphold it. It came from none, and it is sustained by none, but itself. Immortality may be imparted to creatures, but God only *hath* it in and of himself. And when Christ delcares himself to be THE LIVING ONE, he claims and asserts a consubstantiality with the self-existent God, from whom all things proceed, and on whom all creatures depend."[232]

In His message to Thyatira Christ identified Himself as "he which searcheth the reins and hearts: and I will give unto every one of you according to your words" (2:23). Who could read that clear claim of omniscience and not identify it with Jehovah's words in Jeremiah 17:10, "I the Lord search the heart, I try the reins, even to give every man according to his ways, and according to the fruits of his doings"? And this becomes doubly significant when we realize, as we read in I Kings 8:39, that knowing the hearts of men is *exclusively* the right of Almighty God: "Then hear thou in heaven thy dwelling place, and forgive, and do, and give to every man according to his ways, whose heart thou knowest; (for thou, **even thou only**, knoweth the hearts of all the children of men)."

And what should we say of the manner in which the Lamb of God is portrayed in the Revelation? Sir Robert Anderson put it well: "No careful reader can fail to see that if 'the Lamb' of these visions be not God, He has everywhere supplanted God. From the fourth chapter to the end 'the Father' is never named but once; and then it is not in contrast with 'the Lamb,' but in closest union with Him. . . .

"To drag these visions down to the level of religious controversy would be deplorable. Let us ponder them until our minds are saturated with the very words in which they are revealed, and all doubt will be dispelled as to the Godhood of the Christ who died for us."[233]

In this regard, Anderson told of a provincial community where the ministers were having a discussion on "the Trinity." The village had a retarded man whom everyone called "Silly Billy" and he was present, laboriously working his pencil throughout the sessions. When it was all over, someone asked to see his "notes."

While a good share of the paper did not merit notice, three lines stood out:

> **"This can Silly Billy see,**
> **Three in One and One in Three,**
> **And One of them has died for me."**

Well did Anderson comment: "The poor town fool had got hold of what many who are 'wise and prudent' miss!"[234] The teaching is so clear in the Word of God that any and every individual, even a Silly Billy, should see it.

Leon Morris sums it up for us: "It is open to twentieth-century man to reject the Biblical evidence and to build his religion on some other foundation. But it is not open to him to accept the New Testament and yet to deny that Jesus was God incarnate."[235] This is because, "The writers of Scripture have used every conceivable form of terminology in setting forth the deity of the One who came down from heaven to take away our sins."[236] Yes, "Jesus Christ the same yesterday, and to day, and for ever" (Heb. 13:8), the Eternal One!

The saintly yet scholarly brother who wrote this writer's favorite gospel song ("Only a Sinner, Saved by Grace"), James M. Gray, a former president of the Moody Bible Institute, wrote another number, "No Other Jesus," which will serve nicely to conclude this chapter—already much, much longer than originally planned:

> **I know no other Jesus**
> **Than He who died for me;**
> **The Saviour of lost sinners,**
> **The Christ of Calvary.**
> **I know no 'ideal' Jesus**
> **That human minds invent;**
> **The only Jesus Christ I know**
> **Is whom the Father sent.**
>
> **That human Christ should save me**
> **Is inadmissible;**
> **My Jesus is the image**
> **Of God invisible.**

234. Ibid., p. 54
235. LH; quoted in DIS, Vol. VIII, No. 1 , July-September, 1976, "Aberrations Evangelicals Face: The Way and Victor Paul Wierwille" by David L. Larson, p. 9
236. WGBM, p. 64

My Christ became incarnate
And of the Virgin born;
He left a crown of glory
To wear the platted thorn.

The Infant of the manger,
The village Carpenter,
The Teacher sent from Heaven
To men to minister;
The true historic Jesus,
Who died and rose again,
He only is the Jesus
That I proclaim to men.

## Chapter Two
## ONLY A SYNONYM:
## THE HOLY SPIRIT

The little Kansas community was buzzing with open astonishment shortly after TWI took over the College of Emporia. Several shocked citizens phoned the local paper to report that the huge cross which had adorned the chapel steeple when the Presbyterians controlled the campus was being hauled down. A quick check by the *Gazette* proved that the cross, indeed, had already been removed.

When the media contacted director Craig Martindale, he explained the action had taken place because "the cross in our culture symbolizes a denomination. We do not consider ourselves a denomination—we are a research and teaching ministry. If there is a symbol that we rally around, we consider that to be a dove, representing the power of the holy spirit, as you can see because of the beautiful lighted dove on the top of Kenyon Hall."[1]

This was the reason my little Ramada Inn waitress friend, mentioned in our Preface, had a full-color dove tatooed on the back of her hand. And this is why Victor Paul Wierwille wears a gold pin shaped like a dove prominently displayed on his lapel, and a ring on his hand with the same dove emblem.[2]

Yet the honor the cult expresses for the blessed Holy Spirit is no credit to Him. It reminds one of Lincoln's story about the fellow who was tarred and feathered, then ridden out of town on a rail. Honest Abe quoted him as declaring, "If it weren't for the honor of the thing, I believe I'd just as soon walk." This is the kind of honor TWI offers the Holy Spirit. To paraphrase an old expression, "With friends like TWI, the Holy Spirit doesn't need enemies!"

Why do we say this? Because, like their treatment of the Son, Wierwille and TWI deny the *deity* of the Holy Spirit. Even more tragic, going beyond their treatment of the Son, Wierwille and TWI deny Him personality![3]

---

1. EG, October 28, 1974
2. October 22, 1974; " 'The Way' Founder Tells His Story: Part II," by E. N. Earley.
3. In this matter, Wierwille imitates another cult, the Jehovah's Witnesses. It teaches, ". . .the holy spirit is the invisible active force of Almighty God which moves his servants to do his will" (*Let God Be True,* Watchtower Bible & Tract Society, Copyright 1946; Second Edition, Revised April 1, 1952); p. 108

Does it seem strange to deny the personality of the one being honored? No more so, perhaps, than having a nonperson as a religion's representative symbol.

*Time,* in its write-up of TWI, reported: "Wierwille dismisses the doctrine of the Trinity as a throwback to paganism, because it proposes, he says, 'three Gods.' . . .And the Holy Spirit, says Wierwille, is just a synonym for God."[4]

Actually, one discovers when he digs into the cult's theology, the term has dualistic meaning for them. Wierwille explains it:

"God is Holy and God is Spirit. The gift that He gives is holy spirit.

"First of all we must note that in the Greek manuscripts and texts the word *pneuma,* 'spirit,' is never capitalized. Therefore, when the word *pneuma* is translated 'Spirit' with a capital 'S' or 'spirit' with a small 's,' it is an interpretation and, as such, is of no higher authority than the person or translator giving it.

"By recognizing this practice, it is understandable why so many people confuse the Giver, Holy Spirit, with the gift, holy spirit. The Giver is God who is Spirit, *pneuma,* and Holy, *hagion.* God, who is the Holy Spirit, can only give that which He is. Therefore, the gift of the Giver is of necessity holy, *hagion,* and spirit, *pneuma.*"[5]

The principal problem with this theory is that it is all in Wierwille's mind. There is not even the slightest basis, when limited to the Word of God itself, for making such a distinction. There is not one single place in the entire Bible where *Holy Spirit* (or *Holy Ghost,* as some translations express it) cannot intelligently be understood as a Person. This entire argument is seemingly advanced by Wierwille solely to undermine the clear biblical teaching of the Trinity.

---

4. September 6, 1971
5. JCNG, pp. 127,128; see also RHST, pp. 4-5, 273-358. In this latter text, Wierwille draws heavily, without giving credit, from *The Giver and His Gifts* by E. W. Bullinger—although going far beyond Bullinger's conclusions. While we did not see his article until this manuscript was already in the hands of the printer, we noted that John Juedes reached the same conclusion, giving 6 pages of parallels and observing that Wierwille "draws thought after thought—indeed, nearly word after word—from E. W. Bullinger's *The Giver and His Gifts.* Never once in his book does Wierwille give Bullinger credit for the material he derives from him. . . . Although Wierwille takes up some topics that Bullinger does not, *Receiving the Holy Spirit Today* is heavily based on the content, structure, and general conclusions of *The Giver and His Gifts.* In addition, *every* section of Bullinger's book has been incorporated into Wierwille's book in some form" (JPP, Vol. IV, No. 1, "Wierwille's Way With the Word," pp. 115-120, emphasis in original)

The verse Wierwille offers to illustrate his theory proves just the opposite of what he wants it to teach. He quotes Luke 11:13 ("If ye then, being evil, know how to give good gifts unto your children: how much more shall your heavenly Father give the Holy Spirit [*pneuma hagion*] to them that ask him?"), then comments: "This verse clearly shows that *pneuma hagion* is the gift from God the Father, therefore, should be translated with a small 'h' and a small 's.' The gift is not the Giver, and the Giver is not the gift."[6]

While there is obviously a difference between gift and giver, why must that nullify either the *personality* or the *deity* of this gift? In one of the best-known, best-loved verses in the Bible, John 3:16, we are told that the Son is one of God's gifts to man. Does that mean that the Son does not have personality because He is a gift? Does that mean He is not deity? A resounding **"NO!"** is the answer to both questions!

Wierwille enlarges on this theory in another book, saying:

"At this point a law is involved. God cannot give mashed potatoes and gravy or books or houses. God can only give that which He is. Since God is Holy Spirit, He must give this as His gift. On Pentecost He gave holy spirit. The same words are used in the critical Greek text and in the Aramaic; and these texts have not differentiated between the Giver and His gift. That is where the confusion has come in. God is Holy Spirit with a capital *H* and a capital *S*; His gift which was given on the day of Pentecost was *pneuma hagion* which is holy spirit and should always be translated with a lower case *h* and a lower case *s*. God gave what He is— Holy and Spirit; His gift is the power from on high, holy spirit."[7]

There are several fatal flaws in this reasoning. In the first place, there is no "law" involved, as Wierwille says, teaching that "God can only give that which He is." God can give *anything* that is good. James 1:17 very distinctly teaches, "Every good gift and every perfect gift is from above, and cometh down from the Father of lights, with whom is no variableness, neither shadow of turning." He *can* give "mashed potatoes and gravy" and He *can* give "books or houses."

Apparently these things were specifically mentioned because Wierwille considered them extremes in the ridiculous, but the Saviour distinctly listed food and shelter as definite gifts to expect from God. He told His disciples to pray daily, "Give us this day our daily bread" (Matt. 6:11). He enlarged on this thought

6. JCNG, p. 128
7. PAL, p. 358

later in the same chapter, saying: "Take no thought for your life, what ye shall eat, or what ye shall drink; nor yet for your body, what ye shall put on. Is not the life more than meat, and the body than raiment? Behold the fowls of the air: for they sow not, neither do they reap, nor gather into barns; yet your heavenly Father feedeth them. Are ye not much better than they? Which of you by taking thought can add one cubit unto his stature? And why take ye thought for raiment? Consider the lilies of the field, how they grow; they toil not, neither do they spin: And yet I say unto you, That even Solomon in all his glory was not arrayed like one of these. Wherefore, if God so clothe the grass of the field, which today is, and tomorrow is cast into the oven, shall he not much more clothe you, O ye of little faith? Therefore take no thought, saying, What shall we eat? or, What shall we drink? or, Wherewithal shall we be clothed? (For after all these things do the Gentiles seek:) for your heavenly Father knoweth that ye have need of all these things. But seek ye first the kingdom of God, and his righteousness; and all these things shall be added unto you" (Matt. 6:25-33). In other words, He is telling His followers that if they will put His work first, He will give them whatever "mashed potatoes and gravy or books or houses" they need. Remember, He provided the children of Israel with "mashed potatoes and gravy" in the form of heavenly manna every morning, six days a week, for the forty years of their wilderness wanderings.

We also fail to understand Wierwille's statement, "Since God is Holy Spirit, He must give this as His gift." We deny neither that God is Holy Spirit nor that the Holy Spirit is a gift the Father gives, but the logic in the statement escapes us. Why not say, for example, "God is Consuming Fire (Heb. 12:29), so He must give consuming fire as His gift"?

But to pursue Wierwille's own reasoning to a logical conclusion, if God must give of Himself and thereby gives Holy Spirit, would that gift be an impersonal, non-divine spirit? No, God is a *personal* Spirit, a *living* Spirit, a *divine* Spirit, and if "He can only give that which He is," then the Holy Spirit which is His gift must be personal, living, deity!

Perhaps Wierwille should examine more closely what he wrote in admitting, "The same words are used in the critical Greek text and in the Aramaic; **and these texts have not differentiated between the Giver and His gift**." The reason they have not differentiated is that, in this case, Gift and Giver are *both* living, personal, divine Spirit of God—one in essence, two members of the same Godhead! Other Scriptures, as we shall see, abundantly prove this.

Who is the Holy Spirit? In a previous volume dealing with another cult teaching basically the same as TWI about the Holy Spirit, we quoted the theologian Henry C. Thiessen as follows: "But the *Holy Spirit* is also called God. Before we present the proof of this fact, we wish to show that the Holy Spirit is a person. And first, we note that personal pronouns are used of Him (John 14:17; 16:13, etc.). In the last reference the neuter substantive *pneuma* is referred to by the masculine pronoun *ekeinos,* recognizing the Spirit's personality. The neuter 'itself' in Rom. 8:16,26 has in the A.S.V. been properly changed to 'himself.' Again we prove His personality by the name Comforter. The term occurs only in John 14:16,26; 15:26; 16:7 of the Spirit. It is applied to Christ in John 14:16; I John 2:1 (Greek); and since it expresses personality when applied to Christ, it must do so also when applied to the Spirit. Thirdly, we prove it by the personal characteristics ascribed to Him. He has the three essential elements of personality: Intellect (I Cor. 2:11), sensibilities (Rom. 8:27; 15:30) and will (I Cor. 12:11). Fourthly, we prove the same thing by the personal acts which are said to be performed by Him. He works (I Cor. 12:11), searches (I Cor. 2:10), speaks (Acts 13:2; Rev. 2:7), testifies (John 15:26), teaches (John 14:26), reproves (John 16:8-11), regenerates (John 3:5), prays (Rom. 8:26), guides into truth (John 16:13), glorifies Christ (John 16:14), calls man into service (Acts 13:2), and directs him in service (Acts 16:6,7). Fifthly, His personality is established by the fact of His association with the Father and the Son. This is the case in the baptismal formula (Matt. 28:19), in the Apostolic benediction (II Cor. 13:14), and in His office as Administrator of the Church (I Cor. 12:4-6). And finally, we prove His personality by the fact that He is susceptible of personal treatment. He can be tempted (Acts 5:9), lied to (Acts 5:3), grieved (Eph. 4:30; Isa. 63:10, A.S.V.), resisted (Acts 7:51), insulted (Heb. 10:29), and blasphemed (Matt. 12:31,32). An influence, manifestly, is not susceptible of such treatment. All these things prove that the Holy Spirit is a Person.

"But He is a divine Person. This is evident from a number of things. First, attributes of Deity are affirmed of Him, as eternity (Heb. 9:14), omniscience (I Cor. 2:10,11; John 14:26; 16:12,13), omnipotence (Luke 1:35), and omnipresence (Ps. 139:7-10).

Secondly, works of Deity are ascribed to Him, such as creation (Ps. 104:30; Gen. 1:2; Job 33:4), regeneration (John 3:5), the inspiration of the Scriptures (II Pet. 1:21), and the raising of the dead (Rom. 8:11). Thirdly, the way in which He is associated with the Father and the Son proves not only His personality, but also His Deity, as in the baptismal formula (Matt. 28:19), the Apostolic benediction (II Cor. 13:14), and in the administration of the Church (I Cor. 12:4-6). Fourthly, the words and works of the Holy Spirit are considered as the words and works of God. See Isa. 6:8-10 and Acts 28:25-27; Ex. 16:7; Ps. 95:8-11; Heb. 3:7-9; Gen. 1:27 and Job 33:4. And finally, He is expressly called God (Acts 5:3,4 cf. II Cor. 3:17,18, where we read in the A.S.V., 'the Lord the Spirit'). All these references prove that the Holy Spirit, equally with the Father and Son, is God."[8]

Some of the above could be explained away through Wierwille's convenient musical chairs for the term *Holy Spirit,* perhaps, making it *gift* in one passage and *Giver* in another, but it is utterly impossible to do so throughout. We stand amazed that anyone could read the above collection of Scriptures about the Holy Spirit and deny *either* His personality or His deity. As William E. Biederwolf expressed it, "How the idea of the Holy Spirit as a distinct personality could be more clearly set forth than is done in the Word of God is impossible for an unbiased mind to conceive."[9]

The scholarly Bishop Handley C. G. Moule, in his work on the Holy Spirit, waxes eloquent in describing the "Vicar of Christ" (a phrase he ascribes to Tertullian) as a personal *Him* in Scripture, not an impersonal *It.* He enthuses: "With the Paschal Discourse in our heart and mind, we know that it was He, not It, who 'brooded' over the primeval deep. He, not It, 'strove with man,' or 'ruled in man,' of old. He, not It, was in Joseph in Egypt, and upon Moses in the wilderness of wandering, and upon judges and kings of after-days. He, not It, 'spake by the prophets,' 'moving' those 'holy men of God.' He, not It, drew the plan of the ancient Tabernacle and of the first Temple. He, not It, lifted Ezekiel to his feet in the hour of vision. He, not It, came upon the Virgin, and anointed her Son at Jordan and led Him to the desert of temptation, and gave utterance to the saints at Pentecost, and caught Philip away from the road to Gaza, and guided Paul through Asia Minor to the nearest port for Europe.

8. LST, pp. 144,145; quoted in ARMS, pp. 119-121
9. HSHS, p. 27

He, not It, effects the new birth of regenerate man, and is the Breath of his new life, and the Earnest of his coming glory. By Him, not by It, the believer walks, and mortifies the deeds of the body, filled not with It, but Him. He, not It, is the Spirit of faith, by whom it is 'given unto us to believe on Christ.' He, not It, speaks to the Churches. He, not It, says from heaven that they who die in the Lord are blessed, and calls in this life upon the wandering soul of man to come to the living water."[10]

Wierwille, in trying to explain away the tremendous impact of the use of masculine pronouns to describe the Holy Spirit in John 16:13,15 (and it is that 15th verse, incidentally, which the noted Greek scholar Dean Alford said "contains the plainest proof by inference of the orthodox doctrine of the Holy Trinity"[11]), argues, "In Greek the gender of a word does not necessarily denote the actual gender of the object. If this verse really meant that the spirit is masculine (and therefore a person and part of the trinity), what about Romans 8:26 where the pronoun 'itself' which refers back to 'spirit' is the *neuter* form."[12]

That is a fair question and we are delighted to call one of the greatest Greek scholars of history to the witness stand for an honest answer. The late Dr. Archibald Thomas Robertson, in his classic *Word Pictures In the New Testament,* said: "The grammatical gender of *pneuma* is neuter as here, but the Greek used also the natural gender as we do exclusively as in John 16:13 *ekeinos* (masculine *he*), *to pneuma* (neuter). See also John 16:26 (*ho-ekeinos*). It is a grave mistake to use the neuter 'it' or 'itself' when referring to the Holy Spirit."[13]

Dr. W. A. Criswell, pastor of one of the world's largest and most influential churches, enlarges on this fact of Greek grammar, first calling attention to the cause of the problem. He notes: "This attitude of defining the Holy Spirit as an impersonal 'it' has been furthered because of a way of translation found in the King James version of the Holy Scriptures. The original Greek language in which the New Testament was written possesses what is called 'grammatical gender.' Any object can be either masculine, feminine or neuter; a 'he,' 'she' or 'it.' Other languages beside the Greek also possess what is called 'grammatical gender.' German is one of those languages. The word for

---

10. PWHS, pp. 9-11
11. Quoted in CJG, p. 1,075
12. JCNG, pp. 143,144
13. Vol. IV, p. 374

'girl' in German is *das madchen,* neuter gender. That sounds so strange to us in English to refer to a girl in the neuter gender, but it is a part of the formation of the German language which possesses 'grammatical gender.' It is not that the girl is actual neuter, but that in the spoken language the correct reference is in the neuter gender. Greek also possesses that same grammatical structure. The word for spirit, *pneuma* (our word 'pneumatic' comes from it), is neuter. The translators of the King James version of the Bible were following the exact grammatical construction when they wrote in Romans 8:16: 'The Spirit itself beareth witness with our spirit, that we are the children of God'; and in Romans 8:26: 'Likewise the Spirit also helpeth our infirmities: for we know not what we should pray for as we ought: but the Spirit itself maketh intercession for us with grownings which cannot be uttered.' But in no sense, and in no way, and at no time did the inspired apostles refer to the Holy Spirit as a 'it.' In writing correct Greek the Apostle Paul, in these passages in Romans, merely was following the proper construction of the language. The Holy Spirit is always a 'he,' a 'his' or a 'him.' "[14]

While Wierwille surely refers to it somewhere, we could not find any reference to Romans 8:26,27 in his writings—including his appendix on the Holy Spirit in the book, *Jesus Christ Is NOT God*—other than the passing question concerning the first verse as reported above. One of the rare passages where the Holy Spirit is referred to as "It" in the KJV, the verses together read: "Likewise the Spirit also helpeth our infirmities: for we know not what we should pray for as we ought: but the Spirit itself maketh intercession for us with groanings which cannot be uttered. And he that searcheth the heart knoweth what is the mind of the Spirit, because he maketh intercession for the saints according to the will of God."

We do not know whether TWI considers this to be Spirit (God the Father) or spirit (an impersonal force), but Wierwille's position is shot down either way. If Spirit (God) is intended, then we have the Father described as It and any argument against personality through its use is destroyed. On the other hand, if it is considered spirit (impersonal force), the twenty-seventh verse annihilates such a thought by referring to "the mind" of the

14. HSTW, p. 53

Spirit. No impersonal force could have a mind![15]

But suppose for a moment that Wierwille is right and the proper Greek grammatical translation should be an impersonal It, not Him. He is saddled with his impersonal It making "intercession for us with groanings which cannot be uttered." "Maketh intercession" is *huperentunchano* and is a composite of *huper*, meaning "on behalf of," and *entunchano,* meaning "to plead with." The same *entunchano* is used of our Lord in Hebrews 7:25, "he ever liveth to make *intercession* for them." So both Spirit and Son have a dual ministry of making intercession for the children of God. In fact, the same word is used in the same passage to describe the ministry of both (Rom. 8:27,34).

Would Wierwille and TWI have us believe that *an impersonal force* like the wind is making intercession, pleading, begging in the same manner as *a personal force* like the Son of God? The thought would be blasphemous on the surface and really too absurd to consider, were it not the position which they have voluntarily chosen for themselves.

What honest, unbiased person could read the account of Ananias and Sapphira, then deny absolute deity, to say nothing of personality, to the Holy Spirit? When Ananias lied about the price of the land, "Peter said, Ananias, why hath Satan filled thine heart to lie to the Holy Ghost" (vs. 3), then added, "thou hast not lied unto men, but unto God" (vs. 4). That lie to the Holy Spirit was called a lie to God. As F. F. Bruce notes, "A comparison of the language of v. 3 with that of v. 4 shows that the Holy Spirit is not only regarded as personal, but as God Himself present with His people."[16] And the observant student will note the close connection between the biblical command of Deuteronomy 6:16, "Ye shall not tempt the Lord [*Jehovah*] your God," and the biblical question with which Peter faced Sapphira in the Acts 5 passage: "How is it that ye have agreed together to

---

15. Since writing this paragraph we located, in an Appendix of RHST, his "musical chairs" interpretation. It is like this: "Likewise the [Giver] also helpeth our infirmities: for we know not what we should pray for as we ought: but the [gift] itself maketh intercession for us with groanings which cannot be uttered. And he that searcheth the hearts knoweth what is the mind of [the believer himself, or the gift; it is uncertain], because he maketh intercession for the saints according to the will of God." This makes the understanding of the passage a meaningless mumbo-jumbo, dependent upon the whim of the interpreter.

16. NICNT, *The Book of the Acts,* p. 113

tempt the Spirit of the Lord?" (vs. 9).

Perhaps one of the strongest passages in the Word of God emphasizing both the personality and the deity of the Holy Spirit is John 14, 15 and 16—the instructions, counsel and encouragement our Lord gave His disciples when He told them He would be returning to the Father, but would send One to take His place, a Comforter. No one could read these chapters with an unbiased mind and not be overwhelmingly convinced of His personality and deity. While Wierwille has very little to say about this section of Scripture, he does use a portion in an attempt to show the "difference" between the Holy Spirit as God (Giver) and holy spirit as impersonal force (gift). He writes:

"Still another good illustration of the difference between the Giver, God, and the gift is found in John 14.

"John 14:16,17,26:

"And I will pray the Father, and he shall give you another Comforter, that he may abide with you for ever;

"*Even* the Spirit of truth; whom the world can not receive, because it seeth him not, neither knoweth him: but ye know him; for he dwelleth with you, and shall be in you.

"But the Comforter, *which is* the Holy Ghost, whom the Father will send in my name, he shall teach you all things, and bring all things to your remembrance, whatsoever I have said unto you."[17]

Although it should be obvious even to the casual reader that the only *difference* between the Father and the Comforter is *one of Person,* Wierwille would have his followers think it proves *impersonality* on the part of the "gift," even though personal, masculine pronouns are used to speak of Him. He cannot dismiss the matter that simply, however.

Herschel H. Hobbs points out clearly that while the Father and the Comforter are different in being, they most certainly are not different in nature, in essence. He writes: "Still further, He is 'another' Divine Helper. 'Another' (*allos*) means 'another of the same kind' as Jesus. Dods calls Him 'Jesus' *alter Ego,* or 'Jesus' other Self.' B. H. Carroll calls Him 'the other Jesus.'

"The Holy Spirit is to be 'another of the same kind of Divine Helper' as Jesus had been. He is not to replace Jesus. But through the Holy Spirit the continuing life of Jesus is to be made evident in His church. The disciples were grieved because Jesus was going away. But He promised them an even greater privilege

17. JCNG, pp. 128,129

than His bodily presence. He had been with them; the Holy Spirit will be within them. He had spoken through their ears; the Spirit will speak in their hearts. They had felt the touch of Jesus' hand; now they will feel the Spirit's inward presence. At times they were away from Jesus' bodily presence. They will never be away from the Spirit. Jesus had been with them in body for about three and one-half years. The Holy Spirit will abide with them forever.

"Jesus had just called Himself 'the truth.' Now He called this Divine Helper 'the Spirit of truth' (vs. 17). Thus He is intimately identified with Jesus. Yet He is a Person of the Godhead in His own right. A study of this truth in the Scriptures shows both this distinction and this identity. While the Holy Spirit acts as the Spirit, yet His work is so identified with that of Jesus that often they are spoken of in the same sense of identify. The Holy Spirit is called both the Spirit of God and the Spirit of Christ."[18]

W. Graham Scroggie, in his Foreword to W. E. Vine's *An Expository Dictionary of New Testament Words*, calls attention to the same truth. He writes: "A case in point will be found on page 60, under *Another*. The use of *allos* and *heteros* in the New Testament should be carefully examined, for *another numerically* must not be confounded with *another generically*. Mr. Vine points this out in John 14:16. When Christ said, 'I will make request of the Father, and He shall give you another Helper (allon Parakleton),' He made a tremendous claim both for Himself and for the Spirit, for *allos* here implies the personality of the Spirit, and the equality of both Jesus and the Spirit with the Father."[19] In other words, this one verse of Scripture, by and in itself, is proof positive of the Trinity.

Turning to the item Scroggie made reference to on page 60 of Vine's work, we find: "ALLOS and HETEROS have a difference in meaning, which despite a tendency to be lost, is to be observed in numerous passages. *Allos* expresses a numerical difference and denotes another of the same sort; *heteros* expresses a qualitative difference and denotes another of a different sort. Christ promised to send 'another Comforter' (*allos,* another like Himself, not *heteros*), John 14:16. Paul says 'I see a different (A.V., "another") law,' *heteros*), a law different from that of the spirit of life (not *allos*, a law of the same sort), Rom. 7:23. After Joseph's death 'another king arose,' *heteros,* one of quite a dif-

18. EGJ, pp. 222,223
19. P. 2

ferent character, Acts 7:18. Paul speaks of 'a different gospel (*heteros*), which is not another' (*allos,* another like the one he preached), Gal. 1:6,7." Vincent points out the same fact, saying: "Note also that the word *another* is [*allos*], and not [*heteros*], which means different. The advocate who is to be sent is not *different* from Christ, but *another* similar to Himself."[20]

Someone has blundered inexcusably! Either God horribly erred when He used *allos* instead of *heteros* in describing the Holy Spirit, or Victor Paul Wierwille has committed an irremediable *faux pas* in trying to identify the Holy Spirit as something entirely different in nature or being from God the Father and God the Son.[21] Like Joshua of old, "as for me and my house," we, without question or reservation, take our stand with God. It is impossible for Him to err.

Wierwille makes another brief stab at dispensing with the Trinity in his treatment of Galatians 4:6 ("And because ye are sons, God hath sent forth the Spirit of his Son into your hearts, crying, Abba, Father"), merely noting, "In one of the earliest extant manuscripts of the New Testament, one of the Chester Beatty Papyrii known as P[46] (c. 200 A.D), the word 'son' is deleted. The manuscript reads, '. . .God has sent forth His spirit into your hearts. . . .' "[22] It seems incredible that Wierwille would expect anyone—even his most fanatical follower—to ignore the evidence of thousands of other manuscripts in favor of one single manuscript wherein the word "son" is missing! But such is his desperation to remove the Trinity from a verse which speaks clearly of Father ("God"), Spirit and Son.

What is really missing, however, is the apostle's *thought* in the passage from Wierwille's theology. Note how clearly all three Persons of the Godhead are seen working in unity, with or without the word "Son" in verse six. Paul wrote: "But when the fulness of the time was come, God sent forth his Son, made of a

20. WSNT, Vol. II, p. 244

21. Wierwille attempts to blunt this devasting evidence by claiming *allos* means "more than two may be involoved" while *heteros* means "*only* two are involved" (RHST, p. 174). No Greek authority would agree and even he admits, in a footnote, his theory is not always true. In the passage Wierwille notes, I Corinthians 12:8-10, Paul simply uses *allos* and *heteros* to break down the gifts he is listing into three classifications, two in the first, five in the second, and two in the third. *Heteros* is used when the classification differs; *allos* when it remains the same.

22. JCNG, p. 146

woman, made under the law, To redeem them that were under the law, that we might receive the adoption of sons. And because ye are sons, God hath sent forth the Spirit of his Son into your hearts, crying, Abba, Father" (Gal. 4:4-6). Here is God the Father making gifts of both God the Son and God the Holy Spirit. God the Father is giving, God the Son is living and dying, and God the Spirit is regenerating. What beautiful harmony as the Trinity works in perfect unison to provide man's redemption!

Note also the identical descriptive language concerning the Son and the Holy Spirit. Verse 4 says, "God *sent forth* his Son." Verse 6 says, "God hath *sent forth* the Spirit." If the Son is a Person (and He *is*), then the Spirit is a Person. If the Spirit came from Heaven, sent by God (and He *did*, speaking of preexistence before earthly ministry), then the Son also came from Heaven, sent by God (demanding *His* preexistence before earthly ministry as well). No wonder Wierwille would like to blunt the force of this passage through the slight variant rendering of one manuscript among thousands!

Clark H. Pinnock also calls attention to the Trinity in this passage. He writes: "The trinitarian cast of Paul's teaching is noteworthy. The Son is sent forth, and then the Spirit. In this double sending we get a glimpse into the internal constitution of the Godhead. The church's doctrine of the Trinity was arrived at because the New Testament revelation required it. The Trinity was the most adequate model for expressing what Christians wanted to say about God. The Old Testament, while not without strong hints as to internal diversity within the Godhead, emphasized the unity of God over against the polytheism of surrounding cultures. The doctrine of the Trinity became visible only after events occurred which required a trinitarian God as their cause. The revelation in word, such as we find here, had to await the revelation in fact, namely the incarnation and Pentecost.

"In the ministry of Jesus Christ and in the experience of the early church, trinitarian divine reality was encountered. God the Father, Jesus the Lord, and the Holy Spirit all designate a single divine reality, and yet operate in such a way as to imply a personal distinction between them. New Testament theism is trinitarian theism. This doctrine is an inference we have to draw as to the nature of God from what we know God to be in His own self-disclosure. If we give full cognitive authority to the apostle here, we have to be trinitarian in our theology."[23]

The same trinitarian emphasis is given when Paul speaks of the "gifts of the Spirit" in I Corinthians 12, but let us note first Wierwille's comments about those gifts. He writes: "The Holy Spirit gives one gift to a receiving believer, but this one gift has nine parts or manifestations. There are no more and no less than nine manifestations of the spirit. These are set forth in I Corinthians 12."[24] Then he quotes verses 7 through 10. We remind our readers that when Wierwille capitalizes Holy Spirit he is speaking of God the Father, using Holy Spirit as a synonym, and when he speaks of "one gift" and refers to spirit in the lower case, he is talking about the Holy Spirit as an impersonal force.

In the first place, however, he errs when he says there are "no more and no less" than nine of these gifts ("manifestations" is his term) of the Holy Spirit. While there are only nine mentioned in the passage he quotes, other gifts are listed in Ephesians 4:7-11, Romans 12:3-8 and even in the latter part of I Corinthians 12. And perhaps we should also point out his confusion in saying there is only one gift when the passages use the plural ("gifts").

When Wierwille speaks of the believer having one gift, he means that all nine manifestations are included in the one. They are lying dormant, so to speak, but any believer, if he has faith and desire enough to do so, could manifest all nine. He says: "All nine manifestations are energized in every believer by the Holy Spirit, who is God, by way of the indwelling presence of the gift, *pneuma hagion,* the holy spirit."[25] And again, "Every spirit-filled believer has all nine manifestations, but all nine are not always operative in the same person because he may not believe sufficiently."[26] Anything less, he says, would make God a "respecter of persons." But if, as the Bible teaches by direct statement ("For unto whomsoever much is given, of him shall be much required: and to whom men have committed much, of him they will ask the more," Luke 12:48), and by illustration (parable of the talents, Matthew 25:14-30; parable of the pounds, Luke 19:11-27), rewards are given on the basis of abilities and responsibilities, such an objection disappears like snow in the blazing sunlight of July.

Wierwille's reasoning does horrible violence to the context of

---

23. TOF, pp. 56,57
24. PAL, p. 359
25. RHST, p. 178
26. Ibid., p. 181

the "nine gifts" passage in I Corinthians 12. There we are accorded an illustration of how the Holy Spirit's action in giving different gifts to different believers, "dividing to every man severally as he will" (vs. 11), is far from being in 'respect of persons.' Each plays a vital part in the program of God and the fact one believer has a different gift and a different role to play than some other believer is of little consequence, since all are dependent upon each other. Paul's use of a physical body to illustrate the church body shows that the foot cannot say, "Because I am not the hand, I am not of the body"; the ear cannot say, "Because I am not the eye, I am not of the body"; and the eye cannot say to the hand, "I have no need of thee." In fact, the members of the body "which seem to be more feeble, are necessary." This entire passage becomes meaningless in the light of Wierwille's teaching and it is significant that in his verse-by-verse study of this chapter he offers no comment to speak of, merely quoting verses 12 through 27 and passing on.[27]

Not only so, the word "gifts" is plural, not singular. Wierwille seeks to sidestep this fact by saying of I Corinthians 14:12 ("Even so ye, forasmuch as ye are zealous of spiritual gifts, seek that ye may excel to the edifying of the church"): "The word 'gifts' is in italics and should be deleted."[28] While we are quick to agree that "gifts" is italicized in this verse, hence not in the original, we are just as prompt in insisting that it belongs. When the King James translators added italicized words it was, in their judgment, to make the meaning of the passage clearer and yet still in conformity with the context. They did not err here! The three chapters of I Corinthians 12, 13 and 14 are all concerned with the matter of gifts—as even Wierwille himself acknowledges. And the opening chapter speaks of spiritual gifts [Greek, charismata, lit., "gifts of grace"] no less than five times. The first reference is to "diversities of gifts" (vs. 4) and the final one urges to "covet earnestly the best gifts" (vs. 31). So the translators were well within their right in adding gifts in the 14th chapter.

Not only so, but, as Grosheide points out about the diversities of gifts, "The Greek word [diairesis] has the sense of distributing. This accounts for the plural here, for Paul does not refer to the one work of the Spirit as He is distributing His gifts but rather to the various distributions of these gifts. Whether this refers to the fact that the Holy Spirit, every time a charism

27. Ibid., pp. 186-188
28. NDC, p. 114

is given is dispensing that gift at that very moment, or to the different gifts that are given to different persons is irrelevant here. The thought conveyed is that there are various charismata and that all those charismata are given by one Spirit. The idea is one of distribution and this implies that no one gets everything."[29]

However, we are principally interested here in pointing out the strong, positive trinitarian aspect of this *gifts* passage. It is introduced, in the very three verses before the ones Wierwille quoted: "Now there are diversities of gifts, but the same Spirit. And there are differences of administrations, but the same Lord. And there are diversities of operations, but it is the same God which worketh all in all" (vss. 4-6). What a declaration of Trinity working in unity: "the same Spirit" (vs. 4), "the same Lord" (vs. 5), and "the same God" (vs. 6)! What wonderful tri-unity "which worketh all in all" (vs. 6)!

This chapter also has a scathing denunication of Wierwille's theology—plus an explanation, perhaps. Paul declared, "Wherefore I give you to understand, that no man speaking by the Spirit of God calleth Jesus accursed: and that no man can say that Jesus is the Lord, but by the Holy Ghost" (I Cor. 12:3). When one teaches heretical doctrine about the Person of Jesus Christ, he does not do so by the Holy Spirit. On the other hand, it is only through the blessed Holy Spirit that one can give Jesus Christ proper honor; that is, call Him "Lord." This word "Lord" is the Greek *kurios,* the word used in the Septuagint (the Greek translation of the Old Testament Hebrew; the "Bible" used by Jesus and His apostles) for the principal title of the one God, "Jehovah." It is only through the Holy Spirit that one can properly acknowledge the Lord Jesus Christ as Jehovah, the deity of the Old Testament!

Previously we noted how nonchalantly Wierwille passed off the use of masculine, personal pronouns for the Holy Spirit, indicating—*falsely,* we might add—that their use has no significant import whatsoever. To him, the Holy Spirit is still only an impersonal gift. But where else in the Word of God are masculine, personal pronouns used of impersonal gifts from God? Where do we find "he," "him," or "himself" with reference to such gifts as discerning of spirits or the word of knowledge? Kindly cite chapter and verse for the use of such pronouns about the gift of teaching, or the gift of languages, or the gifts of heal-

---

29. NICNT, *The First Epistle to the Corinthians,* pp. 282,283

ing, or the pastor gift. While such pronouns are used with reference to those who possess them, of course, nowhere are the gifts themselves so designated. Masculine, personal pronouns are not used of impersonal gifts in Greek, Hebrew, English—or any other language. Unless, that is, you count Wierwillese! It is the language of one caught short with a theology he cannot substantiate from the Word of God.

### Other Passages of Emphasis

Contrary to what Wierwille tells his followers in TWI, the teaching of the Holy Spirit's personality and deity—hence, the doctrine of the Trinity—is not confined to an obscure reference here and there.

Consider, for example, Paul's teaching that the believer's body is the temple of the Holy Spirit. He asks the Corinthians, "What? know ye not that your body is the temple of the Holy Ghost which is in you, which ye have of God, and ye are not your own? For ye are bought with a price: therefore glorify God in your body, and in your spirit, which are God's" (I Cor. 6:19,20). Robert G. Gromacki points out, "The word for 'temple' (*naos*) was used for the inner sanctuary, the most holy place where God dwelt, not for the general temple area." Then he added this footnote: "Indirectly, this serves as a proof for the deity of the Holy Spirit. Note the logic: The temple was where God dwelt; the Holy Spirit indwelt the temple; therefore the Holy Spirit must be God."[30]

If one is still not convinced that the One indwelling the believer is deity, consider I John 4:12, "If we love one another, God dwelleth in us. . . ." *Who?* **God!** How do we know it is deity who dwells within us? Because it is "his Spirit" God has given us! And consider the next two verses, "We have seen and do testify that the Father sent the Son to be the Saviour of the world. Whosoever shall confess that Jesus is the Son of God, God dwelleth in him, and he in God." What is true of one confessing Christ? God dwelleth in him! *Who?* **GOD!**

To return to Paul, remembering his teaching that the believer's body is "the temple of the Holy Ghost," in II Corinthians 6:16 he argued for personal holiness and separation in the life of the child of God, saying, "What agreement hath the temple of God with idols? for ye are the temple of the living God; as God hath said, I will dwell in them, and walk in them; and I

---

30. CBS, p. 84

will be their God, and they shall be my people." Who did God say would dwell in the believer's body? He said, "I will dwell in them." *Who abides in that temple?* **"The living God!"**

What could be plainer?

Another link in this irrefutable chain of divine evidence for the deity of the Holy Spirit is seen in Isaiah 6:8-10, where the prophet says, "Also I heard the voice of the Lord [*Jehovah*] saying, Whom shall I send, and who will go for us? Then said I, Here am I; send me. And he said, Go, and tell this people, Hear ye indeed, but understand not; and see ye indeed, but perceive not. Make the heart of this people fat, and make their ears heavy, and shut their eyes: lest they see with their eyes, and hear with their ears, and understand with their heart, and convert, and be healed."

Who gave that message to Isaiah? **Jehovah God!**

Yet Paul, in Acts 28:25-27, when quoting that very passage, started out: "Well spake the Holy Ghost by Esaias the prophet unto our fathers, . . ." *Who gave the message to Isaiah?* **The Holy Spirit!**

The interchangeable use of names ("Jehovah," "Holy Spirit") drives any honest seeker after truth to the irrefutable conclusion that the two names refer to the same deity. The Jehovah of the Old Testament is identified in the New Testament as the Father, as the Son, and as the Holy Spirit. There are three blessed Persons in the one Godhead.

Here is another example. In Jeremiah 31:31-34 we read: "Behold, the days come, saith the Lord [*Jehovah*], that I will make a new covenant with the house of Israel, and with the house of Judah: Not according to the covenant that I made with their fathers in the day that I took them by the hand to bring them out of the land of Egypt; which my covenant they brake, although I was an husband unto them, saith the Lord [*Jehovah*]: But this shall be the covenant that I will make with the house of Israel; After those days, saith the Lord [*Jehovah*], I will put my law in their inward parts, and write it in their hearts; and will be their God, and they shall be my people. And they shall teach no more every man his neighbour, and every man his brother, saying, Know the Lord [*Jehovah*]: for I will forgive their iniquity, and I will remember their sin no more."

*Who gave that message to Jeremiah?* **Jehovah God!**

Yet the writer of Hebrews, making reference to the same covenant in the same passage of Jeremiah, started out, "Wherefore the Holy Ghost also is a witness to us: for after that he had said before. . ." (10:15). Who gave the message through Jeremiah? **The Holy Spirit!**

Another trinitarian example from the Old Testament is seen in Isaiah 63. Sir Robert Anderson tells of a conversation he had one time with Alfred Edersheim, author of the widely read and quoted *Life and Times of Jesus the Messiah.* Anderson says: ". . .he impressed on me that, when we bring the truth of 'the Trinity' before a Jew, it is to his own Scriptures we should appeal. And to exemplify his words he quoted the middle verses of Isaiah 63. Jehovah, the prophecy declares, became the Saviour of His people. But how? '*The Angel of His presence* saved them.' The word to Moses was, 'Behold I send an angel before thee. . . Take ye heed of him and hearken unto his voice; provoke him not, for he will not pardon your transgressions, for my name is in him.'

"If doubt be possible as to who it is that is here indicated, surely it is dispelled by the terms in which the promise was renewed—'*My* presence shall go with thee.' Hence the prophet's words, 'the Angel of His presence.' And mark what follows: 'But they rebelled, and vexed *His Holy Spirit.*' Thus we have Jehovah, the Angel of His presence, and His Holy Spirit, as the God of the Covenant people in the Old Testament dispensation; and in the New Testament we have the Father, the Son, and the Holy Spirit. The nomenclature is changed, but it is the same God."[31]

Perhaps just a few of the many New Testament passages we might add will illustrate how commonly interwoven throughout Scripture is the trinitarian idea. In Ephesians 2:18 we read, "For through him we both have access by one Spirit unto the Father." The "him" refers back to Christ Jesus. Here is the Trinity working in behalf of the child of God: *through* Christ, *by* the Holy Spirit, *unto* the Father.

Consider also Ephesians 2:22, "In whom ye also are builded together for an habitation of God through the Spirit." The "whom" refers back to Jesus Christ. It is *in* Christ, *for* the Father, *through* the Holy Spirit.

Then in Ephesians 3:14-17 we are told: "For this cause I bow my knees unto the Father of our Lord Jesus Christ, Of whom the whole family in heaven and in earth is named, That he would grant you, according to the riches of his glory, to be strengthened

---

31. LFH, p. 53

with might by his Spirit in the inner man; That Christ may dwell in your hearts by faith. . . ." Here is the Father, Christ Jesus and the Holy Spirit working in harmony in behalf of believers.

Again in Ephesians, referring to the "unity of the Spirit in the bond of peace" all believers are to endeavor to keep, we read: "There is one body, and one Spirit, even as ye are called in one hope of your calling; One Lord, one faith, one baptism, One God and Father of all, who is above all, and through all, and in you all" (4:4-6). It is one *Spirit,* one *Lord,* one *God and Father* of all. Again, it is Trinity in unity.

John 15:26 is still another example of the trinitarian idea. Talking to His disciples about the coming of the Holy Spirit, Christ promised: "But when the Comforter is come, whom I will send unto you from the Father, even the Spirit of truth, which proceedeth from the Father, he shall testify of me." Here are three persons—*"the Comforter"* (further identified here as "the Spirit of truth"); *"I,"* meaning Jesus Christ Himself; and *"the Father"*—working together harmoniously and in tri-unity. Christ sends the Comforter to do His work, who, in turn, came to do the Father's work. The will and work of the Holy Spirit is the will and work of Jesus Christ, and the will and work of Jesus Christ is the will and work of the Heavenly Father.

### TWI and Speaking With Tongues

The study of the Holy Spirit as taught by Wierwille and his followers would not be complete without calling attention to their position on tongues. When TWI leaders tell their devotees to SIT, it has no reference to a canine obedience school. S.I.T., in popular TWI vernacular, stands for the perennial command of the movement: "Speak In Tongues!" And *command* is the proper word since Wierwille tells them: *"What* you say when you speak in tongues is God's business, but *that* you do speak is your responsibility."[32]

Yes, strange as it may seem to some, this unitarian cult advocates the Pentecostal tongues phenomena. Jane Howard, writing in *Life* magazine nearly a decade ago, described the cult's group at Rye, New York. Among other things, she reported: "Speaking in tongues—an ancient practice technically called 'glossolalia' and recently voguish in many new Christian

---

32. NDC, p. 109, emphasis in original

circles—is always a feature of the Sunday night meeting. At [Steve] Heefner's bidding a worshiper will rise to utter a divinely inspired message that sounds, to an unsaved ear, like: 'Alokar shamalsh frolaniuk asapolikaj shantih. . . .' The prompt translation, by the same speaker, is usually along the lines of 'Be bold, my children, in spreading the Word. Thus saith the Lord.' "[33]

Wierwille, in the Epilogue of his book on abundant living, challenges his flock: "Never be satisfied with just being a minimal Christian. Be clothed with the whole armor. You are going to have to speak in tongues frequently in your private prayer life; you are going to have to speak in tongues and interpret in believers' meetings; you are going to have to bring forth words of prophecy in a believers' meeting; you are going to have to learn how to receive word of knowledge, word of wisdom and discerning of spirits, so that you can carry out faith (believing), miracles and healing in your day-by-day living."[34] In fact, he says one *cannot* worship God *unless* he speaks in tongues. He insists: "There is only one way we can worship God 'in spirit' and that is by speaking in tongues. . . . As John 4:24 pointedly declares, 'God *is* a Spirit: and they that worship him must worship *him* in spirit and in truth.' To worship Him in spirit can only be by speaking in tongues."[35] But such a statement is absurd, of course.

Already mentioned, in our Preface, is the Emporia barber's experience with the Way follower who spoke in tongues for his entertainment or amusement. Yet the founder, Victor Paul Wierwille, told the news media the "second most important day in his life was the day 'I received into manifestation the Holy Spirit and spoke in tongues.' "[36] That something so sacred could be treated so casually is a parable too deep for us to fathom.

How Wierwille learned to speak in tongues is highly interesting and should cause all modern-day tongues advocates to consider it—and their own involvement—very carefully. Here is the account of his experience, which followed a message by Oral Roberts, just as Mr. Wierwille described it to a news reporter:

"In 1951, Mr. Wierwille went to a pentecostal convention in Tulsa. Evangelist Oral Roberts was to speak there, and Mr. Wierwille asked several pentecostal leaders to help him receive

---

33. May 14, 1971; quoted in EG, August 27, 1974
34. PAL, p. 366
35. NDC, pp. 176,177
36. EG, October 22, 1974, op. cit.

'the Holy Spirit.' Their attempts failed.

"Disillusioned, he tried to leave Tulsa 'but I was snowed in, and that rarely happens in Tulsa.' The next morning at breakfast he met a man 'who had been told by God to come to Tulsa and help someone receive the Holy Spirit. He helped me and that night—I spoke in tongues all night."[37]

Does it not seem strange to you—as it does to this writer—that the kind of tongues-speaking experienced by the Oral Roberts people, the PTL people, the Pentecostal people, can be spoken as easily and freely by a unitarian who denies emphatically and repeatedly that Jesus Christ is God, denies the Trinity, and denies that the Holy Spirit is God *or even a person*—simply an impersonal force? Obviously, this kind of speaking with tongues takes no spirituality, no doctrinal discernment, no right relationship with God whatsoever—not even a new-birth experience! It is merely something "learned," and an unconverted individual can "learn" it as easily as can one who is saved and orthodox in belief. Wierwille has been babbling in the tongues he learned from the Oral Roberts group for about three decades now—and has taught thousands of others (people in over 30 denominations he claims), to do the same. Strange, strange doctrine (or, rather, *practice*) is this!

Make no mistake about it, the tongues speaking of TWI definitely *is* a learned behavior. Wierwille admits as much when, discussing the nine gifts of the Spirit, he says, "The reason we see so little (if any at all) manifesting of the spirit today is that we have never been taught. We have the gift, holy spirit, **but the manifestations must be operated by us;** and this most believers know nothing about."[38]

Since people must be taught how to speak in tongues, does Wierwille have a method of instruction? Yes, but he warns his followers: "Do exactly what I tell you to do down to the most minute detail."[39] Here is the Wierwille secret, summed up in three brief positives and one negative:

"I instruct people to receive the holy spirit in the following manner. It is only a method, but God has blessed it and people have received thereby.

---

37. Ibid.; see also WLL, pp. 196-201, where the man is identified as J. E. Stiles
38. PAL, p. 360, emphasis added
39. NDC, p. 116

"1. Get quiet and relaxed. 'Be still and know that I am God.' The greatest cargoes of life come in on quiet seas.

"2. Do not beg God for the holy spirit. It is here. The power has been here ever since Pentecost. There is no waiting and no tarrying necessary.

"3. Rest your head back and breathe in deeply. The word 'inspiration' also means 'inbreathing.'

"By believing, you can breathe in the spirit. Opening your mouth and breathing in deeply is an act of believing which God honors. . . .

"4. Finally, pray this prayer: 'Father, I now receive the holy spirit, the power from on high, which you made available through Jesus Christ.'

"Having carried out these four simple steps to receiving the power of the holy spirit, you must now by your own will, move your lips, your tongue, your throat; you must make the sounds, form the words."[40]

The reader will note—keeping in mind that Wierwille's instructions are not for *receiving* the indwelling Holy Spirit, but for *manifesting the power* of that Spirit—not one of the four steps he offers is found in the Word of God with regard to obtaining the power of the Holy Spirit, while one is a direct contradiction (see Luke 11:5-13). We are especially intrigued with the advice to rest the head back and breathe in deeply, being assured by Wierwille that one "can breathe in the spirit." The only Scripture he offers for any of his four steps relates to this third one, and they are horribly taken out of context (such as God's admonition to Israel about material things in Psalm 81:10, ". . .open thy mouth wide, and I will fill it," and Job's reference to his glory days in Job 29:23, when the people "opened their mouth wide as for the latter rain" to await his gems of wisdom)!

Does the reader marvel at the seeming simplicity of Wierwille's steps? Do you wonder how such an approach brings the desired result of tongues speaking? The answer lies in the fact that the four steps are not taken until the cult's new disciple has been properly conditioned. Marie Leonetti, a member of TWI for approximately two years before being delivered, points out that the tongues issue doesn't come up until "Lesson 12" of the Power for Abundant Living course, and by that time the convert has heard others so often there is no problem when his turn comes— and remember he had been taught it is something he does *by his*

---

40. RHST, pp. 60-62; see also NDC, Chapter Ten, "How to Speak in Tongues," pp. 115-125. (In this passage he even has a long black place on the page, indicating a break for the seeker to speak in tongues, then picks up the narrative again, saying, "Isn't God wonderful!")

*own will.* She explains, "It's very much like when you're a child in kindergarten learning a song: all you have to do is hear it enough times and you know all the words, you know all the notes."[41]

She adds: "You do it automatically, because you don't have to think about it. Once you learn how to do it, it's just a bunch of babbling. Some Way children also speak in tongues as soon as they are old enough to talk. I personally knew of two young boys, aged three and four, who had been taught to speak in tongues."[42]

We found it amusing that Wierwille said much the same: "The only difference between speaking in tongues and speaking in English is that when I say, 'I love the Lord Jesus Christ,' I have to think. When I speak in tongues I do not think. . . ."[43] Tongues, in the TWI movement, is for people who do not think. In fact, the less you use your brain the better it works, apparently!

In his book, *Receiving the Holy Spirit Today,* Wierwille frankly calls the operation of all the sign gifts the "direct action of the human will," not something supernatural. He says:

"The Spirit does not do the speaking. *We do the speaking, but what we speak is the Holy Spirit's choosing.*

"If we do the speaking we can stop at will and start at will. We have complete control over the speaking in tongues at all times. . . .

"The Holy Spirit *never* does the speaking. The Bible plainly teaches that man by *his own will* does the speaking. . . .

"Speaking in tongues by a born-again believer is absolutely based on an act of the human will. There is nothing supernatural about the fact that man may speak in tongues. Man's will is always in control. . . .

"We can start any time; we can stop any time. By our wills we are always in absolute and perfect control of speaking in tongues."[44]

While not talking about tongues, this philosophy is rebutted by our Lord's words to His disciples in Matthew 10:18-20, "Ye shall be brought before governors and kings for my sake, for a testimony against them and the Gentiles, But when they deliver you up, take no thought how or what ye shall speak: for it shall be given you in that same hour what ye shall speak. For it is not ye that speak, but the Spirit of your Father which speaketh in you." And the words of Christ in John 15:5 certainly come to mind when thinking of anything spiritual being done for God: ". . .without me ye can do nothing."

41. YBEC, p. 125
42. Ibid.
43. NDC, p. 117
44. Pp. 48,49,52, emphasis in the original

It is interesting that another cult founder, Joseph Smith, taught his Mormon followers to speak with tongues, just as Wierwille has his.[45] In fact, Jehovah's Witnesses, Muslims, occult worshipers, all kinds of pagan cults, demon worshipers, and any other number of non-Christian peoples have freely spoken in "unknown" tongues.[46]

Strangely, however, even though the use of tongues in devil worship and among many non-Christian religions is well documented, Wierwille assures his followers that it simply is not possible! He writes: "Devils *cannot* speak in tongues. Thus, when one speaks in tongues one can never speak devilish or wrong things. Devils can possess people to prophesy, but devils never speak in tongues. Those who teach that devils can inspire one to speak in tongues have been misled. Every verse in the Bible dealing with speaking in tongues says that the speakers glorified God."[47] And again, in answering the question, "Is it possible for a Christian to receive false tongues or a false spirit when believing for the holy spirit?" he says: "The answer is a loud and clear no. As a matter of fact, speaking in tongues is the only manifestation which basically Satan cannot counterfeit."[48]

However, Wierwille contradicts himself about *every* reference to tongues in the Bible "says that the speakers glorified God" when he observes, in his discussion of I Corinthians 14, "Paul was alarmed about the misuse and abuse of these manifestations ['tongues, interpretation of tongues and prophecy'] in the Church."[49] And in his treatment of the same three gifts later in the book he says, "The Church in Corinth had been misusing these manifestations. . . ."[50] Obviously, if the gifts were being *misused* and *abused,* they were not glorifying God!

---

45. Although best known for the language he called "reformed Egyptian hieroglyphics" (!), Smith nonetheless told his followers, "Arise upon your feet, speak or make some sound, continue to make sounds of some kind, and the Lord will make a tongue or language of it" (see TMA, p. 222). A recent writer, an ex-Mormon herself, says: "Speaking in tongues was common in the early Mormon church. Brigham Young and others claimed that they could speak in the unknown or 'Adamic' language that God speaks. . . . Today Mormons still claim the gift of tongues and interpretation. . ." (see TMM, p. 253).
46. See CDP, pp. 175,178-179; SIT, pp. 172,173; etc.
47. RHST, pp. 4,48, italics in original
48. Ibid., p. 253
49. Ibid., p. 178
50. P. 207

But who says demons/Satan cannot counterfeit tongues speaking? The Bible certainly does not and Wierwille offers no Scripture to support his blanket claim. Furthermore, the idea of "tongues" in the Word of God certainly would make it a simple matter for them to do so. The word translated *tongues* is the Greek *glossa* and simply means "language."[51] Those who spoke in tongues spoke in definite languages, not some unknown gibberish or babble. The Septuagint, the Greek translation of the Old Testament Hebrew which was in use during New Testament days, used *glossa* a score and ten times; *in every instance* it referred to a definite human language. While it is sometimes used in the New Testament of the literal organ of speech, the human tongue, when used of languages it is always a definite, specific language. In the Corinthian passage the translators added the word "unknown" in several places (it is not in the original), but even doing so is not necessarily an indication of a nonlanguage—simply one unknown either to the speaker or the hearer. While Wierwille and others refer to the "tongues. . .of angels" in I Corinthians 13:1 as being a nonhuman language, every time in Sacred Writ that an angel spoke to man it was in a definite, *known* human language.

With this in mind—that biblical "tongues" were definite, specific languages—would Wierwille or anyone else associated with TWI deny that demons could speak the language or dialect of any people? If they could, it would be utterly ludicrous to deny their ability to counterfeit the gift of tongues. And Wierwille himself acknowledges that biblical tongues—*at least part of the time*—refer to definite human languages. He says: "A person speaking in a tongue will always be speaking a tongue of men or of angels. If he speaks a tongue of men, it is a known language somewhere on earth; if he speaks a tongue of angels, it cannot be a known language anywhere on earth."[52] So why would "tongues" be "the only manifestation which basically Satan cannot counterfeit"?

In fact, according to Wierwille's own biblical interpretation, Satan counterfeited a tongue on at least one occasion. His under-

---

51. Strangely, Wierwille, who loves to refer to the Greek about almost everything—often inventing "unique and original" definitions unknown to Greek scholarship—fails to mention the Greek *glossa* in any of his discussions of tongues we could locate, even in his chapter, "What Is Speaking in Tongues?"

52. RHST, p. 201

standing of the sorceress of En-dor "bringing up" Samuel for
Saul in I Samuel 28:7-25 is that "Satan used the prophetess of
Endor who had a familiar spirit, a spirit obedient to the woman's
own beck and call, to counterfeit Samuel by materialization and
impersonation."[53] If so, Satan was not only able to make the
materialization *look* like Samuel, but imitate his *tongue* and
*sound like him* as well! If Satan could counterfeit the tongue of
Samuel sufficiently to deceive, why could he not counterfeit *any*
tongue?

This is especially true since Wierwille says the counterfeit
would not have to be the real thing, only *deceptively* so. He
writes:

"The one fact to keep uppermost in our minds is that Satan *always*
produces a counterfeit, never a genuine. A counterfeit always resembles
the genuine so perfectly that only a qualified person in that certain field
can distinguish between them. Therefore, Satan's deceit can often be so
effective.

"Satan can imitate and counterfeit anything so long as he is familiar
with the original. Satan has access to the knowledge of everything that a
man does while on earth."[54]

So, according to Wierwille's own teaching about Satan and his
power, it would be a simple thing for him to counterfeit the gift of
tongues. In fact, he would only have to hear *one person* speak
with tongues *one time* to be able to counterfeit it!

In Wierwille's case, he teaches that Christians *must* speak
with tongues; there is no option. Referring to Paul's statement in
I Corinthians 14:5, "I would that ye all spake with tongues," he
tells his followers in TWI that this is a *command* to do so.

But, as with many of Wierwille's conclusions, problems immediately arise. Joseph Dillow points out: "(1) The Greek verb
*thelo* is present indicative active (that's a mouthful but it's important!) and not imperative. It is a statement of personal desire
and not a command to be obeyed.

"(2) In I Corinthians 7:7 Paul says, 'I wish that all men were as
I am. . . .' He is here expressing his personal desire that all people remain unmarried. He uses the same verb, *thelo*, in the present indicative active. Now obviously that is not his command.
But if you take I Corinthians 14:6 (sic) as a command you must
also take I Corinthians 7:7 as a command."[55] We seriously doubt

---

53. ADAN, p. 95
54. Ibid., pp. 94,95
55. SIT, p. 72

Wierwille tells his disciples it is a biblical command that they remain unmarried.

Continuing his insistence that tongues speaking is a command, Wierwille says in discussing Acts 2:38: "In other words, Peter said that the one who repents receives remission of sins, and he then should absolutely manifest, *lambano,* by speaking in tongues."[56] And again: "There is no Scripture that teaches that when people are born again they do not speak in tongues. The Word teaches just the opposite."[57]

Wierwille's main support for his tongues thesis is the Day of Pentecost as described in Acts 2:1-4, the heart of that account being summed up in the nine words of verse 4: "And they were all filled with the Holy Ghost." In addition to that "filling" was "a sound from heaven as of a rushing mighty wind" which filled the house where they were assembled, the appearance of "cloven tongues like as of fire" which sat upon each of them, and the miracle of those present beginning to "speak with other tongues, as the Spirit gave them utterance" (vss. 2-4). These three *outward* phenomena were incidental to the one *inward* experience of being filled with the Holy Spirit. Wierwille acknowledges that the cloven tongues like as of fire was a phenomenon,[58] so why not the wind and the tongues? Especially since the same identical nine words of Acts 2:4 are repeated about a second experience in Acts 4:31 *("And they were all filled with the Holy Ghost"),* without any mention whatsoever of the outward phenomena of fire, wind or tongues?

Wierwille goes on to answer the question, "Is it possible for one to receive the gift from the Holy Spirit into manifestation without speaking in a tongue?" by declaring dogmatically: "No, it is not, for the mighty movement from the Spirit will be expressed in *all nine* manifestations from time to time and speaking in tongues is one of these manifestations."[59]

When one checks with the Word of God, however, this claim will not be borne out. For example, in the Book of Acts there are nineteen separate accounts of conversion and even Wierwille acknowledges the Bible to teach one receives the Holy Spirit at the time of his new-birth experience. Yet in those nineteen dif-

---

56. RHST, pp. 98,99
57. Ibid., p. 157
58. Ibid., pp. 83-85; incidentally, Wierwille interprets the sound "as of a rushing mighty wind" as "heavy breathing by the apostles"!
59. Ibid., p. 252

ferent conversion accounts in Acts, only one refers to the new converts speaking with tongues! Without quoting all the passages here, the conversion accounts are: (1) The "about three thousand souls" of Acts 2:41; *no mention of tongues.* (2) The "about five thousand" men of Acts 4:4; *no mention of tongues.* (3) The "multitudes both of men and women" of Acts 5:14; *no mention of tongues.* (4) The Samaritans of Acts 8:12; *no mention of tongues.* (5) The Ethiopian eunuch of Acts 8:26-39; *no mention of tongues.* (6) The conversion of Saul of Tarsus in Acts 9:1-20; *no mention of tongues.* (7) The conversion of Cornelius and his household in Acts 10:34-48; the only time in Acts new converts spoke with tongues. (8) The "great number" at Antioch in Acts 11:21; *no mention of tongues.* (9) The deputy on the Isle of Paphos, Sergius Paulus, in Acts 13:12; *no mention of tongues.* (10) The Gentiles at Antioch of Pisidia in Acts 13:46-48; *no mention of tongues.* (11) The "great multitude both of the Jews and also of the Greeks" at Iconium in Acts 14:1; *no mention of tongues.* (12) Timothy's salvation, mentioned in Acts 16:1; *no reference to tongues.* (13) The conversion of Lydia and her household in Acts 16:14,15; *no mention of tongues.* (14) The conversion of the Philippian jailor and his household in Acts 16:30-34; *no mention of tongues.* (15) The conversion of the Thessalonians in Acts 17:1-4; *no mention of tongues.* (16) The conversion of the Bereans in Acts 17:10-12; *no mention of tongues.* (17) the conversion of "some" following Paul's sermon on Mars' Hill in Acts 17:22-34; *no mention of tongues.* (18) The conversion of the chief ruler of the synagogue, Crispus, and many of the other Corinthians in Acts 18:1-8; *no mention of tongues.* (19) The conversion of many Jews and Greeks at Ephesus in Acts 19:17-20; *no mention of tongues.*[60] Surely no unbiased mind could read these conversion stories and conclude that everyone born again speaks in tongues the moment he is saved—or even has such a gift! Wierwille tries to escape the force of this argument, for example, in the case of the Samaritans in Acts 8 where Simon "saw that through laying on of the apostles' hands the Holy Ghost was given," by arguing: "Let me ask you, 'What did Simon see?' One cannot see spirit."[61] To which we respond, "Neither can one see words, the sound of tongues!"

---

60. We omitted the account of John's disciples in Acts 19:1-7 because we do not consider that a conversion experience; but even counting it, it would only be two cases of tongues out of twenty!

61. RHST, p. 113; see also NDC, pp. 106-108

Wierwille says about Saul of Tarsus in Acts 9, "It does not say Paul spoke in tongues, but he must have, because the task that Ananias set out to do was not only to minister healing, but also to minister to him the gift from the Holy Spirit into manifestation."[62] This is typical Wierwillese: "If it doesn't *say* what I want it to say, then it must *mean* what I want it to say." He "reads into" any text anything he wants that text to teach. It is hardly honest, but it suits his purpose.

Incidentally, not only is the conversion of Cornelius and his household the only time speaking with tongues is mentioned in the nineteen conversion experiences recorded in Acts, it is also the only one about which the statement is made by one who had been present at Pentecost as a man converted prior to that time, "God gave them the like gift as he did unto us" (Acts 11:16,17). The gift for those at Pentecost in Acts 2:1-4 had nothing to do with their conversion—they were already converted! In light of all this, how strange that Wierwille would say, "Speaking in tongues immediately upon one's salvation clearly is a standard of behavior from the Word of God."[63]

Also strange is his unique insistence that only the one who has spoken in tongues can interpret the message. Purporting to answer the question, "Can one person speak in tongues and another give the interpretation?" he writes: "No. We are specifically told in I Corinthians 14:27 and 28 that the person speaking must give the interpretation or else remain siient."[64] However, when one reads the two verses listed he discovers we are not "specifically told" any such thing. They say: "If any man speak in an unknown tongue, let it be by two, or at the most by three, and that by course; and let one interpret. But if there be no interpreter, let him keep silence in the church; and let him speak to himself, and to God." In language as plain as day, two or three would be permitted to speak in another language, while one would act as the interpreter. This is a far cry from Wierwille's "the person speaking must give the interpretation."

How does he attempt to harmonize what he says with what the Scripture says? He tells his followers it means this: "If the one who desires to speak in a tongue in the Church lacks either the believing in his ability or the willingness to interpret what he is about to speak, he is to remain silent. His lack of readiness to in-

---

62. RHST, p. 125
63. Ibid., p. 126
64. Ibid., pp. 255,256

terpret, either because of insufficient instruction or refusal to speak forth the interpretation is reason for him to keep silent in the Church."[65] Reread carefully the Scripture, then reread Wierwille's explanation. That should suffice to show how far he has missed the boat.

He also delves into *his* Greek to support his theory, saying in a footnote: "The Greek uses the word *heis* meaning 'the one and the same,' not someone else. Thus, 'let each one who speaks in tongues, that one and the same interpret. I Corinthians 14:5,13; Luke 12:52; Romans 3:10.'"[66] Once again we are embarrassed in his behalf over such shoddy scholarship. Does *heis,* translated as simply "one" nearly 300 times in the New Testament, mean "one and the same"? Let's check some samples of its use. In John 6:70 our Lord said to His disciples, "Have not I chosen you twelve, and one [*heis*] of you is a devil?" There is a strong parallel here because of the contrast in numbers. In I Corinthians 14:27 it is "two or three" offset by "one." Here it is "twelve" offset by "one." If we were to follow Wierwille's interpretation, we would understand John 6:70 to be saying, "Have not I chosen you twelve, and each one I have chosen, that one and the same is a devil." We hardly think *that* is what Jesus meant and we believe we are safe in saying Wierwille doesn't think so either!

Another numerical illustration is found in Matthew 27:47,48, which says: "Some of them that stood there, when they heard that, said, This man calleth for Elias. And straightway one [*heis*] of them ran, and took a spunge, and filled it with vinegar, and put it on a reed, and gave him to drink." While the first number here is indefinite ("some"), the principle is still the same. According to Wierwille's understanding of *heis,* the meaning would be: "Some of them that stood there, when they heard that, said, This man calleth for Elias. And straightway each one of the some, the one and the same, ran, and took spunges, and filled them with vinegar, and put them on reeds, and gave him to drink." Such an interpretation would be absurd!

Other illustrations could be multiplied, but we have offered sufficient to establish our point that Wierwille's interpretation is faulty. Incidentally, the scholar Godet writes here: "The third rule fixes the *mode;* the tongue ought to be followed by an interpretation. The expression [*heis*], *one,* seems to signify that one and the same interpreter ought to act for the two or three dis-

---

65. Ibid., p. 235
66. Ibid., p. 234

courses in tongues; no doubt to prevent discussions as to the meaning of any one of the discourses."[67] And as for the idea that the same man who spoke in a tongue should interpret it, he says: ". . .this meaning is contrary to verses 5 and 28, which expressly exclude the use of a tongue without interpretation."[68] Obviously, if one were to speak in one language and then interpret it in another, he could just as easily have spoken in the second language in the first place! Wierwille's understanding makes the entire matter of tongues a meaningless exercise.

Our purpose here, however, is not to deal with the theological matter of tongues either pro or con. We are presenting it only to show that it is part and parcel of TWI teaching and practice—a very vital part in fact.

Suffice it to say now that the holy spirit supposedly honored in Wierwille's TWI is not the blessed Holy Spirit of the Bible. His holy spirit is a nonpersonal, nondivine force. The Holy Spirit of the Word of God is a living, personal, eternal member of the Godhead. As Peter said in rebuking Ananias and Sapphira for lying to the Holy Spirit: ". . .thou hast not lied unto men, but unto God" (Acts 5:4).

Hail to the Spirit—the Spirit of might;
Strength for the marching and strength for the fight;
Power for witnessing, strength to endure;
Might to be patient and noble and pure!

Hail to the Spirit—the Spirit of peace,
Peace that abides and will nevermore cease;
Peace the world cannot give or take away,
Peace for the ages and peace for the day!

Hail to the Spirit—the Spirit of joy;
Bliss that earth's troubles can never annoy;
Happiness passing humanity's plan;
Blessings exceeding the knowing of man!

Hail to the Spirit—the Spirit of grace;
Beauty of bearing and beauty of face;
Loveliness lying on all that we do;
Winsomeness filling us all through and through!

Hail to the Spirit—the Spirit of God,
Heaven's high majesty linked to the sod;
Heaven's dear beauty reborn on the earth,
All things renewed with an infinite birth!

Hail to the Spirit—a Witness of Christ,
Sacrifice perfect, unmeasured, unpriced;
Love of the Father, the Spirit, the Son;
Glory and praise to the Infinite One!

—*Amos R. Wells*

---

67. CFC, Vol. II, p. 301
68. Ibid.

## Chapter Three
# A RIGHT CLAIM:
# THE WRONG USAGE!

"The Bible is the irrefutably accurate word of God, containing no contradictions, and solving all problems," Victor Paul Wierwille was quoted as claiming in a newspaper interview.[1]

"We believe that the Word of God is the will of God. That it means what it says and says what it means. That God has a purpose for everything He says, where He says it, why He says it, and how He says it," he insisted to the same newsman. A typical Wierwille locution is, "God means what He says and says what He means and has a meaning for everything He says."[2]

"The first and most basic key for power for abundant living is that *the Bible is the revealed Word and Will of God*" is the way he expressed it in one of his books.[3]

"The original, God-given Word literally contained no errors or contradictions," Wierwille enthused in the same volume.[4]

In fact, the official doctrinal statement of TWI declares as its initial item: "We believe the scriptures of the Old and New Testaments were **Theopneustos**—'God-breathed' and perfect as originally given; that the Scriptures or the Word of God is of supreme, absolute and final authority for believing, for all life and godliness."[5]

No one who loves the Lord and His Word will object in the slightest to any of these statements, taken at face value. They could easily be from the faithful pen of the most ardent fundamentalist or evangelical. Yet, just as all is not gold that glitters, neither can any such claims about the Bible by TWI be taken to mean what they seem to be saying.

There is an old proverb, "Pictures don't lie, but liars use pictures." In the same vein, Wierwille and his followers use evangelical words but have meanings quite contrary to evangelical understanding.

*Wierwille frankly admits this!*

Discussing the deity of Christ, he says: "Before we proceed

---

1. EG, October 21, 1974; " 'The Way' Founder Tells His Story: Part I" by E. N. Earley
2. For example, see RHST, p. 3
3. PAL, p. 5
4. Ibid., p. 79
5. From an information sheet, "For Those Who Want to Know," released by TWI headquarters

further, we must define our terms. **Many people may be misled because while using the same language or words, we don't mean the same thing.**"[6] So when TWI leaders speak high-sounding words about the Word of God—or any other matter—those statements need to be taken with a grain of salt and evaluated by other remarks found elsewhere. It is as Humpty Dumpty said to Alice in Wonderland, "When I use a word, I mean just what I choose that word to mean, nothing more, nothing less."

Actually, Wierwille and his TWI do not want to be considered as part of historic Christianity. One of the leaders of the cult at New Knoxville expressed it, "There have been very few organizations like us in history that want a perfectly Biblical view."[7] In other words, the position of TWI and the position of historic Christianity are two entirely different entities. What is white to historic Christianity is black to TWI and what is white to TWI is black to the Christianity of the centuries.

This is true when the full teaching of biblical inspiration and inerrancy become known—as understood by Wierwille and his followers.

### TWI's Understanding of Inspiration

For one thing, historic Christianity has always held to a position of *verbal* inspiration for the Word of God. Wierwille's position, which he apparently got from Karl Barth, under whom he claims to have studied, is neo-orthodoxy's *thought* inspiration.

Here is how he describes it: "God being Spirit spoke to the spirit upon the holy men and told them what He wanted said. Then the men of God used their vocabularies in speaking what God had revealed."[8] Ignoring for the moment the contradiction with what he teaches elsewhere (that man is only body and soul, receiving spirit only when born again—yet no one was born again before Pentecost, hence no Old Testament prophet could have spirit), we merely point out now that this is "thought inspiration," pure and simple. Wierwille is saying that God gave the gist of what He wanted written, then the Bible writers put those thoughts into their own words.

But the Bible insists *the very words* holy men wrote were the

---

6. JCNG, p. 4, emphasis added
7. DIS, April/June, 1977; quoted by Kevin N. Springer in "Victor Paul Wierwille and the Way"
8. PAL, p. 79

words of God. Jehovah said to Isaiah, "I have put **my words** in thy mouth" (Isa. 51:16). He proclaimed to Jeremiah, "Behold, I have put **my words** in thy mouth" (Jer. 1:9). And to Ezekiel He voiced, "Thou shalt speak **my words** unto them" (Ezek. 2:7).

The Apostle Paul was decidedly dogmatic about the method God used in writing the Bible, declaring it to be "not in the words which man's wisdom teacheth, but which the Holy Ghost teacheth" (I Cor. 2:13). It was the very "words. . .which the Holy Ghost" taught, not merely the thoughts. Our Lord punctuated the same truth when He rebuked Satan, saying, "Man shall not live by bread alone, but by every word that proceedeth out of the mouth of God" (Matt. 4:4). The very words of Scripture came from the mouth of God, Jesus said.

In trying to establish his own brand of inspiration, Wierwille is not entirely honest in how he pictures the claims of historic Christianity. For example, he tells his readers: "Many theologians and religious leaders have taught that whenever a Biblical writer wanted to write he sat down and penned a part of the Word of God. The Word of God does not say that. Moses never sat down in the desert and said, 'Well, now I think I am going to write the Word of God,' and then got out his shorthand pad. He did not scratch his head and write, 'In the beginning God created the heaven and the earth.' 'I like that.' No."[9] We will agree that it didn't happen like that. In fact we will go even further and say no "theologians and religious leaders" teach it as happening that way today—or ever have taught it. Not even liberals teach thus!

Wierwille continues manufacturing his strawmen, saying, "Some people teach that God took the arm of Moses and shoved it around and, in this way, made Moses write what God wanted written."[10] Who does? We know of none.

Wierwille's understanding of inspiration bogs down a little when he says, "God being Spirit can only speak to what He is— spirit. Things in the natural realm may be known by the five senses—seeing, hearing, smelling, tasting and touching. But God is Spirit and, therefore, cannot speak to brain cells; God cannot speak to a person's mind. It is a law and God never oversteps His own laws."[11] There are no exceptions, he tells us, to this form of God's revelation.

---

9. Ibid., p. 73
10. Ibid., p. 75,76
11. Ibid., p. 78

How embarrassing then, for example, is the story of Balaam's ass (Num. 22:28-30). Did that beast of burden have the Spirit from God within him? Was that donkey a part of what God is— spirit? To *suggest* such a thought is to *dismiss* it!

Illustrations contradicting Wierwille's claim can be multiplied. Caiaphas, the high priest, gave a clear prophetic message about the death of Jesus Christ (John 11:49-52), yet no Spirit from God was upon him. He was one of the most responsible of all the Christ-killers, the men plotting the crucifixion, yet his message has no explanation if God did not speak to his mind with the revelation.

It was the same with Abimelech, the pagan king of Gerar to whom God appeared and spoke His message of warning regarding Sarah, Abraham's wife (Gen. 20:3-7). That heathen king had no Spirit from God within him and it is impossible to understand the story if, as Wierwille says, God "cannot speak to brain cells; God cannot speak to a person's mind."

Then there is the case of Necho, the raiding, plundering, wicked pharaoh of Egypt. The message of warning he issued to King Josiah and Judah, we are told, "came from the mouth of God" (II Chron. 36:22). Surely he had no Spirit from God within him or upon him in the sense that Wierwille claims. If God did not speak to Necho's mind, from whence came the message?

And what about Saul of Tarsus, the man who eventually became the mighty Apostle Paul? God spoke to him on the road to Damascus at the very time he was "breathing out threatenings and slaughter against the disciples of the Lord" (Acts 9:1) and making "havock of the church" (Acts 8:3). An interchange of conversation between a holy God and a lost sinner took place on that highway, resulting in the conversion of the one who was "a blasphemer, and a persecutor, and injurious" (I Tim. 1:13). Yet there was no Spirit from God within Saul of Tarsus. If God did not speak to his mind, how was His will revealed?

### Wierwille Versus Christ

Like most cult founders, Wierwille has a very high view of himself and his teaching. Since he and his followers consider him to be an apostle, it is not surprising that he would claim inspiration for at least some of his writings.

Note how he tucks this thought in a passage which otherwise could be accepted *totis viribus* by any fundamentalist or evangelical in the world: "The Bible was written so that you as a believer need not be blown about by every wind of doctrine or theory or ideology. This Word of God does not change. Men change, ideologies change, opinions change; but this Word of God lives and abides forever. It endures, it stands. Let's see this from John 5:39, 'Search the scriptures. . . .' It does not say search Shakespeare or Kant or Plato or Aristotle or V. P. Wierwille's writings or the writings of a denomination. No, it says, 'Search the scriptures. . .' because all Scripture is God-breathed. **Not all that Wierwille writes will necessarily be God-breathed**; not what Calvin said, nor Luther, nor Wesley, nor Graham, nor Roberts; but the Scriptures—they are God-breathed.''[12]

Note how cleverly Wierwille wrote what we have placed in boldface type. Since "not all that Wierwille writes will necessarily be God-breathed," the clear implication is that *some* will be—in fact, the way it is worded leaves the impression that more will be God-breathed than is not thus inspired. And note the change in wording when he mentions the writings of others. All of his words, we are told, are "not necessarily God-breathed." But the "not necessarily" is dropped for the words of Calvin, Luther, Wesley, Billy Graham and Oral Roberts—their words are definitely not God-breathed.

Wierwille does not have the high view for the words of Christ, apparently, that he has for his own. In his magazine is the astounding claim, made by one of his writers, "Basically, when the lord Jesus Christ came, most of the things that he taught the people of the East they'd known for thousands of years."[13] And again, "Many people had come before and taught the same spiritual truths."[14]

Our first impression is one of shock that Wierwille and TWI would stoop to describe our Lord as a teacher of "warmed over" truth with which His hearers were already, for the most part, familiar. But on second thought, when one has discarded like a dirty word the absolute deity of the Lord Jesus Christ, perhaps such a conclusion is logically a matter of course.

Like most other cult founders and teachers of heresy, Wierwille had to cut all his ties with historic Christendom before discovering his "new truth." Telling about it later, he said: "When I

12. Ibid., p. 83, emphasis added
13. WM, March/April, 1977, p. 26; "lord" is in the lower case in the original
14. Ibid.

started my research, the first thing I did was throw away all my Bible commentaries. I just learned to work from texts. I can read Hebrew and Greek, and I used the King James for my basic text—you have to start someplace. That became my version and then I would work the Hebrew and Greek texts, and if I found something which I could not find in the text work, I would hold it and wait. At the research center we are continuing to work on some verses."[15]

How many books did he throw away? It depends upon which source you accept. *Time* says "he shucked his academic background by burning more than 1,000 religious books 'to clean myself out' before starting his own research."[16] But in one of his own books, he says, "One day I finally became so disgusted and tired of reading around The Word that I hauled over 3,000 volumes of theological works to the city dump."[17] In another publication he calls reading "outside works" confusing, saying, "I suffered from a common disease called basic mental confusion. . . ."[18] Scholars who have read *his* writings feel he still suffers grievously from the same malady, concluding that perhaps the wrong books were burned.

A corresponding contempt for the greatest minds of Christendom is shared by his followers. As one TWI leader expressed it, "We're not concerned with what somebody else taught."[19] While we strongly believe in the final and absolute authority of Scripture, we are not so naive as to think scriptural insight starts and stops with us, or that we are the only one in the last 1900 years to whom God has given illumination about His Word.

Paul did not share that disregard for the writings of others. In his very last inspired letter to a brother preacher he was pleading, "The cloke that I left at Troas with Carpus, when thou comest, bring with thee, and the books, but especially the parchments" (II Tim. 4:13). And his wide reading range is evidenced by his quotations from the Cretians (Titus 1:12) and the Grecian poets (Acts 17:28).

### What Scripture Is for Today?

Actually, Wierwille's low view of Scripture does not present a

15. EG, October 22, 1974; " 'The Way' Founder Tells His Story: Part II" by E. N. Earley
16. September 6, 1971; "Fellow Traveling With Jesus"
17. PAL, p. 120
18. TWW, p. 46
19. Quoted in DIS, op. cit.

practical problem of much magnitude since he thinks very little of it applies in our day. All of the Old Testament and more than one-third of the New is theoretically dismissed with a wave of the hand, saying, "All Scripture before Pentecost is not addressed to us but is for our learning. No one could be born again and belong to the Church of God until the Church was established on Pentecost. That is why The Word says in I Corinthians 10:11 that all Scripture before Pentecost is an admonition to those of us who belong to the Church of God."[20]

We could find a lot to quarrel with in that brief comment. For one thing, the Bible does not say that the church was established at Pentecost. Some earnest Bible students believe it existed in the Old Testament, some believe it was established during Christ's earthly ministry, others that it was founded at Pentecost, and some even after Pentecost. We are not interested in that debate now; we simply point out that the Word of God is silent and any conclusion about it is an inference at best.

Second, Wierwille's proof text, I Corinthians 10:11, says nothing of Pentecost. The fact of the matter is that the illustrations Paul gives in this passage are all found in the Pentateuch, not even going beyond the Book of Numbers—*which is a long, long way from Pentecost!*

In the third place, Wierwille is wrong about who was born again when he says no one could be born again before Pentecost. Quite the contrary, the Old Testament speaks of many who received a new heart, had sins completely forgiven, were both children of God and saints of God, and otherwise bore evidence as ones who had experienced biblical regeneration.

Incidentally, Wierwille makes an interesting comment about the division of the Old Testament, saying: "Jesus Christ, God's only-begotten Son, rightly divided The Word. According to Luke 24:44 Jesus divided the Old Testament into the Law, the Prophets and the Psalms. 'Psalms' means 'writings' in Biblical usage. I had been taught to divide the Old Testament into the books of the Law, the books of History, the books of Poetry, the Major Prophets and the Minor Prophets. I put them into five categories whereas Jesus Christ put them into three. Who do you think was right?"[21]

We are perfectly willing to go along with Jesus Christ on this (although Wierwille's definition of "Psalms" as "writings" is er-

20. PAL, p. 209
21. Ibid., p. 122

roneous; it means sacred songs, sung to musical accompaniment), but, alas and alack, we discover Wierwille is not. He insists on at least four divisions of the Old Testament. Here is his argument:

"To whom were the Gospels addressed? To a period before or after Pentecost? The Bible indicates that the four Gospels—Matthew, Mark, Luke and John—basically took up with the birth of Christ and terminated with His ascension ten days before the day of Pentecost. So are the Gospels addressed to us? Not if the Word of God is right for Romans says that all Scripture before the day of Pentecost is for our learning, and the Gospels obviously come before the founding day of the Church of God. The records in the Gospels are addressed at times to Israel and at other times to the Gentiles, but never to the Church of God. One of the greatest errors in the translation of the Bible was placing the four Gospels in the New Testament. The Gospels logically belong in the Old Testament. Jesus came to Israel, His own people. He was the prophet who fulfilled the law of the Old Testament; therefore, the Gospels complete the Old Testament."[22]

Note several things about these conclusions which Wierwille has based upon his false premise:

(1) He makes the infallibility of the Word of God rest on his theories, saying that if he is wrong the Word of God is wrong because "Romans says that all Scripture before the day of Pentecost is for our learning." But he is wrong about Romans, of course. *Pentecost is not even once mentioned in the Book of Romans!*

Later, in what appears to be a proof text for the above, he quotes part of Romans 15:8 as follows: "Now I say that Jesus Christ was a minister [to] the circumcision. . . ." It is easy to see why he did not quote more of the passage because it goes on to say, ". . .for the truth of God, to confirm the promises made unto the fathers: And that the Gentiles might glorify God for his mercy; as it is written, For this cause I will confess to thee among the Gentiles, and sing unto thy name. And again he saith, Rejoice, ye Gentiles, with his people. And again, Praise the Lord, all ye Gentiles; and laud him, all ye people. And again, Esaias saith, There shall be a root of Jesse, and he that shall rise to reign over the Gentiles; in him shall the Gentiles trust" (vss. 8-12).

So, contrary to what Wierwille wanted emphasized, the early ministry of our Lord Jesus Christ was *not* just to the circumcision, but to the uncircumcision as well. In fact, in the above pas-

---

22. Ibid., p. 210

sage from Romans the emphasis is far more on His ministry to the uncircumcision—the word "Gentiles" is used six times in four verses, an average of one and a half times per verse—than to the circumcision!

(2) He is also in error when he says, "The records in the Gospels are addressed at times to Israel and at other times to the Gentiles, but never to the Church of God." Quite the contrary, the Gospels contain instructions for the church regarding church government and church discipline, prayer, the mission of the church in getting out the gospel to all the world, and a host of other matters.

(3) There is a fatal flaw in Wierwille's reasoning that the Gospels belong to the Old Testament because they tell of events *before* Pentecost. They were not written until *after* Pentecost! In fact, merely to return to his questions, "To whom were the Gospels addressed? To a period before or after Pentecost?" is to realize how faulty is his premise. While the events and teachings found in the Gospels historically took place chiefly from a few months to a few years before Pentecost, to whom were those Gospels addressed? To Christians! To the church of God! To those who had been born again of the Holy Spirit of God! Wierwille is wrong in trying to relegate the Gospels to the Old Testament.

However, when the truth is known, Wierwille really doesn't want all of the New Testament after the Gospels for today. Acts also suffers from his Jehudian penknife and he tells his followers, "The New Testament actually begins with the book of Romans, with Acts being the book of transition between the Old Covenant and the New."[23]

But even this is not all he wants sacrificed by today's church. He writes, "Hebrews is not addressed to the Church in the sense that we know the Church established on Pentecost. Hebrews is addressed to believers who are born again of God's Spirit but who have never walked in the freedom or the greatness of the new birth; Hebrews is written for those who are still zealous for the law. Likewise the book of James is addressed to the same Old Testament-minded believers."[24]

So, for all practical purposes, other than merely being examples for our admonition, Wierwille dismisses the Old Testament as we know it, the four Gospels, Acts, Hebrews and James. He

23. Ibid., p. 211
24. Ibid., p. 213

thus ends up with a mere 143 chapters of the New Testament out of a total 260 chapters (barely half), which he feels are truly pertinent for today's church. And, we hasten to add, this is a total of only 143 chapters out of the 1,189 chapters in the Bible. Eighty-eight percent of the Bible he has relegated to the background.

It is not what Wierwille *says* about the Scriptures, however, as much as it is how he *uses* them that bothers us most.

### Examples of Wierwille's Handling The Word

Paul's instructions in II Corinthians 4:1,2 are most pertinent here. He testified, "Therefore seeing we have this ministry, as we have received mercy, we faint not; But have renounced the hidden things of dishonesty, not walking in craftiness, nor handling the word of God deceitfully; but by manifestation of the truth commending ourselves to every man's conscience in the sight of God." Wierwille, one finds upon studying his writings, has not renounced the hidden things of dishonesty. Rather, he walks in craftiness, handling the Word of God deceitfully.

Here are just a few illustrations, taken at random. Not all of them relate to what would be called heresy, but all do involve "hidden things of dishonesty."

Wierwille, obviously seeking to destroy the impact the passage has for the deity of Christ, attempts to put the Bible, the written Word, into John 1:1,2. He writes:

"The key to understanding John 1:1 and 2 is the word 'with.' If any other Greek word were used for the word 'with' except *pros*, the whole Bible would crumble. The word *pros* means 'together with, yet distinctly independent of.' That is exquisite semantic accuracy. Jesus Christ in the beginning was together with God, yet He was distinctively independent of Him. The written Word was originally with God, yet distinctively independent of God. This is its remarkable usage because it refutes the erroneous teaching that in the beginning Jesus Christ was with God to start everything. This is not what The Word says. It says that He was with Him, but the written Word was also with Him. How? In what you and I would express as 'in the mind of God.' God in His foreknowledge knew of the coming of the Lord Jesus Christ. He knew of the prophets to whom He could give The Word, and of their faithfulness in writing and speaking The Word. This was all with God because of His foreknowledge."[25]

Before commenting on this statement, let us hastily concur that the Bible was in God's foreknowledge. He, who is om-

---

25. Ibid., p. 102

niscient, knew every book, every chapter, every verse, every word, every jot and tittle which would eventually appear in the original autographs. That is not the issue. The issue here is whether or not this is what John 1:1 and 2 are teaching.

First of all, note Wierwille's comments about the Greek word *pros*, the preposition translated "with" in our English versions. He says it means "together with, yet distinctly independent of." We do not know who taught Wierwille Greek, but his body would be whirling in his grave, to use a familiar figure of speech, if he were aware of how his pupil was using this language today.

The word *pros* means "toward, by, near."[26] The Greek word for "together with" is *hama*, although *pros* certainly includes the idea of togetherness. The famous Greek scholars, Robertson and Davis, say that the root meaning of *pros* is "to be near," pointing out that in I Corinthians 13:12 it is used three times together, literally "face facing face," and noting especially that its use in John 1:1 is literally "the Logos was face to face with God."[27] This was no mere foreknowledge; it was two distinct persons having face-to-face fellowship and communion in eternity past.

That *pros* means near, not merely in foreknowledge, can be seen by its New Testament usage:

*Matthew 13:55,56*, "Is not this the carpenter's son? is not his mother called Mary? and his brethren, James, and Joses, and Simon, and Judas? And his sisters, are they not all with [*pros*] us?" They were nearby, not merely in God's foreknowledge—or, more to the point of this preposition's use here, in the foreknowledge of the people of Nazareth.

*Mark 14:49*, "I was daily with [*pros*] you in the temple teaching, and ye took me not: but the scriptures must be fulfilled." Jesus was not telling the religious multitude that He had been in their foreknowledge all along, but that He had been nearby on a daily basis, giving them many opportunities to take Him, had they so desired.

*First Corinthians 16:6,7*, "And it may be that I will abide, yea, and winter with [*pros*] you, that ye may bring me on my journey whithersoever I go. For I will not see you now by the way; but I trust to tarry a while with [*pros*] you, if the Lord permit." Paul was not speaking of being in the Corinthians' foreknowledge—although he was, no doubt, in their minds often—but being near them, close by for fellowship, communion and instruction.

---

26. YAC, p. 1,061
27. NSG, p. 260

*Second Corinthians 11:9*, "And when I was present with [*pros*] you. . . ." Here, again, Paul was referring to being near them; it had to do with his actual face-to-face presence in their midst.

*Galatians 1:18*, "Then after three years I went up to Jerusalem to see Peter, and abode with [*pros*] him fifteen days." That was abiding, being with or near Peter for two weeks and one day of close communion and face-to-face fellowship.

*Galatians 4:18,20*, "But it is good to be zealously affected always in a good thing, and not only when I am present with [*pros*] you. . . .I desire to be present with [*pros*] you now, and to change my voice; for I stand in doubt of you." This had nothing to do with foreknowledge, it was no mere matter of the mind; it related to nearness, with actual presence and fellowship.

*First John 2:1*, "My little children, these things write I unto you, that ye sin not. And if any man sin, we have an advocate with [*pros*] the Father, Jesus Christ the righteous." John's entire argument is based upon the fact that the believer's representative is actually in the presence of God the Father; He is near the Father, able to make effective face-to-face intercession in our behalf. And if *pros* means He is actually in the presence of the Father on this side of His earthly ministry, then He was actually in the Father's presence in the time before that ministry. The exact same word describes them both!

Other illustrations from the New Testament, taken at random from the hundreds of times *pros* is used, are Mark 9:19, Luke 9:41, I Thessalonians 3:4 and II Thessalonians 2:5. *Pros* always carries the thought of nearness, never the idea of mere foreknowledge.

Suffice it now to simply state dogmatically that not one single verse in the Word of God says the Bible was with the Father "in the beginning" in His foreknowledge. This is entirely a figment of Wierwille's imagination, a vain attempt to discredit John 1:1 and 2 as a statement of the pre-existence and absolute deity of Jesus Christ. Furthermore, we are bold and positive in saying that this passage has nothing whatsoever to do with the written Word. It is a case of Wierwille's dishonestly, craftily "handling the word of God deceitfully."

Another example, which we dealt with more in detail in a previous chapter but mention again now because it is such flagrant abuse, relates to his making John 1:13 refer to the physical birth of Jesus Christ, not the spiritual birth of those who "receive" and "believe." He uses his large supply of brackets to present John 1:13 as follows: "Which were [who was] born [conceived], not of blood, nor of the will of the flesh, nor of the will of man, but of God."[28]

He is forced to do this because his brackets have already changed the meaning of the previous verse. In fact, he says, "A literal translation according to usage of verse 12 would be: 'But as many as walked according to the revealed Word given to the prophets and later the revealed Word, Jesus Christ, to them God gave the privilege of adoption as sons of God, to those who continued believing unto the name of Jesus Christ.' "[29] Is this a literal translation? **Absolutely not!** The very kindest thing that could be said is that it is a wild, irresponsible paraphrase, not even remotely in harmony with the Greek.

Yet he justifies his bracket-rendering of verse 13 on the basis of his changing of verse 12, saying, "The first word, 'which,' must be the word 'who,' referring to the 'namesake' of verse 12, Jesus Christ. There are no manuscripts indicating this. . . ."[30] His conclusion has absolutely no manuscript authority of any kind, he freely admits, and it is completely contrary to the context of the passage, yet he teaches it as fact because it fits his views. What deceitful handling of the Word of God!

Wierwille will, strangely for a self-professed Bible scholar, argue that a verse should be changed in some way so that it harmonizes with some point he wishes to make, then very shortly thereafter he will seek to establish some other point, using the original wording of the verse before he changed it! By way of example, he tells his students that Genesis 1:1 ("In the beginning God created the heaven and the earth") ". . .properly reads, 'God created the heavens and the earth in the beginning.' Placing 'God' first in the verse and the Word of God puts Him in His proper position."[31]

While he is not correct in this assumption (the Hebrew gives it *"Bereshith bara Elohim eth hashamayim waeth ha' aretz"*; the word *bereshith* means "in the beginning" and thus the Hebrew opens exactly as the English, not with "God" but with "In the beginning"), just three pages farther in the same book he is seeking to establish another thought, this time arguing from the same verse as it is in the King James, having already forgotten his

---

28. JCNG, p. 99
29. Ibid.
30. Ibid.
31. TWW, p. 3

"improved" translation! He writes: "The last three words of Genesis 1:1 are 'and the earth.' [*Note above that the last three words in his* improved *translation are "in the beginning"*— R.L.S.] Immediately following, verse 2 begins with the same phrase, 'And the earth. . . .' This is a figure of speech called *anadiplosis,* meaning that the next thought begins with the same words ending the previous thought, a repetition."[32] Obviously, Wierwille cannot have it both ways. While doctrine is not the issue here, we offer it merely as a sample of how loosely and carelessly he handles the blessed Word of God—and all in the name of research and scholarship!

In fact, Wierwille is not at all adverse to a little outright deception if it will enhance his cause. For example, trying to prove his "Paradise is always on earth" theory, he writes: "The unorthodox teaching we have had is that paradise is an intermediate state, a purgatory. This is total error."[33] To insinuate that Bible believers teach that Paradise and purgatory are synonymous terms for the same place is "hitting below the belt," a flagrantly dishonest deception on his part. Purgatory means "any condition or place of temporary punishment, suffering, expiation, or the like." Yet Paradise is a place of peace, blessedness, sinlessness and joy. They are not equivalents; they are exact opposites.

In an earlier chapter we referred to Wierwille's lifting of the phrase "children are partakers of flesh and blood" out of Hebrews 2:14, reversing its thought with reference to Christ. In another book he sought to enlarge on that attempt, handling it like this:

"Hebrews 2:14:

"Forasmuch then as the children are partakers of flesh and blood, he also himself likewise took part of the same. . . .

"All children are of Adam, and all partake of Adam's flesh and blood. The word 'partake' is the Greek word *koinoneo* and means to 'share fully.' So all of Adam's descendants *share fully* in his flesh and blood, thereby transmitting sinfulness to all Adam's children. But Jesus just 'took part' of the same, the Greek word is *metecho* which means to 'take only a part, not all.' Jesus took some part, but not all; He did not partake, *koinoneo,* share fully. Ordinarily all children share fully in Adam's flesh and blood, but Jesus did not share fully."[34]

---

32. Ibid., p. 6
33. Ibid., p. 95
34. Ibid., p. 159

Once again Wierwille is guilty of defining Greek to suit his own purposes. (Perhaps he will soon publish his own Greek and Hebrew lexicons, since his definitions are so radically different from the consensus of historic Greek and Hebrew scholarship!) The Greek word *koinoneo* simply means "to have in common," but Wierwille has added his idea of "fully." That the word does not necessarily mean "fully sharing" can easily be seen by its use in I Peter 4:13, "But rejoice, inasmuch as ye are partakers [*koinoneo*] of Christ's sufferings. . . ." Do Christians, even in the most intense forms of persecution, "fully share" in the sufferings of Christ on the cross? To ask the question is to recognize the absurdity of the suggestion.

Nor is he correct in his definition of *metecho* as "take only a part, not all." While the two English words "take part," by themselves, can mean taking only a portion of something (although we do not think the average English reader would understand it as such in Hebrews 2:14), the Greek word *metecho* simply means "to hold along with." Even with Wierwille's understanding of "take only a part," it would still be taking a part of "flesh and blood," which he interprets as "sinfulness." And we note further that "also" [*kai*] and "likewise" [*paraplesios*] are used about Christ; that is, "children are partakers of flesh and blood," and Christ "also, likewise." *Paraplesios* means "in like manner" and that thought is evidenced in most modern versions.

We are not saying that the writer's use of *metecho* and *koinoneo* in Hebrews 2:14 was accidental or without purpose; far from it, the distinction between the two is very real and very important. We are just saying that Wierwille's false and manufactured definitions of the words belie his pretense of scholarship. Let us quote Wuest on what he calls "a careful distinction" between the words: "The words 'took part of' are the translation of a different word from that translated 'partakers.' It is *metecho*, made up of *echo* 'to hold' and *meta* 'with,' thus, 'to hold with.' Thus, our Lord took hold of human nature without its sin in the incarnation, and held it to Himself as an additional nature, thus associating Himself with the human race in its possession of flesh and blood. He took to Himself, something with which by nature He had nothing in common. Human beings possess human nature in common with one another. The Son of God united with Himself something that was not natural to Him. God, as to His nature, is spirit, that is, incorporeal Being (John 4:24). Vincent says that Westcott states the matter correctly. He says that *koinonia* (partakers) marks the characteristic sharing of the common fleshly nature as it pertains to the human race at large, whereas *metecho* (took part of) speaks of the unique fact of the incarnation as a voluntary acceptance of humanity. What light this throws upon the Bible's attitude towards the dual nature of our Lord, Very God and true Man."[35] Instead of being "wholly" and "partly," the difference is "necessity" and "voluntarily."

Perhaps part of what appears to be Wierwille's deceitful handling of the Word of God is due to his lack of familiarity with what the Bible really says. For example, with the help of his unlimited bracket supply he writes:

"Colossians 1:13:

"Who hath delivered us from the power of darkness, and hath translated *us* into the kingdom of [by] his dear Son.

"This kingdom cannot be the 'kingdom of his dear Son' for the Son has no kingdom of His own; the 'kingdom is the kingdom of God. The word 'of' should be 'by.' It is the genitive of origin."[36]

While possession is the most common use of the genitive case, meaning the King James translators were correct in making it "of" and not "by," it is his erroneous statement that "the Son has no kingdom of His own" to which we now call attention. While not discounting at all His coming *political* kingdom, there is a sense in which King Jesus is ruling right now over a very real and definite *spiritual* kingdom, entrance into which depends upon a new-birth experience (John 3:3,5)—sometimes called His body and sometimes called His church—and He will continue to reign until "the end," when He hands the kingdom over to the Father. First Corinthians 15:24,25 explain it like this: "Then cometh the end, when he shall have delivered up the kingdom to God, even the Father; when he shall have put down all rule and all authority and power. For he must reign, till he hath put all enemies under his feet." Peter speaks of "the everlasting kingdom of our Lord and Saviour Jesus Christ" (II Pet. 1:11), called by Paul "the King of kings, and Lord of lords" (I Tim. 6:13-15). Other passages speaking of a kingdom for Christ include Matthew 16:28, Luke 1:31-33, Luke 22:30, John 18:36 (3 times) and Ephesians 5:5.

In the same book Wierwille has a chapter on baptism, setting

---

35. HGNT, p. 63
36. BTMS, p. 64

forth his views on this subject. It is amazing—and, if not so serious, amusing as well—the manner in which he reaches his conclusions. Starting with various Greek words for baptism, he multiplies shades of meaning and usage until he reaches the conclusion, "From every Biblical usage of the word 'baptism,' we can only conclude that the root meaning and the basic thought in baptism is washing."[37] While we strongly disagree with his idea as to both the root meaning and the basic thought, his summary opens the door for him to look at different Greek words meaning "to wash," finally concluding that baptism had to do with ceremonial cleansing for Israel and all water baptisms ended with the passing of the Old Testament dispensation, being supplanted by the baptism of the Holy Spirit.

He quotes Acts 1:4,5, then says:

"In other words, with the coming of the greater (holy spirit), the lesser (water) came to an end. This replacement was initiated on Pentecost
. . . .

"Being baptized into the body of Christ doesn't mean baptized with the old physical element of water, but with the new spiritual element of holy spirit."[38]

While we have no quarrel with his statement that the baptism of the Holy Spirit is greater than the baptism of water, why does the introduction of the former mean the eradication of the latter? Jesus gave His disciples a new commandment ("That ye love one another; as I have loved you, that ye also love one another"; John 13:34), but did that remove such old commandments as "Honour thy father and thy mother" or "Thou shalt not steal" (Exod. 20:12,15)? Of course not!

The scholarly E. Y. Mullins and Geoffrey W. Bromiley, discussing this issue, were quick to point out: "The baptism of the Spirit was not meant to supersede water baptism. This is clear from the whole history of Acts, where water baptism is uniformly administered to converts after the pentecostal baptism of the Spirit, as well as from numerous references in the Epistles (cf. Rom. 6:3; I Cor. 1:14-17; 10:2; 12:13; Gal. 3:27; etc.). On the contrary, the baptism of the Spirit brings out the true significance of the rite, inward baptism being the regeneration that the work of the Spirit accomplishes on the basis of the death and resurrection of Christ and through the ministry of the gospel."[39]

---

37. Ibid., p. 130
38. Ibid., p. 134
39. ISBER, Vol. I, p. 428

Does Wierwille have any proof for his theory? He thinks he does, but his evidence leaks more than mere water. He says: "The records of baptism in Acts, the book which records the events of Pentecost and immediately thereafter, do not mention water at all; thus to say there is water involved in baptism can only be private interpretation."[40] He then offers Acts 2:38; 8:16; 9:18 and 19:5, which refer to baptism without using the word water, as if they alone spoke of baptism in Acts, concluding, ". . . we have just seen by examination of the above verses of Scripture that water is never stated."[41]

He admits to a problem with another passage, however, the one dealing with the conversion of Cornelius and his household, where Peter said of the new converts, "Can any man forbid water, that these should not be baptized, which have received the Holy Ghost as well as we?" then "commanded" them to be baptized. Since the divine record states very clearly that these new believers had received the Holy Spirit, it is obvious that Peter referred to a baptism in water. In fact, he said so!

Here is Wierwille's explanation and we admit, for originality, it is a humdinger:

"This is the same Peter who spoke in Acts 2:38. Why did he include water in Acts 10 when earlier he did not? In Acts 2:38 he did not have time to go to his office and prepare a sermon; he spoke by revelation and inspiration. But after the day of Pentecost, Peter was preaching in the synagogue and was still influenced by it. He simply reverted to his previous doctrine and added water. Peter himself clarifies this same account later in Acts 11.

"Acts 11:16:

"Then remembered I [after I had ordered water baptism] the word of the Lord, how that he said, John indeed baptized with water; but ye shall be baptized with the Holy Ghost.

"This record indicates he did not baptize the Cornelius household of believers in water."[42]

Does this explanation and re-writing of Scripture seem incredible to you? It is typical of Wierwille, not in the least out of character. He expects his devotees to swallow—hook, line and sinker—as "gospel truth" such conclusions as: (1) Peter did not "have time to go to his office and prepare a sermon" (what office?) in Acts 2, so he "spoke by revelation and inspiration." But

40. BTMS, p. 135
41. Ibid., p. 136
42. Ibid., p. 136,137

the time element between conversion and baptism was the same in Acts 2 and Acts 10; both immediately followed conversion. How did Peter have any more "time to go to his office and prepare a sermon" in the case of Cornelius and his household? (2) Wierwille implies Peter "forgot" about the baptism of the Holy Spirit and "reverted to his previous doctrine and added water." Since, depending upon which chronology you follow, there was a time span of between 8 and 11 years from the event at Pentecost and the event at Caesarea, where Cornelius was stationed in the Roman army, Wierwille is asking his followers to believe that after all those years—and the hundreds of thousands of conversions that had followed Pentecost—it just "slipped Peter's mind" that he wasn't baptizing in water any more! (3) The bracket insertion he places in Acts 11:16 is purely his own imagination; there is absolutely no basis for it whatsoever—other than Wierwille's need to prop up a theory. One thing is certain: no one would ever read the Bible record and arrive at such a conclusion, unless he received prompting from some highly imaginative soul like Wierwille.

However, since he seems to have conveniently forgotten the most telling case of water baptism in the Book of Acts, we will point it out. It relates to the conversion of the prominent Ethiopian, treasurer for Queen Candace, and the full account is found in Acts 8:26-39. Without going into the details of his new-birth experience, we will just note the evidence as to whether his baptism was in water. The Ethiopian, when "they came unto **a certain water**," asked Philip, "See, here is water; what doth hinder me to be baptized?" (vs. 36). Did Philip say, "Listen, brother, you don't understand; we don't baptize with water anymore"? No, he responded immediately, "If thou believest with all thine heart, thou mayest" (vs. 37). When the Ethiopian confessed his personal faith in Christ, we are told: "And he commanded the chariot to stand still: and they went down both **into the water**, both Philip and the eunuch; and he baptized him" (vs. 38). As if that were not enough, the record gives the following detail about the baptism, "And when they were come up **out of the water**. . ." (vs. 39). What kind of baptism did the Ethiopian have? One that (1) required water; (2) involved going down into the water; (3) ended by coming up out of the water. Perhaps Wierwille and his associates can conclude a "baptism of the Holy Spirit" from this account, but we cannot. (Does Wierwille think Deacon Philip had a lapse of memory, too, and "forgot"?)

Wierwille gives full vent to his imaginative genius again in a study on Judas Iscariot. He opens with this mindboggling statement: "God's Word teaches that Judas Iscariot not only was alive at the time of the crucifixion, but he saw the resurrected Christ and was also an eye-witness of Christ's ascension."[43] If you can believe that, you probably have no trouble with the tooth fairy, Santa Claus and Rudolph, the Easter bunny that lays eggs, or even Charlie Brown's Great Pumpkin!

His chain of reasoning goes something like this: (1) We are told in I Corinthians 15:5, about the resurrection appearances of Christ, "And that he was seen of Cephas [Peter], then of the twelve," so "If the resurrected Christ was seen of the twelve as verse 5 states, then Judas had to be alive during the appearances of Jesus."[44] (2) On our Lord's appearance to the disciples in the upper room on the first Easter Sunday night, John 20:24 tells us, "But Thomas, one of the twelve, called Didymus, was not with them when Jesus came." Wierwille says of this: "Thomas was absent; the other eleven apostles assembled when Jesus came; thus Judas Iscariot had to have been living and present."[45] (3) A week later, Jesus appeared to the disciples in the upper room again. Wierwille offers the account, with his brackets, like this: "John 20:26:. . .again his disciples were within, and Thomas with them [eleven and Thomas made the count twelve]: *then* came Jesus, the doors being shut, and stood in the midst, and said, Peace *be* unto you."[46] (4) As for the divine record in Matthew 27:3-5 ("Then Judas, which had betrayed him, when he saw that he was condemned, repented himself, and brought again the thirty pieces of silver to the chief priests and elders, Saying, I have sinned in that I have betrayed the innocent blood. And they said, What is that to us? see thou to that. And he cast down the pieces of silver in the temple, and departed, and went and hanged himself"), Wierwille says: "This account does not say that these events happened in quick succession. This simply summarizes Judas' life."[47] (5) Acts 1:3 says, "To whom also he shewed himself alive after his passion by many infallible proofs, being seen of them forty days, and speaking of the things pertaining to the kingdom of God," so Wierwille concludes: " 'To

43. Ibid., p. 151
44. Ibid., p. 152
45. Ibid., p. 153
46. Ibid., p. 154
47. Ibid., pp. 154,155

whom' refers back to the apostles (of verse 2) whom He had chosen. To the twelve apostles He showed Himself alive after His passion by many infallible proofs, being seen of them—the twelve apostles—forty days."[48] (6) By tracing "them," "they," "ye" and other pronouns down Acts 1, he arrives at verses 9 and 10 to conclude, with his bracket insertions: "And when he [Jesus] had spoken these things, while they [the twelve apostles] beheld, he was taken up; and a cloud received him out of their [the twelve apostles'] sight. And while they [the twelve apostles] looked stedfastly toward heaven as he went up, behold two men stood by them [the twelve apostles] in white apparel."[49] So Judas witnessed the ascension, Wierwille says. (7) He points out that Judas was the lone apostle not a Galilean, then climaxes his account with Acts 1:11, "Which also said, Ye men of Galilee, why stand ye gazing up into heaven?" Wierwille says: "In verse eleven the 'two men' addressed their remarks to 'men of Galilee,' the eleven apostles—not to Judas, the Judean. Note the *time* of verse ten, when the two men stood by them (the twelve), and verse eleven when the two men spoke to men of Galilee (the eleven)."[50] Then he adds, "Judas Iscariot departed the scene at this time. There is a passing of time between verses ten and eleven which allows for this departure. . . ."[51]

No doubt this reasoning sounds unanswerable to the uninformed, but although a chain merely needs one weak link to be faulty, we think we can show that *all* his links have chinks. Using the same numbering system as in the previous paragraph, note the following: (1) the term "the twelve" does not necessarily mean twelve people. It is a generic term referring to the apostles chosen by our Lord, much as "the Sanhedrin" was a generic term referring to the 71 rulers of Israel at the time of Christ. Second Chronicles 10:16 speaks twice of "all Israel" when only 10 of the 12 tribes is meant. So I Corinthians 15:5 uses "the twelve" in its generic term; actually, there may have been more than twelve people present. (2) Once again, in John 20:24, the generic term "the twelve" is used, not as a head count but as an indication that this group was meeting. As with the previous reference, perhaps there were actually many more than the members of "the Twelve" present. (3) As for John 20:26, there is no mention

---

48. Ibid., p. 155
49. Ibid., p. 157
50. Ibid., pp. 157,158
51. Ibid., p. 158

of a head count nor even reference this time to "the twelve"; it merely says "his disciples"—it could well have included a host of believers. (4) Who says these events did not happen in quick succession? We dare say no intelligent person could read those three verses and conclude otherwise. This means the burden of proof is on Wierwille to prove differently, and he cannot. And does he really think the brief events of this passage "summarizes the life" of Judas? (5) We agree, "whom" points back to the apostles chosen by Christ. However, they are not numbered as to "eleven" or "twelve" or anything else. Just as I might say I visited with my children and mean three of them, not all five, so it simply speaks of our Lord's appearing to apostles He had chosen. We presume eleven are meant, but it does not definitely say. (6) This argument collapses because of his faulty premise— that all twelve of the original apostles were meant in Acts 1:2, something the verse does not definitely state. (7) His point about the "time," which he begs us notice, is incredible. If indeed there were a "passing of time" between verses ten and eleven, the eleven apostles must have had very sore necks the next day, gazing upward for that length of time. They were looking "stedfastly toward heaven" while Christ ascended and they were still "gazing up into heaven" when they were called Galileans by the two in white apparel. And we would consider the fact that they were called Galileans stronger evidence that only Galileans were present the whole time, not that it meant a Judean had suddenly slipped off into the sunset!

Do you realize what Wierwille is teaching when he argues that Judas was with the other eleven apostles from the resurrection to the ascension? He is saying that our Lord commissioned Judas, "Go ye into all the world, and preach the gospel to every creature" (Mark 16:15). He is saying that our Lord promised Judas, ". . .lo, I am with you alway, even unto the end of the world" (Matt 28:20). He is saying that Jesus said to Judas, "Peace be unto you" (Luke 24:36). He is saying that our Lord opened the understanding of Judas, that he might understand the Scriptures (Luke 24:45). He is saying that the Son of God breathed on Judas and said, "Receive ye the Holy Ghost" (John 20:22). He is saying that Jesus Christ gave Judas the authority symbolized in the words, "Whose soever sins ye remit, they are remitted unto them; and whose soever sins ye retain, they are retained" (John 20:23). He is saying that Judas was one of those promised the enduement of power by the Son of God, "But ye shall receive power after that the Holy Ghost is come upon you; and ye shall be witnesses unto me both in Jerusalem, and in all Judaea, and in Samaria, and unto the uttermost part of the earth" (Acts 1:8). This fanciful flight of unreality is further compounded when you realize that just before the betrayal and crucifixion, Jesus said of Judas, ". . .it had been good for that man if he had not been born" (Matt. 26:24).

No, we cannot join Wierwille and his TWI followers in giving Judas such an exalted position and honor *after* his betrayal of the Lord Jesus Christ. That story is fancy, not fact; it is fiction, not truth.

Another example of his loose handling of Scripture is seen in his comment about the word *throughly* in II Timothy 3:17. He writes,

"Then in II Timothy 3:17 comes the next word: 'That the man of God may be perfect, throughly. . . .' The word is 'throughly,' not 'thoroughly.' I have asked hundreds of people in classes to read this verse of Scripture, and 99 out of 100 will read that word 'thoroughly.' When we do not read what is written, how can we expect to understand the Word of God? People are constantly reading into it. Our minds project rather than read. It is basic that we read what is written. II Timothy 3:17 does not say 'thoroughly;' it says 'throughly.' You may ask, 'What is the difference?' You see, I can wash hands thoroughly, but I cannot wash my hands throughly. 'Throughly' implies an inside job whereas 'thoroughly' is for the external. The purpose of the Word of God is that the man of God may be perfect, not on the outside, but on the inside.

"If the word 'thoroughly' is in your Bible, it is a proofreader's oversight. If it were typed accurately, the word would always be printed 'throughly.' One cannot have perfection on the outside unless he first has perfection on the inside. The purpose of the Word of God is that the man of God may be perfect on the inside as a starting point."[52]

If ever a self-appointed Bible teacher made a mountain out of a molehill, this is it!

While we are quick to agree that the Word of God must penetrate to the inside for effectiveness and that the job must be accomplished inwardly before permanent outward results are seen—there are amply other Scriptures which teach it—this most definitely is not the difference between *throughly* and *thoroughly* in II Timothy 3:17. And we are astounded that anyone would make it an issue.

The Greek word in question is *exartizo*. Strong defines it: "to

---

52. PAL, pp. 90,91

*finish out* (time); fig. to *equip fully* (a teacher);—accomplish, thoroughly furnish."[53] Wuest comments, " 'Throughly furnished' is *exartizo*, 'to complete, finish.' It has the same root as *artios*, the word for 'perfect.' The prefixed preposition *ex* means 'out,' and makes the compound verb mean, 'fitted out.' "[54]

Is Wierwille justified in trying to make his distinction between thoroughly and throughly? Not in the slightest. In fact, almost all other translations fail to follow his thought; the King James is unique in its rendering of throughly. The translation of which he speaks so highly, prepared by a former teacher at his research center, George M. Lamsa's version from the Peshitta, gives it as "thoroughly." So do the New International Version, the Amplified Bible, and the New Testament in the Language of the People (Williams). The New Berkeley has "adequately equipped," the Centenary Translation of the New Testament (Montgomery) "completely furnished," the Revised Version of 1881 "furnished completely," Weymouth "perfectly equipped," Young's Literal Translation "completed," and both the Christian Counselor's New Testament (Adams) and Phillips' paraphrase give it as "fully."

The point is clear: Wierwille's distinction is completely unwarranted and unjustified from the standpoint of the Greek. In fact, the only other time the word is found in the New Testament, Acts 21:5, the King James translators rendered it "accomplished." It certainly has nothing to do with "inside" as contrasted with "outside." This is merely another example of Wierwille's deceitful, dishonest, crafty handling of the Word of God.

In discussing the gift of the Holy Spirit in Acts 2:38, he says: "We should know, if we are reading the Scriptures accurately, that the phrase 'baptized with the Holy Ghost' is never used in The Word after the day of Pentecost."[55] To which we respond: "*It wasn't used on the day of Pentecost, either!*" Wierwille has a footnote here to explain, "Acts 11:16 uses these words, but as a quote in recalling the occurrence recorded in Acts 2."[56] But let us quote Acts 11:16, along with the 17th verse, and we will note a serious contradiction to what he is claiming: "Then remembered I the word of the Lord, how that he said, John indeed baptized

---

53. SEC, "Greek Dictionary of the New Testament," p. 29, #1822
54. PEG, p. 151
55. RHST, p. 100
56. Ibid.

with water; but ye shall be baptized with the Holy Ghost. Forasmuch then as God gave them the like gift as he did unto us, who believed on the Lord Jesus Christ; what was I, that I could withstand God?" Note that, contrary to what Wierwille is saying, if verse 16 is referring to being "baptized with the Holy Ghost," then what Cornelius and his household experienced was also being "baptized with the Holy Ghost," for Peter says, "God gave them the like gift as he did unto us." What happened to the disciples at Pentecost happened to Cornelius and his household!

Wierwille also has a thing about omitting, adding or changing punctuation whenever it suits his purpose. Talking about Paul's insistence on going to Jerusalem when he had been warned against it, Wierwille said:

"Another example of a grave punctuation error is in Acts 21 which, when I first saw it, I found difficult to believe. I had been taught that the men of God in the Bible—like Abraham, and Paul, and John—never made mistakes. . . .

"After translators accurately gave The Word thus far, they reached verse 14. The translators tried to help Paul save face in the modern translations by simply putting in commas.

"Verse 14:

"And when he would not be persuaded, we ceased, saying, The will of the Lord be done.

"If the commas are left in, there is error upon error for the truth of the record is clearly obvious. Four times the word of the Lord to Paul was not go to Jerusalem. If that was the Word of God, then it has to fit with verse 14 too. What did the translators do? They put in commas to substantiate their theology because they could not believe that the Apostle Paul ever made a mistake."[57]

First of all, we do not know who taught Wierwille that men of God in the Bible never made mistakes. We know of no reputable Bible teacher who propagates such foolishness. All within our sphere of acquaintance teach that Jesus Christ was the only sinless one who ever walked the face of this earth. And we can assure Wierwille that the translators did not think Paul errorless; they had no compunction in scores of places about accurately translating the sinfulness of all mankind, saints as well as sinners.

Second, he is most dishonest in implying—as he does repeatedly—that the Greek is without rules of grammar. His picture is that the Greek is something like this:

---

57. PAL, pp. 135,140-141

## VICTORPAULWIERWILLESAYS
## ROBERTLSUMNERISADIRTYRAT

Then translators can make it say anything they so desire by deciding *where* and *what* punctuation to use. Pro-Wierwillites would make it: *Victor Paul Wierwille says, "Robert L. Sumner is a dirty rat!"* On the other hand, anti-Wierwillites could make it, *"Victor Paul Wierwille," says Robert L. Sumner, "is a dirty rat!"* In other words, the meaning would depend upon the translator's whim—or bias.[58]

Nonsense! While early Greek manuscripts did have the words written together and without punctuation, in Greek, just as in English and other languages, there are definite, positive rules of grammar to guide translators. And in Acts 21:14 the King James men were not trying to get Paul out of a pickle by adding commas. They expressed it, instead, "And when he would not be persuaded, we ceased, saying, The will of the Lord be done." Wierwille would have it, instead, "And when he would not be persuaded, we ceased saying The will of the Lord be done."

However, if Paul's traveling companions and his friends at Caesarea had been saying, "The will of the Lord be done," there is no record of it. How could they cease saying something they had not said?

Second, "The will of the Lord be done" is a *positive* statement; their arguments had been *negative*, "not to go" (vs. 12). Taking out the commas, as Wierwille wants, does not fit the context. "The will of the Lord be done" was not something they *stopped* saying; it was something they said for the first time.

Rather than the King James translators trying to help Paul out, it was these disciples who were guilty. Their reaction in the light of the context, seems to be: "Paul, we think highly of you as a man of God. Perhaps you are right and these men who are warning you against going are wrong. At any rate, we are only interested in the will of God being done. So be it!"

By the way, once again his teacher, George M. Lamsa, does not agree with him. His translation from the Peshitta of this verse is, "And when he would not listen to us, we ceased, saying, Let the will of our Lord be done." In fact, we know of no translator—evangelical, liberal or cultist—who agrees with Wierwille on the punctuation of this verse. His rendering is com-

---

58. In a personal notation to the author, Dr. Robert Gromacki illustrated this with the phrase: **HEISNOWHERE,** giving the choice of "He is nowhere" or "He is now here"—certainly extremes in opposites!

pletely without justification. Unless, of course, you count the justification of making it conform to Wierwille's theories.

Another illustration of how Wierwille toys with the Greek, making claims and assertions no real Greek scholar would dare advance, is seen in his comment about Acts 10:44 ("While Peter yet spake these words, the Holy Ghost fell on all them which heard the word"), where he says: "Here the word 'heard' is not the Greek word meaning to hear only with the physical ears, but to hear to the end of believing by acting on it."[59] But the truth of the matter is that the Greek is the word *akouo* and it is the primary word for "hear" in the New Testament, used over 400 times and repeatedly for merely hearing "only with the physical ears." In fact, just two verses on, in Acts 10:46, it says: "For they heard [*akouo*] them speak with tongues, and magnify God." Surely Wierwille does not understand it here to mean that Peter and the others with him "believed by acting on it." But perhaps the real clincher proving his mishandling of the Greek is seen in Acts 9:7 and Acts 22:9, dealing with Saul of Tarsus' dramatic meeting of Christ on the road to Damascus. The first verse tells us, "And the men which journeyed with him stood speechless, hearing [*akouo*] a voice, but seeing no man." That "hearing" is further described in the second verse: "And they that were with me saw indeed the light, and were afraid; but they heard [*akouo*] not the voice of him that spake to me." The hearing [*akouo*] for Saul was an intelligible message in the Hebrew tongue (Acts 26:14), yet for his companions that same hearing [*akouo*] was an unintelligible noise completely devoid of meaning. Surely the latter did not "hear to the end of believing by acting on it."

Perhaps one of Wierwille's most amazing twistings of Scripture relates to Deuteronomy 18:15, which says, "The Lord thy God will raise up unto thee a Prophet from the midst of thee, of thy brethren, like unto me; unto him ye shall hearken." After quoting this, Wierwille says: "Moses was this man of God. He was a prophet, one who speaks for God."[60] Thus he negates one of the greatest Old Testament prophecies about Messiah to be found anywhere in the 39 books.

Yet it seems a junior boy, reading the context in Deuteronomy, would know that the reference was not to Moses. Two verses on Moses said, "And the Lord **said unto me**, They have well spoken that which they have spoken. I will raise them up a Prophet from

59. RHST, p. 145
60. PAL, p. 89

among their brethren, **like unto thee**, and will put my words in his mouth; and he shall speak unto them all that I shall command him" (vss. 17,18).

We have added boldface type in the above verses to emphasize that the Lord told Moses this Prophet whom He would raise up would be **like** Moses in His ministry. Now, if He would be **like** Moses, He obviously wouldn't **be** Moses!

Furthermore, that the passage speaks of Christ is settled by Peter beyond controversy in Acts 3:20,22, when he said in his second sermon at Jerusalem: "And he shall send Jesus Christ, which before was preached unto you. . . .For Moses truly said unto the fathers, A prophet shall the Lord your God raise up unto you of your brethren, like unto me; him shall ye hear in all things whatsoever he shall say unto you." We have no idea what possessed Wierwille to apply this clear Messianic prophecy to Moses.

Another illustration of how Wierwille handles the Word of God deceitfully to advance his own ends is seen while trying to establish his theory of Holy Spirit versus holy spirit, along with his own brand of speaking with tongues. Tying it in with the English word "receive," he says:

"There are two Greek words translated 'receive' which must be accurately defined and understood. These Greek words are *dechomai* and *lambano*. From checking each usage in the New Testament the following are the exact meanings: *dechomai* is a subjective reception indicating that by a person's own decision something spiritual has taken place; *lambano* is an objective reception indicating that by a person's decision he manifests outwardly that which has been received inwardly. In other words, to receive spiritually is *dechomai*, and to receive into manifestation in the senses world is *lambano*. Thus, one can receive something spiritually, *dechomai*, without receiving it into manifestation, *lambano*, in the senses world.

"In Acts 8:14 and 15 both Greek words for 'receive' are used.

"Acts 8:14,15:

"Now when the apostles. . .heard that Samaria had received [*dechomai*—spiritually] the word of God [in other words, they were spiritually saved, for they believed according to verses 12 and 13], they sent unto them Peter and John:

"Who, when they were come down, prayed for them, that they might receive [*lambano*—manifest in the sense world] the Holy Ghost [*pneuma hagion*].

"Thus, one can readily see that a knowledge of the exact word is necessary to understand the significance of the word 'receive.' It is possible to receive something spiritually without ever receiving it into manifestation; however, one must receive [*dechomai*] spiritually before one can receive into evidence or manifestation [*lambano*] in the senses world."[61]

However, such a distinction between *dechomai* and *lambano* is not justified, as any qualified Greek scholar would quickly point out. Wierwille dogmatically states that the "exact" meaning of *dechomai* is subjective, dealing with the spiritual, and *lambano* is objective, relating to the senses world of see, smell, hear, taste and touch. It is easy to prove that such is not the case, with *dechomai* used in the Bible of the senses world and *lambano* used of the spiritual.

In the case of *dechomai*, here are some examples of it being used of the senses: (1) In Acts 22:5 ("I *received* letters") and Acts 28:21 ("We neither *received* letters") the emphasis is on the senses—see, touch—not on the spiritual. It is objective, not subjective. (2) Hebrews 11:31 says of Rahab, ". . .she had *received* the spies with peace." This did not relate to the subjective, but involved the senses of see, hear, touch—as the record in Joshua bears out. (3) Paul speaks of "having *received* of Epaphroditus the things which were sent from you" in Philippians 4:18. These "things," as the context shows, were not subjective spiritual matters; they were material provisions which he was able to see, touch, and perhaps smell and taste as well. (4) In Luke 2:28, when Simeon saw the baby Jesus, it says: "Then took [*dechomai*] he him up in his arms, and blessed God." This was not a spiritual receiving, but a physical one involving the senses of see and touch—and, since our Lord's humanity as a baby was involved, it probably related to hearing as well! (5) In our Lord's parable of the unjust steward, the latter twice said to his lord's debtors, "Take [*dechomai*] thy bill" (Luke 16:6,7). It involved the senses: seeing, touching. (6) When Christ instituted what we call "the Lord's Supper," He said to His disciples, with reference to the cup containing the fruit of the vine, "Take [*dechomai*] this, and divide it among yourselves" (Luke 22:17). The senses of seeing, touching and tasting were involved. It was objective, not subjective. And these are just illustrative cases of how *dechomai* is used.

But what about *lambano*? Does it always refer to the world of senses, as Wierwille claims? No, it is repeatedly used of what

---

61. RHST, pp. 9,10

Wierwille calls "to receive spiritually." In John 1:16 *lambano* is used of receiving "his fulness," in John 5:41 of receiving "honor," in Romans 1:5 of receiving "grace and apostleship," and in Hebrews 4:16 of receiving "mercy." None of these refers to the senses.

Wierwille used Acts 8:14 as his illustration of *dechomai* referring to the spiritual and especially emphasized that it proved "they were spiritually saved, for they believed." Yet the Greek *lambano* is used for receiving the same identical experience of salvation. Both Acts 10:43 and Acts 26:18 use *lambano* about salvation from sin, the former saying "*receive* remission of sins" and the latter "*receive* forgiveness of sins." And Romans 5:11 triumphantly shouts, "And not only so, but we also joy in God through our Lord Jesus Christ, by whom we have now received [*lambano*] the atonement."

Wierwille's contrived definitions of *dechomai* and *lambano* cannot survive the scrutiny of New Testament usage. Instead, they merely offer one more example of how he "handles the Word of God deceitfully" to advance his own philosophies and ends. And since he has literally saturated *Receiving the Holy Spirit Today* with this argument, proving him wrong here has the effect of annihilating the force of his book.

One of Wierwille's strangest interpretations relates to "Christian unbelievers." Dealing with the tongues passage in I Corinthians 14, he quotes part of verse 22 ("Wherefore tongues are for a sign, not to them that believe, but to them that believe not"), then comments:

"This verse is addressed to the Church, and the Church is composed of born-again believers. Yet, in the Church there are some born-again Christians who are 'unlearned' (verse 16) and are still 'children in understanding' (verse 20). They have become members of the Church and have been instructed, but not sufficiently to fully believe. They are 'babes in Christ,' referred to here as 'them that believe not.'

" 'Unbeliever,' is the Greek word *apistos*: having been instructed but not sufficiently to fully believe."[62]

We think the context clearly refutes such an understanding, since the very next verse says: "If therefore the whole church be come together into one place, and all speak with tongues, and there come in those that are unlearned, or unbelievers, will they not say that ye are mad?" (vs. 23). These "unlearned" and

---

62. Ibid., pp. 228,229

"unbelievers" are those who would come into the assembly and behold what the professing Christians were doing, concluding them to be insane.

However, his problem is more serious than ignoring the context; it is a case of faulty Greek. *Apistos* does not mean a Christian who does not "fully believe"; it is the negative adjective of *pistos* and means **one who does not believe.** A quick sampling of its New Testament usage should convince anyone that it does not refer to a Christian with weak faith. For example, discussing the sin of Christian going to law against Christian, I Corinthians 6:6 says, "But brother goeth to law with brother, and that before the unbelievers [*apistos*]—those who are not brethren! Second Corinthians 6:14,15, talking about separation, says: "Be ye not unequally yoked together with unbelievers [*apistos*]: for what fellowship hath righteousness with unrighteousness? and what communion hath light with darkness? And what concord hath Christ with Belial? or what part hath he that believeth with an infidel [*apistos*]?" Is the Word of God forbidding Christians to yoke up with other Christians who are merely weak in the faith? We are elsewhere told to "receive" such (Rom. 14:1). And is "infidel" another term for a Christian who is merely weak in faith? (First Timothy 5:8 also translates *apistos* as "infidel"!) And Revelation 21:8 warns, "But the fearful, and unbelieving [*apistos*], and the abominable, and murderers, and whoremongers, and sorcerers, and idolaters, and all liars, shall have their part in the lake which burneth with fire and brimstone: which is the second death." Does Wierwille really think that Christians who are weak in the faith will be cast into the lake of fire along with murderers, whoremongers, sorcerers and the rest of that Christ-denying crowd? Surely not!

His interpretation gets a little sticky even for him when he tries to explain the meaning of verse 23. Using his plentiful supply of brackets to alter the meaning, he writes:

"Verse 23:

"If therefore the whole church [Note the word 'whole' includes the faithful, the unfaithful, and the unlearned.] be come together into one place, and all [Note the word 'all.'] speak with tongues. . .

"Everyone speaking in tongues at the same time in the Church, without interpretation, has so discredited the speaking in tongues for some born-again Christians that they have refused to believe anything worthwhile or good could possibly come from speaking in tongues or receiving the gift of the Holy Spirit. But note what The Word says,

". . .and there come in *those that are* unlearned, or unbelievers, will they not say that ye are mad?

"The unlearned are those who, though born again, have not yet been sufficiently instructed to be transformed by the renewing of their minds. The unbelievers are those who have been instructed but not sufficiently to believe to the end of manifesting. When they, the unlearned and the unbelievers, hear everyone speaking in tongues at the same time, they will indeed say 'that ye are mad.' "[63]

Note his dilemma. He has placed into the first half of the verse, as part of the "whole" church, the "unfaithful" and the "unlearned"—with "all" speaking in tongues. Then the latter part of the verse has the unlearned and unbelievers coming into the assembly and "they" saying "ye are mad." He can't have it both ways; if these unbelievers are part of the "whole" church in the first clause, they cannot be "coming in" and accusing *themselves* of being mad!

Do you recall that we opened this chapter with quotations by Wierwille and his leaders about the Word of God, including the one, "We believe that the Word of God is the will of God. That it means what it says and says what it means"? For our final illustration of TWI's dishonest, deceitful handling of the Scriptures, consider an article written by Rev. Bo Reahard, TWI's Trunk leader for the United States and its "researcher on Orientalisms in the Bible," which appeared in the cult's official publication, *The Way Magazine.*

His article was about treasures in Heaven and his basic text was Matthew 6:19-21, "Lay not up for yourselves treasures upon earth, where moth and rust doth corrupt, and where thieves break through and steal: But lay up for yourselves treasures in heaven, where neither moth nor rust doth corrupt, and where thieves do not break through nor steal: For where your treasure is, there will your heart be also."

How does TWI, which says the Bible means what it says and says what it means, explain this passage? Believe it or not, this is what readers were told: " 'Treasures' means thoughts. . . .'Upon earth' means the flesh, the things of the flesh, carnal things, things of the world. 'Moth and rust' mean fear and worry. 'Thieves' are doubts."[64]

No fooling; that is exactly what Bo Reahard, with Founder Wierwille's obvious approval, told the cult's disciples. According

---

63. Ibid., p. 231
64. March/April, 1977; p. 24

to Reahard, *treasures* does not mean treasures, *earth* does not mean earth, *moth* does not mean moth, *rust* does not mean rust, and *thieves* does not mean thieves. And probably no one would ever guess, unless a TWI researcher explained it to him, that "moth and rust" really mean "fear and worry." If the reader thinks he denotes a touch of sarcasm in our words, he is right!

There are several things wrong with this form of fanciful interpretation. In the first place, it violates the context of the entire chapter, a portion of our Lord's Sermon on the Mount. This section has much to say about material things. The opening verses have to do with money and instructions about how to give. The next section relates to prayer, but our Lord includes praying for such material things as our daily provisions. The conclusion to the verses Reahard quotes is, "Ye cannot serve God and mammon." If the God is *literally* "God," then the mammon is *literally* "riches." And the final section of the chapter, covering ten verses, relates to God's guarantee of providing material things such as food, clothing and shelter for those who put God's kingdom and God's righteousness first in their daily lives. There is no way, in the light of the context, verses 19-21 can be understood in any manner but their literal meaning.

In the second place, the TWI interpretation is exploded by the commands to "Lay up" and "Lay not up." This is literally a storing away, a setting aside—not merely thinking some thoughts. The Greek is *thesaurizo* and means "to treasure up." Barnes says it "denotes a laying by in a place of security of property that may be of use to us at some future period."[65] Noting its other usage in the New Testament will prove that it carries the thought of setting something aside for the future. Consider the following:

*Second Corinthians 12:14*, ". . .the children ought not to lay up [*thesaurizo*] for the parents, but the parents for the children." This is not saying that the children should not do the thinking for the parents, but that it is the responsibility of parents to set aside provisions for the children, and not vice versa.

*Luke 12:21*, "So is he that layeth up [*thesaurizo*] treasure for himself, and is not rich toward God." This was our Lord's conclusion in the parable of the rich fool. It had to do with one storing up earthly riches for future use and our Lord simply said that anyone who did so to the neglect of wealth toward God was equally foolish. It had nothing to do with thinking thoughts; it

---

65. NNT, *Romans,* p. 61

was entirely a matter of setting aside wealth for the future.

*Romans 2:5*, "But after thy hardness and impenitent heart treasurest up [*thesaurizo*] unto thyself wrath against the day of wrath and revelation of the righteous judgment of God." Here Paul speaks of lost sinners, through their wicked and rebellious actions, setting by in store the wrath of God's judgment to befall them at a later time. It has nothing to do with thoughts.

*First Corinthians 16:2*, "Upon the first day of the week let every one of you lay by [*thesaurizo*] him in store, as God hath prospered him, that there be no gatherings when I come." Paul was not telling the Corinthians he would gather up their thoughts when he arrived. No, no. He was talking about "the collection for the saints" (vs. 1) and he wanted them to set it aside every Sunday so it would be available when he got to Corinth. It was to be set aside ahead of time, not gathered after his arrival.

The same Greek word is also used in James 5:3 and II Peter 3:7, carrying the same idea of setting aside, storing up. Never does it have the idea of thinking thoughts!

Incidentally, Reahard explains the "heaven" of Matthew 6:20 as "spiritual things" and "the things of God's Word,"[66]—fitting in with his thought-process interpretation. But why should "heaven" in verse 20 be something different from "heaven" in verse 9, "Our Father which art in heaven, Hallowed be thy name"? If the latter usage refers to the Father's dwelling place on high—and we know of no one who denies this—why wouldn't the *same* word, used in the *same* passage, have the *same* meaning?

But this is simply a sampling of Wierwille's and TWI's "dishonesty. . .craftiness. . .[and] handling the word of God deceitfully."

---

66. Op. cit., p. 25

## Chapter Four
# THE WAY'S "WAY" TO HEAVEN:
# SAVING SOULS BY THE BARRELFUL!

Tina Ranyak left her home in Rye, New York to attend an art school in Kansas City. While there she became involved with TWI through a classmate and eventually dropped out of school, going to live at the cult's communal house in Wichita. It was with regard to this latter place that a Way leader enthused, "We've saved souls by the barrelful!"[1] As an evangelist, how such a statement would thrill and excite our heart if it were not for the positive knowledge we possess that TWI means something entirely different from what the Word of God suggests when it speaks of "saving souls." And the "barrel" of TWI is not filled with redeemed, blood-bought, Heaven-bound, Spirit-filled individuals who are only a heartbeat's failure from the Glory Land. Quite the contrary!

How could TWI's method of salvation be correct when it is wrong about redemption's foundational truth: the cross of Christ and the Christ of the cross? Essential to TWI's understanding of the cross is an absolute denial of the dying, atoning Redeemer's deity. Wierwille says, "Our very redemption, the crucial point on which all of Christianity rests, is dependent on Jesus Christ's being a man and not God. . . .To understand our redemption through Christ our passover, we must know that the perfect sacrifice had to be a man and not God."[2] No, man's redemption depended upon Jesus Christ being **both** God and man. If He had been only perfect man, it would have resulted merely in His *own* salvation. It would have simply made *Him* fit for Heaven. God might as well have sent Adam back to earth for a retrial! Our redemption hinges on Christ's absolute deity!

W. H. Griffith Thomas, in his summary of Colossians, lists this as the third of six major teachings in the epistle: "**The Epistle Teaches that Redemption Is Founded on the Deity of Christ.** The work of Christ for us must of necessity spring from His person, and only a divine person (1:15-19) can do a redemptive work. The possibility of Jesus Christ's being anything less than God would make redemption absolutely unthinkable, since

---

1. *Life,* May 14, 1971, article by Jane Howard; quoted in EG by John Cook, August 27, 1974; the former high-ranking TWI official, Dave Anderson, described it the same way, saying, ". . .the people were coming in by the barrelsful" (IS, April 5, 1981)
2. JCNG, pp. 7,76

the death of a mere man may not and cannot purchase even his own salvation. It is here that all modern systems fail which do not accept and emphasize the deity of Christ, for without His membership in the Godhead there can be no salvation, no forgiveness, for men."[3]

The noted scholar, J. Gresham Machen, professor of New Testament at both Princeton and Westminster seminaries, spoke of the tragic truth if our Redeemer be anything less than the eternal God. He wrote:

"This great beyond of mystery—can Jesus help us there? Make Him as great as you will, and still He may seem to be insufficient. Extend the domains of His power far beyond our ken, and still there may seem to be a shelving brink with the infinite beyond. And still we are subject to fear. The mysterious power that explains the world still, we say, will sweep in and overwhelm us and our Saviour alike. We are of all men most miserable; we had trusted in Christ; He carried us a little on our way, and then left us, helpless as before, on the brink of eternity. There is for us no hope; we stand defenseless at length in the presence of unfathomed mystery, unless—a wild, fantastic thought—unless our Saviour, this Jesus in whom we had trusted, were Himself in mysterious union with the eternal God. Then comes the full, rich consolation of God's Word—the mysterious sentence in Philippians: 'who, being in the form of God, thought it not robbery to be equal with God'; the strange cosmology of Colossians: 'who is the image of the invisible God, the firstborn of every creature: for by him were all things created, that are in heaven, and that are in earth, visible and invisible, whether they be thrones, or dominions, or principalities, or powers: all things were created by him, and for him: and he is before all things, and by him all things consist'; the majestic prologue of the Fourth Gospel: 'In the beginning was the Word, and the Word was with God, and the Word was God'; the mysterious consciousness of Jesus: 'All things are delivered unto me of my Father: and no man knoweth the Son, but the Father; neither knoweth any man the Father, save the Son, and he to whomsoever the Son will reveal him' [Philippians 2:6; Colossians 1:15-17; John 1:1; Luke 10:22].

"These things have been despised as idle speculation, but in reality they are the very breath of our Christian lives. They are, indeed, the battle ground of theologians; the Church hurled

---

3. SCP, p. 144, boldface in original

anathemas at those who held that Christ, though great, was less than God. But those anathemas were beneficent and right. That difference of opinion was no trifle; there is no such thing as 'almost God.' The thought is blasphemy; the next thing less than the infinite is infinitely less. If Christ be the greatest of finite creatures, then still our hearts are restless, still we are mere seekers after God. But now is Christ, our Saviour, the One who says, 'Thy sins are forgiven thee,' revealed as very God. And we believe."[4]

Wierwille adds to his own confusion about the crucifixion, saying in a footnote on the same page as the above, "The Word of God says that Jesus Christ was dead for 72 hours. How could Jesus Christ be God for God cannot die? He is Alpha and Omega."[5]

Our initial impulse is to ask, regarding the claim that the Word of God says Christ was dead for 72 hours, **"Where?"** We are familiar with no such statement. Wierwille is guilty of making his *interpretation* of a biblical claim *an actual statement* of the Bible. Nowhere does the Bible say, "Jesus Christ was dead for 72 hours." While we, personally, understand "three days and three nights" to be three *full* days and three *full* nights (in the grave, incidentally, not just "dead"), many outstanding, competent scholars take it to mean any part of three days and three nights. And, contrary to cultists like Wierwille and the Armstrongs—who have a special axe to grind in their interpretation—there are strong, logical arguments for this limited understanding of the biblical phrase.

But that is not our main concern here. We are taking issue with the claim, "How could Jesus Christ be God for God cannot die?" In the first place, Wierwille is confusing the idea of death as he understands it with what is taught in the Word of God. He is implying that death is some sort of "ceasing to be" and that Christ was "out of existence" for 72 hours. No, the primary meaning of death is *separation* and when our Lord died at Calvary, His soul and spirit were simply separated from that human body which had been prepared for Him by the Father. Was He out of existence? Had He ceased to be, even temporarily? **Of course not!** He went, in soul and spirit, to Hades (the Sheol of the Old Testament), the unseen world. There was no dying of deity in the sense Wierwille implies.

---

4. WIF, pp. 115-116
5. JCNG, p. 76, footnote 11

However, because of his refusal to accept the truth of the incarnation—that deity clothed Himself with human form, becoming the God-Man, **both** Man and God—Wierwille misses the point completely. The very fact that He **is** God, and thereby *could not* experience physical death, was the very reason for the incarnation! Hebrews 2:9,16-18 describes it: "But we see Jesus, who was made a little lower than the angels for the suffering of death, crowned with glory and honour; that he by the grace of God should taste death for every man. . . .For verily he took not on him the nature of angels; but he took on him the seed of Abraham. Wherefore in all things it behoved him to be made like unto his brethren, that he might be a merciful and faithful high priest in things pertaining to God, to make reconciliation for the sins of the people. For in that he himself hath suffered being tempted, he is able to succour them that are tempted." He took upon Himself a body, clothed Himself with humanity, "for the suffering of death."

Strangely, Wierwille dramatically insists, "What difference does it make whether Jesus Christ is God or the Son of God? The difference and the importance of this difference is the basic reason for writing this book. *If Jesus Christ is God and not the Son of God, we have not yet been redeemed.* The difference is that important, that critical."[6] Yet, in fact, the converse is true. If Jesus Christ is not God, no one ever *has been* or ever *can be* redeemed! Only deity could make an atonement for sin. And we hasten to point out most emphatically that the Word of God declares the atonement to be the blood of deity—"purchased with his own blood" is the way Paul described it (Acts 20:28).

Wierwille pursues this thought later in the same book when discussing Christ as our Passover Lamb. He says: "Furthermore, the male passover lamb was to be taken out from among the sheep. This is why Jesus Christ had to be a man. He had to be one of the flock. God could not have died for our sins; God could never have been nailed to a cross. God is Spirit; God is not a sheep from the flock. Jesus Christ, His only-begotten Son, was the lamb from the flock."[7]

Part of what he says is true, of course. Jesus Christ *did* have to be a man; in His Spirit form He *could not* be nailed to a cross. But when He became Man He did not cease to be God! It was necessary not only that He be "a sheep from the flock," but that

6. Ibid., pp. 5,6
7. Ibid., p. 78

He be *more* than just a sheep. While Wierwille is correct in say-ing, "It took the shed blood of a lamb to save the Israelites from destruction"[8] at the first passover, he ignores the fact that the sacrifice of that "one of the flock" was only good for a single household. Hundreds of thousands of lambs had to be slain for the deliverance of all the nation. One mere lamb, even though without blemish or spot, was not sufficient. And so our Passover Lamb could not merely be "one of the flock" (although that was essential), and "without blemish and without spot" (which was also essential), but it was imperative that He be above human worth, not simply a fellow mortal of sinners. *To take away sin, He had to be God!*

E. S. Bickersteth notes along this line, commenting about the Suffering Servant of Jehovah in Isaiah 53: "Nay more—It is, not only that he was (ver. 3) acquainted with grief, but (ver. 10) the Lord hath put him to grief: not only (ver. 5) he was bruised for our iniquities, but (ver. 10) it pleased the Lord to bruise him: not only (ver. 12) he bare the sin of many, but (ver. 6) the Lord hath laid on him the iniquity of us all: not only (ver. 7) he is brought as a lamb to the slaughter, but (ver. 10) thou shalt make his soul an offering for sin. If Jesus were only a spotless, sinless man, of-fering no vicarious atonement, how was it that a holy and just God—we will not say permitted such sufferings to light upon a perfectly innocent being—but himself caused him to suffer?"[9] Such a view would be at variance with all the rest of the biblical teaching about the character of God.

Incidentally, is it not strange that Wierwille and TWI should emphasize so strongly the biblical truth—and it *is* truth—of our Lord's absolute sinlessness, that as our sacrifice for sin it was re-quired He be without spot or blemish? Wierwille is asking us to believe that a mere man, a mere mortal of flesh and blood like you and me, lived some 30-odd years on this sin-cursed earth without committing one single sin in action, in speech, or even in thought. Such an idea is absolutely preposterous, even if that mere mortal be a Son of God in some unique sense! And we stand all amazed that anyone could give the matter five minutes' thought and not realize it. Only as we know Him to be *God* can we understand Him to be *sinless.*

Wierwille's misunderstanding of the crucifixion is seen also in his denial that the Son was forsaken by the Father. Accusing the

---

8. Ibid.
9. TT, p. 33, footnote

traditional text of error, he says, "Yet Matthew 27:46 says, 'Jesus cried with a loud voice, saying, Eli, Eli, lama sabachthani? that is to say, My God, my God, why hast thou forsaken me?' This verse contradicts the rest of The Word."[10] No, it only contradicts Wierwille's theories—but this is his typical reaction to anything in the Bible out of harmony with his views.

Rather than Jesus crying, "My God, my God, why hast thou forsaken me?" Wierwille tells his followers that He was really saying just the opposite: "My God, my God, for this purpose was I reserved, for this purpose was I spared."[11] For proof, he offers the Aramaic translation from the Peshitta by George M. Lamsa.

He explains it like this: "First of all, the foreign words inserted in that verse are Aramaic words. Jesus spoke Aramaic. . . .These Aramaic words are left in this particular Scripture because the translators really did not know what to do with them. They let the verse set and added the English interpretation. There are a few other examples in the New Testament to this day where the translators have allowed the Aramaic words to remain in the text."[12]

There are two language rebuttals to Wierwille's theory of "the Aramaic language": one is Hebrew and one is Greek.

The Hebrew language convincingly proves Wierwille to be in error. The cry of Christ from the cross, "My God, my God, why hast thou forsaken me?" was a word-for-word quotation of Psalm 22:1, a Messianic Psalm of no little repute. And, unfortunately for Wierwille's position, the Hebrew leaves no doubt whatsoever as to the correct meaning. The Hebrew for "forsake" is *azab*. Wilson's Hebrew Lexicon tells us it means "to leave, forsake, in a forlorn, destitute condition, without any further care, but not in the strong sense of" *natash*.[13] The Hebrew word *azab* never has even the slightest hint of "spared" or "reserved."

Anyone with doubts or questions about its meaning need but check its Old Testament usage. Here are some samples from the Psalms, for the benefit of any doubting Thomases:

Psalm 9:10, ". . .thou, Lord, hast not forsaken [*azab*] them that seek thee."

Psalm 27:9, ". . .leave me not, neither forsake [*azab*] me, O God of my salvation."

---

10. PAL, p. 154
11. Ibid., pp. 155,156
12. Ibid., p. 154
13. OTWS, p. 175

Psalm 27:10, "When my father and my mother forsake [*azab*] me. . . ."

Psalm 37:8, "Cease from anger, and forsake [*azab*] wrath . . . ."

Psalm 37:28, "For the Lord loveth judgment, and forsaketh [*azab*]not his saints; they are preserved for ever. . . ."

Psalm 38:32, "Forsake [*azab*]me not, O Lord. . . ."

Psalm 71:9, ". . .forsake [*azab*]me not when my strength faileth."

Psalm 71:11, "Saying, God hath forsaken [*azab*]him. . . ."

Psalm 71:18, "Now also when I am old and grayheaded, O God, forsake [*azab*] me not. . . ."

Psalm 94:14, ". . .neither will he forsake [*azab*] his inheritance."

Psalm 119:8, ". . .O forsake [*azab*] me not utterly."

Psalm 119:53, ". . .because of the wicked that forsake [*azab*] thy law."

Psalm 119:87, ". . .I forsook [*azab*] not thy precepts."

Not by the wildest flight of imagination could the Old Testament Hebrew passage Christ quoted on the cross mean what Wierwille seeks to make it mean. The Hebrew language refutes him.

So does the Greek! And, in this, Wierwille is guilty of dishonestly distorting the facts to his English readers. Remember his claim, "These Aramaic words are left in this particular Scripture because the translators really did not know what to do with them. They let the verse set and added the English interpretation"? That is a gross misrepresentation of Matthew 27:46 and it implies that only "Eli, Eli, lama sabachthani?" were found in the original. He says *"the translators"* left the Aramaic in and then "added the English interpretation."

No, no! It was not *the translators* who added the interpretation. The truth is that the Holy Spirit of God, through Matthew in the original text, presented it in two languages, adding the Greek interpretation to the Aramaic phrase[14] and giving it,

---

14. While we do not think our Lord's cry was in Aramaic, we do not deem the matter of sufficient importance to debate here. But as Leon Morris [*The Story of the Cross;* Wm. B. Eerdmans Publishing Co., Grand Rapids, 1957; p. 102] points out: "The form in which Mark gives the words might be held to point to Aramaic, though even in the Second Gospel the words are just as much Hebrew as Aramaic. But the way Matthew puts it seems to indicate that our Lord used Hebrew, and this is supported by the fact that the bystanders thought He was calling for Elijah. The Hebrew 'Eli' would be more likely to be confused with the name Elijah ('Eliyah') than the Aramaic (which is 'Elahi')."

"*Theos mou, Theos mou, hinati me egkataleipo?*" That this clearly means "forsaken" and not "spared" is seen by its usage elsewhere in the New Testament. Paul used it twice in II Timothy 4, saying in verse 10, "For Demas hath forsaken [*egkataleipo*] me, having loved this present world, and is departed. . . ." Then, in verse 16, he lamented, ". . .all men forsook [*egkataleipo*] me: I pray God that it may not be laid to their charge." And Hebrews 13:5 highlights its meaning with the guarantee from God, ". . .for he hath said, I will never leave thee, nor forsake [*egkataleipo*] thee."

Like the Hebrew, the Greek refutes Wierwille's position.

Regarding strange interpretations of the crucifixion, Wierwille has one that surely must be unique in all of Christendom. Wierwille says that *five* crucifixions took place on the brow of Calvary's hill that day. Instead of *one* on either side of the Saviour, he says there were *two* on each side. His head count shows two robbers, two malefactors, and Jesus Christ. Nor does he merely mention this theory in passing, either; twelve pages are devoted to expounding it in just one of his books—and those pages are located in a section purporting to show what a great Bible teacher he is, illustrating how he makes difficult passages simple!

His argument, summed up, is: (1) Two thieves (lit., *robbers*) were crucified with Christ, according to Matthew 27:38. (2) Luke 23:32-33 says two malefactors were put to death with Him. (3) His conclusion: "According to the accurate Word of God, how many men were crucified with Jesus? Two malefactors plus two thieves makes four people."[15] If that seems like asinine reasoning, perhaps it is only because it is! In fact, after nearly 2,000 years of the Gospel records being read and studied by literally millions of people, Wierwille is the only one, so far as we have been able to ascertain, who reached such a conclusion from the Scripture itself. And since he quotes no authority, we presume the thought is original.

Actually, there is no problem whatsoever in the inspired account. Matthew and Luke merely use different descriptive nouns for the same men. You and I might refer to Babe Ruth as *an athlete*; someone else might call him *a baseball player*. Is there a contradiction? Are we speaking of two different men? Of course not! Wierwille acknowledges as much when he admits: "A robber, for instance, would be a malefactor; but not every malefac-

---

15. PAL, p. 163

tor would be a robber."[16] Just as a baseball player would be an athlete but not every athlete would be a baseball player, so we have two malefactors who, no doubt along with many other crimes, were robbers. There is no confusion in the Gospel accounts; it is entirely in Wierwille's mind.

Wierwille and his disciples do have a problem, however, when they come to the statement of John 19:18, which says (without identification as to robbers or malefactors), "Where they crucified him, and two other with him, on either side one, and Jesus in the midst." To be consistent with his other conclusions in Matthew and Luke, Wierwille ought to make a new crucifixion number total of seven: two robbers, two malefactors, two who were unidentified, and Jesus! Instead he merely admits, "Now we have an apparent discrepancy."[17]

What is his solution to this "apparent discrepancy"? He says: "One small word from John 19:18 should immediately attract our attention, and that is the word 'midst.' It means 'middle.' The word 'midst' is a key word because grammatically one individual would not be crucified in the 'midst' of two. With the use of the word 'midst,' four, six or eight are indicated. When a person is situated with one on either side, he is not in the midst; he is between. A person is between two, but in the midst of four."[18]

This is a case of semantics running wild and we add again that the only discrepancy is in Wierwille's mind. The Greek word translated "midst" here is *mesos*. It is merely an adjective denoting "middle" and Wierwille acknowledges this fact. He is wrong, however, when he tries to say that one person cannot be in "the middle" of three. He argues, "A person is *between* two . . . ." Well, that is exactly the word a host of translators used when translating *mesos* in John 19:18. This is the exact word used by the New American Standard Bible, The Amplified Bible, the Revised Standard Version, Today's English Version, the New English Bible, Jay E. Adams and H. B. Montgomery, just to name a few. Even George M. Lamsa, used by Wierwille as his authority in Matthew 27:46, gives it as "between."

But Wierwille is not finished. He tries a little Greek gymnastics in an attempt to show that the phrase in John 19:18, *enteuthen kai enteuthen*, is the same as in Revelation 22:2,

16. Ibid., p. 161
17. Ibid., p. 164
18. Ibid., p. 165

where it is translated "on either side."[19] However, Wierwille asks his readers to note that in John's Gospel it also has the word *duo* (two), so he reasons it must equal "two on this side and two on that side and Jesus in the midst." There is one major flaw in his deduction: *"duo"* refers to "other with him," not "on either side." Instead of proving him right, it proves him wrong.

The plain simple truth of the matter is that no reputable Greek scholar in the world, to our knowledge, agrees with him. Scholars of evangelical, liberal, and even cultist backgrounds conclude that John 19:18 refers to three—*and only three*—men. Here are some samples, quoting only the portion of the verse which is pertinent: "with Him two other men, one on either side, and Jesus in between" (NASB); "with Him two others, one on either side and Jesus between them" (AMP); "with Him two others, one on each side, with Jesus in the center" (BERK); "with him two others, one on either side, and Jesus between them" (RSV); "and with him two others, on this side, and on that side, and Jesus in the midst" (YOUNG); "with two others, one on each side, and Jesus in the middle" (WILL); "with him two others, one on either side, and Jesus between" (HBP); "and with him two others—one on each side and Jesus in the middle" (NIV); "with two others, one on each side and Jesus in the middle" (BECK); "with him two others, one on the right, one on the left, and Jesus between them" (NEB); "With Him were two others, one on each side with Jesus in between" (ADAMS); "with two others, one on each side and Jesus in the middle" (CB); "two others at the same time, one on each side and Jesus in the middle" (WEY); "and two others, one on either side of him with Jesus in the middle" (PHIL); "with him two others, on either side one, and Jesus in the midst" (RV); "they also nailed two other men to crosses, one on each side, with Jesus between them" (TEV); "with him two others, one on either side, and Jesus between them" (MONT); "with him two others, one on each side and Jesus in the center" (CON). Even TWI's fellow cultists, the Jehovah's Witnesses—who hate equally with Wierwille the deity of Jesus Christ—render it in their New World Translation, "and two other [men] with him, one on this side and one on that, but Jesus in the middle." We challenge Wierwille and his TWI "research" team to produce one translation anywhere—reputable or disreputable—which renders John 19:18 as "two on this side and two on that side and Jesus in the

---

19. Ibid., p. 166

midst." It does horrible violence to the Greek.

Perhaps, though, you are like this writer when he first read Wierwille's strange claims, thinking, "Never mind, for a moment, how many the Roman soldiers hung 'up' on crosses; how many did they take 'down'?" John 19:32-33 limit it clearly to a total of three: "Then came the soldiers, and brake the legs of the first, and of the other which was crucified with him. But when they came to Jesus, and saw that he was dead already, they brake not his legs."

Once again Wierwille is ready with a solution—a real humdinger, complete with all his bracket insertions and wild, high-flying imagination. First, here is his rendering of John 19:32: "Then came the soldiers, and brake the legs of the first [one of the robbers], and of the other [one of the malefactors] which was crucified with [The prefix *sun* means 'in close proximity with.'] him [meaning the first robber]."[20] He then argues from this verse, whose meaning he has completely changed with his brackets: "To illustrate how we have been mistaught about how the soldiers went about breaking the legs of the miscalled two thieves: the soldiers broke the legs of the first; then they must have by-passed Jesus and gone around His cross which was really a tree to the second miscalled thief. Finally these soldiers came back to Jesus and said, 'My goodness, he is dead already.' This type of routine is not very reasonable. As a matter of fact, it is senseless."[21]

Quite the contrary, it is very sensible and reasonable when one understands the facts. Breaking the legs of the crucified was not some additional torture dreamed up by already sadistic men; it was an act of mercy. Gerald L. Borchert describes it: "But the mechanism of crucifixion, as physicians will affirm, is such that the weight of the body fixes the rib cage; and respiration can take place only in diaphragmatic action. After a prolonged period of suspension, however, fatigue of the diaphragm will occur; and, finally, complete paralysis of this muscle will supervene. The fastening of the legs enables the victim to relieve this respiratory failure by providing a point of leverage to raise the body and thus alleviate the paralyzing tension of the thorax set up by the body weight hanging on the arms. No matter how agonizing the process, the victim may continue to surge and plunge in this way for amazingly long periods of time. When the legs are broken,

20. Ibid.
21. Ibid.

however, the point of leverage is removed and the victim dies because of respiratory failure. The breaking of the legs is not to be understood, therefore, merely as an act of torture, but rather as an act of mercy, or expediency, directed to the accelerated dispatch of the victim."[22]

Understanding this, wouldn't it have been logical for the soldiers—who had been watching the entire event and noting that two were still fighting for breath and one was not—to have gone *first* to the struggling ones, to put them out of their misery, leaving the still form of the third until last? We think so.

And anyway, according to Wierwille's version, what happened to the other two crucified men? Were they already dead, too? Did the soldiers break their legs? The silence of the Scripture clearly indicates, to all who have no "two on this side and two on that side" axe to grind, that the job had been completed when the soldiers pierced the side of the Saviour with the spear.

Wierwille does not give up easily, however, and he next seeks to make a case from the word "other." He writes: "The word 'other' in verse 32—'and of the other which was crucified with him'—is another key to add to the proof that four men were crucified with Jesus. There are two different words translated 'other' in John 19 and Luke 23. One word is *heteros*, and the other Greek word is *allos*. Both *heteros* and *allos* are translated 'other,' but *heteros* means 'other when only two may be involved,' while *allos* means 'other when more than two may be involved.' The word 'other' in John 19:32 is *allos*."[23]

This simply is not true; such a distinction between *heteros* and *allos* is merely a figment of his highly productive imagination. That they are words pretty much interchangeable is indicated by the fact that the principal rendering for both is "another" (*heteros* 42 times; *allos* 62 times) and "other" (*heteros* 41 times; *allos* 74 times).

Does *allos*, as Wierwille says, mean "more than two may be involved"? Let's see some of the ways it is used in the Word of God. The very first time is in Matthew 2:12, "they departed into their own country another [*allos*] way." Were more than two ways involved? Certainly not; merely the way they went home as contrasted to the way they came. Matthew 5:39, "whosoever shall smite thee on the right cheek, turn to him the other [*allos*] also."

---

22. CT, Vol. VI, No. 12, March 16, 1962, "They Brake Not His Legs"; quoted in LID, p. 211, footnote #28
23. PAL, p. 167

Are more than two cheeks involved? Hardly; man only has two! Matthew 12:13, "Then saith he to the man, Stretch forth thine hand. And he stretched it forth; and it was restored whole, like as the other [*allos*]." Were more than two hands involved? No, the man only had two hands. Mark 14:58, "We heard him say, I will destroy this temple that is made with hands, and within three days I will build another [*allos*] made without hands." Were more than two temples involved? No, only two. John 14:16, "And I will pray the Father, and he shall give you another [*allos*] Comforter." Were more than two involved? No, just Jesus and the Holy Spirit.

Wierwille's case for *heteros*, that it means "only two may be involved," is equally weak. Note a few samples. Matthew 12:45, "Then goeth he, and taketh with himself seven other [*heteros*] spirits more wicked than himself." Were only two spirits involved? No, a total of eight! Matthew 15:30, "And great multitudes came unto him, having with them those that were lame, blind, dumb, maimed, and many others [*heteros*]." Were only two in need of healing? No, it was many in addition to the lame, blind, dumb and maimed. Luke 3:18, "And many other [*heteros*] things in his exhortation preached he unto the people." Did John the Baptist's preaching have only two points? No, he dealt with many things. Luke 4:43, "I must preach the kingdom of God to other [*heteros*] cities also." Was our Lord planning to preach in only two cities? No, in cities all over Judaea, Samaria and Galilee. Luke 10:1, "the Lord appointed other [*heteros*] seventy also." Were only two disciples involved? No, a total of seventy to be added to the original twelve! Philippians 2:4, "Look not every man on his own things, but every man also on the things of others [*heteros*]." Are only two people to be involved in a Christian's concern? No, everyone within his sphere is counted! Hebrews 11:36, "and others [*heteros*] had trial of cruel mockings and scourgings." Were only two involved? No, it speaks of a host of Old Testament saints who suffered grievously for God throughout the centuries. On numerous occasions, *heteros* is joined with the adjective "many," showing a great number to be involved. Wierwille's Greek here, as in so many other cases we have checked, turns out to be a sieve; *it doesn't hold water!*

But now that we have shown his confusion about the cornerstone of Christian salvation, the person and crucifixion of Christ, let us look more closely at what he teaches about how one can obtain salvation.

### Repentance and Faith

Any discussion of a group's views regarding the way to Heaven would call for a consideration of Paul's statement to the Ephesian church elders, "I kept back nothing that was profitable unto you, but have shewed you, and have taught you publickly, and from house to house, Testifying both to the Jews, and also to the Greeks, repentance toward God, and faith toward our Lord Jesus Christ" (Acts 20:20,21). With reference to the Father, *repentance*; with reference to the Son, *faith*.

Surely no one in his right mind would deny the necessity of repentance for salvation. Our Saviour said twice in the span of three verses, "I tell you, Nay: but, except ye repent, ye shall all likewise perish" (Luke 13:3,5). The Lord Jesus Christ, just as John the Baptist before Him, came preaching, "Repent ye, and believe the gospel" (Mark 1:15). Peter warned, "Repent ye therefore, and be converted, that your sins may be blotted out . . ." (Acts 3:19). It is, beyond dispute, turn or burn!

Yet, what is repentance? Since it is a necessity, an imperative for redemption, one's understanding of it must be correct. Wierwille offers this strange definition: "After the Church was started on the day of Pentecost, Peter preached a tremendous sermon. He closed in Acts 2:38, 'Then Peter said unto them, Repent. . . .' He didn't say repent of your sins. 'To repent' is simply to confess the Lord Jesus and believe that God raised Him from the dead."[24] On another occasion he wrote: "How do you repent? Repentance is doing the will of God. It is not crying your eyes out, singing hymns or running to an altar."[25]

He is wrong. We are certainly in favor of confessing the Lord Jesus, but that is not repentance. We are positively on the side of one believing that God raised Jesus Christ from the dead, but that is not repentance. We overwhelmingly support doing the will of God, being obedient to His Word, but neither is that repentance. And we concur that "crying your eyes out, singing hymns or running to an altar" is not repentance. All these things are the *fruits*, the *results* of repentance, not the repentance itself.

What is repentance? The word is the Greek *metanoeo* and literally means "to have another mind." Vine says it "signifies to change one's mind or purpose, always, in the N.T., involving a change for the better, an amendment, and always, except in

24. Ibid., p. 308; see also RHST, p. 98, footnote
25. BTMS, p. 18
26. EDNTW, Vol. III, p. 280

Luke 17:3,4, of repentance from sin."[26] So biblical repentance takes place when a lost sinner has another mind about sin, about Jesus Christ, about the Word of God, about Heaven and Hell. Up to the point of repentance he has been rejecting Christ, preferring sin, and choosing his own way. But in repentance *his attitude* is changed and he now is willing to turn his life over to the Lord Jesus Christ in complete surrender. This is biblical repentance as it relates to salvation. After repentance, of course, the new creature in Christ will evidence that reality through a revolutionized life, including obedience to the will of God (II Cor. 5:17).

However, biblical repentance is involved in things other than the act of salvation. Since repentance is simply a change of attitude or mind, it becomes a repeated thing in the Christian life. When a Christian does wrong, as he often will, repentance is a change of attitude about that wrong; it involves a forsaking of the sin, of course (but, again, this is rightfully a *fruit* of that repentance, not the repentance itself).

We find it amazing, therefore, when Wierwille calls repentance a once-for-all happening, never to be repeated. Drawing his conclusions from Hebrews 6:4-6, which he takes out of context, he writes:

> "What is impossible according to these verses? To renew the sinners again unto repentance. If a person could repent a second time, it would have to be a renewal. It says very plainly that it is impossible to renew a saved man again to repentance.
> ". . .How many times can he repent? Once. . . .It is impossible to be renewed unto repentance because repentance is a one-time event."[27]

By limiting repentance to something taking place only at salvation, and at the same time misunderstanding what repentance is, Wierwille is forced to ignore many passages of Scripture. Christ's messages to the churches of Asia Minor offer a good illustration of this point. To the Christians at Ephesus, He said, "Remember therefore from whence thou art fallen, **and repent**, and do the first works: or else I will come unto thee quickly, and will remove thy candlestick out of his place, **except thou repent**" (Rev. 2:5). To the Christians at Pergamos, He said, "**Repent**; or else I will come unto thee quickly, and will fight against them with the sword of my mouth" (Rev. 2:16). The Christians at Sardis heard the warning, "Remember therefore how thou hast

---

27. PAL, p. 309

received and heard, and hold fast, and **repent**" (Rev. 3:3). And the instruction to the Christians at Laodicea was, "As many as I love, I rebuke and chasten: be zealous therefore, and **repent**" (Rev. 3:19). Obviously, biblical repentance is not a "one-time event."

Wierville is equally confused, if not more so, about the other ingredient of God's salvation: "faith toward our Lord Jesus Christ." For one thing, he tries to distinguish between "faith" and "believing." He writes:

> "Before going further, let us clarify the difference between the two words 'faith' and 'believing.' These two words are not synonymous though the King James and other translations have used them interchangeably. Faith is an inner spiritual development, while believing is an action of the human mind. The natural man of body and soul can believe; but the natural man cannot have faith."[28]

We will be discussing his understanding of the natural man later, but let us first explode his false theory about faith and believing. While the words most definitely *are* used interchangeably in the Word of God, it is not, as Wierwille tells his followers, an error for which "the King James and other translations" are to blame. Their interchangeable use was by the Divine Author when He wrote the original manuscripts through human instrumentality. The principal word used for faith is the Greek *pistis* and the main word translated believe is *pisteuo*; the reason for any difference lies merely in the fact that *pistis* is a noun and *pisteuo* is a verb.

That the two are used interchangeably is easy to prove. In Matthew 8:10, referring to the centurion, Jesus said, "I have not found so great faith [*pistis*], no, not in Israel." Yet He said moments later about that faith, "Go thy way; and as thou hast believed [*pisteuo*], so be it done unto thee" (vs. 13). In Matthew 9:28, Jesus asked the blind men, "Believe [*pisteuo*] ye that I am able to do this?" When they said yes, He responded, "According to your faith [*pistis*] be it unto you" (vs. 29). In Matthew 21:21, He said, "If ye have faith [*pistis*]"; then in the next verse explained it, "believing [*pisteuo*], ye shall receive." About moving

---

28. Ibid., p. 271. John Juedes notes: "We must ask: what wholesale confusion would result if we would distinguish love from loving, repentance from repenting, and sin from sinning, just as he distinguishes faith, or belief, from believing? Each of these pairs has a common Greek root. Wierwille would have to assign contrasting meanings to each if he were consistent" (JPP, Vol. IV, No. 1, "Wierwille's Way With the Word," p. 101)

mountains, He said, "Have faith [*pistis*] in God," then in the next two verses He explained that faith: "believe [*pisteuo*] that those things which he saith shall come to pass. . . .believe [*pisteuo*] that ye receive them" (Mark 11:22-24). In Acts 15:7, Peter reminded his fellow apostles "that the Gentiles by my mouth should hear the word of the gospel, and believe [*pisteuo*]," then in verse 9 he pointed out that God had done it, "purifying their hearts by faith [*pistis*]." Discussing Abraham, Paul said in Romans 4:3, "Abraham believed [*pisteuo*] God, and it was counted unto him for righteousness." He rephrased the same thing in verse 9, "we say that faith [*pistis*] was reckoned to Abraham for righteousness." Discussing Israel's failure to obtain righteousness, Paul said in Romans 9:32, "Because they sought it not by faith [*pistis*]," then in the next verse changed the negative to a positive, "and whosoever believeth [*pisteuo*] on him shall not be ashamed." Talking of the Gospel he preached, Paul said in Romans 10:8, "that is, the word of faith [*pistis*], then he explained what that faith was in the next verses: "believe [*pisteuo*] in thine heart. . . .with the heart man believeth [*pisteuo*]. . . . Whosoever believeth [*pisteuo*] on him" (vss. 9-11). Later in the chapter he referred to Isaiah's statement, "Lord, who hath believed [*pisteuo*] our report" (vs. 16), then explained in the next verse, "So then faith [*pistis*] cometh by hearing, and hearing by the word of God." He opened Romans 14 by speaking of "Him that is weak in the faith [*pistis*]," explaining, "For one believeth [*pisteuo*]." In Galatians 3:6, Paul spoke of Abraham again, "Even as Abraham believed [*pisteuo*]," then explained in the next verse, "they which are of faith [*pistis*], the same are the children of Abraham." Paul told the Thessalonians they "were ensamples to all that believed [*pisteuo*] in Macedonia and Achaia" (I Thess. 1:7). Why? Because "in every place your faith [*pistis*] to God-ward is spread abroad" (vs. 8). In Hebrews 4:2 it speaks of those to whom the Word of God was not profitable, "not being mixed with faith [*pistis*] in them that heard it," then contrasts that in the next verse, "we which have believed [*pisteuo*]." Peter uses the words interchangeably in three consecutive verses, "the trial of your faith [*pistis*]. . .yet believing [*pisteuo*], even the salvation of your souls" (I Pet. 1:7,8,9). John, in I John 5:4, said, "this is the victory that overcometh the world, even our faith [*pistis*]." Then he explained the overcomer in the very next verse. "Who is he that overcometh the world, but he that believeth [*pisteuo*] that Jesus is the Son of God."

Often in the Word of God *pisteuo* and *pistis* are used interchangeably in the very same verse, not just the same context. Here are some samples: Romans 3:22, "Even the righteousness of God which is by faith [*pistis*] of Jesus Christ unto all and upon all them that believe [*pisteuo*]." Romans 4:5, "But to him that worketh not, but believeth [*pisteuo*] on him that justifieth the ungodly, his faith [*pistis*] is counted for righteousness." Second Corinthians 4:13, "We having the same spirit of faith [*pistis*], according as it is written, I believed [*pisteuo*], and therefore, have I spoken; we also believe [*pisteuo*], and therefore speak." Galatians 2:16, "Knowing that a man is not justified by the works of the law, but by the faith [*pistis*] of Jesus Christ, even we have believed [*pisteuo*] in Christ Jesus, that we might be justified by the faith [*pistis*] of Christ, and not by the works of the law: for by the works of the law shall no flesh be justified." Hebrews 11:6, "But without faith [*pistis*] it is impossible to please him: for he that cometh to God must believe [*pisteuo*] that he is, and that he is a rewarder of them that diligently seek him." First Peter 1:21, "Who by him do believe [*pisteuo*] in God, that raised him up from the dead, and gave him glory; that your faith [*pistis*] and hope might be in God." The idea that faith and believing mean different things, that they cannot be used interchangeably, simply is not true and an examination by honest people clearly shows it.

Why would Wierwille try to make them different? Simply to support another erroneous idea: that the unsaved man, whom he says has no spirit, can *believe*, but cannot have *faith*. He writes:

"Having only a body and soul, how does a natural man ever again have a connection with the spiritual realm? Spiritual things can only be known by the spirit, even as things in the natural realm can only be known by the five senses. Since natural man cannot know God, what is the bridge that spans the chasm between the natural man and God? The bridge is faith.

"But the natural man does not have faith because faith is a spiritual element. How then does he get faith to span that chasm?

"Romans 10:17:

"So then faith *cometh* by hearing, and hearing by the word of God.

"Faith comes to the natural man by hearing. The man of body and soul can hear. The man has freedom of will and he has a mind so that he can believe if he wants to. . . .

"Galatians 3:22:

"But the scripture hath concluded all under sin, that the promise by faith of Jesus Christ might be given to them that believe.

"The natural man of body and soul, the unsaved man, does not have faith. Faith is spiritual and the natural man cannot have it. But the man of body and soul can believe."[29]

This, of course, is merely a rambling of contradictory words seeking to support an erroneous idea about a supposed difference between faith and believing. Apparently Wierwille does not even notice the two contradictory statements in the above quotation. First he says, "Faith comes to the natural man by hearing." Then he says, "Faith is spiritual and the natural man cannot have it." So he manufactures a supposed difference between believing and faith, making believing a chasm through which a natural man can pass into faith.

He has quoted Romans 10:17, which rightly says, "So then faith [*pistis*] cometh by hearing, and hearing by the word of God." *Period.* Not so, says Wierwille. His interpretation of Romans 10:17 would be, in effect: "The natural man cannot receive faith directly from the Word of God, so he must hear, then believe, then receive faith."

This understanding, in turn, forces him into another error: the faith which saves is not the individual's faith, but the faith of Jesus Christ. He writes:

"Galatians 3 continues, 'but before faith came. . . .' Then there must have been a time when faith did not exist.

"Galatians 3:23,24:

"But before faith came, we were kept under the law, shut up unto the faith which should afterwards be revealed.

"Wherefore the law was our schoolmaster *to bring us* unto [until] Christ, that we might be justified by faith.

"The law was the schoolmaster until Christ, that we might be justified by faith. Whose faith? The faith of Jesus Christ. We, natural men of body and soul, are to be justified by faith."[30]

But was Paul saying, as Wierwille claims, that no one had faith before Christ came to earth? *Hardly!* There are a host of Scriptures speaking of those who had faith from the very time of earth's earliest creatures, come 6,000 or more years ago. Paul was not speaking of faith in general when he said "before faith came," he was referring to the faith spoken of in the context, described in the previous verse: "that the promise by faith of Jesus Christ might be given to them that believe." He speaks here of a specific faith. In fact, although the King James

29. PAL, pp. 270,271
30. Ibid., pp. 271, 272

translators do not acknowledge it, there is a definite article before faith in the Greek. Numerous translations—Amplified, Adams, Montgomery, Young's, Revised Version of 1881 (margin), to mention a few—give it as "the faith." Others—for example, the New International Version, Goodspeed, Weymouth, Williams, the New English Bible—render it "this faith."

Wuest comments about this: "The correct understanding of the expression, 'Before faith came' is found in the fact that the definite article is used before the word *faith*, namely, 'before the faith came.' The article here identifies the faith mentioned in this verse with the faith spoken of in verse 22, personal faith in Jesus Christ as Saviour, exercised in this Age of Grace. That faith is fundamentally alike so far as its character goes, to the faith Abraham exercised, but different in that it looks back to an accomplished salvation at the Cross, whereas the faith of Abraham looked forward to the accomplishment of that salvation at Calvary. The former is faith in a historic Christ, whereas the latter was faith in a prophetic Christ. Faith has been the appointed means of obtaining the salvation of God since Adam's time. Faith itself did not begin to be exercised on the occasion of the Cross. Faith as such did not come then. But the particular faith in Jesus Christ as exercised in this Age of Grace came at the beginning of the age."[31]

So obsessed is Wierwille with the idea that saving faith is the faith of Christ, not the individual's faith, he actually rewrites Scripture—thanks to his unlimited supply of brackets—in an attempt to bolster that theory. He offers Ephesians 2:8,9 like this: "For by grace are ye saved through faith [the faith of Jesus Christ]; and that not of yourselves; it is the gift of God."[32]

But, to return to his main argument in Galatians 3:22, does "faith of Jesus Christ" mean our Lord's faith? According to the best Greek scholarship, it does not. Vine, for example, dealing with the preposition "of," explains: "In the A.V. 'the faith of' is sometimes ambiguous; with reference to Christ it is objective,

---

31. GGNT, pp. 108,109
32. PAL, p. 293; incidentally, although Wierwille professes to believe in a salvation by grace, apart from works, in ADAN he speaks of "the reward of going to Heaven" (p. 44). Our unabridged office dictionary gives the primary definition of *reward* as "something given or received in return or recompence for service, merit, hardship, etc." In all the definitions listed, "recompence" is the key to the meaning. Heaven is hardly a "reward" for anyone!

i.e., faith in Him, not His own faith, in the following passages in which the R.V., 'in' gives the correct meaning; Rom. 3:22; Gal. 2:16 (twice), 20, R.V., 'I live in faith, the faith which is in the Son of God;' 3:22; Eph. 3:12; Phil. 3:9, (cp. Col. 2:12, 'faith in the working of God')."[33] Note that this very text, Galatians 3:22, is one of those singled out for emphasis by Vine as being objective: faith *in* Christ, not the faith of Christ!

It is simple to show, using Wierwille's strange definitions of *believing* and *faith*, that a sinner is justified before God on the basis of his own faith, not the Lord's faith. Wierwille says that believing is the act of the natural man (something different from faith). Yet Acts 13:39 clearly states, "All that believe [*pisteuo*] are justified from all things." He is justified! If faith is something different, then he is justified before he has faith!

And the biblical interchangeable use of faith and believing is seen when the Word of God, after saying man is justified by believing [*pisteuo*], turns right around and says he is justified by faith [*pistis*] in Romans 3:28, "Therefore we conclude that a man is justified by faith [*pistis*] without the deeds of the law." Wierwille's theory simply does not pass the test of biblical examination.

Since he makes Christ the bringer of faith, yet denies Christ had any existence before Bethlehem, he is compelled to compound error upon error and say that faith did not exist in the Old Testament. He writes:

"If faith came by Jesus Christ, was there faith in the Old Testament? Was there then faith in the Gospels? There must not have been because Jesus Christ came to make it available, and the law was not entirely fulfilled until Pentecost. Absolutely nobody could have faith until Jesus Christ made faith available.

"Jesus did not bring it when He was born in Bethlehem; He did not bring it when He died upon the cross; He brought it when all was fulfilled on the day of Pentecost. There is no faith in the Gospels or in the Old Testaments. When we read the word 'faith' before the book of Acts, we are simply reading an error in translation. How many times do you think the word 'faith' appears in the Old Testament in the King James Version? It appears only twice, once in Habakkuk 2:4 and once in Deuteronomy 32:20. . . .Most people think there is faith in the Old Testament because of Hebrews 11: 'By faith Noah,' 'By faith Abraham,' 'By faith Isaac,' 'By faith Jacob,' 'By faith Sara.' Yet in the Old Testament, it does not say that Abraham had faith. It says that Abraham believed God, Isaac believed God, Jacob believed God. These men had

33. EDNTW, Vol. III, p. 128

body and soul; they could believe for they had a mind; they could hear The Word; they could see the Ten Commandments and believe what they saw. Galatians 3:6 says of Abraham, 'he believed God, and it was accounted to him for righteousness.' Hebrews 11 should accurately read, 'By believing Noah,' 'By believing Abraham,' 'By believing Isaac,' and so forth."[34]

Note several inconsistencies and flaws in the above. (1) He describes any mention of faith in the Old Testament as "an error in translation," his favorite trick whenever the Bible and Wierwille disagree. Yet this would not be an error in translation, it would be an error in the original manuscripts (God's mistake!)—translation has nothing whatsoever to do with it. (2) His statement that the word "faith" appears only twice in the Old Testament contradicts his own definition of the Old Testament, which he claims includes the 4 Gospels—and faith is mentioned more than a score of times in Matthew, Mark, Luke and John. In fact, the noun *pistis*—used in Galatians 3:23, "before *faith* came"—is found at least two dozen times in the Gospels and the corresponding verb *pisteuo* is found almost ten dozen times! Wierwille follows his own definitions when it suits his purpose to do so; when it does not, he abandons them. (3) He notes that the Old Testament says Abraham (and others) "believed God," not had faith in God. Yet, as we have already seen, when Paul, in Romans 4, referred to Abraham believing God (vs. 3), he interpreted that by saying, "his faith [*pistis*] is counted for righteousness" (vs. 5). Abraham *believing* and Abraham *having faith* are one and the same. (4) He says Hebrews 11, speaking of Old Testament giants of faith, should be rendered "by believing" instead of "by faith." But the Greek in Hebrews 11 is *pistis* and that is exactly the very same word found in Galatians 3:23, "But before faith [*pistis*] came." If Wierwille is right in Galatians, then it must be translated "faith" in Hebrews 11 as well. If he is right in Hebrews, then Galatians 3:23 should be, "But before believing came"—and out the window goes his whole theory. He is trying to have his cake and eat it too, but it is not possible.

It is apparently Wierwille's determination to make Christ the bringer of faith—and have it available only after Pentecost—that causes him to end the Old Testament after the Gospels. In fact, as we have already seen, he really doesn't want it to end even there. Wierwille says: "All Scripture before Pentecost is not addressed to us but is for our learning. No one could be born

---

34. PAL, pp. 272,273

again and belong to the Church of God until the Church was established on Pentecost. That is why The Word says in I
Corinthians 10:11 that all Scripture before Pentecost is an admonition to those of us who belong to the Church of God."[35]

When one turns to I Corinthians 10:11, however, he finds it
does not make the wild claim Wierwille pretends. Is there
anything in this verse which speaks of "All Scripture before
Pentecost"? No, it merely says, "Now all these things happened
unto them for ensamples: and they are written for our admonition, upon whom the ends of the world are come." When one ex-
amines the context to discover what "these things" are, he learns
nothing is mentioned that did not happen during Israel's
wilderness wanderings under Moses! Yet Wierwille even finds
the four Gospels in this verse!

On this faulty premise, here is his conclusion:

"To this point, people usually understand. But now take this key a
step further in accurately dividing God's Word. To whom were the
Gospels addressed? To a period before or after Pentecost? The Bible indicates that the four Gospels—Matthew, Mark, Luke and John—
basically took up with the birth of Christ and terminated with His
ascension ten days before the day of Pentecost. So are the Gospels addressed to us? Not if the Word of God is right for Romans says that all
Scripture before the day of Pentecost is for our learning, and the Gospels
obviously come before the founding day of the Church of God. The
records in the Gospels are addressed at times to Israel and at other times
to the Gentiles, but never to the Church of God. One of the greatest errors in the translation of the Bible was placing the four Gospels in the
New Testament. The Gospels logically belong in the Old Testament."[36]

In addition to this conclusion being based upon a false foundation, note the following: (1) The four Gospels were not written
until *after* Pentecost. Wierwille would have his followers believe
that four vital books for the Old Testament dispensation were
not made available until **after** that dispensation was over completely! (2) He uses his usual "error in translation" to sidestep
the fact that the Word of God does not agree with his theories.
Actually, what he is arguing would be a *canon* problem, not a
*translation* matter. (3) This division would rule out, for the
Church of the 20th century, the Great Commission, various instructions by our Lord as to church government and church discipline, His teaching about prayer, and a host of other vital, im-

35. Ibid., p. 209
36. Ibid., p. 210

portant truths of the church age.

Wierwille next quotes part of the opening phrase in Romans 15:8, where the Lord Jesus is called a minister of the circumcision, and concludes from this:

"I do not belong to the circumcision, and neither do you if you are born again of God's Spirit; for if we are born again of God's Spirit, we belong to the Church of God in which there is neither Jew nor Gentile. Jesus Christ did not come to start the Church on the day of Pentecost; Jesus Christ came as a minister to the circumcision. He was the completion, the fulfillment of the Old Covenant, the Old Testament."[37]

We can well understand why Wierwille only quoted part of the first phrase in Romans 15:8, stopping in the middle of a sentence, since the context is concluding exactly the opposite to what he is teaching. It is showing that Jews and Gentiles are one in Christ— and that the Son of God came to minister to *both* Jews and Gentiles in order to make it possible. Let us read what Wierwille does not quote, adding some emphasis to call attention to what the Word of God is really saying: "Now I say that Jesus Christ was a minister of the circumcision for the truth of God, to confirm the promises made unto the fathers: **And that the Gentiles might glorify God for his mercy**; as it is written, For this cause I will confess to thee **among the Gentiles**, and sing unto thy name. And again he saith, **Rejoice, ye Gentiles**, with his people. And, again, Praise the Lord, **all ye Gentiles**; and laud him, all ye people. And again, Esaias saith, There shall be a root of Jesse, and **he that shall rise to reign over the Gentiles; in him shall the Gentiles trust.** Now the God of hope fill you with all joy and peace in believing, that ye may abound in hope, through the power of the Holy Ghost" (Rom. 15:8-13). Wierwille has completely misunderstood the ministry of our Lord Jesus Christ in saying He came only as a minister to the circumcision.

Yet, as mentioned previously, Wierwille really is not satisfied to have the New Testament commence with Acts. He writes: "The New Testament actually begins with the book of Romans, with Acts being the book of transition between the Old Covenant and the New."[38] Here, apparently, is another "error in translation."

All of this maneuvering and reclassifying of Scripture is just to support his theory that no one had faith in the Old Testament (or the Gospels) and, hence, no one was saved during that time.

37. Ibid., p. 211
38. Ibid.

Habakkuk 2:4, "the just shall live by his faith," is a mistranslation, he says. Statements by our Lord, such as the one to the woman who was a sinner in Luke 7:50, "Thy faith hath saved thee; go in peace," are mistranslations! Evidently the apostle made a miskake when he wrote about those who rejected God's message in the Old Testament and those who had accepted it in the Gospels, "For unto us was the gospel preached, as well as unto them: but the word preached did not profit them, not being mixed with faith in them that heard it" (Heb. 4:2). The word "faith" here is *pistis*, which Wierwille says did not come until Christ and was not appropriated until after Pentecost. Yet the inspired writer of Hebrews blames the rejection on Old Testament sinners, not the unavailability of faith. And he pointedly declares that it was mixed with faith on the part of himself and others.

Wierwille, however, is dogmatic in insisting that this could not be true. He says, "The new birth was not available until the day of Pentecost."[39] Even the apostles were not born again when they labored for and with the Lord. Wierwille writes: "Jesus Christ came to make the new birth available. Some people believe that the apostles were born again while Jesus was here; but if the apostles could have been born again while Jesus was on earth, Jesus Christ wouldn't have needed to die upon Calvary's cross; God wouldn't have needed to give the holy spirit. . . .No one, absolutely no one, was born again until the day of Pentecost. Everyone until that time was just body and soul, without eternal life."[40]

Ignoring for the moment the fact that the most complete and thorough discussion of the new birth in the Bible is in what he calls the Old Testament (John 3:1-15), the reader will note that Wierwille is abandoning his favorite doctrine of "foreknowledge" here. We have seen that all the statements in the Word of God about the preexistence of Jesus Christ are passed off by Wierwille as His existing only in "foreknowledge." Well, why couldn't Old Testament people, when they placed faith in God, be born again *on the basis of God's foreknowledge about Calvary?* Especially when that very thing is spelled out so clearly in Scripture! While not one single word is given in Scripture about Christ existing in the Father's foreknowledge, Revelation 13:8 speaks of those "whose names are not written in the book of life of the

39. JCNG, p. 130
40. PAL, p. 289

Lamb slain from the foundation of the world." While this verse highlights those whose names were *not* written, it clearly indicates that the names of the saved, the born again, *were* written. Here are names written before the fact! Even more clearly, it speaks of "the Lamb slain from the foundation of the world." When God *decrees* something, He considers it as good as *done*— so saying none could be saved before the historical act is absurd.

Wierwille says no one was a son of God before Pentecost. "This is the reason men in the Old Testament were not sons of God. Abraham was a servant of God and Moses was a servant of God because sonship was not yet available."[41]

His explanation of this is as follows:

"From time to time in the Old Testament, Israel is referred to as a son. But reading it carefully, one will see that Israel is not a son by birth but by adoption. If you adopt someone, he does not have your blood in him; he does not have your seed in him. . . .

"Now we are sons of God because of birth.

"Galatians 4:6,7:

"And because ye are sons, God hath sent forth the Spirit of his Son into your hearts, crying, Abba, Father.

"Wherefore thou art no more a servant, but a son; and if a son, then an heir of God through Christ."[42]

But this confusion Wierwille espouses about adoption is contradicted by the very context of the Galatians passage he quotes. The two previous verses say: "When the fulness of the time was come, God sent forth his Son, made of a woman, made under the law, To redeem them that were under the law, that we might receive the adoption of sons" (4:4,5). So it is the "we" of the New Testament dispensation who are sons by "adoption," according to this passage, not those of the Old Testament.

Not only so, but when God described the spiritual relationship of His sons in the Old Testament, He said in Exodus 4:22 (a verse, strangely, Wierwille uses to prove his unusual view of adoption[43]), "And thou shalt say unto Pharaoh, Thus saith the Lord, Israel is my son, **even my firstborn**." This is birth, not adoption. The word translated firstborn is the Hebrew *bekeh*, which comes from the root *bakar*, meaning "to burst the womb." In fact, *bekeh* is used in Numbers 3:12, "the firstborn [*bekeh*] that openeth the matrix." There is no thought of adoption in Exodus 4:22.

41. Ibid., p. 314
42. Ibid.
43. TWW, p. 71

The entire problem, of course, is that Wierwille does not understand the meaning of adoption. He gives the word a 20th century English interpretation when the true understanding hinges on the first century meaning, usage and practice. The word adoption, biblically, is *huiothesia* and comes from *huios*, meaning son, and *thesis*, meaning placing. It literally means "son placing."

According to today's English, adoption is taking someone else's son and legally making him yours. The meaning of first century Greek was one of placing for *privileges*, not *relationship*. Those who by faith have been *born* into the family of God through a second birth are also *placed* in a position (legalized, you might say, by the courts of Heaven) entitling them to be heirs of God and joint-heirs with Jesus Christ. They become sons the moment they trust Christ, but not all the privileges are realized in this life. That is why, in Romans 8:23, one aspect of this adoption is described as future: "to wit, the redemption of our body." As we wrote elsewhere: "The word *adoption* here is 'son-placing.' It refers to the custom in ancient times wherein a man took to the forum the children he wanted as heirs and had them recognized as legally his. They were his children both by birth and by son-placing. So we are born into the family of God (children by birth), and are legally placed as sons before the courts of Heaven (adopted as children)."[44]

A recent writer expressed it: "The Greek word literally means 'the placing of a son.' Notice that it is not the *making* of the son, but the *placing* of a son. Therefore, it is not the taking of a child of another family and making him one's own. That is not spiritual adoption. This adoption takes a child who is God's own, a son, and places him as an *adult* son with all its privileges and responsibilities."[45]

Earlier in this book, dealing with the deity of Jesus Christ, we examined Wierwille's teaching as it related to a key verse, John 1:12, but we wish to mention it again here because he make it appear to endorse a salvation by works. He writes: "A literal translation according to usage of verse 12 would be: 'But as many as walked according to the revealed Word given to the prophets and later the revealed Word, Jesus Christ, to them God gave the privilege of adoption as sons of God, to those who continued

---

44. SGS, p. 39
45. GNB, September, 1979, "Adoption—The Placing of a Son" by John F. Fletcher; emphasis in the original

believing unto the name of Jesus Christ."[46]

In the first place, that is not a literal translation at all, it is a wild paraphrase (at best). In the second place, he is making this "adoption as sons" only for those who "walked according to the revealed Word," walked according to "the revealed Word, Jesus Christ," and "who continued believing." Quite apart from an instantaneous salvation the moment the sinner believes, this is a progressive redemption of works and human effort. Wierwille is even more open about this salvation by works for pre-Pentecost converts, saying, "Before the accomplishments of Jesus Christ, the law had to be kept by man for his salvation."[47]

Is this true? Not if you believe the Apostle Paul! Quite the contrary, Paul said it was impossible for one to be saved by the law and that, anyway, that was not why God gave it. He wrote to the Romans: "Now we know that what things soever the law saith, it saith to them who are under the law: that every mouth may be stopped, and all the world may become guilty before God. Therefore by the deeds of the law there shall no flesh be justified in his sight: for by the law is the knowledge of sin" (Rom. 3:19,20). This impossibility of salvation through keeping the law was highlighted by Paul on this ground: "For as many as are of the works of the law are under the curse: for it is written, Cursed is every one that continueth not in all things which are written in the book of the law to do them. But that no man is justified by the law in the sight of God, it is evident: for, The just shall live by faith" (Gal. 3:10,11). Note carefully that Paul insisted "no man" could be saved by the law, also pointing out that the Old Testament plan of salvation was exactly the same as the New Testament, "The just shall live by his faith" (Hab. 2:4). James explained this inability to gain salvation by law-keeping, pointing out: "For whosoever shall keep the whole law, and yet offend in one point, he is guilty of all" (2:10). The breaking of *one* commandment would forfeit *any* hope of salvation! Yet Wierwille is stuck with his idea of man having to keep the law to gain salvation—because of his erroneous claim that there was no faith before Jesus Christ came; in fact, none before Pentecost.

One reason for his confusion about salvation, perhaps, is that he does not understand what it is. In attempting a definition, he wrote: "What does the word 'salvation' mean? It means

46. JCNG, p. 99
47. Ibid., p. 105
48. NDC, p. 28

wholeness or soundness: mental, physical, spiritual."[48] While wholeness may be included as a fringe benefit, that is not its meaning. The word translated salvation is the Greek *soteria* and it simply means deliverance, preservation. The believer has part of his salvation, the spiritual, the moment he trusts Christ (Acts 16:30,31). The physical phase awaits the second coming (Rom. 8:22-25).

Regarding the new birth, Wierwille has a strange twist, teaching that some are "born again" of the Devil! After discussing his idea of the new birth for those who trust Christ, he continues: "However, there is another possibility for John. Rather than confessing Jesus as Lord, he believes the Devil is the true god. Then John Doe, a man of body and soul, is born again of the seed of the serpent. He is born again of seed, and seed cannot be removed. Because this seed cannot be removed, it is an unforgivable sin.

"When John Doe accepts the Devil as god, he is born again of the seed of the serpent, the seed of the Devil. He then has the hate of the Devil, even as he who accepts the God and Father of the Lord Jesus Christ has the love of God. One man has eternal death, while the man born again of God's seed has eternal life. The households of the two gods are complete opposites. There are two seeds and two antithetical essences.

"It is possible for a man of body and soul to go through life and never accept either god. A person does not always make this choice. But if he does choose, he has only two alternatives. He can either accept the Lord Jesus Christ as his personal Lord or accept the Devil. If he accepts the Devil he is born again of the seed of the serpent, it is unforgivable (unrepentable) because a person cannot get rid of seed. It is permanent."[49]

There are a lot of things wrong with this statement, the most obvious being that Wierwille made it all up. The Word of God says absolutely nothing about a new birth whereby one is born into the family of Satan. In the second place, the people to whom Jesus spoke in John 8:44 had not confessed the Devil as their god, yet Christ said to them: "Ye are of your father the devil, and the lusts of your father ye will do." In fact, these people, as far as "confessing" was concerned, were loud and long in confessing Jehovah God as their Father. The thought of their confessing Satan as father is totally absurd. Third, some have received the Devil as their god—they literally became Satan worshipers—yet

---

49. PAL, pp. 319,320; see also TWW, pp. 58,59

later came to receive Christ as Lord and Saviour, loving and serving Him faithfully. One tells her gruesome story in the book, *We Found Our Way Out.*[50] This young woman signed a vow in her own blood, "I give to thee, O Satan, my heart, body and soul." The very day she was to end her life, at the instruction of Satan, she surrendered to Jesus Christ, was born again, and happily serves Christ today in a Bible conference center, helping to publish and distribute gospel tracts. Thank God, there are *no* impossible cases! As our Lord said, ". . .him that cometh to me I will in no wise cast out" (John 6:37). And we are assured in Hebrews 7:25, "He is able also to save them to the uttermost that come unto God by him, seeing he ever liveth to make intercession for them."

Can children of Satan become the sons of God? The Word of God says they can! Paul, writing to "the saints" and "faithful in Christ Jesus" at Ephesus (1:1), reminded them of what they were before conversion. He called them "the children of disobedience" (2:2) and said they "were by nature the children of wrath" (2:3). In fact, he pointed out that "the spirit" that worked in them was that of Satan, "the prince of the power of the air" (2:2). Remember that Wierwille says for one to have the "spirit" of Satan in him is to be born of Satan; yet these Ephesian saints once lived with his spirit operating in them, but now they were the children of God. While being born again of Satan is a thought foreign to the Bible, absolutely *anyone who wants to come* to Christ for salvation *may come* and be saved. A correct understanding of the unpardonable sin would show it not in contradiction to our Lord's "whosoever will" guarantees in any way whatsoever.

Before we leave the matter of Wierwille's understanding of the new birth, perhaps we should remind the reader that he equates it with "speaking in tongues"—a matter he picked up from the Oral Roberts group. After quoting Acts 2:1-4, he comments: "In these four verses, we have the complete record of the receiving of the gift, *pneuma hagion*, power from on high, by twelve apostles. The speaking in tongues was the external manifestation of the receiving of the gift of holy spirit. In Mark 16:17, Jesus says that believers in His name 'shall [absolutely] speak with new tongues.' The new birth was available for the first time with Pentecost."[51]

---

50. Chapter 13, "I Worshiped Satan," pp. 107-113
51. JCNG, p. 131

Without going into detail here, we reply: (1) A host of people were born again in the Bible without speaking in tongues. They received the Holy Spirit without any outward manifestation such as tongues. (2) If, as Wierwille has inserted with his brackets, one who is born again shall "absolutely" speak with new tongues, he is stuck with teaching successful snake handling on the same occasion. The next five words after the verse Wierwille quoted—and they are part of the same sentence—say "they shall take up serpents" (vs. 18). Remember, Wierwille says the "shall" means "absolutely." And, since the latter part of the verse (and still the same sentence) says "they shall lay hands on the sick, and they shall recover," if speaking in tongues is the external manifestation of being born again, so is laying hands on the sick and seeing them recover! In other words, a Wierwille experience of the new birth would instantly result in the new convert's becoming, as an outward manifestation of that birth, an instantaneous divine healer! We seriously doubt that Wierwille believes this, but it is the forced conclusion of his "tongues" claim.

It is time, perhaps, to examine a teaching the reader will have noted all through Wierwille's discussion of salvation: that the natural man does not have a spirit. After quoting Ephesians 2:1, he says: "What does *dead* mean? Man appeared to be lively. He had body and soul, but was dead in trespasses and sins because he had no spirit."[52] Not until a man is saved does he have a spirit, Wierwille teaches. "When a man is born again of God's Spirit, this man of body and soul then has spirit."[53] And he explains, "When the Bible speaks of the man of body and soul, it refers to the man who is *not* born again of God's Spirit."[54]

The word for spirit in the Old Testament, when man did not possess a spirit according to Wierwille, is the Hebrew word *ruach*. This word is used no matter the *kind* of spirit: God's, man's, or beast's. For example, of God's Spirit Genesis 1:2 says, "and the Spirit [*ruach*] of God moved upon the face of the waters," and Genesis 6:3 declares, "And the Lord said, My spirit [*ruach*] shall not always strive with man." Examples of *ruach* being used of man are in Genesis 45:27, ". . . .and when he saw the wagons which Joseph had sent to carry him, the spirit [*ruach*] of Jacob their father revived," and in Psalm 77:6, "I call

52. PAL, p. 270
53. Ibid., p. 299; note Wierwille's small "s" on spirit, indicating that he considers it to be an impersonal gift, not God the Holy Spirit.
54. JCNG, p. 64, footnote #3

to remembrance my song in the night: I commune with mine own heart: and my spirit [ruach] made diligent search." And it is even used with reference to an animal in Ecclesiastes 3:21: "Who knoweth the spirit [ruach] of man that goeth upward, and the spirit [ruach] of the beast that goeth downward to the earth?"

Without going into the deep theological ramifications involved, it will suffice our purpose now just to show Wierwille wrong in denying that the natural man has a spirit. In Numbers 16:22, Moses and Aaron said to Jehovah, "O God, the God of the spirits [ruach] of all flesh, shall one man sin, and wilt thou be wroth with all the congregation?" Note that "all flesh," all men, have spirits.

Wierwille says there is no spirit in man unless he has been born again—and he says none had spirit in the Old Testament. Yet Job 32:8 says, "But there is a spirit [ruach] in man: and the inspiration of the Almighty giveth them understanding." Not only does man have a spirit, that spirit is capable of intelligence (understanding). And remember that God said to Moses about Joshua the son of Nun, "a man in whom is the spirit [ruach]" (Num. 27:18).

Even the lost of the Old Testament had a spirit within them. Of a wicked enemy of Israel, Deuteronomy 2:30 says, "Sihon king of Heshbon would not let us pass by him: for the Lord thy God hardened his spirit [ruach], and made his heart obstinate, that he might deliver him into thy hand, as appeareth this day."

Wierwille says that if man has spirit within him, it is God's Holy Spirit. We have some serious, earnest questions for him about this. Does Job 15:12,13 ("Why doth thine heart carry thee away? and what do thy eyes wink at, That thou turnest thy spirit [ruach] against God, and lettest such words go out of thy mouth?") mean that man can turn God's Holy Spirit against God? Does Psalm 78:8 ("And might not be as their fathers, a stubborn and rebellious generation; a generation that set not their heart aright, and whose spirit [ruach] was not stedfast with God") mean that God's Holy Spirit in a man can become "not stedfast with God"? Does Proverbs 16:18 ("Pride goeth before destruction, and an haughty spirit [ruach] before a fall") mean that God's Holy Spirit can be haughty? Does Proverbs 16:32 ("He that is slow to anger is better than the mighty; and he that ruleth his spirit [ruach] than he that taketh a city") mean that God's Holy Spirit can be ruled by man and that it is good for man to do so—even better than capturing a city? Does Isaiah

57:16 ("For I will not contend for ever, neither will I be always wroth: for the spirit [*ruach*] should fail before me, and the souls which I have made") mean that God's Holy Spirit can fail? What is the "new heart and a new spirit [*ruach*]" of Ezekiel 18:31 if the "old spirit" would be God's Spirit? Our question is the same in Ezekiel 36:26,27. And what is the "walking in the spirit [*ruach*] and falsehood" of Micah 2:11?

Let us sum up this chapter by saying The Way's "way" to Heaven leads to Hell because:

1. It has a wrong, non-biblical understanding of repentance.

2. It has a wrong, non-biblical understanding of faith.

3. It has a wrong, non-biblical understanding of the Saviour's sacrifice on Calvary.

4. More vital than any of the above, it has a saviour who is merely human, a fellow man. Only a Saviour who is deity has power to redeem!

Instead of saving souls by the barrelful, TWI and its founder/head Wierwille are damning them, giving them a false hope that leads to the same slavery of mind and will as all other cults. The only solution is found in the Saviour's words: "Ye shall know the truth, and the truth shall make you free. . . .If the Son therefore shall make you free, ye shall be free indeed" (John 8:32,36).

## Chapter Five
# LIFE AFTER DEATH

Moses, Elijah, David, Jeremiah, Mary, Daniel, Peter, Lydia, Paul, James, John, Matthew and Barnabas all have one thing in common, according to TWI theology: *they are all nonexistent!* Victor Paul Wierwille says, "Not one person in the Bible is living except the Lord Jesus Christ, and God raised Him from the dead. All the rest are dead."[1]

Dogs, goats, hogs, horses, birds, fish and elephants pass into oblivion when they die. So, TWI teaches, do men, women and children! Wierwille expresses it like this: "The Bible says that when a man dies, he is dead and he stays dead until the return of Christ and the resurrection. Nobody who has died is living with the exception of the Lord Jesus Christ, whom the Bible declares God raised from the dead."[2]

In another book he uses strong language to describe anyone who disagrees with his position, saying: "The teaching that when a person dies he immediately goes to God in heaven is one of the many doctrines of Satan and his fallen angels. Such erroneous thinking can be inspired only by Satan and believed and taught by broken-down clerical institutions and by all other religions which are inaugurated and formed by natural man, and directed by Satan."[3]

The position of Wierwille and TWI is identical on this point with that of the Jehovah's Witnesses, the Armstrongites, the Seventh-day Adventists, and numerous other cults. They also teach the sleep of the soul from the point of death to the hour of the resurrection at Christ's second coming.

In the section of his book, *Power for Abundant Living,* where he lists fancied misinterpretations of Scripture on the part of the historic Christian church, Wierwille pounces on the psalmist's treasure of comfort as a prime example, saying:

"Psalms (sic[4]) 116:15 is another verse which is frequently wrongly

1. PAL, p. 192
2. Ibid, p. 189
3. ADAN, p. 97
4. We find it amusing that one who boasts of his scholarship would refer to an individual psalm as "psalms." Since the Book of Psalms was the official hymnbook of the Jewish people, to refer to "Psalms" 116 would be like a song leader in a church today saying, "Turn to 'hymns' number 116!" As a collection, they are "psalms"; individually, each is a "psalm." He makes other grammatical blunders, too, such as writing, "Does he have a million dollars laying in front of him?" (TWW, p. 228). What would the money be laying? Eggs?

divided. This is a verse of Scripture which we often hear at a funeral when a good man of God has died.

"Psalms (sic) 116:15:

"Precious in the sight of the Lord *is* the death of his saints.

"We say, 'It is precious, it is good, in the sight of the Lord that he is dead.' Talk about wrongly dividing the Word! It is not good in the sight of the Lord that Herman died or that John died or that Mary died because they cannot help God any after they are dead. The only time they could help God is when they were alive. The word 'precious' in the text is 'costly.'

"We speak of a diamond as a precious stone because it is costly and rare. The more costly it is, the more precious it is. This is what is meant by 'precious in the sight of the Lord *is* the death of his saints.' It does not cost God anything when an unbeliever or a God-rejector dies. They have not done anything for God anyway. But if a believer died, it would be costly to God. That is why the Psalmist said, 'Costly in the sight of the Lord *is* the death of his saints.' "[5]

First of all, the English word "costly" infers something for which a price is paid, something very expensive. On the other hand, the Hebrew word is *yokar*, which Pick's dictionary of Old Testament words defines as "dear, rare, valuable."[6] The thought is not that God must pay a high price, but that He considers it something very valuable to Him.

Wierwille is understanding it to mean, "Costly *to* the Lord is the death of His saints." While this may be true, it most definitely is *not* what the psalmist is saying. He is speaking of how the Lord *views* that death, it is "in the eyes of" which receives the emphasis. The Hebrew for "sight" in this verse is *ainayim* and simply means "eyes." The Lord's emotions are involved as He beholds something very dear happening to one of His very own redeemed ones. Spurgeon said: "The Lord watches over their dying beds, smooths their pillows, sustains their hearts, and receives their souls. Those who are redeemed with precious blood are so dear to God that even their deaths are precious to him. The death-beds of saints are very precious to the church, she often learns much from them; they are very precious to all believers, who delight to treasure up the last words of the departed; but they are most of all precious to the Lord Jehovah Himself, who views the triumphant deaths of his gracious ones with sacred delight."[7]

5. Pp. 122,123
6. DOTW, p. 333
7. TOD, Vol. III, p. 71

Another noted commentator of the 19th century, the Presbyterian Albert Barnes, observed: "It is of value or importance in such respects as the following:—(1) As it is the removal of another of the redeemed to glory—the addition of one more to the happy houses above; (2) as it is a new triumph of the work of redemption,—showing the power and the value of that work; (3) as it often furnishes a more direct proof of the reality of religion than any abstract argument could do. How much has the cause of religion been promoted by the patient deaths of Ignatius, Polycarp, and Latimer, and Ridley, and Huss, and Jerome of Prague, and the hosts of martyrs! What does not the world owe, and the cause of religion owe, to such scenes as occurred on the death-beds of Baxter, and Thomas Scott, and Halyburton, and Payson! What an argument for the truth of religion,—what an illustration of its sustaining power,—what a source of comfort to those who are about to die,—to reflect that religion does not leave the believer when he most needs its support and consolation; that it can sustain us in the severest trial of our condition here; that it can illuminate what seems to us of all places *most* dark, cheerless, dismal, repulsive—'the valley of the shadow of death.' "[8]

The idea in Psalm 116:15 is not so much *tragedy for God*, as indicated in Wierwille's idea of God's loss of useful service from the saint, as it is a *triumph for God* in His redemptive process. It is something He highly esteems.

Comparing other instances in the Bible where the same word is translated "precious" bears out this truth. For example, I Samuel 3:1, referring to the days of Eli, says, "And the word of the Lord was precious [*yokar*] in those days; there was no open vision." A message from Jehovah was not "costly," but it was highly esteemed, it was rare. Psalm 139:17 quotes David as saying to Jehovah, "How precious [*yokar*] also are thy thoughts unto me, O God! how great is the sum of them!" God's words, God's thoughts were not "costly" to David, but, oh, how highly esteemed, how sweet and precious they were to him! And the use of "precious" in Psalm 72:14 is much as it is in Psalm 116:15: "He shall redeem their soul from deceit and violence: and precious [*yokar*] shall their blood be in his sight." Not "costly," but "highly esteemed."

*Yokar* is rendered "excellent" in Psalm 36:7 and Proverbs 17:27, "honorable" in Psalm 45:9, and "prized" in Zechariah

---

8. Quoted in TOD, Vol. III, pp. 88,89

11:13. It is only translated "costly" four times and all four relate to the stones in the Temple of Solomon (I Kings 5:17; 7:9,10,11). It is safe to say that Wierwille is wrong in his understanding of "precious" in Psalm 116:15.

But why does he make an issue of this? Because, in his understanding of a saint's death, there is absolutely nothing precious about it. To him it is merely a "ceasing to be," a being blotted out of existence until the resurrection morning. He teaches that the entire man, not just the body, sleeps in the grave, awaiting the blowing of the resurrection trumpet. So he *must* understand "precious" as "costly."

Is Wierwille right or wrong? Does or does not the redeemed person go to Heaven when he dies? In speaking of Luke 23:43, he says:

"If a man is going to heaven today, heaven must be available. Some teach that heaven is available. If they had studied The Word, they would know that heaven is not available. However, this verse talks about paradise—and paradise is not heaven. Heaven is heaven and paradise is paradise. When the Word of God says 'paradise,' it means 'paradise.' Paradise is present in Genesis chapters 1 and 2, at the end of which paradise is no longer accessible. It is not again available until the book of Revelation which speaks of a new heaven and a new earth wherein dwells righteousness.

"Paradise is always a place upon earth. If we are going to paradise, it has to be available. . . . Since paradise was nonexistent on the day of the crucifixion, Jesus had to say to the malefactor that sometime in the future he would be with Him, not in heaven, but in paradise."[9]

There are so many things obviously wrong with the above statement it is amazing that TWI followers cannot see at least some of them. For example, Wierwille says that Paradise is not Heaven. But what says the Scripture? In the case of the Apostle Paul, in II Corinthians 12, he told of one "caught up to the third heaven" (vs. 2), which is where God dwells, "the heaven of heavens" (Deut. 10:14). Yet, still speaking of the same wonderful experience, he went on to say that this one was "caught up into paradise" (vs. 4). In other words, "Heaven" and "Paradise" are interchangeable words for the same place. Just as people today refer to the largest city in the Empire State as "Fun City," "The Big Apple," "Sin City" and "New York City," so in the Word of God there are often several designations for the same place.

Wierwille seeks to refute the force of the II Corinthians passage

---

9. PAL, pp. 134,135

by arguing that the words "caught up" are a translation of the Greek *harpazo* and the latter simply means "snatcheth away," not necessarily "up."[10] But whether the one of whom Paul spoke was caught up, down, in, or around is not the specific issue; the point is that he was taken to Paradise, the third Heaven. Anyway, it is the prepositions Paul uses here which determine direction. As Philip E. Hughes writes: "The Apostle was caught up '*as far as* [*heos*] the third heaven': this specifies the 'height' or 'distance' of his rapture. Also, but not separately, he was caught up '*into* [*eis*] Paradise': this specifies the 'depth' of his rapture, and is a more precise disclosure of the particular 'part' or nature of the third heaven into which he was taken."[11]

Incidentally, Hughes gives abundant evidence that the idea of Christians' going immediately at death to Paradise dates back to New Testament times and can be seen from the wealth of apocryphal writing on the subject. He refers to the *Gospel of Nicodemus, Narrative of Joseph, Revelation of Esdras, Revelation of Paul* and *Revelation of Moses* as speaking of various saints already there, then notes: "These are, of course, apocryphal writings, full of fancies and discrepancies; **but they do at least supplement the unanimous voice of the Church of the early centuries that Paradise is a place of rest and bliss for those who enter it after death.**"[12]

Another obvious error in Wierwille's statement is his claim that "Paradise is always a place upon earth." As we have just noted in the Corinthian passage, Paradise is very clearly described as "the third heaven" and the one who went was "caught up" (both verses 2 and 4 use the phrase "caught up").

Again, Wierwille says, "Paradise is present in Genesis chapters 1 and 2, at the end of which paradise is no longer accessible." But Genesis 1 and 2 do not speak of Paradise (the name Paradise is not found anywhere in the Old Testament). How strange that Wierwille would call the Garden of Eden "Paradise" when God does not, yet refuse to call Heaven "Paradise" when God does!

We are quite willing to concede that the Garden of Eden was *an* "earthly paradise," and the Septuagint renders it thus, but it was most definitely not *the* Paradise of God. If one were to base his argument upon the Septuagint usage, he would also be com-

---

10. TWW, pp. 88,89
11. NICNT, *The Second Epistle to the Corinthians,* p. 437
12. Ibid., emphasis added

pelled to describe as "Paradise" Solomon's garden (Song of Sol. 4:13; Eccl. 2:5), Asaph's forest (Neh. 2:8), the Jordan valley (Gen. 13:10), the gardens of Balaam's vision (Num. 24:6), the gardens of the Jewish captives in Babylon (Jer. 29:5), and even Judah's mythical garden without water (Isa. 1:30)—since they are all rendered thus in the Septuagint.

Actually, the term "Paradise" is only found three times in the Word of God. In addition to the two references already listed, the third and final time is Revelation 2:7. Once again it speaks of Heaven, promising to believers at Ephesus some 1,900 years ago: "To him that overcometh will I give to eat of the tree of life, which is in the midst of the paradise of God." So the Paradise of God was then existing, nearly two millenniums ago.

How does Wierwille evade the clear teaching of Luke 23:43 that the dying thief would go with Christ that day to Paradise? He uses a little hanky-panky! He juggles the punctuation, inserts a comment with his plentiful supply of brackets—and changes the meaning of the verse entirely. Here is what he comes up with: ". . .Verily, I say to you To day, thou shalt [the day is coming in the future when you are going to]    be with me in paradise."[13]

The idea is not original with Wierwille and other cultists with soul sleep theories have done so before him. He speaks of other translations putting the comma after today, as he has, but we know of none save the "New World Translation" of the Jehovah's Witnesses—which seems to have been translated exclusively to bolster the false teachings of that heretical cult. And we recall the words of William Hendriksen about that: "And what shall we say with respect to Rutherford's translation or interpretation of Christ's word to the penitent thief? How utterly childish! Jesus, then, is supposed to have said, 'Verily I say unto thee today.' Well, of course, he said it *today*. When else would he be saying it?"[14] That kind of redundancy is not typical of the Saviour's speech.

Perhaps it would help show Wierwille's error if we did to other passages what he has done to Luke 23:43. It would be like translating Luke 4:21 ("And he began to say unto them, This day is this scripture fulfilled in your ears") as, "And he began to say unto them this day, Is this scripture [the day is coming in the future when it is going to be] fulfilled in your ears?" Or Luke 19:9

---

13. PAL, p. 135
14. BLH, p. 43

("And Jesus said unto him, This day is salvation come to this house, forsomuch as he also is a son of Abraham") as, "And Jesus said unto him this day, Is salvation [the day is coming in the future when it will be] come to this house, forsomuch as he also is a son of Abraham?" Or Hebrews 3:7 ("Wherefore (as the Holy Ghost saith, To day if ye will hear his voice") as, "Wherefore (as the Holy Ghost saith today, If ye will [the day is coming in the future when you will] hear his voice." Hebrews 3:15 ("While it is said, To day if ye will hear his voice, harden not your hearts, as in the provocation") as, "While it is said today, If ye will [the day is coming in the future when you will] hear his voice, harden not your hearts, as in the provocation."

Examples could be multiplied but, since Wierwille's position here is the same as that of Armstrongism and the Worldwide Church of God, permit us to quote from our book on that movement:

"Dr. George Lawlor, professor of Greek and Bible at Cedarville College, dealt with this charge in our magazine, *The Biblical Evangelist*, some time ago. His article is too lengthy to reproduce in its entirety, but here is the heart of it:

". . .the text of Luke 23:43 is so assured by reliable evidence that *any* change based on textual grounds must be rejected. All is clear where *seimeron* ['today'] and the punctuation of the sentence are concerned. The KJV is right: the comma belongs where it is—after the pronoun 'thee' [the Greek order reverses the pronoun and the verb, but retains the same sense]. Again, as previously in the Gospel records, we meet the seal of verity and sovereignty in '*Amen*' ['Verily' in the KJV] coupled with the declaration of authority: '*I say unto thee*' [the Greek text places the dative pronoun before the verb: 'To thee I say'], followed correctly by the comma. Any attempt to join the word 'today' with the clause 'to thee I say' **violates common sense, ignores the textual evidence, and destroys the force of the Lord's promise.**

"It should not even be necessary to explain that the comma is not to be moved so that the word 'today' must be construed with 'I say to thee.' To be sure the Lord is saying these words TODAY—*this is self-evident!* When else would He be saying them? The thief heard the words and knew the Lord was talking to him AT THAT MOMENT—today—and believed what the Lord said. Never did Christ so redundantly and emphatically express Himself. Hence the [Wierwille] insinuation is groundless—

yea, dangerous, for the Lord's great promise in this remarkable statement would lose all of its precision, meaning and blessedness if based upon the [Wierwille] interpretation that there is no passage of the soul into the presence of the Lord.

"Without doubt, the adverb 'today' is an essential part of the Lord's promise to the thief. In fact, its place forward in the last clause bears a degree of emphasis. While it is perfectly obvious that the Lord is making this remarkable statement TODAY and not YESTERDAY or TOMORROW, the stress is upon the fact that TODAY, *this very day, today already—the thief will be with Christ in paradise.* Frequently, in the normal course of things, it would take perhaps two or three days until a man would die hanging on a cross, so lingering was death by crucifixion. But our Lord Jesus Christ assures this thief that his sufferings will cease TODAY, *and that the thief will be with the Lord, where He is—* TODAY.

"The adverb 'today' [Greek, *seimeron*] stands first and immediately with the prepositional phrase 'with Me' [*met' emou*], which is followed by the rest of the sentence in order: 'shall be in paradise' [*esei en to paradeiso*], so that the whole clause reads literally: 'Today with Me (pronoun emphatic) thou shalt be in the paradise.' The position of 'today' [*seimeron*] in immediate proximity with the words 'with me' [*met' emou*] argues for the fact that it belongs to the second clause. . . .

"Our Lord's reply to the thief's humble plea assured the thief of continued existence in the state of blessedness into which he would enter immediately after death—that state of conscious union and perfect fellowship with Christ. The thief would not have to wait until the Lord returned to be with Him—TODAY HE WOULD BE WITH HIM WHERE HE WAS. Such is the true meaning of the Lord's promise and it imparts consolation and comfort to every believing heart since it assures all true believers of the immediate translation of their spirits into the presence of the Lord at the instant of physical death. The scheme of transferring the comma and thus making the word *'today'* a part of the first *'I say to thee'* dishonors the Lord and belongs to a subtle, satanically-devised system of teaching that denies Heaven *ad interim* to the soul that dies in Christ. But let no true Christian be troubled or disturbed. The Scriptures leave no doubt for us on this point."[15]

Other scholars say the same. For example, Norval

15. ARMS, pp. 235-237

Geldenhuys, the late South African authority, quotes Godet and Plummer at this point: " 'In our Lord's answer, the word *today* stands foremost, because Jesus wishes to contrast the nearness of the promised happiness with the remote future to which the prayer of the thief refers. *Today*, before the setting of the sun which is shining on us' (Godet, *in loc.*). To take together with *I say*, as some interpreters do, is altogether unjustifiable, for then *today* has no force here (cf. Plummer *in loc.*).' "[16]

Part of Wierwille's problem about what happens at death is due to his confusion about immortality. He writes: "What ultimately happens to the soul? As the body goes back to dust, the soul is passed on from one person to his progeny. If a person has no offspring, his soul is gone when he dies; it is no more. If my soul is gone, I am a dead person and the Bible speaks of me as a dead soul. There is nothing immortal about the soul, no more so than there is anything immortal about dust. Man's body is made of dust and it goes back to dust. When man takes his last breath, his soul life terminates."[17]

Ignoring for the moment his strange understanding of what happens to a soul at death, consider this matter of immortality. In the Word of God, the Greek for "mortal" is *thnetos* and means "subject to death." The word for "immortality" is simply the negative, *athanasias*, and literally means "not subject to death," or deathless (see Vine, Young, *et al*). Never does it carry the thought of ceasing to be, or, as Wierwille expresses it: "his soul life terminates."

For the *soul* to "terminate" would be for the *individual* to terminate since the soul is the personality, the ego of an individual. It is soul that thinks, wills, decides, loves, hates and manifests other emotions. The Word of God speaks of the soul being hungry (Ps. 107:9), loathing (Lev. 26:11), being thirsty (Ps. 42:2), being grieved (Job 30:25), finding rest (Matt. 11:29), loving (Matt. 22:37), being weary (Jer. 4:31)—just to mention a few of its emotions.

Nowhere in Scripture does it speak of the soul terminating or ceasing to be. It does speak of *death*, but death is never ceasing to be; death in the Word of God is simply separation. Physical death is the *separation* of the soul and the spirit from the body. Spiritual death is the *separation* of the individual from God because of sin and rejection of Christ. The second death is a com-

16. NICNT, *The Gospel of Luke,* p. 615
17. PAL, p. 237

plete and final *separation* from God in the lake of fire forever. We repeat: *death is never a ceasing to be!*

Quite the contrary, death is a departure (II Tim. 4:6), a going somewhere. That departure, we learn from our Lord in the story He told in Luke 16:19-31, involves two destinies. For the one, the rich man who remained unrepentant throughout life, the destiny was a place of punishment. Jesus said: ". . .the rich man also died, and was buried; and in hell he lift up his eyes, being in torments. . ." (vss. 22, 23). For the other, the repentant beggar named Lazarus, death was a departure "carried by the angels into Abraham's bosom," another expression for Paradise (vs. 22). For neither was it soul sleep or soul termination.

This thought abounds in the Word of God. The psalmist reminded God, "Thou shalt guide me with thy counsel, and afterward receive me to glory" (Ps. 73:24). He expected the Lord's counsel and direction for his earthly walk; and he expected to be received into Glory "afterward," as soon as that pilgrimage down here had been completed. David, in his beautiful Shepherd Psalm, declared, "Yea, though I walk through the valley of the shadow of death, I will fear no evil: for thou art with me" (Ps. 23:4). Was death termination? Not for King David; he was *going* somewhere. It was not a place of *inactivity*, it was a place of action, of *walking!* It was not unconsciousness, it was a place where his *emotions* were active, a place of experiencing calm and comfort rather than fear. And it was a place where he was confident he would experience *conscious fellowship* with the Good Shepherd; *Jehovah would walk with him!*

Solomon, after one of the most beautiful figurative pictures of old age and death found in any literature, sacred or secular, said: "Then shall the dust return to the earth as it was: and the spirit shall return unto God who gave it" (Eccles. 12:7). When he died he expected a separation between his body and his spirit. The body would be placed into the ground and return to dust; the spirit would "return unto God who gave it." No termination was expected; no, it would be a departing, a returning to God.

Paul was conscious of this truth and, when writing to the saints at Corinth, spoke of the body as a house, a tabernacle, a dwelling place for the real person. He spoke of being "absent from the Lord" while living in the body, then explained his heartfelt expectation: "We are confident, I say, and willing rather to be absent from the body, and to be present with the Lord" (II Cor. 5:8). When Paul's soul left his body at death, what did he expect to happen? Did he think his soul would be terminated? No, he fully expected to be "present with the Lord" the very moment he became "absent from the body." Incidentally, the New International Version translates II Corinthians 5:8,9: "We are confident, I say, and would prefer to be **away from the body** and at home with the Lord. So we make it our goal to please him, whether we are at home in the body **or away from it**" (emphasis added).

In his book, *Are the Dead Alive Now?* Wierwille devotes a chapter to these two verses (II Cor. 5:8,9; largely ignoring the chapter's opening verses), but it is less than four pages in length and consists mostly of merely quoting verses in the 4th and 5th chapters, plus other verses which relate to Christians being "present with the Lord" when He comes again—the latter being something no one would deny and only "muddies the water" when Wierwille attempts to connect it with the passage in question. Too, it disregards the plain fact that when the Word of God speaks of being present with the Lord at His coming, it plainly identifies it as such (for example: I Thessalonians 4:13-18; John 14:2,3).

As a summary of *what* Wierwille says—and an illustration of *how* he says it—we offer this conclusion from his pen:

"The return of Christ is the enveloping context of II Corinthians 5:8, which says,

"We are confident, I say, and willing rather to be absent from the body [so long as we are in the body, the return has not come so we are naturally absent from the Lord] and to be present with the Lord.

"When will we 'be present with the Lord'? At the *parousia*, the return."[18]

Of course we will be present with the Lord at His return, but that is not the issue. Wierwille's theology leaves unanswered the question: "When will we be 'absent from the body'?" And note how Wierwille used his plentiful bracket supply to dull the force of the passage and change the clear intent of Paul's meaning: when the *real* person leaves his body/tabernacle on earth he is immediately "present with the Lord."

Paul enlarged on this thought in Philippians 1, declaring: "For to me to live is Christ, and to die is gain" (vs. 21). Was death to the beloved apostle a termination? No, no! It was profit, it was gain. He went on to say, "For I am in a strait betwixt two, having

18. P. 59

a desire to depart, and to be with Christ; which is far better: Nevertheless to abide in the flesh is more needful for you" (vss. 23,24). No wonder he called it gain: *it was "to be with Christ"!* His body would be in some earthly tomb returning to dust, but he, himself, would already be in the wonderful presence of the Redeemer. Hallelujah!

If the Wierwille philosophy of "termination" be true, why would Paul have been in a "strait betwixt two"? If he would merely be nonexistent, sleeping in an Italian hillside near Rome for nearly 2,000 years thus far, why the hurry to die? Why not have a single-minded goal of service to saints and sinners? After all, the longer he could live down here the more good he could do for the Lord Jesus Christ—and he would not get to Heaven even the twinkle of an eye sooner anyway! Ah, but that was not how Paul understood it. The moment he died he expected to be "with Christ." And, praise God, he was!

Johnstone enlarges on this thought: "Paul says that he felt himself 'in a strait,' hemmed in by conflicting motives and feelings, so that he found it difficult to decide whether he should definitely long for life or death. Had there been any thought in his mind of a time of unconsciousness following death, I can hardly suppose that for a man of his principles and temperament there would have been any 'strait.' His decision would have been clear and unhesitating,—'Better, immeasurably better, to remain here, enjoying communion with my Lord, and labouring in His service, than to pass into a torpor, in which I can neither hold fellowship with Him, nor in any way consciously magnify Him.' There is broad and firm scriptural ground, my brethren, for the precious doctrine set forth in the familiar words of the Westminster Divines, that 'the souls of believers are at their death made perfect in holiness, and do *immediately* pass into glory.' "[19]

Wierwille has an answer, he feels. He writes: "Contortionists of The Word also come with the reference from Philippians 1:21 where Paul says, 'For to me to live *is* Christ, and to die *is* gain.' Philippians does not say that the gain is immediate. Paul says that the return of Christ is better than living or dying; for when Christ returns the mortal shall put on immortality."[20]

We suggest readers take time right now to turn in the Word of God to Philippians 1 and carefully read the context of the passage in question. Note that there is absolutely no mention or sug-

19. LEPP, p. 106
20. PAL, p. 192

gestion whatsoever of the second coming of Christ in the context. In fact, Wierwille's interpretation makes "to die" the resurrection, something *completely foreign* to the context. Paul is simply speaking of living and dying. If he lived, it would be to serve and honor Christ. If he died, it would be "gain" and being "with Christ." We ask this of our readers because, believe it or not, after horribly taking Paul's words out of their context and attempting to relate them to the second coming, Wierwille says, just two paragraphs later: "We must always go to The Scripture and its context and find out exactly what it says before we make any other statement or we shall be led into confusion by the wrong dividing of The Word."[21]

One thing is certain: *he isn't lacking in nerve!*

Nor does he seem to be lacking in deliberate deception and falsehood. Speaking of Philippians 1:22 ("But if I live in the flesh, this is the fruit of my labour: yet what I shall choose I wot not"), he dares to write: "On the surface, as the verse reads in the Authorized King James Version, it seems to indicate that Paul was in a dilemma, not knowing which choice to make. '. . .what I shall choose I wot not.' The word translated 'I wot' is *gnorizo* used 24 times in the A.V.: 16 times 'to make known'; 4 times 'declare'; 1 each 'to do wit,' 'certify,' 'give to understand' and 'wot.'

"Thus clearly *gnorizo* means 'to make known.' Paul did not know what his choice really was. The context indicates that while Paul's personal preference was in one direction, his decision had to benefit others for Christ's gain."[22]

We have no quarrel, for once, with Wierwille's Greek (other than to note inverted words in the phrase "to do wit," which should be "do to wit"; a typesetter's error, no doubt); it is his dishonesty here that troubles us. While he is right in saying *gnorizo* can mean "to make known" [and it can *also* mean "to know"], we have no idea what Wierwille means by Paul's "personal preference" being in one direction, but "his decision had to benefit others." Obviously, Paul had no decision in the matter of living or dying; that was completely in the Lord's hands. As he expressed it in Romans 14:7,8: "For none of us liveth to himself, and no man dieth to himself. For whether we live, we live unto the Lord; and whether we die, we die unto the Lord: whether we live therefore, or die, we are the Lord's."

---

21. Ibid., p. 193
22. ADAN, p. 53

We think it is interesting in this verse that Paul said "if I live in the flesh." The inference is that he would never cease to live—didn't his Lord say "whosoever liveth and believeth in me shall never die" (John 11:26)?—it was merely a preference as to whether he would live "in the flesh" or live "absent from" the flesh (II Cor. 5:8).

That Paul was indeed speaking of the uncertainty of his personal preference is seen from the continuation of his thought in verse 23, which Wierwille wants to dismiss as parenthetical. Paul says, "I am in a strait betwixt two, having a desire to depart, and to be with Christ; which is far better." The phrase "I am in a strait" is the Greek *sunechomai* and means to be pressured from both sides. It could be translated "I feel the pressure" (BERK), or "I am torn" (NIV), or "I am hard pressed" (NASB and NKJB). Wierwille's friend, Lamsa, translates the verse: "For I am torn between two desires, the one to depart, that I may be with Christ, which is far better" (HBP). The reason Paul *didn't* make his preference known was that he *couldn't;* he didn't know himself!

One of Wierwille's major problems with this verse is Paul's stated "desire to depart," to leave for some place else. He passes it off like this:

"The word *depart* in verse 23 is in the Greek the word *analuo*. It is used only once in another passage in the Bible, namely in Luke 12:36: '. . .when he will return from the wedding. . . .' In Luke, *analuo* is translated 'return.' Thus the word *analuo* does not mean 'to depart' in the sense of leaving the place where one is, but it is a return to the place which was left. The word *analuo* does not mean to depart in the sense of starting off from this place and going to another place, but it means to return to the place which has been left earlier. This gives us the absolute meaning of the word *analuo* without any private interpretation."[23]

While Wierwille is correct that *analuo* is used only twice in the New Testament, he fails to mention the fact that *analuo* is actually a very common Greek verb and that the literal meaning is "to unloose, to undo." Vine calls it "a metaphor drawn from loosing moorings preparatory to setting sail, or, according to some, from breaking up an encampment, or from the unyoking of baggage animals."[24] What Wierwille is suggesting regarding our understanding of *analuo* is that we determine the meaning of the usual ("depart") from the rare and unusual ("return"), rather

23. Ibid., p. 55
24. EDNTW, Vol. I, pp. 294,295

than understanding the rare by the normal. Whatever else you may call such reasoning, it certainly is not good biblical hermeneutics. In fact, Luke 12:36 reads very logically when so understood ("And ye yourselves like unto men that wait for their lord, when he will depart from the wedding; that when he cometh and knocketh, they may open unto him immediately"), while to understand Philippians 1:23 by Luke 12:36 would not make sense ("For I am in a strait betwixt two, having a desire to return, and to be with Christ; which is far better"). Robertson suggests that understanding Luke 12:36 as departure may well be true, commenting: "Perhaps here the figure is from the standpoint of the wedding feast (plural as used of a single wedding feast in Luke 14:8), departing from there."[25]

Wierwille also refers to the departure of II Timothy 4:6 ("For I am now ready to be offered, and the time of my departure is at hand"), saying: "The word *departure* is the Greek noun *analusis*, and again means 'returning.' 'For I am now ready to be offered, and the time of my "returning to dust" is at hand.' For further corroboration which can be checked in any good concordance, the words translated 'depart' occur around 130 times in the New Testament."[26]

We certainly trust readers will check the word "depart" in a good concordance; they will discover that it means "go somewhere" in New Testament usage, not "return from somewhere." And did you note how cleverly Wierwille changed the meaning of II Timothy 4:6, inserting foreign words into the verse, giving the idea of "returning *to dust*." (He has a footnote quoting Genesis 3:19, ". . .dust thou art, and unto dust shalt thou return.") It would be just as logical—and far more in harmony with the context—to insert Ecclesiastes 12:7, ". . .the spirit shall return unto God who gave it," and that verse implies the spirit's returning to God takes place at the same time the body returns to dust.

Incidentally, the noted scholar who served as dean of Trinity College at Cambridge and principal of Ridley Hall, the late Handley C. G. Moule, has an interesting comment here: "The word rendered 'departure,' *analusis*, is the Greek original of our 'analysis.' An analysis means a setting free, a detachment, a separation of things or thoughts from one another. The original noun here, like the kindred verb in Phil. i.23, denotes the undo-

25. WPNT, Vol. II, p. 179
26. ADAN, pp. 55,56

ing of a connexion, as it were the untying of a cord, the weighing of an anchor, so as to set the voyager free to seek the further shore. To the Philippians, in that earlier day, St. Paul had owned that his 'desire' was 'to unmoor, and to be with Christ' (Phil. i.23). And here the desire is about to become fact; 'the season of his unmooring is upon him.' "[27]

One problem facing Wierwille in his "going out of existence" philosophy of death is the statement by Peter: "For Christ also hath once suffered for sins, the just for the unjust, that he might bring us to God, being put to death in the flesh, but quickened by the Spirit: By which also he went and preached unto the spirits in prison; Which sometime were disobedient, when once the longsuffering of God waited in the days of Noah, while the ark was a preparing, wherein few, that is, eight souls were saved by water" (I Pet. 3:18-20).

He comments: "Jesus paid the full legal price for man's sin and the consequences of sin. He descended into hell (the grave), and sometime between the resurrection and His appearance to Mary, in His resurrected body, He preached to the imprisoned spirits."[28]

Do you see his dilemma? Those "imprisoned spirits" were the people of the time of Noah who rejected God and His Word, perishing in the flood. Wierwille says they are nonexistent, that they are dead and will stay dead "until the return of Christ and the resurrection." Too, he says Hell is only "the grave" anyway! Yet he claims that Christ, in His resurrection body, "sometime between the resurrection and His appearance to Mary," preached to them! Did He go to the grave and "preach" to nonexistent dead spirits? Presumably, with that kind of a preaching service, no altar call was given—and no hands were even raised for prayer!

One of Wierwille's problems is that he tries to make immortality synonymous with the resurrection. He writes, "When do we have immortality? With the second coming of Christ. . . . It is then—with the return of Christ—that we have victory over death. Then we have immortality and incorruption. Until that time, the dead remain in gravedom in corruption and unconsciousness."[29] His proof text is I Corinthians 15:53-57, but, apart from the weird understanding he offers that the corruptible put-

27. SST, p. 140
28. NDC, pp. 61,62
29. WM, March-April, 1977; "Are the Dead Alive Now?" p. 10

ting on incorruption refers to the bodies of the *dead* believers and the mortal putting on immortality is the bodies of the *living* believers, the entire passage is talking about *bodies*, not souls and spirits! The body will not put on incorruption or immortality until that time, but, for the believer, it is the only part of him which *can* experience death and corruption.

Note here two things: (1) If the physical resurrection of the body is experiencing immortality for the real person (the soul), then the unsaved will receive immortality too, since they will also experience the resurrection of the body (John 5:28,29; Dan. 12:2; Rev. 20:5-6,11-12). (2) As far as the soul is concerned, believers *already have* immortality, they are "not subject to death." Quite the contrary, as Jesus told Martha in John 11:25,26 (when she, like Wierwille, mistakenly connected immortality with "the resurrection at the last day"), "I am the resurrection, and the life: he that believeth in me, though he were dead, yet shall he live: And whosoever liveth and believeth in me shall never die. Believest thou this?"[30] We can only echo the question to Wierwille and TWI followers: "Believest thou this?" Do you believe, as Jesus insisted, that the one who puts his faith and trust in Jesus Christ "shall never die," that immortality, deathlessness, is already his, a present possession—as far as the soul is concerned? It is what our Lord declared and we are quite willing to believe Him about the matter. He said elsewhere, "Verily, verily, I say unto you, He that heareth my word, and believeth on him that sent me, hath everlasting life, and shall not come into condemnation; but is **passed from death unto life**" (John 5:24, emphasis added). Such a believer's soul cannot die; it is immortal! While in a different context and without any of his uncertainty, we say with Cicero: "If I err in my belief that the soul of man is immortal, I err with pleasure."[31]

Part of Wierwille's problem is his misunderstanding about death. He says, "The word *death* in the Bible is the Greek word *thanatos*, which is defined as 'the natural end of earthly human existence.' *Thanatos* is not merely an instantaneous occurrence when one expires but a continuing state. Release from this continuing state of death hinges upon the return of Christ."[32]

---

30. Believe it or not, in ADAN, Wierwille has the audacity to use his bracket insertion method to change the meaning of this passage, rendering it: "And whosoever liveth and believeth in me shall never die [After the resurrection]" (p. 98). Is *nothing* sacred to him?
31. Quoted and translated from the Latin by Johnstone, LEPP, p. 86
32. ADAN, p. 22

About the only thing correct in his statement is that the most common word for death in the Bible (he means the New Testament; the most common word for death in the Old Testament is the Hebrew word *maveth*) is the Greek *thanatos*. As for his definition of the meaning of *thanatos*, he is way off base! What he has done is refer to the *Greek* word and then give a common *English* definition. The meaning of Greek words are determined by Greek usage!

Perhaps the simplest way to show how erroneous Wierwille's definition is would be to insert it for the word death in passages which speak of death. For example, the verse just quoted would become, "He that heareth my word, and believeth on him that sent me, hath everlasting life, and shall not come into condemnation; but is passed from *the natural end of earthly human existence* unto life." Is that what happens the moment someone trusts Christ? Absolutely not; Wierwille's definition does fit here!

How about John 8:51,52, which would become: "Verily, verily, I say unto you, If a man keep my saying, he shall never see *the natural end of earthly human existence*. Then said the Jews unto him, Now we know that thou hast a devil. Abraham is dead, and the prophets; and thou sayest, If a man keep my saying, he shall never taste of *the natural end of earthly human existence*." If the Jews understood death as does Wierwille, no wonder they thought our Lord had a devil!

Or how about Paul's triumphant statement in Romans 8:1,2: "There is therefore now no condemnation to them which are in Christ Jesus, who walk not after the flesh, but after the Spirit. For the law of the Spirit of life in Christ Jesus hath made me free from the law of sin and *the natural end of earthly human existence*." Did Paul think his conversion freed him from any eventual "natural end of earthly human existence"? If so, like the followers of Mary Baker Patterson Glover Eddy in our day, he was pitifully mistaken, as he discovered when he laid his head upon the Roman chopping block to die a martyr's death.

In the same passage, consider Wierwille's definition in the light of Romans 8:6: "For to be carnally minded is *the natural end of earthly human existence*; but to be spiritually minded is life and peace." The very thought is absurd! How much simpler to understand death as "separation," determining the type of separation by the context in which it is used.

Another illustration would be I John 3:14, which, according to

Wierwille's understanding, would read: "We know that we have passed from *the natural end of earthly human existence* unto life, because we love the brethren. He that loveth not his brother abideth in *the natural end of earthly human existence.*" Are we really to understand that our assurance of present salvation and life comes from having ended earthly human existence, or that if we do not love our brother we are in a state where our natural earthly human existence has ended? To ask those questions is to answer them. And keep in mind that the Greek word in all the above passages is *thanatos.*

By the way, for the believer in Christ, death has been "abolished" through His death on the cross. Second Timothy 1:10 assures the Christian, "But is now made manifest by the appearing of our Saviour Jesus Christ, who hath abolished death, and hath brought life and immortality to light through the gospel." Notice that Paul writes of death's abolishment as a past reality and life and immortality for the believer as a present possession: *hath* abolished death and *hath* brought life and immortality to light. It is something the believer can claim for the here and now.

Where are saints who "die in the Lord" (Rev. 14:13)? In the Revelation of Jesus Christ the veil hiding the unseen world is pulled back and we are given a glimpse of some of them. Revelation 6:9-11 pictures them in Heaven with the Lamb of God, saying: "And when he had opened the fifth seal, I saw under the altar the souls of them that were slain for the word of God, and for the testimony which they held: And they cried with a loud voice, saying, How long, O Lord, holy and true, dost thou not judge and avenge our blood on them that dwell on the earth? And white robes were given unto every one of them; and it was said unto them, that they should rest yet for a little season, until their fellowservants also and their brethren, that should be killed as they were, should be fulfilled."

Perhaps we should emphasize that this is not a portrayal of eternity after the return of our Lord Jesus Christ and the end of the world as we now know it, but it is a picture of a scene in Heaven while saints are being persecuted and martyred on earth. In fact, the martyring is not finished and the talk relates to others "that should be killed" and the fulfillment of prophecy still to come. Yet the martyred ones are in Heaven—even though there as souls without bodies!

To be consistent, Wierwille teaches that our Lord Jesus Christ "terminated" for three days and three nights after the crucifixion. He writes: "Jesus Christ likewise descended into gravedom when He died. If anyone should have gone to Heaven immediately after death, surely it should have been Jesus. But even He went to *sheol* or *hades*. For three days and three nights He had no consciousness, as Matthew 12 and Acts 2 state."[33] He then quotes Matthew 12:40, "For as Jonas was three days and three nights in the whale's belly; so shall the Son of man be three days and three nights in the heart of the earth."

But had Jonah "terminated" during those three days and three nights? Was he in a state of "no consciousness"? Surely Jonah, writing under the God-breathed inspiration of the Holy Spirit, would be the one most qualified to answer. During those three days and nights "Jonah prayed" (Jonah 2:1). He said, "I cried by reason of mine affliction unto the Lord, and he heard me; out of the belly of hell [*sheol*] cried I, and thou heardest my voice" (vs. 2). Instead of *sheol* being a place of unconsciousness, it was a place where Jonah prayed and God heard. It was a place where Jonah's soul was faint [Hebrew, *otaph*, literally "overwhelmed"] (vs. 7). It was a place of memory (vs. 7, "I remembered the Lord"). And it was a place where Jonah reaffirmed his covenant with the Lord (vs. 9, "I will pay that that I have vowed"). Wierwille's proof text leaves more than a little to be desired in support of his position.

What about the Scriptures which clearly picture the Christian going to be with Christ at the moment of death? That is merely something like an optical illusion, Wierwille tells us. He writes: "Because there is no consciousness in death, there is no awareness of time for the dead person. Thus the moment of a man's death becomes, *in a sense of time for him*, the moment of the return of Christ. But *within the dimension of time*, the moment of a man's death is *neither* his gathering together unto Christ *nor* his resurrection. In a sense of time he does not go immediately to Heaven, but descends into gravedom, *sheol*."[34] But this interpretation does horrible violence to the force of Paul's argument in Philippians 1:21-23, noted above. If Wierwille's understanding were true, there would have been no urgency in Paul's heart to "depart"; the call of the work on earth would have possessed sole priority in his feelings. Not only so, according to the Word of God the return of Christ is *His coming for*

---

33. Ibid., pp. 24,25
34. Ibid., pp. 23,24, italics in original

*believers*; death is *the believer going to Christ!* They are entirely different.

All of this leads us to note how Wierwille defines the Hebrew *sheol* and the Greek *hades*. He says:

> "If release from death comes with the return of Christ, where are the dead until that time? The Bible says that they are in the 'grave' (*hades* in Greek; *sheol* in Hebrew.) These words are interchangeably translated 'hell,' 'grave,' and 'pit.' *Hades* or *sheol* is never the place of destruction; it is always the continuing state of the dead. The most accurate translation of *hades* and *sheol* would be 'gravedom.' Gravedom is the state in which all dead dwell; it is not a *geber*, a spot where the body is buried on land or sea. The Biblical description of gravedom (the kingdom of all those in the grave—the dead), *sheol* or *hades*, is a place where there is no consciousness and thus no remembrance."[35]

The problem with this definition is that very few real Greek or Hebrew scholars agree with him—apart from those supplied by the various cults who sympathize with Wierwille's theology. Speaking of *sheol*, Vine says: "It never denotes the grave, nor is it the permanent region of the lost. . . ."[36] And he identifies *hades* as "the region of departed spirits of the lost (but including the blessed dead in periods preceding the Ascension of Christ)."[37] *Young's Analytical Concordance of the Bible* gives "the unseen state" as the meaning of *sheol* and "the unseen world" for the meaning of *hades*.[38] These words can be understood to refer to the grave only in the sense that it is part of the unseen state, the unseen world. *The International Standard Bible Encyclopedia* offers as the meaning of *hades* "not to be seen."[39] And it says of *sheol*, "It means really the unseen world, the state or abode of the dead, and is the equivalent of the Gr *Haides*, by which word it is [translated in the Septuagint]."[40]

In a book published exactly one century ago, Junius B. Reimensnyder observed that *hades* was ". . .the term in common use among the Greeks for the under-world, the realm of the dead in general. It comprised two apartments: the upper, the *Elysian fields*—the abode of the righteous, and the lower, *Tartarus*—the prison of the wicked. In the New Testament it bears to some extent the same signification. That is, it denotes the whole empire

---

35. Ibid., pp. 22,23
36. EDNTW, Vol. II, p. 188
37. Ibid., p. 187
38. P. 474
39. Vol. II, p. 1,314
40. Vol. IV, p. 2,761

of the dead, i.e., disembodied spirits, in one apartment of which, Abraham's bosom, or Paradise, the righteous, while indeed happy and rejoicing with their Lord, are still deprived of that full, blissful re-union with their bodies to take place at the resurrection; and in the other of which, the wicked are already reaping a bitter foretaste of their final doom"[41]

Wuest, the Greek professor at Moody when Wierwille was supposedly taking everything he could get his hands on through its correspondence department, notes this about *hades*: "The word *haides* is from the Greek stem *id* which means 'to see,' and the Greek letter Alpha prefixed which makes the composite word mean 'not to see,' the noun meaning 'the unseen.' The word itself in its noun form refers to the unseen world made up of all moral intelligences not possessing a physical body. These would include the holy angels, the fallen angels, the demons, the wicked dead, and the righteous dead. As to the inhabitants in the unseen world, the holy angels are in heaven, the fallen angels in Tartarus, the wicked dead in Hades, the righteous dead in heaven, and the demons in the atmosphere of the earth and in the bottomless pit. All these are included in the unseen world."[42]

That these words do not carry the idea of nonexistence should be obvious from checking their usage. In Deuteronomy 32:22, where *sheol* is used, it speaks of the fire of God's anger burning there, a clear indication of judgment. Would God's judgment fire be burning in the "lowest" part of a grave? The New Testament counterpart, *hades*, is described as a place of torment, fire, memory, prayer, vision, speech and a spirit of hopelessness (Luke 16:19-31).

No consciousness, no existence, no knowledge beyond the grave? Then explain Luke 16:29, where Abraham said to the rich man in *hades*, "They have Moses and the prophets; let them hear them." How did Abraham even know Moses existed? Abraham died two centuries before the birth of Moses! And how did he know about the Old Testament? Not a single one of the 39 Old Testament books had been written at the time of his death. Or explain John 8:56, where our Lord said to the Jews, "Your father Abraham rejoiced to see my day: and he saw it, and was glad." When did Abraham see Jesus' day and rejoice?

The words of Christ to the Sadducees are pertinent here. When they, who taught as Wierwille that at death one is nonexistent,

41. DE, pp. 185,186
42. SVG, p. 49

tried to trip the Saviour in His position with the story of a maiden who had been married to seven brothers, He replied: "As touching the resurrection of the dead, have ye not read that which was spoken unto you by God, saying, I am the God of Abraham, and the God of Isaac, and the God of Jacob? God is not the God of the dead, but of the living" (Matt. 22:31,32). Wierwille says, "Not one person in the Bible is living except the Lord Jesus Christ. . . .All the rest are dead."[43] According to him, Abraham, Isaac and Jacob are all dead. This would make our Lord "the God of the dead"; He said He is "the God of the living." Will you believe Him or Wierwille?

Wierwille tries to escape the force of this scriptural argument by looking to the future. He says: "When is God not the God of the dead but of the living? Not now, but at the time of the resurrection. . . . At the time of the resurrection, Abraham, Isaac and Jacob will be made alive."[44]

There are two serious flaws in this interpretation: (1) At the time the words Christ quoted were originally given to Moses, in Exodus 3:6, the illustrious trio had long since been "gathered to their fathers." (2) In both passages, the original in Exodus and the statement of Christ in Matthew, the present tense is used. He said "I **am** the God of" and "God **is**." He did not says, "I **will be** the God of" or "God **will be**." He was clearly and unmistakably talking about the immediate, not the future. Wierwille is grossly guilty of twisting the biblical statements to conform to his own false theories.

Perhaps we should take a closer look at Abraham, whom Wierwille says is nonexistent and whom God says is living. At the time Jehovah confirmed His covenant with him, He said: "Thou shalt go to thy fathers in peace; thou shalt be buried in a good old age" (Gen. 15:15). Two things were promised here: (1) He would go to his fathers in peace; that is, die a nonviolent death. (2) He would not be buried until he had lived a full life. The two statements, while related, are separate. And keep in mind that Abraham's fathers were "buried" far away in Babylon.

When Abraham died many years later, at the age of 175, the record tells us: "Then Abraham gave up the ghost, and died in a good old age, an old man, and full of years; and was gathered to his people. And his sons Isaac and Ishmael buried him in the

43. PAL, p. 192
44. Ibid., p. 187

cave of Machpelah, in the field of Ephron the son of Zohar the Hittite, which is before Mamre" (Gen. 25:8,9). Once again there are two separate yet related statements: (1) He was gathered to his fathers. (2) He was buried. Note carefully that he was *first* "gathered to his people" (vs. 8), and then "buried" in the cave of Machpelah by his sons (vs. 9), far from the tomb of his fathers. In other words, he was first united with his relatives, then his body was buried in a place completely separate from where their bodies were buried.

The Hebrew scholar Keil notes about the thought of being gathered to his people: "The phrase is constantly distinguished from departing this life and being buried, denotes the reunion in Sheol with friends who have gone before, and therefore presupposes faith in the personal continuance of a man after death."[45] And Dean Alford adds: "This does not relate to burial, for this was not so: Abraham's 'people' dwelt at this time in Haran, and he was buried at Hebron. . .Nor is it a mere synonym for dying . . .The only assignable sense, therefore, is that of reference to a state of further personal existence beyond death; and the expression thus forms a remarkable testimony to the O.T. belief in a future state."[46]

Coming back to Luke 16:19-31, Wierwille dismisses it as nothing but a mere parable. He says: "We must note first of all that this Scriptural passage is a parable, which again is a figure of speech. In fact, in two ancient Greek manuscripts—the Bezae Caulabrigiensis and the Koridethain-Caesarean text—words are included which have been deleted in other translations. Both of these ancient manuscripts begin Luke 16:19 with the words: *eipen de kai heteran parabolen*, which translated means, 'And He said also another parable.' "[47]

First of all, we question the textual authority of these two "ancient" manuscripts. The Codex Bezae—containing only the Gospels, Acts, and a few verses from the Catholic epistles—consists of Greek and Latin texts on facing pages. Sir Frederic Kenyon writes of it: "This is undoubtedly the most curious, though certainly not the most trustworthy, manuscript of the New Testament at present known to us. . . .It is remarkable. . . . on account of the many curious additions to and variations from the common text which it contains; and no manuscript has been

45. PC, Vol. I, p. 313
46. GABC, Vol. I, p. 73
47. ADAN, p. 73

the subject of so many speculations or the basis of so many conflicting theories. . . .The manuscript has been corrected by many hands, including the original scribe himself; some of the correctors are nearly contemporary with the original writing, others are much later. . . .The general result is that the evidence of D, whether for the Greek or Latin text, must be used with some caution; and care must be taken to make sure that any apparent variation is not due to some modification introduced by the scribe. . . .Its special characteristic. . .is the free addition, and occasional omission, of words, sentences, and even incidents."[48]

So much for his first textual authority. His other authority, Codex Koridethianus, is described by Kenyon as "a curious new discovery. . . .a manuscript of the Gospels, of uncouth appearance, probably of the ninth century, written in late, rough uncials by a scribe who knew very little Greek. . . ."[49]

Second, as for it being a parable according to New Testament usage, it contradicts every passage that is labeled *parable* from the standpoint that none in the Bible gives names; all characters in biblical parables remain anonymous. Yet in Luke 16:19-31, both Abraham and Lazarus are specifically identified.

Third, even if the passage were a parable, that would not change the truth it embodies. No biblical parable describing persons or places was a myth, a fairy story. For example, in the previous chapter, Luke 15, our Lord gave the parable popularly known as the prodigal son (vss. 11-20). He said, "A certain man had two sons" (vs. 11). Even though an indefinite pronoun [*tis*] is used,[50] we understand this to mean there really was a "certain" man who had "two sons." The events surrounding the younger son really happened and our Lord told the story of this true experience to illustrate spiritual truth. Such is the idea of a biblical parable: *an earthly story with a heavenly meaning.* Both the *story* and the *meaning* were true. So, regardless of the spiritual truth being taught in the story of the rich man and Lazarus, even if taken as a parable the facts of the story are to be considered true: two men lived and died, at death one of the men went immediately to a place of torment and suffering, at death the other man was carried by angels to a place of blessing and consciousness where Abraham was.

Fourth, our Lord specifically identified the man who went to

---

48. OBAM, pp. 144-146
49. Ibid., pp. 151,152
50. Vine says, "*tis* signifies anyone, some one, a certain one" (Vol. I, p. 178)

Hell as "a certain rich man," and he identified the other man as "a certain beggar," even adding his name, "Lazarus." Would Wierwille tell us that such "a certain rich man" or such "a certain beggar" named Lazarus never existed—that our Lord simply made up the story? We are neither ready nor willing to make such an accusation against our Lord, even if Wierwille is. Perhaps the difference lies in the fact that we believe Jesus Christ to be Almighty God and Wierwille does not.

But he is not content to merely dismiss the passage as a parable, he must perform a little retranslating and verse juggling also, a matter to which the reader of this volume has become so accustomed by now. He writes:

> "Although Luke 16 must be understood as a parable, further clarity is achieved with a more accurate translation of verses 22 and 23.
>
> "Verse 22:
> "And it came to pass, that the beggar died, and was carried by the angels into Abraham's bosom: the rich man also died, and was buried; also in hell [*hades*, the grave].
>
> "The first three words of verse 23 'And in hell. . .' belong as the last words in verse 22. The word 'and' must be translated 'also.' Verse 23, begins with the words:
>
> ". . .he [the rich man] lifted up his eyes, being in torments, and seeth Abraham afar off, and Lazarus in his bosom."[51]

Why does switching the first three words of verse 23 give "further clarity" and "a more accurate translation"? Why "must" the word *and* be changed to *also*? Only because it suits the Wierwille theology—**and for absolutely no other reason whatsoever!** He simply wants to make the rich man and Lazarus both in "the grave," conforming to his understanding of *hades*. However, such an idea flatly contradicts what our Lord quoted Abraham as saying—they were separated by "a great gulf fixed: so that they which would pass from hence to you cannot; neither can they pass to us, that would come from thence" (vs. 26). Like all other cultists, Wierwille fails miserably to defuse the explosive force of Luke 16:19-31. Nor can he escape the truth that in this *hades*, which he passes off as the grave, the inhabitants see, feel, talk, listen, pray and otherwise react in much the same manner as do inhabitants on this side of *hades*.

What about the "nonexistent" Moses and Elijah appearing on the Mount of Transfiguration and talking with our Lord about

---

51. ADAN, pp. 75,76

His coming crucifixion? According to Wierwille it was merely something like a hallucination. He writes: "People try to confuse the accuracy of God's Word by giving the example of Moses and Elijah who appeared to Jesus and three of His disciples on the Mount of Transfiguration and with whom Jesus talked. The Word of God says that they saw Moses and Elijah *in a vision*. A vision is not producing the men themselves."[52]

One might wonder why Wierwille dismisses Elijah and Moses so quickly, giving them and their witness such brief attention. Merely "a vision," he says. But let's examine the record more closely. The account is found only in the first three Gospels. Matthew describes the appearance: "And, behold, there appeared unto them Moses and Elias talking with him" (17:3). *No mention of "a vision" here!* In Mark, the account says: "There appeared unto them Elias with Moses: and they were talking with Jesus" (9:4). *No thought of "a vision" here!* Luke describes it: "And, behold, there talked with him two men, which were Moses and Elias: Who appeared in glory, and spake of his decease which he should accomplish at Jerusalem" (9:30,31). *No indication of "a vision" here!*

In fact, the only mention of "a vision" was after the transfiguration was past and our Lord and the disciples were on the way down the mountain. Then "Jesus charged them, saying, Tell the vision to no man, until the Son of man be risen again from the dead" (Matt. 17:9). Matthew alone calls it a "vision" and the Greek word he uses is *horama*. It simply means "that which is seen." The same word is translated "sight" in Acts 7:31.

What is Wierwille saying? Is he charging our Lord with pulling off a fraud, a fake, a sham, the kind of hokus-pokus a Houdini might present? Did He "fake out" Peter, James and John with an unreal Moses and Elijah who, at the time, were really nonexistent? We find such a thought most abhorrent. No, He was simply saying, in Matthew 17:9, "Tell the *sight* [what you saw] to no man, until the Son of man be risen again from the dead."

Notice also that in all three Gospels it clearly says Elijah and Moses "appeared" unto them. This word is the Greek *optomai* and it means "to see, be seen." The same word is used to describe the post-resurrection appearances of Christ by the eleven, when they said, "The Lord is risen indeed, and hath appeared [*optomai*] to Simon" (Luke 24:34). Would Wierwille say that these appearances were not real, that they were only visions? And if

---

52. PAL, p. 190

they were only visions, would that mean Christ might still be non-existent?

We would also call attention to the fact that Hebrews 9:28, speaking of Christ, says, ". . .and unto them that look for him shall he appear [*optomai*] the second time without sin untó salvation." Does this mean, according to Wierwille's thinking, that Christ will return only in a vision, not actually or personally? If His post-resurrection appearance to His disciples were *real*, and His second coming will be *real*, what rule of biblical interpretation can be brought to bear which denies that the appearance of Moses and Elijah at the transfiguration was any less real? The vision (sight) they had of Moses and Elijah was of a *real* Moses and a *real* Elijah—not a fake presentation of two non-existent personages.

In his work, *Are the Dead Alive Now?* Wierwille gives an entire chapter to "The Vision at the Transfiguration," but it consists only of barely four pages and well over half of that is simply reproducing the Scriptures in Matthew 17 and II Kings 2 which give the record. We call attention to one paragraph (which is a full one-fourth of all *his* comment in the chapter):

"Elijah and Elisha moved ahead over the Jordan at Jericho. While the fifty sons of the prophets and Elisha watched, Elijah was taken up into heaven as The Word discloses. However, this 'taken up' cannot mean he was transported into the presence of God to abide with Him forever, because the fifty sons of the prophets looked for Elijah for three days in the rocky slopes. If II Kings 2:11 meant that Elijah went 'straight up,' the fifty sons of the prophets would never have looked for him on the land. 'And Elijah went up by a whirlwind into heaven' means that God took Elijah. Elijah died away from Elisha and the fifty prophetic sons · and is buried awaiting the resurrection."[53]

We do not share Wierwille's alarm over the "straight up" idea. In the first place, the Bible merely says "up," not *straight up*. Second, not long ago we read of two men who went *straight up* in a balloon, failed to return, and search parties went looking for them "in the rocky slopes." So the idea is not as far-fetched as Wierwille indicates. Third, the Scripture plainly states that Elijah was transported in "a chariot of fire, and horses of fire." While balloons go *straight up*, the picture envisioned by horse-drawn chariots relates to ascending on a slant, more like a jet plane. Fourth, that chariot was hurtled through the skies "by a whirlwind." Although this whirlwind was supernatural and

---

53. P. 65

perhaps cannot be compared with a natural one, the latter would not go *straight up*.

However, the clincher lies in the misreading of the divine record by Wierwille. He says, "the fifty sons of the prophets and Elisha watched" Elijah being "taken up into heaven." No, only Elisha watched; the fifty sons of the prophets were back on the other side of Jordan and did not see what happened. The one who witnessed it, Elisha, knew there was no need or use to look for him "in the rocky slopes." Only those who did not see exactly what happened wanted to send—and *did* send—out a search party.

We think what happened is quite clear in the record of II Kings 2. Both Elisha and the sons of the prophets knew that "the Lord will take away thy master" on that very day (vs. 3). While Elisha refused to leave Elijah's side, the fifty sons of the prophets "stood to view afar off" where they could see what happened at Jordan (vs. 7). From that distant vantage point they were able to see Elijah smite the river, the waters divide, and the two prophets walk to the other side on "dry ground" (vs. 8). However, the men of God did not remain by the banks of the Jordan and the record says, "they still went on, and talked" (vs. 11), apparently walking out of the vision range of the sons of the prophets—who were a long way ("afar off") from the river. At that time, out of sight of the sons of the prophets, Elijah was caught up "into heaven" (vs. 11). As Elisha returned he came back into sight of the fifty, since the record says, "when the sons of the prophets. . .saw him" (vs. 15). They no doubt saw both dividings of Jordan, first by Elijah and then by Elisha, but what happened between was not witnessed by them.

Wierwille gives a little more space to Enoch, regarding whom the Bible plainly says did not die. Here is his explanation of that biblical account:

"Unknowing people say Enoch was such a good man that he never saw death because God translated him. Let us read the record in context.

"Hebrews 11:5:

"By faith Enoch was translated that he should not see death; and was not found, because God had translated him: for before his translation he had this testimony, that he pleased God.

" 'By faith Enoch was translated.' The word 'translated' is the word 'transported,' meaning 'taken from one place to another.' He was not taken from one spot *up* to another place; he was taken from one place *over* to another '. . .that he should not see death.' The word 'see' is *anablepo*, which means to 'look with one's eyes' or literally to see someone die. In checking the Old Testament, we discover that Enoch had never seen anybody pass away. He pleased God all the time for which God so loved him that God took him from the place where Enoch's loved ones would die and put him at a place where he should not see death. Enoch did not see anyone else die, but he himself died. The Bible says so in Hebrews 11:5, 'By faith Enoch'; verse 7 says, 'By faith Noah'; verse 8 says, 'By faith Abraham'; verse 11 says, 'By faith Sara. . . .'" Then in verse 13, after listing Enoch, Noah, Abraham, and Sara, Hebrews 13 says, 'These all died. . . .' All without exception died. If they all died, then Enoch is dead. That is what The Word says and that is what it means."[54]

There are several flies in this reasoning ointment, however, and we would like to point out some of them. In the first place, his interpretation does violence to reason; it flaunts the sense of the passage. Bible students universally have understood the clear meaning to be that Enoch escaped physical death. For example, E. W. Bullinger, whom Wierwille himself quotes on numerous occasions as an authority, offers typical comments: "When He explains that, '*God took him*,' and '*he was not found*,' He means that Enoch did 'NOT SEE DEATH' at all, but that he was translated without dying, and was taken bodily from the earth.

". . .in Enoch's case, his body 'was not found:' because 'God took him,' and he did not die at all. . . .

"It required no faith on the part of Enoch to believe that he would die. It does not say Enoch died by faith. That would have been a matter of 'sight.' He saw death on every hand.

"Of each of the six patriarchs before him, it is recorded 'and he died' (Gen. v. 5,8,11,14,17,20). But of Enoch it is written, that he did 'not see death,' and the reason given is that 'God, took him,' and 'he was not found.'

"This implies that men looked everywhere for him, but the search parties could not find him dead or alive.

"They could not find Enoch, for God had translated him. They could not find his corpse, for he had not died."[55]

In the second place, whether Enoch was translated "up" or "over" is all in Wierwille's imagination; the Bible doesn't say.[56] Third, the idea of merely "seeing," as he describes it, com-

---

54. PAL, pp. 190,191
55. GCW, pp. 95,96, italics in original
56. In ADAN, Wierwille actually tries to compare Enoch's translation to an Episcopal, Anglican or Roman Catholic bishop's reassignment! (p. 68)

pietely ignores the miraculous disappearance of Enoch: "he . . . was not found." Fourth, Wierwille's interpretation ignores the Genesis account, that "Enoch walked with God: and he was not; for God took him" (5:24). The word "took" is the Hebrew *lokakh* and means, according to Pick, "to take, receive."[57] God **received** him! It was not merely that He translated or transported him, but that He translated him unto Himself—and that is the way it has been understood for thousands of years, ever since Moses penned the passage. The same word, *lokakh*, is used four times in II Kings 2 about the translation of Elijah and he "went up by a whirlwind into heaven" (vs. 11). Both Enoch and Elijah were **received** by Jehovah **without dying**.

The Scottish scholar, Thomas Whitelaw, says of the expression *God took him*: "Though the writer to the Hebrews (ch. xi.5) adopts the paraphrase of the LXX, yet his language must be accepted as conveying the exact sense of the words of Moses. Analysed, it teaches (1) that the patriarch Enoch did not see death, as did all the other worthies in the catalogue; and (2) that in some mysterious way 'he was taken up from this temporal life and transfigured into life eternal, as those of the faithful will be who shall be alive at the coming of Christ to judgment' (Keil)."[58]

Fifth, Wierwille made a horrendous mistake when he referred to the Greek word in this passage which the KJV translated "see." As the kids say, "He really blew it!" Wierwille wrote: "The word 'see' is *anablepo*, which means to 'look with one's eyes' or literally to see someone die." But the word used is not *anablepo*, it is *idein*; what caused him to blunder in this way we do not know, but blunder he did![59] Anyway, *anablepo* does not mean "literally to see someone die," as he says, it means to "receive sight" and is translated thus 15 of the 26 times it is used in the King James. (It is rendered "look" or "look up" 10 times.) The only time *anablepo* is translated "see" in the Authorized Version is in Luke 7:22, where Jesus told them to tell John "the blind see"—and it correctly becomes "receive their sight" in the revised version. The normal Greek words for see, or "look with one's eyes" as Wierwille puts it, are *theoreo* ("be a spectator of") and *theaomai* ("view attentively"). The word that is used, *idein*, comes from *eidon*, which Young tells us means "to know, be ac-

57. DOTW, p. 471
58. PC, Vol. I, p. 96
59. Apparently someone called his attention to this *faux pas* and in another book, ADAN, he came closer—although still missing it— calling it *eidon* (p. 68)

quainted, see."[60] Translated literally it is saying: "By faith Enoch was translated that he should not get acquainted with death!" The New International Version expresses it, "he did not experience death." Wierwille's friend and teacher, Lamsa, has it, "did not taste death." Others render it: "he did not experience dying" (WILL), "without experiencing death" (CB), "without experiencing death" (PHIL), "taken away without dying" (BECK), "without passing through death" (NEB).

Sixth, Wierwille says, "In checking the Old Testament we discover that Enoch had never seen anybody pass away." We simply inquire: "where" in the Old Testament? For the convenience of our readers we will list every Old Testament reference to Enoch: Genesis 4:17,18; 5:18,19,21,22,23; plus the geneological record of I Chronicles 1:3, where he is called Henoch. We invite the reader to examine each reference carefully and minutely to see if he can discover any place where it is said—or even implied—that "Enoch had never seen anybody pass away." The whole idea is a figment of Wierwille's imagination. Does he infer it by "silence"? If so, he might as well claim that the Old Testament teaches Enoch had never seen anybody eat dinner, or ride a camel, or shoot an animal with a bow and arrow, or marry a wife, or anything else. In fact, it doesn't say *anything* about his "seeing" or "not seeing" *anything*!

Finally, Wierwille's biggest blunder—or attempt at deception with regard to what the Word of God actually says—relates to his use of the words in Hebrews 11:13, "these all died," with reference to Enoch. We are not at all unfamiliar with this tactic on the part of those who would like to get Enoch "dead"; in fact, Herbert W. and Garner Ted Armstrong used the same argument. We said at that time: "As for the writer's dishonest attempt to prove his point through tying Hebrews 11:13 with Enoch (vs. 5), saying, 'it is clearly stated in Hebrews that Enoch *died* in faith, not having received the promises,' it is necessary only to turn to the passage and read the context. Rather than speaking of Enoch (or Abel, or Noah), this statement pertains only to those who 'sprang' from Sarah's seed 'as the stars of the sky in multitude, and as the sand which is by the sea shore innumerable' (vs. 12). Shame on the Armstrongites for trying to pretend that Enoch was a descendant of Abraham and Sarah!"[61] And shame on Victor Paul Wierwille and his TWI for copying the Armstrongs in

60. YAC, p. 851
61. ARMS, p. 302

this flagrant perversion of what the Scripture is saying.

Thank God, Wierwille is wrong in his conclusion—after summing up correctly the historic Christian position—when he writes:

"One area we must check carefully in God's Word has to do with death. Most Christians hold the belief that upon death those who belong to Christ are immediately received up into glory, commonly called heaven or paradise, to appear before the Father. There they are alive and conscious and have a joyous existence with Him and their loved ones. Such a belief is contrary to the teachings in the Word of God."[62]

Ah, but it is not contrary! The individual who has placed his faith and trust in Jesus Christ, experiencing what the Bible calls "the new birth," will never die. Spiritually, he is already immortal!

"Then Martha said to Jesus, 'Lord, if You had been here, my brother would not have died, and I know that even now whatever You ask of God, He will grant You.' Jesus said to her, 'Your brother will rise again.' Martha replied, 'I know that he will rise again in the resurrection on the last day.' Jesus said to her, 'I am the Resurrection and the Life; He who believes in Me will live even when he dies, and no one who lives and believes in Me will ever die. Do you believe this?' "[63]

Will you respond, as did Martha, **"Yes, Lord, I have faith . . ."?**[64]

---

62. WM, March-April, 1977; op. cit., p. 4
63. John 11:21-26, BERK
64. John 11:27, BERK, emphasis added

## Chapter Six
# OTHER MATTERS

A college professor of our acquaintance was writing recently about his 9-year-old daughter's delight in dining. He related a rather humorous incident which occurred during a Sunday night after-church get-together in their home when refreshments consisted of soft drinks, hamburgers and potato chips—real delicacies for a normal child. She enthusiastically dove into the trimmings, intending to make her hamburg sandwich a masterpiece. She stacked tomato, pickles, onions, lettuce and other extras high on her bun, mentally savoring the taste until the time she could actually clamp her teeth into that culinary work of art.

Some time later the bubbling, enthusiastic conversation of family and friends was punctuated with the little lass' exclamation of despair: "Oh, no! I ate my whole sandwich and *forgot* the hamburger!" She had left out the main ingredient!

We were working on this book when we read that account and thought immediately of Victor Paul Wierwille and his disciples in TWI. Since they have omitted the main ingredient of Christianity—the deity of Jesus Christ, foundation rock of the entire movement (Matt. 16:13-18)—it naturally is to be expected that their entire "sandwich" will taste different from the genuine article.

This is, indeed, the truth and TWI is wrong on many other matters as well. In fact, it is wrong on so many issues we cannot devote full attention to them all. In this chapter, we plan simply to mention a few in passing.

For one thing, as with numerous other cults appealing mainly to youth, standards against worldliness are almost nil—you may have your religious cake and eat the desserts of the world at the same time! TWI devotees are free to participate in almost anything nonreligious youth do. Dances are sponsored, boozing is permissible (we overheard some of the college youth at the cult's Kansas school joking about the champagne they drank at a party the night before), rock music is featured, and even the use of tobacco is not frowned upon. In fact, regarding the latter, when W. N. Earley was interviewing Wierwille for his newspaper, he quoted the latter's enthusiasm for the Word of God as follows: " 'I got excited over every iota of truth, every fragment. I just thrilled and thrill still at its inherent accuracy, its dynamic reality, its living truth. In those years of working the Word, it became my food, my life, my very breath,' Mr. Wierwille explained, tapping the ashes off his cigaret as he spoke."[1] But perhaps we should not be too surprised that he sees nothing wrong—since he does not think the Holy Spirit who indwells a believer's body is anything more than an impersonal force, not a personal God—with a Christian inhaling 19 different kinds of deadly poison (including pyridine, carbon monoxide gas, furfural, nicotine, wood alcohol and arsenic) into a body described in the Word of God as "the temple of the Holy Ghost" (I Cor. 6:19,20). Incidentally, Wierwille blames his rejection by the denominational leaders on his use of tobacco, saying, ". . . the denominations were beginning to dislike me because I smoked or I didn't smoke enough."[2] No, we rather think denominational dislike resulted from his "doctrines of devils" (I Tim. 4:1) regarding the Person of Christ, the Trinity, the Holy Spirit and other matters—not his personal lifestyle.

A woman's dress is incidental for female followers of TWI. Wierwille tells them, "It does not make any difference to God whether one wears a long dress or a short one. . . ."[3] Yet the Word of God teaches exactly the opposite: "In like manner also, that women adorn themselves in modest apparel, with shamefacedness and sobriety; not with broided hair, or gold, or pearls, or costly array; But (which becometh women professing godliness) with good works" (I Tim. 2:9,10). One of the modern English translations renders that first phrase, "I also want women to dress modestly, with decency and propriety" (NIV). Short skirts do not fit the "decency and propriety" mold.

An illustration of how this worldly attitude effects TWI members was seen recently in the author's locality. Since she is deceased, we will only identify her by the name "Linda." Described by friends and acquaintances as "very religious," Linda was a member of TWI and very active in the group, even "soliciting contributions" for the organization.[4] Married twice and divorced twice from the same man, the 28-year-old Linda

1. EG, October 22, 1974; " 'The Way' Founder Tells His Story: Part II
2. WLL, p. 207
3. PAL, p. 125
4. We found it interesting, to say the least, that TWI leadership, in a sworn statement to the Ohio Attorney General's Office, said it did not "solicit money from other than its existing membership"—yet it *has* no membership! Its public relations director, Lonnell Johnson, insists: "We are not a church. We have followers, but not members" (CE, January 27, 1980)

was the mother of a small pre-school daughter.

Since TWI encourages dancing, Linda not only "frequently went dancing" according to police investigators, she even taught classes in disco dancing—the most vulgar and obscene dance to come down the pike in the 20th century! *Los Angeles Times* music critic Robert Hilburn described it: "Disco is a temporary thrill—a night in a bordello." Gay Talese, who has been working on a comprehensive study of sex in America for almost a decade, calls disco music to the ear what pornography is to the eyes. He described it as an aural kind of porno film and says: "Of course the beat is sexual, the rhythm is sexual. The whole fantasy is that sex is easy." Even a magazine like *Esquire* said of it: "What differentiates disco-mania from most of its predecessors is its overt tendency to spill over into orgy. All disco is implicitly orgy. By offering the instant and total gratification of all sexual desires in an atmosphere of intense imaginative excitement, the disco-inspired orgy premotes the dawning of an exalted state of consciousness of literal extasis, or standing outside of the body." *Parade* described one disco dance: "The Freak is danced by partners who bend their knees, spread their legs, advance upon each other with whirling hips until they touch. At this point, some couples retreat while others improvise." One husband shot his wife after seeing her do the Freak at a neighbor's house. Another man became so incensed when he watched another man dance the Freak with his girlfriend he got a gun and shot him three times. Most of the music is "explicity sexual" and homosexuality, sex looseness and drugs are an admitted and accepted part of the disco scene.[5]

One Friday night Linda dropped off her daughter at a babysitter's, apparently for the weekend, then went to The Arrangement, a discotheque on the far east side of Indianapolis. She taught her Free University disco dancing course and then danced until the wee hours of Saturday, leaving the discotheque about 3 a.m., going to a nearby restaurant with friends for breakfast. About four a.m. she was back at The Arrangement to pick up her automoble and left, presumably, for home.

That was the last time she was seen alive. At about 5:30 Saturday evening her lifeless body—clad only in shoes, underpants and a simulated leather coat—was found in an abandoned house.

---

5. Quotes about disco music and dancing are taken from the October, 1979 issue of BE, both from a sermon by Don Ohm, "Disco Damnation," and the author's editorial column, "Off the Cuff!"

She had been beaten, sexually assaulted and strangled. Strangely, she was not identified until the following Monday because the couple with whom she lived did not think it unusual when she did not return home over the weekend. Even stranger, the man of the house had seen her car parked along the road about 9 on Saturday night, stopped to check, found the window on the driver's side down and Linda's purse lying on the front seat. He removed the purse, rolled up the window and locked the car, but did not become concerned when she didn't come home several nights in a row—because Linda was "on the go" a lot, as he put it!

The man later arrested as her killer had gotten acquainted with her at the discotheque. Dancing is a way of life with TWI members; in Linda's case, it was also a way of death.

This lack of personal standards against worldliness is one factor drawing youth to the TWI movement. One leader in the Jesus Movement—spawned amid the youth rebellion of the '60s that vaulted TWI into prominence—had this to say about it: "Wierwille teaches that since salvation means forgiveness for past, present and future sins, one is free to partake of sinful desires. This idea has been particularly appealing to Christians coming out of the hip scene who still want to take dope or fornicate. This means to us [the author] the major reason why people get into The Way, so that they can have a puny Jesus and their sin also. The message of repentance and obedience is not emphasized by The Way."[6]

Another aspect of worldliness is carnality. Paul tells us that the "works of the flesh are. . .hatred, variance, emulations, wrath, strife. . ." (Gal 5:19,20). The Saviour's instructions are: "Therefore all things whatsoever ye would that men should do to you, do ye even so to them: for this is the law and the prophets" (Matt. 7:12).

One would think that a religious group making the dove of the Holy Spirit its international symbol would seek to follow the highway of charity and good will toward all men. Yet the cult's official magazine published a "first-person account" of an attempt to deprogram a leading TWI couple. They were described: "Dan and Randi Moran are in the Seventh Way Corps. Dan is 25 years old and Randi, 26. They were married in 1975. Both took

6. Quoted by Joel A. MacCollam in "The 'Power for Abundant Living,' An examination of The Way, its leader and his teaching"; LC, October 10, 1976, p. 11

the foundational class on Power for Abundant Living in May 1973. Dan wrote the favorite WOW song entitled 'The Ambassador Song.' "[7] So it is probably fair to consider this couple representative of the youth in the movement, perhaps above average. And we must call attention to the fact that the story was printed in TWI's official magazine without any suggestion—either by the participants or editorially—that their actions or reactions were at all amiss.

The deprogramming attempt was made at the home of Dan's folks in Michigan and, in addition to the parents, involved a widow from across the street who had been a close friend of the family for many years, a couple who were friends of the widow, plus two other men. The widow brought a Christmas gift for Dan and Randi (a box of candy), and while it was being opened the front and back doors were bolted. The couple immediately perceived something was "not right" and made an attempt to get out of the house. It failed.

Here is how this TWI couple reacted: Dan took a cup off the kitchen table and tried to hurl it through a closed window. He missed, but the cup smashed on the sink. Then he walked into the next room and knocked a stereo radio off the table. A free-for-all started.

Randi went over to a woman who was merely sitting on the couch and slapped her face. Dan went back to the kitchen, picked up another cup and threw it at the window—this time successfully. Randi "smacked" one of the men in the face with her purse. While the deprogrammers also acted in a manner we certainly cannot approve, the physical violence started with the TWI couple. One thing is for sure, it was a far cry from the "fruits of the Spirit"—love, joy, peace, longsuffering, gentleness, goodness, faith, meekness, temperance—described in Galatians 5:22,23. Again we emphasize that this was reported with the apparent approval of the Morans' actions by the TWI leadership. And we might add that Russell Chandler, a religion editor for the Los Angeles Times News Service, quotes Wierwille's rationale in this area as: "If a non-believer, an enemy, or anybody else comes in and burns your house down, you have a right to fight to take back what was given you in the first place. If you have to kick a few butts, well, you have to do it. Christians aren't a bunch of lollipops."

Another aspect of worldliness is the irreverence often

---

7. WM, March-April, 1977; "An Attempted Deprogramming," p. 11

manifested in regard to the sacred and holy. For example, the interviews in the *Emporia Gazette* closed with a quote from Wierwille, ". . .when you teach the Way, it's just you and Daddy."[8] We find such reference to our Heavenly Father most reprehensible and inexcuseable.

In our judgment, however, far greater blasphemy is evidenced when Wierwille speaks of our Lord at the age of 12. He writes:

"Luke 2 contains one verse of Scripture that for many years I was not able to understand.

"Luke 2:42:

"And when he [Jesus] was twelve years old, they went up to Jerusalem after the custom of the feast.

"I knew that according to Jewish law, a boy became a man, going through *Bar Mitzvah*, when he was thirteen. But Jesus was taken to the temple when He was twelve. I could not understand it so I considered that there might be a mistake in the text. I looked in every critical Greek text that I could find and checked every other source I could think of; but I never found Jesus to be thirteen when He went to the synagogue. Every text concurred on the age of twelve. Finally I came across an old piece of literature which explained that according to ancient Jewish law when a boy was conceived illegitimately, this child was brought to the temple at the age of twelve instead of thirteen."[9]

Note several things: (1) Wierwille has made a federal case about Jesus going to the Temple at the age of 12, something completely unwarranted by the text. Going to Jerusalem annually for the Passover Feast was simply a matter of course for a pious, godly family such as the family of Joseph, an obedience to the Law of God (Exod. 23:14-17; Deut. 16:16). There is no implication in the text whatsoever that this was Jesus' first time to accompany Joseph and Mary on the trip. Quite the contrary, they went "every year" (vs. 41) and in all probability Jesus and the other children went, too. Except for the fact that this particular incident took place when Jesus was twelve, the record could just as easily have said, "And when he was eleven years old," or "ten," or "nine," or "fourteen," or most any other age.

(2) There is no thought of a *"Bar Mitzvah"* in the text. This is merely one more of Wierwille's imaginations.

(3) Notice how Wierwille confuses the Temple with the synagogue in his account.

(4) Wierwille gives no documentation for his "old piece of

---

8. Op. cit.
9. PAL, p. 57

literature" which supposedly explains that illegitimate boys were brought to the Temple at twelve for their entrance into manhood, their *"Bar Mitzvah"*—becoming a "son of commandment," a "son of the law"—instead of the customary thirteen. In fact, the very age of thirteen is open to dispute. For every scholar who says it was thirteen, another says it was twelve! At the age of three, a Jewish male put on, for the first time, the fringed or tasselled garment suggested by Numbers 15:38-41 and Deuteronomy 22:12. Two years later, at the age of five, he started to learn the Law under his mother's tutelage, memorizing some of the more important passages first, such as the Shema of Deuteronomy 6:4 and the Hallel of Festival Psalms (114, 118, 136), then came catechetical teaching in school. It was at the age of twelve that he became more directly and personally responsible for obedience to the Law and at thirteen he put on, for the first time, the famous phylacteries devout Jewish men wore at daily prayer.[10] However, we have some very serious reservations about whether Joseph and Mary would have participated in any kind of a *Bar Mitzvah*, anyway, because this wearing of the phylacteries, which literally means "safeguards" or "preservatives," was an act of superstition, considered by the wearer as a charm or amulet to protect him against evil spirits. We cannot picture the "holy family" taking part in such a religious charade. Can you?

(5) But far more serious than anything else, and necessitating our charge of blasphemy, Wierwille is openly saying in this interpretation that **Mary and Joseph were thus publicly acknowledging to all Israel and the world that Jesus was illegitimate!** What an affront to the scriptural teaching of the virgin-born Son of God! Perish the thought! It would have *never* happened! Not only so, but according to the "espousal" customs of the time—with both conception and birth taking place during that time period—Jesus was *not* illegitimate in the eyes of Jewish law.

Another aspect of worldliness would relate to money. Already noted, in the tragic story of Linda's murder, is the fact that TWI—like the Moonies, the Hare Khrishnas and other cults—solicit funds from anyone and everyone, disgracing the name of God through begging for material handouts (something David said he had never seen the seed of the righteous doing: Psalm 37:25).

10. See PC, Luke, Vol. I, p. 42; ECWB, Vol. VI, pp. 140,257,258

The "big money," of course, comes from individuals TWI is able to trap in its movement and fleece from the inside in one way or another. Here is one example, taken from our weekly "Incidents and Illustrations" column where we said:

"Like many of the other cults—Armstrongism, Jim Jones, *et al*—The Way has a knack of separating its followers from their 'big money' in short order. Some of its escapades in this area have given The Way cult lots of unfavorable and unwanted publicity recently.

"Take the case of Timothy Goodwin.

"Tim is a quadriplegic. He got that way in an accident. Living in California, he was invited by members of the cult to their meetings in Long Beach, California. As things progressed he was led to believe that some of the cult members possessed healing powers and that he could be fixed up if he cooperated with them. Boy, did he ever cooperate!

"He paid more than $10,000 to provide a Cadillac for one Way official.

"He invested more than $11,000 in a BMW automobile for another Way executive.

"He moved from California to St. Mary's, Ohio to be near the international headquarters at New Knoxville.

"He donated $210,000 to the organization in 1975, acting on what he says was a promise he would be healed sufficiently to walk within one year.

"He parted with more than $13,000 as a result of miscellaneous requests from the group for contributions.

"*Nothing happened! No healing, no nothing!*

"Tim sued for recovery of the almost $300,000 he had given the cult during his association with it, claiming its agents 'falsely and fraudulently' represented things to him in exchange for his gifts.

"The Way countersued for $850,000, saying Goodwin's suit constituted 'libelous harrassment' which had caused The Way and its leaders to be 'caused humiliation and embarrassment.' The counter action acknowledged receiving all the loot from Goodwin, but insisted it gave him 'no reason to believe [The Way] possessed religious powers capable of healing [him], as no human beings have such powers of their own.'

"This, of course, passes the blame to God for the failure in healing, but having read Wierwille's teaching on the subject, we can easily understand how and why Goodwin thought following

The Way philosophy would result in his physical restoration. After all, didn't Wierwille himself say, 'God never meant for the Christian believer to be sick; sickness is never glorifying to God'? *"The court battle ended in a draw!*

"The Way refunded all of Goodwin's contributions in an out-of-court settlement and Tim agreed that neither he nor his attorney, Craig Spangenberg of Cleveland, would ever discuss the matter again.

"Apparently the 'humiliation and embarrassment' factor was too much for The Way officials."[11]

It may be of more than passing significance that the first "substantial gift" the organization received, according to Wierwille's brother Harry, the man in charge of TWI's finances, was from "an old lady [who] came up and said she was clearing out her special savings account that she had put away in case of sickness. She said that now since she had taken the class she didn't need that anymore. She was real grateful and made out a check for exactly $1000."[12] We can only wonder how many others have cleaned out their savings accounts of substantial sums and given it to TWI after hearing Wierwille's teaching about healing!

Most religious organizations are only too happy to dispense their teachings about what they believe to be sacred truth without charge, feeling a moral obligation to thus get out the good news. Contrariwise, TWI has found a way to profit from the "truth" it dispenses. In the same column above, we wrote:

"By the way, the cult is using the facilities of Ohio University next month for a two-week training seminar. It expects 4,000 people, mostly youth, to attend the convocation, paying *a minimum* of $505 for the privilege. Broken down, $10 is for an examination fee, $245 is for room and board, and a 'minimum donation' of $250 constitutes the balance.

"The 'minimum donation' for that number of people comes to a cool [or *hot*] million bucks! And The Way is only one of

---

11. May 4, 1979, "Another 'Vicious' Cult!"; One "big fish" Wierwille landed was John S. Lynn, an executive with Lilly Endowment, who got him a $76,000 Lilly grant and donated tens of thousands of personal funds in addition, but later "identified" as the assailant who wounded him by Charles Leighton, an attorney representing an ex-member suing TWI—the identification dramatically coming on an NBC-TV taping about the cult as the victim looked through a stack of photographs (IS, April 5, 1981)

12. WLL, pp. 74,75

hundreds of cults now busily separating the gullible from their money."

But let us examine for a moment what TWI teaches about healing. We have already seen that Wierwille insists, "God never meant for the Christian believer to be sick; sickness is never glorifying to God."[13] He tells his followers: "It may be said that all sickness is some form of oppression of the devil. . . ."[14] No, it may *not* be said! There are too many statements in the Word of God declaring that God either *sent* disease or that He *threatened* to send disease under certain circumstances and conditions. For example, there is that classic passage in which He warned Israel: "If thou wilt not observe to do all the words of this law that are written in this book, that thou mayest fear this glorious and fearful name, THE LORD THY GOD; Then the Lord will make thy plagues wonderful, and the plagues of thy seed, even great plagues, and of long continuance, and sore sicknesses, and of long continuance. Moreover he will bring upon thee all the diseases of Egypt, which thou wast afraid of; and they shall cleave unto thee. Also every sickness, and every plague, which is not written in the book of the law, them will the Lord bring upon thee, until thou be destroyed" (Deut. 28:58-61). Who would bring the diseases upon them? "He" would: THE LORD THY GOD! The disease of leprosy came from God upon Miriam (Num. 12:9,10), upon Uzziah (II Chron. 26:20), and upon Naaman's servant, Gehazi (II Kings 5:27); Jehovah smote Jehoram with "an incurable disease" (II Chron. 21:18,19); and even godly Job's physical afflictions were possible only because God permitted them (Job 2:6,7).

Wierwille's teaching is that healing for anything and everything is simply waiting to be claimed. He writes:

"If God has delivered us from the power of darkness (that is, the power of Satan) how can we be under that sinister power any longer? If we have been delivered, why look further for deliverance? Why wait for deliverance when it has already been made available. Satan has no legal rights over a believer because all believers have been delivered from Satan's power through Jesus Christ. What God accomplished for us when He rescued us from the power of Satan we can appropriate to ourselves when we believe. So the next time you get sick, say, 'Look here, headache [cold, or whatever negative symptom it may be], you have no power over me. You were defeated over nineteen hundred years

---

13. PAL, p. 12
14. RHST, p. 142

ago. It says so in The Word, and I believe The Word; therefore, be gone from me.' When we have salvation, we have wholeness, even physical wholeness, if we simply accept it."[15]

You will note that Wierwille used simple illnesses like headaches and colds for his illustrations! We can just visualize a TWI member with terminal cancer, walking around the house and saying, "Look here, cancer, you have no power over me. *Begone!*" Or how about saying something like that when afflicted with Hodgkin's disease, multiple sclerosis, or some other killer disease? *Presumption* is a far cry from *faith* and Wierwille's advice is far closer to Mary Baker Eddy's "Christian Science" than it is to biblical Christianity.

One of his young disciples tells of a football player who "had broken his collarbone in four or six places and was in a shoulder brace." Some of the kids prayed for him, "the bones came together and knit up in the name of Jesus Christ," and he left without his brace, "completely healed." In fact, he wanted to play football the following week, but authorities would not permit it. In his case, the healing apparently was not too permanent since he phoned back a little while later to say that he had broken the collarbone again. So the youthful TWIs fixed him up *over the telephone*, "rehealing" the collarbone![16] With gifts like this it would not even be necessary to go to a hospital and visit the patients—just give them a call on the phone!

In a chapter, "The Broken Body and The Shed Blood, Healing in the Holy Communion," in which he makes the cup [blood] stand for bearing sins and the bread [body] represent bearing sicknesses, Wierwille argues from Malachi 3:6, "For I am the Lord, I change not. . . ," to prove "What He was once, He is always. What He did once, He does always."[17] The first part is true; the second is false. That passage relates exclusively to our Lord's *person*, not His *program*; it speaks only of His essence, His attributes, His immutability of character. As for what He *does*, the fact that He had a domesticated mammal, the *Equus*

---

15. NDC, pp. 30,31

16. WLL, pp. 145,146; Another attempt was not so successful: ex-Way Corpsman John Desmond tells of being sent with others by Wierwille to a hospital where fellow Corpsman, Gary Donhoff, was an accident victim ("We were told that we were going to pray this guy out of the hospital because we were spiritual macho men. Dr. Wierwille really believed and had us believing that no one could die while in The Way Corps"), but, alas, Donhoff died a few days later (IS, April 5, 1981)

17. BTMS, pp. 75,76

*asinus*, speak with human language in Balaam's day does not mean He follows the same program in our day.

Yet Wierwille goes on to quote part of Psalm 105:37 (". . .there was not one feeble person among their tribes"), and concludes: "If God can take two and a half million from Egypt without one feeble person among them, then what is there He cannot do in the day in which we live?"[18] Without wanting to minimize God's power in the slightest, we are quick to point out that this was what God did for a *special people* at a *special time* and under *special circumstances*; it is hardly offered in Scripture as a pattern for all people in all of God's dispensations. To illustrate this truth, we call attention to further facts about Israel's wilderness wanderings as recorded in Deuteronomy 29:5, where God reminded them: "I have led you forty years in the wilderness: your clothes are not waxen old upon you, and thy shoe is not waxen old upon thy foot." We seriously doubt that Wierwille teaches his followers that, if their faith is strong enough, their suits, dresses, shoes and other apparel will last for forty years without showing the slightest evidence of wear. Or, since he argues that God is willing to do much more under grace than under law, why not teach that if faith is strong enough an automobile can last a lifetime, never needing repairs, tires, plugs, points, oil change or anything else—running as smoothly the last day as the first. And while we're at it, why not make a tank of gas last forever! Wierwille is claiming more for the text than the context warrants.

Going on with his argument about the meaning of Holy Communion, he quotes a portion of Matthew 8:17 ("Himself took our infirmities, and bare our sicknesses"), then concludes: "How we have neglected to reach God's people with this truth about Jesus' bearing our sickness. We have taught that Jesus bore our sin but have neglected to teach the other half—that He '. . .bare *our* sicknesses.' The Word of God is clear regarding these two definite parts in the death of Jesus."[19]

We are not so quick to agree, at least not on the basis of Matthew 8:17. The noted Greek scholar, Marvin R. Vincent, notes about the word "bare" [Greek, *bastazo*] in this verse: "This translation is correct. The word does not mean 'he *took away*,' but 'he *bore*,' as a burden laid upon him. This passage is the corner-stone of the faith-cure theory, which claims that the

18. Ibid., p. 80
19. Ibid., pp. 84,85

atonement of Christ includes provision for *bodily* no less than for *spiritual* healing, and therefore insists on translating 'took away.' Matthew may be presumed to have understood the sense of the passage he was citing from Isaiah, and he could have used no word more inadequate to express his meaning, if that meaning had been that Christ *took away* infirmities."[20]

In a flagrant twisting of Scripture, Wierwille refers to the sickness of the believers in I Corinthians 11:17-34, then says: "The Apostle Paul, according to the Epistle to the Corinthians, rebuked them and endeavored to correct them for being sick."[21] Nowhere did Paul rebuke them "for being sick." He rebuked them for their sin, their disorders at the Lord's table. The sickness, in this case, was the result of their sinfulness—the direct chastening hand of Almighty God upon their lives. Not one time in the Bible did God rebuke anyone for being sick; on the contrary, He was known to say, "This sickness is for the glory of God, that there might be a manifestation of God's works in him" (See John 9:1-4).

If your child disobeyed your orders not to eat rich candy on his empty stomach, overate and became deathly ill, would you say, "Shame on you for getting sick?" No, your rebuke would not be for vomiting, it would be for his sinfulness in defiantly disobeying your command. So with the Corinthian believers; the apostle's rebuke related to sinfulness at the Lord's Table, not for getting sick (and dying!).

Apparently Wierwille thinks God never meant for unbelievers to be sick, either, since he declares, in dealing with Mark 11:23 ("For verily I say unto you, That whosoever shall say unto this mountain, Be thou removed, and be thou cast into the sea; and shall not doubt in his heart, but shall believe that those things which he saith shall come to pass; he shall have whatsoever he saith"): "This is the great law in the Word of God. '. . .Whosoever. . .' It does not say Christian or non-Christian; *whosoever* means *whosoever*. . . .In other words: say it, believe it, and it will come to pass."[22]

That, again we must insist, is not *faith*; it is *presumption*! However, the falseness of what Wierwille is teaching here is easily seen from an examination of the context (Mark 11:20-26). In the first place, our Lord was not addressing the unconverted, He

20. WSNT, Vol. I, p. 53
21. BTMS, pp. 76,77
22. PAL, p. 35

was speaking to His own—and *only disciples* were involved. It was spoken as He and "the twelve" returned from Jerusalem and several times He spoke to them of God as being "your Father." Only Christians can call God "Father"; nonbelievers are children of the Devil, just as Jesus said (John 8:44).

In the second place, there are plain statements of Scripture stating that biblical promises about answers to prayer are not for the unconverted, they are only for believers. In John 9:31 the man who had been miraculously healed of blindness by Christ told his detractors, "Now we know that God heareth not sinners: but if any man be a worshipper of God, and doeth his will, him he heareth." He based that statement on strong Old Testament authority, too, as we note in Proverbs 28:9, "He that turneth away his ear from hearing the law, even his prayer shall be abomination." Obviously, when Jesus said "whosoever" in Mark 11:23, He referred to the *whosoever* among His *followers*.

But Wierwille makes his case for healing nonbelievers even stronger. In his book, *Power for Abundant Living,* he relates such miraculous healings under his own ministry (which supposedly happened in India) that we can well understand why the Tim Goodwins within the cult would expect great results from their "donations." One case had to do with a high-caste Hindu with paralysis of the arm. He asked Wierwille to pray for the healing of his arm, but emphasized, "I do not believe in your Jesus." Three times he positively and dogmatically declared that he did "not believe in your Jesus."[23] Yet Wierwille supposedly prayed for him in Jesus' Name anyway and the man, we are told, "was totally set free."[24] So, in Wierwille's theology of healing, it not only matters little whether you are believer or nonbeliever, you can just as easily be an avowed enemy of Jesus Christ. . .*and still be healed!*

In another book, Wierwille abandons his idea of healing without faith. This is not altogether surprising, however, as contradicting himself is nothing new or unique in his literature. He says in *The Bible Tells Me So:* "In every Biblical record believing is always required on the part of everyone having a need, with the exceptions indicated above: certain types of mental derangement, dead people and children."[25] This is a false premise, of course, since many were healed in New Testament days apart

---

23. P. 30
24. Ibid.
25. P. 43

from any confession of faith for the miracle. We offer Matthew 8:14,15,16; Acts 3:1-11; Matthew 15:30,31; and Matthew 12:9-14 simply as samples.

Perhaps this about-face in the requirement of faith for healing—and the additional view that it requires the faith of the party wanting the healing, not the faith of the one doing the praying—stems from experiences with individuals like Timothy Goodwin, whose aborted healing was described earlier in this chapter. At any rate, dealing with the healing of the demon-possessed boy in Mark 9:14-27, under the theme, "The Law of Believing," Wierwille blames the failure of the disciples to perform the miracle on the unbelief of the father. He writes:

"The disciples were victims of the blame in this situation. The disciples were caught in this man's trap, but not Jesus. Many people would like for others to do their believing for them; they just do not want to learn how to believe for themselves. . . .Jesus understood the situation clearly and He said to the father of the child, 'If you can believe. I know that my disciples believe, and the fact that they could not remove the cause is not their fault. They could believe until Doom's Day for your child without any result; but if *you* can believe, then something will happen."[26]

*What an absolute reversal of Bible teaching is this!*

Wierwille conveniently closed his reading of the passage with verse 27. The next two verses tell us: "And when he was come into the house, his disciples asked him privately, Why could not we cast him out? And he said unto them, This kind can come forth by nothing, but by prayer and fasting." While this is not strong evidence by itself, perhaps, when the account by Matthew of the same incident is added, it certainly becomes so. The latter writes: "Then came the disciples to Jesus apart, and said, Why could not **we** cast him out? And Jesus said **unto them**, Because of **your unbelief**: for verily I say unto **you**, If **ye** have faith as a grain of mustard seed, **ye** shall say unto this mountain, Remove hence to yonder place; and it shall remove; and nothing shall be impossible **unto you**. Howbeit, this kind goeth not out but by prayer and fasting" (Matt. 17:19-21, emphasis added).

Wierwille says the failure was due to the father's unbelief; Jesus said it was due to lack of faith on the part of the disciples. Wierwille says the disciples had the faith; Jesus said they did not. Wierwille says the disciples were innocent victims of the father's unbelief—they were trapped by him; Jesus said the op-

---

26. Ibid., p. 42

posite, that the fault was the failure of the disciples to believe. Do you prefer to believe Wierwille, or our Lord Jesus Christ?

Part of Wierwille's problem about instant healing may stem from his misunderstanding about prayer. To him, prayer is not *asking* God, it is *demanding!* After quoting Luke 11:13 ("If ye then, being evil, know how to give good gifts unto your children: how much more shall your heavenly Father give the Holy Spirit to them that ask him?"), Wierwille says: "The word 'ask' is the same word as 'demand.' "[27]

That simply is not true! The word *ask* here is the Greek *aiteo* and there is no suggestion in it of making a demand. (The Greek for demand is *eperotao*.) Vine says: "*Aiteo* more frequently suggests the attitude of a suppliant, the petition of one who is lesser in position than he to whom the petition is made; e.g., in the case of men in asking something from God, Matt. 7:7; a child from a parent, Matt. 7:9,10; a subject from a king, Acts 12:20; priests and people from Pilate, Luke 23:23 (R.V. 'asking for' A.V., 'requiring'); a beggar from a passer by, Acts 3:2."[28]

Demanding God? Should a beggar demand from a stranger? Should a subject demand from a king? Should children demand from their parents? No, and neither should believers demand things from God. *Petition*, yes; *demand*, no. How much wiser and safer to pray as did the Saviour, "Father, if thou be willing . . .nevertheless not my will, but thine, be done" (Luke 22:42).

Wierwille follows the charismatic approach on exorcism, too, as well as in healing and tongues. He ties it in with the gift of discernment, summing it up: "discerning of spirits—receiving information by a believer concerning the presence, nonpresence, and identity of spirits; if the spirits be evil, they can then be cast out in the name of Jesus Christ."[29] While we are not sure what he means by the ability to discern the "nonpresence" of spirits, a much better definition of the gift of discernment is given by Jerry Vines: "Discernment is the ability to distinguish between the false and the true, an uncanny ability to put a finger on the situation."[30]

A biblical illustration of this gift is seen when Paul declared to Elymas, "O full of all subtilty and all mischief, thou child of the devil, thou enemy of all righteousness. . . ." (Acts 13:10). And

27. NDC, p. 121
28. EDNTW, Vol. I, p. 79
29. PAL, p. 361
30. GST, p. 190

there is the illustration of Peter, facing first Ananias with the charge, "Why hath Satan filled thine heart to lie to the Holy Ghost, and to keep back part of the price of the land?" (Acts 5:3), then his wife, Sapphira: "How is it that ye have agreed together to tempt the Spirit of the Lord?" (vs. 9).

There is a sense, of course, in which every Christian is to have a spirit of discernment. John wrote: "Beloved, believe not every spirit, but try the spirits whether they are of God: because many false prophets are gone out into the world" (I John 4:1). It is on the basis of this command that we discern Wierwille not to be of God. *No one could deny the deity of our Lord Jesus Christ and be of God!*

One feature of Wierwille's writings relates to misrepresentation. Apparently he got an early start in this abominable habit and one interviewer reported his confession to him: "He married a nurse named Dorothea during his junior year [at Mission House College] but he and his bride kept the marriage a secret so that he could continue to play basketball."[31] He felt then that the end justified the means—even though the means was wrong—and apparently he still feels the same.

An illustration of his dishonest misrepresentation, seeking to bolster thereby his own teaching, is his comment about the evangelical teaching of the Trinity. He says, "Aside from the 'we' of Genesis 1:26, the basic scripture upon which the Jesus-is-God doctrine has been founded is John 1:1. This has been read and interpreted as follows: 'In the beginning was God the Father, God the Son, God the Holy Ghost. All three were with God, and all three were God.' But this is not what the verse says."[32] No, and we do not know any evangelical who says it does! In fact, we challenge Wierwille to quote even one authority for it.

John 1:1 is no proof text for the Trinity. The Holy Spirit is not mentioned at all in the verse. Evangelicals refer to John 1:1 exclusively as proof of the deity of Jesus Christ, never as proof of the Trinity. But Wierwille sets up this strawman because it obviously is "not what the verse says."

Another illustration of what appears to be *deliberate* misrepresentation involves this case Wierwille claims actually happened:

"Acts 17:2 is a verse of Scripture which a minister once handed to me.

---

31. EG, op. cit.
32. JCNG, p. 82

He said, 'Dr. Wierwille, you are always talking about preaching nothing but The Word and not going to outside sources, but do you know that the Apostle Paul did not always use the Word of God, that he reasoned with people logically from outside The Word?' Then he quoted Acts 17:2 to prove to me that the Apostle Paul went outside of the Bible to reason with people about spiritual matters.

"Acts 17:2:

"And Paul, as his manner was, went unto them, and three sabbath days reasoned with them out of the scriptures.

"Did Paul reason with them from outside the Scriptures? That is what the minister said, but that is not what The Word says."[33]

While we cannot imagine any minister, be he ever so un-educated and untrained—or even if "mama called and papa sent"—being that dumb, who are we to say the incident didn't happen? But what we *will* say and *do* say is that Wierwille's use of the incident is an attempt to portray evangelical clergy as either stupid or dishonest. We catagorically deny it. And we are suspicious that this is a fact Wierwille well knows.

However, it is interesting to note that Paul did, in that very 17th chapter of Acts, go "outside the Bible" to reason with people logically about spiritual matters. He said of God, "For in him we live, and move, and have our being; as certain also of your own poets have said, For we are also his offspring" (Acts 17:28). Paul did not go "outside" to establish a thought *foreign* to biblical teaching, but he did logically illustrate what the Word of God was already teaching, just as with the Athenians at Mars' Hill. Another example is in his quote to Titus of a Cretian prophet (1:12).

One reviewer of Wierwille's works describes them as "a hodgepodge of contradictions and misinterpretations and fan-ciful explanations that are unscriptural from start to finish."[34] We think that is an honest and accurate evaluation. As an il-lustration, consider what he says about believing. Wierwille writes: "There are two types of believing: (1) positive and (2) negative. We either have faith or fear. We must recognize that believing has both a negative and a positive side."[35] Then later he adds: "Unbelief is believing; it is negative believing."[36] And in another book he repeats: "Fear, worry and anxiety are types of believing. If you worry, have fear and are anxious you will receive

---

33. PAL, p. 116
34. OIB, June-July, 1974: "The Way" by Karl Gettmann
35. PAL, p. 37
36. Ibid., p. 53

the fruit of your negative believing which is defeat."[37]

We find such statements naive to the point of being incredible, especially when offered to budding theologians as sound biblical teaching. What he is teaching is like saying that non-solid is solid; it is negative solid. It is like saying "darkness is light, it is negative light"; or, "wet is dry, it is negative dryness"; or, "hot is cold, it is negative cold." In a word: *Hogwash!*

Speaking about faith again, Wierwille says, "No one ever rises beyond what he believes and no one can believe more than what he understands."[38] This simply is not true. In the first place, I believe a lot I do not understand. For example, II Corinthians 5:17 declares, "Therefore if any man be in Christ, he is a new creature: old things are passed away; behold, all things are become new." I do not understand all the mystery and miracle of the new birth, how God makes the individual a brand new creation, changing his nature and personality in such a way that "old things are passed away" and "all things are become new," but I believe it explicitly.

Not only do I fail to understand the new creation processes, neither can I begin to fathom the old creation. Hebrews 11:3 says, "Through faith we understand that the worlds were framed by the word of God, so that things which are seen were not made of things which do appear." And Psalm 33:6 describes it: "By the word of the Lord were the heavens made; and all the host of them by the breath of his mouth." God simply spake and the universe sprang into being! *Understand* it? Not in a million years with the mind I now have! *Believe* it? Absolutely and unconditionally! One must take the very first page of Scripture—yea, the very first verse—by faith, completely apart from understanding. Incidentally, Wierwille says faith can only be based upon understanding; Hebrews 11:3, quoted above, says understanding in the matter of creation is based upon faith!

In the second place, however, there is a very real sense in which it would not be "faith" if it were "understood." As the Hebrews passage says, "Now faith is the substance of things hoped for, the evidence of things not seen" (vs. 1). Faith relates to the "unseen." Wierwille is saying, "Seeing is believing." God is saying, "Believing is seeing!" Two thoughts more opposite would not be possible. As Paul said in II Corinthians 5:7, "We walk by faith, not by sight." To walk by understanding would be

---

37. BTMS, p. 44
38. PAL, p. 37

walking by sight. Walking by faith is walking as one would walk *if* he had the knowledge.

Wierwille's "negative believing" leads him down some strange highways. For example, he says: "What one fears will surely come to pass. It is a law."[39] Does he mean that a spinster with all the sex appeal of a telephone pole, who constantly fears she will be raped, will eventually suffer such a fate? And what of all the women who *have been* assaulted who later testified the thought of such a possibility never once entered their mind? If our examples seem ludicrous, they are no more so than Wierwille's assertion—and he, please note, sets no limitations on his "law."

He says again: "If one is afraid of a disease, he will manifest that disease because the law is that what one believes (in this case, what one believes negatively), he is going to receive. People have a fear of the future; they have a fear of death."[40] Yet people will go into the future whether they fear it or not. And they will eventually die, no matter whether they do or do not fear death. But Wierwille says, "If a person makes up his mind that this time next year he is going to be dead, God would have to change the laws of the universe for the person not to be accommodated."[41] Evidently God has had to change the laws of His universe a lot to keep from accommodating people. We have known many pessimistic individuals who gloomily predicted their demise constantly. And many of them outlived the ones to whom they made their dire pronouncements! Wierwille's remarks are not based upon the Word of God, they are founded upon pagan superstition.

As for what one fears surely coming to pass, Wierwille seeks to prove his point, not by Scripture but by an illustration of a mother who had an only child. She was so fearful he would get run over by a car, she always walked him to school, a few blocks from her home. One day, when he was in the fourth grade or so, he came home from school early and his mother had not met him at the corner. He was hit by a car and killed! So Wierwille concluded: "Do you know what killed that little boy? The fear in the heart and life of that mother. She was so desperately afraid something was going to happen to her little boy that she finally reaped the results of her believing."[42] Nonsense! Do you know

---

39. Ibid., p. 44
40. Ibid., p. 38
41. Ibid., p. 44
42. Ibid., pp. 43,44

what probably killed that little boy? The fact that he had not been taught responsibility, how to cross the street by himself and to have a healthy respect for automobiles.

Wierwille offers as evidence another case, this one of an insurance salesman who read statistics that "a traveling salesman is supposed to wreck his automobile every so many thousands of miles." Since he had already driven many thousands of miles more than an average salesman, his fear of a wreck became an obsession with him. Wierwille says: "He was losing business day after day and week after week because of this fear. He came to me and I explained to him the law of believing. The man changed his believing and has not had an accident to this day."[43] But was that the result of "changing his believing," or a fruit of following safe driving principles? We answer by noting that the man in question hadn't had an accident all the time he was "fearing," either! Early in this writer's ministry he traveled hundreds of thousands of miles by auto, sometimes getting into his car and driving day and night for several days until reaching his destination. He remarked on more than one occasion that he expected his ministry might be terminated through an accident while still in his thirties. He is now nearing his sixties and Wierwille's "law of the universe" hasn't caught up with him yet.

Wierwille continues his argument: "The world around us builds fear in people. The psychology prevalent in our society today is fear. If you do not use this brand of toothpaste, you are going to have an increased number of cavities; you are afraid of increasing your cavities so you buy this kind of toothpaste. If you do not do this, you are going to get that. It is all based on fear."[44] We think Wierwille is missing the point for the average individual. It is not a matter of fear, it is a matter of common sense to want to take care of his body. The Christian has an added concern because his body is the very temple of God the Holy Spirit.

While we most certainly are not offering a brief for the sin (and it *is* a *sin*) of fear, we are saying that Wierwille is wrong in insisting that what one fears will come to pass because he fears it.

He attempts to prove his thesis by quoting Isaiah 8:12, "Say ye not, A confederacy, to all them to whom this people shall say, A confederacy; neither fear ye their fear, nor be afraid." Then he observes: "These people were being enslaved as a nation because they were afraid of other people. Yet The Word said, 'Neither

43. Ibid., p. 44
44. Ibid., pp. 44,45

fear ye their fear, nor be afraid."[45] However, he only shows his lack of understanding of the passage in saying this. Isaiah, in this message to Judah from Jehovah, was referring to the confederacy that Pekah, king of Israel, and Rezin, king of Syria, had made against Ahaz and the people of Judah. He was simply assuring them that there was no need for fear and that they should look to Him and His Word for deliverance (See vss. 19,20). When Judah did eventually become enslaved by another nation, it was not the result of fear for another people. No, it was because they didn't fear the Lord, broke His commandments, persecuted and killed His messengers, and turned their backs upon Him in rebellion and defiance, worshiping other gods. As II Chronicles 36:16 says, "They mocked the messengers of God, and despised his words, and misused his prophets, until the wrath of the Lord arose against his people, till there was no remedy." Or, to put it in the words of Jeremiah to Zedekiah: "Many nations shall pass by this city, and they shall say every man to his neighbour, Wherefore hath the Lord done thus unto this great city? Then they shall answer, Because they have forsaken the covenant of the Lord their God, and worshipped other gods, and served them" (22:8,9).

His "positive believing" is just as wierd as his "negative believing" since it works, according to him, for any old reprobate who wants to try it. In one of his pep talks to his kids on the farm, he told of two men in Van Wert who "got together every morning at 5 a.m. and believed together for an hour. Every morning. I don't know what they called it. But they would set their minds on an agreed project. They never spoke; just got together every morning and both concentrated on whatever it was, until it came to pass." These men "never went to church, or hardly ever, anyways," they were "the two meanest guys you could ever want to meet," and he summed up their lives by saying, "I don't know if those guys ever looked at the Word of God. I doubt it. But they knew that law [referring to Mark 11:23, which he had just quoted: 'Whosoever shall say unto this mountain, Be thou removed, and be thou cast into the sea; and shall not doubt in his heart, but shall believe that those things which he saith shall come to pass; he shall have whatsoever he saith']. They operated it, and sure made it work for them. They used it for money, for their profit—not for the glory of God—and that law worked for them."

---

45. Ibid., p. 45

What did God do for those ungodly men through their "positive believing"? Wierwille says:

"I remember they got involved in Cuba some time ago, in sugar. That was before all the changes in Cuba. After a while, they had so much sugar, they decided they needed a distillery to use up that sugar for the most profit.

"Well, they just got together and put their minds on it every single morning for a couple of weeks, and lo and behold, one day suddenly some guy who wanted to sell his distillery just called them up, and asked if they wanted to buy it. They'd never heard of the guy with the distillery before. He found them.

"Yep, they made millions, gambled, won."[46]

Now our readers can believe, if they so desire, that God gave those ungodly men—who merely got aside every morning and psyched up their minds—sugar and a distillery to make damning booze as a reward for their "faith." As for us, we don't think God had one single thing to do with it!

Wierwille makes a strange, unwarranted statement about the Virgin Mary, claiming: "The reason Mary was the one who brought forth the Messiah after thousands of years is that she was the first woman who ever literally and unreservedly believed what God said."[47]

*His proof for this?*

**Absolutely none!**

While we would not for a moment want to minimize the faith, the character, the purity of life, the dedication, or the importance of her service as the handmaiden of the Lord, we find Wierwille's comment an aspersion on such great ladies of faith as Hannah, Ruth, Jochebed, Esther, Deborah, Huldah, Jehosheba and a host of other faithful, godly women of the Bible. We think the Virgin Mary was a great woman, but we concur with the late A. T. Robertson, "I reverence her for her noble womanhood, not for qualities attributed to her beyond the data in the Gospels."[48] Wierwille's assumption goes beyond that data.

Wierwille shows his lack of scriptural understanding also when he says: "Isaiah had prophesied, hundreds of years before, that when the true Messiah came there would be one miracle which He would do that had never been done before. This one miracle,

---

46. WLL, pp. 150-152
47. PAL, pp. 286,287
48. MOJ, p. 67

opening the eyes of a man who was born blind, would prove He was the Messiah of God."[49]

Notice some things about this statement: (1) While it is true that Isaiah prophesied that Messiah would "open the blind eyes" (Isa. 42:7), the reference was to the spiritually blind, not the literally blind. The same passage also says He would be "a light of the Gentiles. . .bring out the prisoners from the prison, and them that sit in darkness out of the prison house." Honest biblical interpretation demands that if the opening of blind eyes refer to the literal, so must the bringing out of prisoners from the prison house. The latter could not have been literal (if so, the prophecy failed), so the other matters must have been figurative also. That the blindness *was* figurative can be seen from the rest of the passage, noting especially verses 16, 18 and 19. Paul's declaration in Acts 26:16-18 strengthens this conclusion.

(2) Wierwille is wrong in saying that the opening of blind eyes would be the "one miracle" Messiah would perform. Recall that when John the Baptist sent messengers to Jesus to inquire, "Art thou he that should come, or do we look for another?" our Lord's response was not alone about blind eyes receiving sight; He declared, "Go and show John again those things which ye do hear and see: The blind receive their sight, and the lame walk, the lepers are cleansed, and the deaf hear, the dead are raised up, and the poor have the gospel preached unto them" (Matt. 11:3-5). The blind receiving sight was just one evidence our Lord offered the Baptist, who wouldn't be around when the "one miracle" proving His Messiahship (deity) would take place.

(3) Note how Wierwille adds the words "born blind" to the prophecy, something Isaiah did not say. He is forced to do this if he is to claim it was a miracle "that had never been done before." Opening blind eyes *had* been done! Without going into any specifics, the psalmist said to Jehovah: "The Lord openeth the eyes of the blind: the Lord raiseth them that are bowed down: the Lord loveth the righteous" (Ps. 146:8). And there is also the case of the Syrians, whom God had first miraculously smitten with blindness in response to Elisha's prayer. Then Elisha, through prayer again, after the warriors had been led into the city of Samaria (II Kings 6:18,20), had opened their blind eyes. So the opening of the eyes of the sightless was not an unknown miracle, one "that had never been done before."

(4) Finally, our Lord Himself said that the "one miracle"

---

49. PAL, p. 38

which would prove His Messiahship (deity) was His resurrection from the dead. When the scribes and Pharisees came to Him demanding, "Master, we would see a sign from thee," He replied, "An evil and adulterous generation seeketh after a sign; and there shall no sign be given to it, but the sign of the prophet Jonas: For as Jonas was three days and three nights in the whale's belly; so shall the Son of man be three days and three nights in the heart of the earth" (Matt. 12:38-40).

Speaking of our Lord's bodily resurrection from the grave, Wierwille is wrong in his understanding of it, too. He says: "Jesus Christ literally fulfilled the law; He carried out the Word of God by being buried on Wednesday afternoon and being raised seventy-two hours later on Saturday afternoon."[50]

He is wrong on both counts: the time of burial and the time of resurrection! Regarding our Lord's burial, He was not buried in the afternoon. Wierwille has confused the time of His *death*, which was in the afternoon, with the time of His *burial*. Regarding the latter, Matthew 27:57-60 tells us: "When the even was come, there came a rich man of Arimathaea, named Joseph, who also himself was Jesus' disciple: He went to Pilate, and begged the body of Jesus. Then Pilate commanded the body to be delivered. And when Joseph had taken the body, he wrapped it in a clean linen cloth, And laid it in his own new tomb, which he had hewn out in the rock; and he rolled a great stone to the door of the sepulchre."

The key to the time element is in the phrase: "the even was come." The word translated "even" is the Greek *opsia*. Vine tells us: "The word really signifies the late evening, the latter of the two evenings as reckoned by the Jews, the first from 3 p.m. to sunset, the latter after sunset; this is the usual meaning."[51] So it was after sunset before Joseph even approached Pilate to request the body and obtained his command to have it delivered. This was followed by preparing the body for burial and the actual interment. All of this would have taken time, of course, and it is obvious that the burial must have taken place well after sunset, not in the afternoon. As for whether the day was Wednesday, the Bible simply does not say. While we are not dogmatic, our personal opinion is that it was Thursday (the crucifixion on Wednesday, but since the burial was not until after sunset, it would have made a Thursday according to Jewish reckoning of

50. Ibid., p. 179
51. EDNTW, Vol. II, p. 44

time). If so, the full three days and three nights would have been completed early Sunday, the first day of the week, sometime before sunrise.

As for the time of His resurrection, Wierwille is mistaken in saying it was on Saturday afternoon. For one thing, as we have already noted, he errs in the starting time for his "seventy-two hours." However, the day of resurrection is much simpler to determine than by adding hours. The Word of God specifically tells us what day He arose, describing it as "the first day of the week." That would be Sunday, not Saturday. Some think the day of the crucifixion was Wednesday, tradition holds for Friday, and a good argument can be made for Thursday. But when it comes to the resurrection, the matter is not debatable for one who accepts what the Scripture teaches.

Note these scriptural facts: In Matthew 16:21 we read, "From that time forth began Jesus to show unto his disciples, how that he must go unto Jerusalem, and suffer many things of the elders and chief priests and scribes, and be killed, and be raised again the third day." Notice carefully He said He would be raised "the third day." Fact number two: the events of Luke 24 took place on "the first day of the week" (vs. 1). Fact number three: when the two on the road to Emmaus were talking to Jesus, without recognizing Him, they told of their hopes that He should have been the one to redeem Israel, the Messiah. Then they said—and note this carefully—"and beside all this **today is the third day** since these things were done" (vs. 21, emphasis added). By putting these three indisputable Bible facts together, we find: (1) Christ was to rise from the dead on "the third day." (2) The accounts of Luke 24 took place "on the third day." (3) That third day was "the first day of the week." Beyond honest controversy, the day of our Lord's resurrection was Sunday, the first day of the week! So Wierwille is wrong when he says: "Not one of the Gospels—Matthew, Mark, Luke nor John—states that Christ arose on Easter Sunday morning. That is tradition, not The Word."[52] The Gospel of Luke *does* clearly state it!

Incidentally, Wierwille seeks to escape the force of Luke 24:21 by referring to the Aramaic and to Moffatt's translation "three days have passed." But that does not change the thought at all; if *more* than three days had passed, they would have said "four days have passed," or "more than three days have passed." Young's literal translation gives it: "this third day is passing to-

---

day, since these things happened."[53] Wierwille's objections simply are not valid.

Often Wierwille will say one thing and, just a few paragraphs later, contradict himself. For example, in one book he says, "I promised the Father that if He would forgive me, as long as I lived I would never preach a negative sermon. I would never condemn anybody."[54] Yet a few pages later he forgets his sweetness and light approach, saying: "We have always taught that if a person is a real Christian the only thing he ever does is love. Don't you think that Jesus Christ loved? Wasn't He all love? Yet, Mark 3 records that He looked around about on those synagogue leaders with anger. Jesus was really irritated. The idea that Christians and men of God have to go around patting everybody on the back all the time is a distorted concept. Sometimes men of God have to take a stand against those obstructing the power of God."[55]

Later in the same book he is saying, "No man has a right to reprove any other man."[56] While that may be good sentiment and sure to be applauded by positive thinkers, it is not very good Bible. First Timothy 5:20 commands, "Them that sin rebuke before all, that others also may fear." And there is the classic illustration of Paul publicly rebuking the great Apostle Peter, because he was not only wrong, he was leading others astray on the same matter (Gal. 2:11-14). He also took out after Hymenaeus and Alexander (I Tim. 1:18-20), along with Philetus (II Tim. 2:16-18).

Again, speaking of negative preaching, Wierwille writes: "For many years I moved among groups in which I constantly heard people preaching sin, condemnation and hellfire, and other negative subjects. These well-meaning ministers were not telling people how to get rid of sin, they were just saying that it was wrong."[57]

But should ministers preach against sin? Isaiah 58:1 says, "Cry aloud, spare not, lift up thy voice like a trumpet, and show my people their transgression, and the house of Jacob their sins." Paul, in instructing a young minister about how to preach, told Timothy: "Preach the word; be instant in season, out of season; reprove, rebuke, exhort with all longsuffering and doctrine" (II

53. YOUNG, Luke 24:21
54. PAL, p. 18
55. Ibid., pp. 27,28
56. P. 85
57. Ibid., p. 16

Tim. 4:2). So one "preaching the word" will have to reprove and rebuke, as well as exhort!

And what should we say of the example of our Lord? He was as strong a sin-condemning, hellfire-and-brimstone preacher as ever ministered in public. Read and reread His scathing denunciation of the scribes and Pharisees recorded in Matthew 23:13-33. He called them hypocrites, fools and blind, whited sepulchres, blind guides, snakes—and summed it up: "How can ye escape the damnation of hell?"

On another occasion, John tells us, ". . .Jesus went up to Jerusalem, And found in the temple those that sold oxen and sheep and doves, and the changers of money sitting: And when he had made a scourge of small cords, he drove them all out of the temple, and the sheep, and the oxen; and poured out the changers' money, and overthrew the tables; And said unto them that sold doves, Take these things hence; make not my Father's house an house of merchandise" (John 2:13-16). Quite frankly, we would say that His actions at that time were about as negative as negative could be!

Wierwille said again: "When I was attending seminaries and being instructed in homiletics and other arts of the ministry, I was told that when a person preaches a sermon he should never say *you*, but to always say *we*. Peter must have gone to the wrong seminary because when he was preaching here he said, '*You* have crucified Him and *you* have slain him.' "[58] However, whether Wierwille is willing to admit it or not, *that* is strong negative preaching and it contradicts what he is teaching.

Wierwille makes a strange accusation against Paul's ministry when trying to support his Greek punctuation theories. He says:

"This mighty man of God, under whose ministry all Asia Minor heard the Word of God in two years and three months, in the following two years won not one soul for the Lord Jesus Christ. The only record is in Acts 26:28 when he witnessed to Agrippa, the king who said to Paul, '. . .Almost thou persuadest me to be a Christian.' If the evangelists who use this text realized what it really implies, they would never use it again. In the context the quote is about the ministry of a man who was outside the will of God. The nearest Paul came to winning anybody for the Lord in all those years was 'almost.' "[59]

We find that conclusion incredible!

Not only so, it is speculation, pure and simple. It is an argu-

---

58. Ibid., p. 48
59. Ibid., p. 141

ment from the *silence* of Scripture and one treads on mighty thin ice when he does this. In fact, one could prove almost anything by what is *not* said. For example, would it be logical to claim that Paul only had one meal in this same period of time because there is only one account in the record of his eating? And even if Paul were out of the will of God in going to Jerusalem, and perhaps he was, he didn't remain in that condition long. Within two weeks of arriving, we find the Lord standing by him and saying, "Be of good cheer, Paul: for as thou hast testified of me in Jerusalem, so must thou bear witness also at Rome" (Acts 23:11). If Wierwille is right in assuming Paul only "almost " won one soul in two years, his failure was while "in" the will of God, not "out" of it!

Another strange statement is Wierwille's comment, referring to II Timothy 3:6 ("For of this sort are they which creep into houses, and lead captive silly women laden with sins, led away with divers lusts"): "When we talk about silly people, we think of people who show little sense. When the King James uses the word 'silly,' it means 'harmless.' "[60]

One wonders how he thinks women "laden with sins" would be harmless, but in truth and in fact he has missed the meaning of "silly" in the King James by a country mile. The word is *gunaikarion* in the Greek and it appears only this one time in the entire Greek New Testament. Vine says it is a diminutive of *gune* and "is used contemptuously."[61] The *Pulpit Commentary* agrees that it is a term of contempt, then adds: "In the passages quoted by Alford from Irenaeus and Epiphanius, the women made use of by the later Knostics are called [*gunaikarion*]. See, too, the striking quotation in the same note from Jerome, specifying by name the women whom Nicolas of Antioch, Marcion, Montanus, and others employed as their instruments in spreading their abominable heresies. So true is St. Paul's forecast in the text."[62] What caused Wierwille to think it only means "harmless" is anyone's guess. Perhaps it was because the women Irenaeus, Epiphanius and Jerome referred to, like Wierwille, denied the deity of Jesus Christ!

## Conclusion

We agree with Kevin N. Springer, who, after a brief evaluation

---

60. Ibid., p. 151
61. EDNTW, Vol. IV, p. 227
62. Vol. XXI, *The Second Epistle to Timothy,* p. 41

of the cult in *The Discerner*, noted, "Is this the abundant life? I think not. The Way is well organized and is emphasizing certain doctrines (i.e., how to be successful, personal 'body life' meetings, 'how to' encounter God, spiritual release through tongues, 'freedom' in Christ) that are sucking many into their sect. Yet, in the final analysis The Way is only abundantly leading people to hell. This sect is not Christian in that it does not assent the Deity of Christ nor worship Him. The sect also rejects the Deity of the Holy Spirit. Dr. Victor Paul Wierwille has accepted responsibility for the sect's teachings and will receive a just penalty of judgment before the throne of God unless he repents. There is nothing original about this heresy, as it has been shown to be a modern day form of Dynamic Monarchianism."[63]

We close with the words of Wierwille himself:

"If my research is wrong-dividing of God's Word, then I stand before God as an unapproved workman. . . .I accept full responsibility."[64]

**We would not be in his shoes for all the gold, silver and precious stones in the world!**

---

63. April-June, 1977; "Victor Paul Wierwille and The Way," p. 13
64. JCNG, p. 3

HE HAS THE ONLY NAME UNDER HEAVEN GIVEN TO MAN — HE IS THE NAME ABOVE EVERY NAME — AT HIS NAME EVERY KNEE SHALL BEND, I THINK HE IS THE GREATEST MOST BEAUTIFUL, LOVING, ALL GIVING, ALL POWERFUL, ALL TRUTH, LIGHT, THE ONLY WAY TO ETERNAL LIFE. THE ONLY TRUE GOD, HE II HIS FATHER EXPRESS IMAGE AND GLORY.

## Chapter Seven

# WHAT THINK YE OF CHRIST?

Near the sunset of our Lord's earthly ministry, winding up a session in which the Herodians, Sadducees and Pharisees had taken turns endeavoring to trap Him with barbed questions, the Saviour Himself turned examiner and asked the Pharisees, "What think ye of Christ? whose son is he?" (Matt. 22:42). The obvious answer to men long schooled in Messianic lore, provoking an instantaneous response, was, "The son of David."

Then came the Lord's fatal thrust to their denial of His deity: "How then doth David in spirit call him Lord, saying, The Lord said unto my Lord, Sit thou on my right hand, till I make thine enemies thy footstool? If David then call him Lord, how is he his son?" (vss. 43-45). They were thoroughly, totally whipped and silenced; in fact, "from that day forth" no man dared ask Him any further questions.

His reference was to the oft-quoted Psalm 110:1, readily acknowledged by the Jews of His day to be both Davidic and Messianic, where King David called the Christ "my Lord," using one of the names of deity, Adonai. Messiah was not merely David's son after the flesh by geneological descent, He was God's Son in eternity past—one known, loved and acknowledged by David. And Jesus pointed out that David called Him Lord "in spirit"; that is, by and through the inspiration of the blessed Holy Spirit. (Incidentally, note the Trinitarian reference in this passage: Jehovah, Adonai, Spirit!)

Why did the Pharisees refuse to answer the question, "If David then call him Lord, how is he his son?" Their difficulty was not unlike that of Wierwille and TWI today for, as Bishop Ryle points out: "It could only be explained by conceding the pre-existence and divinity of the Messiah. This the Pharisees would not concede. Their only idea of Messiah was, that He was to be a man like one of themselves. Their ignorance of the Scriptures, of which they pretended to know more than others, and their low, carnal view of the true nature of Christ, were thus exposed at one and the same time."[1]

"*What think ye of Christ?*" Was He only a prophet, such as Mohammed? In the sacred book of Islam, *The Koran*, Mohammed confessed, "Say, Verily I am only a man like you."[2] And he

1. RETG, Vol. I, *Matthew,* p. 295
2. Translated from the original Arabic by George Sale; American Book Exchange, New York, NY, 1880; p. 257

acknowledged again, "Mohammed is no more than an apostle; the other apostles have already deceased before him: if he die therefore, or be slain, will ye turn back on your heels?"[3]

It is no longer "if he die" since death ushered Mohammed out of time and into eternity back in 632 A.D., while still a middle-aged man in his early sixties. Those who wish to visit his tomb may travel to Saudi Arabia and go to the city of Medina. Mohammed lived, died, and is gone from this earthly scene forever.

*"What think ye of Christ?"* A writer in the 19th century, Herrick Johnson, put it well when he said, "Christ was either the grandest, guiltiest of imposters, by a marvelous and most subtle refinement of wickedness, or He was God manifest in the flesh."[4] There is no middle ground.

*"What think ye of Christ?"* Although we consider C. S. Lewis suspect in several areas of theology, regarding the foundational issue of Christ's deity he was right on target when he declared: "I am trying here to prevent anyone saying the really foolish thing that people often say about Him: 'I'm ready to accept Jesus as a great moral teacher, but I don't accept His claim to be God.' That is the one thing we must not say. A man who was merely a man and said the sort of things Jesus said would not be a great moral teacher. He would either be a lunatic—on a level with the man who says he is a poached egg—or else he would be the Devil of Hell. You must make your choice. Either this man was, and is, the Son of God: or else a madman or something worse. You can shut Him up for a fool, you can spit at Him and kill Him as a demon; or you can fall at His feet and call Him Lord and God. But let us not come with any patronising nonsense about His being a great human teacher. He has not left that open to us. He did not intend to."[5]

*"What think ye of Christ?"* Frederic Louis Godet, referring to the time in John 8 when our Lord told the Jews He existed before Abraham, noting they picked up stones to stone Him, observed correctly: "In the face of this reply, there was indeed nothing left

---

3. Ibid., p. 43
4. Quoted in *Three Thousand Select Quotations,* compiled by Josiah H. Gilbert; The S. S. Scranton Company, Hartford, CT, 1907; p. 57
5. "What Are We to Make of Jesus Christ?" in *God in the Dock: Essays on Theology and Ethics,* edited by Walter Hooper; Wm. B. Eerdmans Publishing Co., Grand Rapids, MI; quoted in JGGG, p. 80

to the Jews except to worship—or to stone him."[6] That choice remains to this hour and there is no neutral position. Either acclaim Him Very God of Very God or stone Him with words of contempt and condemnation.

*"What think ye of Christ?"* We emphasize again that only a Saviour who is deity can redeem from sin, death and Hell. Well did W. H. Griffith Thomas quote Bishop Moule in declaring, "A Saviour not quite God is a bridge broken at the farther end."[7]

Which brings us to the main purpose behind this huge book: what think **ye** of Christ? Do you know Him as Lord and personal Saviour, blessed Redeemer from sin and Giver of eternal life? Richard Fuller was right when he wrote: "What will you do with Jesus? *Do with Him* did I say? O what, what will you *do without him*? What, when affliction and anguish shall come upon you? What, when closing your eyelids in death? What, when appearing before the awful judgment-seat?"[8]

It is not enough to admit the Bible truth that Jesus Christ is God. That very knowledge will only add to your damnation in Hell if you fail to personally receive Him as Lord and Saviour. The one who is God is the one who insists, "Verily, verily, I say unto thee, Except a man be born again, he cannot see the kingdom of God. . . .Marvel not that I said unto thee, Ye must be born again" (John 3:3,7). Will you claim the wonderful promise in Romans 10:13, "For whosoever shall call upon the name of the Lord shall be saved"? *Trust Him today!*

To those who have been following The Way International I make an additional appeal. You have my special sympathy and understanding since you have been following a man and a movement you thought you could trust, depending upon their interpretations of the Bible. In this volume you have been brought face to face with distasteful facts. You have learned that your leader is a scholar in pretense only, a man who cannot be trusted in spiritual matters. He has deceived you, tricked you, lied to you. That revelation is bitter, crushing, despairing. There may be a whispering in your soul now, inspired by Satan, to the effect: "Throw in the towel. Turn your back upon *all* religion. It is all a sham, a mockery, an illusion."

No, the Bible **is** true, Christ **is** real, redemption **is** wonderful, and Bible Christianity **has** proven itself over the march of cen-

---

6. CJG, p. 684
7. SCP, p. 47
8. *Three Thousand Select Quotations,* op. cit., p. 95

turies. Because one man develops error and forms a cult, that does not make truth any less truth.

We suggest the following:

(1) Claim Jesus Christ as Lord and Saviour, acknowledging His absolute deity. Appropriate some promise like the Saviour's guarantee in John 5:24, "Verily, verily, I say unto you, He that heareth my word, and believeth on him that sent me, hath everlasting life, and shall not come into condemnation; but is passed from death unto life." Put your faith *completely* in Him, not in any man or any movement. Make sure of your own salvation.

(2) Completely and totally sever all ties with TWI. Get rid of all its literature and stop attending its meetings. Quitting "cold turkey" is the only way to be delivered from the harmful influence of this Christ-denying cult. Obey II John 9-11 when it says: "Whosoever transgresseth, and abideth not in the doctrine of Christ, hath not God. He that abideth in the doctrine of Christ, he hath both the Father and the Son. If there come any unto you, and bring not this doctrine, receive him not into your house, neither bid him God speed: For he that biddeth him God speed is partaker of his evil deeds."

(3) Start attending a church where the Word of God is preached honestly and accurately, fellowshiping with those who truly honor and love the Lord Jesus Christ.

If the author can be of any additional service in helping you know you are saved, or in breaking with the TWI cult, feel free to write:

> Dr. Robert L. Sumner, Director
> BIBLICAL EVANGELISM
> P. O. Box 1513
> Murfreesboro, TN 37133-1513

*Other Books by Dr. Sumner*

# ARMSTRONGISM

*Some of the most influential and greatly-used leaders in Christendom have highly commended this authoritative study of Herbert and Garner Ted Armstrong's evil cult. For example, consider some of the following:*

". . . detailed, thorough, and comprehensive. It will do much good . . . May God give it wide circulation."

—*Dr. Jack Hyles*

"We recommend this scholarly and important big book. It is true to the Scriptures, and it will be a tremendous revelation to honest readers."

—*Dr. John R. Rice*

". . . an excellent volume! . . . will result in opening the eyes of many . . . I am in hearty agreement with you . . ."

—*Dr. Lee Roberson*

"I am now happy to recommend this book which will answer every question concerning the false teachings of both Herbert and Garner Ted Armstrong."

—*Dr. Jack Van Impe*

". . . well written, well documented, thorough, even kind."

—*Dr. Bob Moore*

". . the largest, the most informative and the most comprehensive book on the American-based cult . . ."

—*Dr. G. Archer Weniger*

". . . very large and detailed book . . . a masterpiece."

—*Dr. Tom Wallace*

"The most documented, thorough examination and expose' of any cult I have ever read . . . superb and extremely helpful . . . a classic work on one of the most insiduous cults of our time and should be read by all pastors and Christian workers."

—*Dr. C. Sumner Wemp*

". . . the finest of this type written . . . clear and scholarly . . . honest, sincere, factual and documented . . . God's answer to one of the greatest religious deceptions of all time. It ought to be in every Christian home, in the library of every Bible-believing preacher and in every fundamental college. I am extremely proud to possess a copy of my own."

**15 Chapters, 424 Pages**

—*Dr. Tom Malone, Sr.*

The Book EVERYONE Is Talking About!

# THE MENACE OF NARCOTICS!

### By Dr. Robert L. Sumner

". . . combines the fervor of an evangelist, the compassion of a pastor, the depth of a theologian, and the love of a father to warn our youth . . . a must for every parent, teenager and child."
—Dr. Jack Hyles, First Baptist Church, Hammond, IN

". . . a 'must' book for the public in general and for the Christian in particular . . . This author has done an excellent job . . . ."
—Information Bulletin, FUNDAMENTAL BAPTIST FELLOWSHIP

". . . should be considered a must for parents, teens, pastors, Sunday school teachers and youth workers."
—Ohio Independent Baptist

". . . a valuable contribution to the libraries of pastors and youth workers."
—Dr. Bob Moore, Marietta Baptist Tabernacle

". . . quite possibly the best treatment on this subject . . ."
—Dr. G. Archer Weniger, THE BLU-PRINT

". . . a tremendous work. The tips to parents and advice to victims are worth any price."  —Dr. Tom Wallace, in THE BEAM

". . . A very practical book . . . certainly needed today . . . well-written, well-illustrated, and true to the Bible . . . should have a very wide circulation."
—Christian Victory

". . . informative, compelling, activating, alarming and convincing. We highly recommend its wide circulation . . . ."
—THE SWORD OF THE LORD

". . . hard-hitting, clear, documented . . . Use it for reference. Read it for facts . . . ."
—The Bible for Today

". . . a good, inexpensive book . . . needs to be read by every fundamental believer."
—The Baptist Bulletin

"An excellent book . . . discusses the drug problem frankly and intelligently . . . ."
—Grace and Life

". . . should be demanded coursebook for every school—Grade School through Post Graduate University—and the students should be made to take an examination in it."
—Dr. Hyman Appelman, Noted Jewish Evangelist

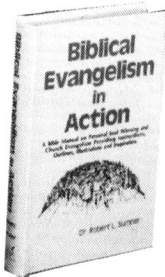

# Biblical Evangelism in Action!

"... ONE OF THE MOST HELPFUL BOOKS ON SOUL WINNING TO APPEAR IN THIS GENERATION... LOADED WITH WORKABLE IDEAS ...BEARS OUR UNCONDITIONAL RECOMMENDATION."

—*Dr. G. Archer Weniger*

**"We do not know of any book similar in nature which is as practical and thorough."**—*The Baptist Bulletin*

*"How I rejoice in the appearance upon the stage of Christian literature of this great book ..."*

—Dr. Tom Malone, President, Midwestern Baptist College; Pastor, Emmanuel Baptist Church, Pontiac, Michigan.

**"I would like to give my full commendation . . . it is interesting reading and convincing in its presentation . . ."**

—Dr. Lee Roberson, Chancellor, Tennessee Temple University; Pastor, Highland Park Baptist Church, Chattanooga, Tennessee.

11 chapters, 344 pages, hard binding.

## EVANGELISM: The Church on Fire

This book comprises a series of ten lectures on evangelism delivered by the author at the Grand Rapids Baptist Bible College & Seminary. The publishers have summed up this significant volume with the words: *"In forceful, practical, stimulating style, Mr. Sumner describes the need for New Testament evangelism, the meaning of New Testament evangelism, personal and pulpit qualifications of New Testament evangelists, regular and special evangelism in the New Testament church, evangelistic preaching, good manners in evangelism, and conserving the results of evangelism."*

*". . . a very challenging book. My own desire to win the lost was intensified by reading it."*—Dr. John G. Balyo, Cedar Hill Baptist Church, Cleveland, Ohio.

*"Several features make this one of the most important books written on evangelism in the last twenty-five or more years."*—Evangelist John R. Rice.

*". . . if churches ever need a book like this and the message it contains, the time is now!"*—Dr. Walt Handford, Southside Baptist Church, Greenville, South Carolina.

10 chapters, 220 pages, paper binding.

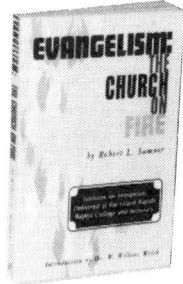

# Four Good Books by

## *Evangelist*

# ROBERT L. SUMNER

### MAN SENT FROM GOD

A Biography of Dr. John R. Rice. An accurate, up-to-date account of the challenging, eventful, fruitful life and ministry of a man referred to therein as "the Twentieth Century's mightiest pen." New, improved edition; many pictures. 17 chapters, plus Appendices. 264 pages.

### MORMONISM!

By Dr. Robert L. Sumner. Subtitled "A Destructive, Soul-Damning Cult," this booklet gives warning to its readers to "watch out for the Church of Jesus Christ of Latter-day Saints (Mormon), currently celebrating its 150th anniversary! Inspired of Satan, conceived in Joseph Smith, enlarged by Brigham Young, it is a non-Christian false cult! Beware!" It is said to be "by far the best small booklet on that subject." 47 pages.

### SAVED BY GRACE. . .FOR SERVICE!

Ephesians, by many Bible "scholars," has been often regarded as so deep, profound and mysterious. But in this masterpiece commentary Dr. Sumner removes this misconception.

The subjects in the 6 chapters of Ephesians are covered thoroughly in 16 refreshing chapters in this volume. A big book of 333 pages.

### POWERHOUSE

This book contains 95 different "precious promises" (II Peter 1:4). Each study has promise, point, proof and poem. Preachers will find a wealth of illustrative material.
203 pages, paperbound.

## BIBLICAL EVANGELISM PRESS
### Murfreesboro, Tennessee 37133-1513

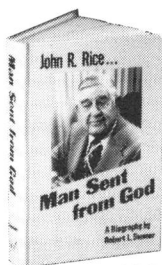

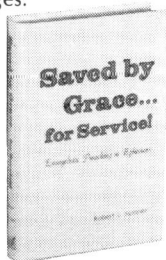